# Paper Trails

# Paper Trails

## *The US Post and the Making of the American West*

CAMERON BLEVINS

OXFORD

UNIVERSITY PRESS

Oxford University Press is a department of the University of Oxford. It furthers
the University's objective of excellence in research, scholarship, and education
by publishing worldwide. Oxford is a registered trade mark of Oxford University
Press in the UK and certain other countries.

Published in the United States of America by Oxford University Press
198 Madison Avenue, New York, NY 10016, United States of America.

Library of Congress Cataloging-in-Publication Data
Names: Blevins, Cameron, author.
Title: Paper trails : the US Post and the making of the American West / Cameron Blevins.
Description: New York : Oxford University Press, 2021. | Includes index. |
Identifiers: LCCN 2020033035 (print) | LCCN 2020033036 (ebook) |
ISBN 9780190053673 (hardcover) | ISBN 9780190053697 (epub)
Subjects: LCSH: Postal service—West (U.S.)—History—19th century. |
United States—Territorial expansion | West (U.S.)—History
Classification: LCC HE6376.A1 W476 2021 (print) | LCC HE6376.A1 (ebook) |
DDC 383/.497809034—dc23
LC record available at https://lccn.loc.gov/2020033035
LC ebook record available at https://lccn.loc.gov/2020033036

DOI: 10.1093/oso/9780190053673.001.0001

3 5 7 9 8 6 4 2

Printed by Sheridan Books, Inc., United States of America

# Contents

# Acknowledgments

I've been lucky enough to work at a series of wonderful institutions. This book began while I was a graduate student at Stanford University, where I learned from Jim Campbell, Gordon Chang, Zephyr Frank, Estelle Friedman, Annelise Heinz, Ryan Heuser, Allyson Hobbs, Ben Hoy, Matt Jockers, Gabriel Lee, Natalie Marine-Street, Sara Mayeux, Casey Nichols, Andy Robichaud, Scott Spillman, Erik Steiner, Ben Stone, Caroline Winterer, and Glen Worthey. The Spatial History Lab, the Literary Lab, and the Center for Spatial and Textual Analysis provided community and institutional support, while the Bill Lane Center for the American West supported my final year of graduate school. The Andrew W. Mellon Foundation funded a one-year postdoc at the Center for Historical Analysis at Rutgers University, where I benefited from the mentorship of Ann Fabian, Francesca Giannetti, Toby Jones, and Jamie Pietruska. Christof Mauch welcomed me as a visiting scholar at the incomparable Rachel Carson Center for Environment and Society, which gave me the opportunity to wrestle my dissertation into a book. I finished working on the book at Northeastern University, where I enjoyed some truly exceptional colleagues, including Moya Bailey, Marty Blatt, Victoria Cain, Sarah Connell, Ryan Cordell, Elizabeth Maddock Dillon, Julia Flanders, Gretchen Heefner, Laura Nelson, Élika Ortega, Chris Parsons, Bahare Sanaie-Movahed, Heather Streets-Salter, Ben Schmidt, Philip Thai, and Louise Walker. Finally, thank you to the people who kept all of these institutions running: Celena Allen, Kirsten Bilas, Matt Bryant, Carmen Dines, Shari Haun, Arielle Helmick, Bonne Knipfer, Art Palmon, Lynn Shanko, Priscilla Trojino, and Monica Wheeler.

Like any work of history, this one was only possible because of libraries, archives, and the talented people who work in them. I benefited in particular from Alexander Library, the Bancroft Library, the Beinecke Library, the California State Library, Green Library, the Huntington Library, the National Archives, and Snell Library. Historians like to fetishize physical archives over digital ones, but I spent just as many hours researching this book in the virtual spaces of the California Digital Newspaper Collection, the David Rumsey Historical Map Collection, the Library of Congress's Chronicling America database, Google Books, HathiTrust, and Wikipedia.

Thank you to my editor, Susan Ferber, for her sharp eye and for guiding this project through the entire publication process. The production team at Oxford did exceptional work with copy-editing, indexing, and laying out such an unreasonable number of figures. I am grateful to Richard Helbock, whose research and data collection made so much of my research possible. Many thanks to Zephyr Frank and Caroline Winterer, who were instrumental in the early stages of this project as dissertation readers and mentors. A series of talented research assistants contributed to this project: Tara Balakrishnan, Jenny Barin, Dina Hassan, Jocelyn Hickox, Alex Ramsey, and Varun Vijay. Jason Heppler patiently worked with me to create an interactive visualization of post offices that has proven endlessly helpful over the years. Steven Braun provided consulting for the accompanying online narrative for this book, and a seedling grant from the NULab for Texts, Maps, and Networks helped me hire someone to actually build it: Yan Wu, who is the single most talented designer I've ever met. Many thanks to Richard R. John for his groundbreaking work on this topic and for providing a wealth of ideas, contacts, sources, and suggestions over the years. Patty Limerick wrote a truly unforgettable review of my manuscript and helped shepherd the book to completion. Victoria Cain swooped in like the superhero that she is to drag me across the finish line. Finally, this book joins countless others that were made possible by the mentorship of Richard White. Richard has influenced the book and my career in too many ways to list, so I'll keep this as succinct as one of his emails: thank you.

Acknowledgments often use some variation of "any of this book's flaws or shortcomings are entirely my own." I have the same attitude toward my parents and sister for the way they raised me; any flaws or shortcomings are entirely my own. My mom in particular taught me much of what I know about how to be a teacher, scholar, and colleague. I appreciate the many friends in my life who indulged my need to not talk or think about this book when I wasn't working on it. Most of them have only the vaguest sense of what it's about, and I am a much happier person because of it. This project began around the same time as my relationship with Erica. A decade later, one of them has ended while the other continues to be the single best part of my life. Thank you.

# Note on Methods

*Paper Trails* is a work of digital history, a field that revolves around the use of computational methods to understand the past. This approach produced new findings and interpretations about the nineteenth-century American state and the western United States, while also allowing me to communicate those findings through maps, charts, and other data visualizations. In the interests of readability, I have tried to avoid detailed technical discussions about the data and methods of this approach within the main text of the book.

Many of the maps in this book rely on a particular dataset: post office records transcribed by the philatelist and postal historian Richard Helbock. The Post Office Department recorded the names of all post offices in the country and the dates for when they were established, discontinued, or reopened along with any time they changed names. The vast majority of this information is housed by the National Archives through microfilmed "Records of Appointment of Postmasters." Helbock spent years poring over these records and consulting other local sources in order to build a dataset of every post office that existed in the United States, including their names, the states and counties in which they were located, and their dates of operation. Helbock passed away in 2011, two years before I discovered his work and purchased a CD-ROM of the dataset from his wife, Catherine Clark. I am indebted to Helbock, without whom this book would have been impossible.[1]

The Helbock dataset is a remarkable source of historical information, but it required several additional steps to turn it into a spatial dataset. This involved a process known as geocoding, or assigning geographical coordinates to each post office so that they could be placed on a map. Instead of trying to locate all 166,000 post offices by hand, I wrote a computer program to try to do this automatically. Generally speaking, the program took the name, county, and state of each post office and attempted to locate a corresponding record in the Geographic Names Information System (GNIS), a database of several million geographical features compiled the US Board on Geographical Names. This process allowed me to locate roughly two-thirds of the post offices in Helbock's dataset, which I then used to generate the maps in this book.[2]

There are limitations to this approach. Most obviously, a lack of geographical coordinates for such a large portion of the data hinders precise quantitative analysis, such as measuring the exact geographical distribution of post offices in different parts of the country. I have largely avoided this kind of analysis and instead used the dataset to visualize spatial patterns more generally. Even so, a map that is missing thousands of post offices can paint an equally misleading picture. To mitigate this, I assigned semi-random coordinates to each post office with a missing location, but confined these coordinates to an area within the surrounding county's boundaries. These semi-random post office locations only appear on national maps of the contiguous United States and regional maps of the American West, and are indicated by a lighter, semi-transparent shade of gray in order to convey their uncertain status. The accuracy or inaccuracy of any individual post office is largely undiscernible to the human eye at this scale and with this symbology. In aggregate, the inclusion of these semi-random post office locations provides a more accurate impression of the network than if I had left them out entirely.

Several other features of this dataset should be kept in mind. First, individual post offices changed names with surprising frequency in the nineteenth century. Helbock recorded these events in his dataset as if the existing post office with the old name had closed and a new post office with a new name had opened. Because of this, maps of "established" or "discontinued" post offices in this book include some post offices that had simply changed names. Second, in addition to changing names, an individual post office might repeatedly close and then reopen within the span of a few years or even months. Rather than recording every one of these closures, Helbock only recorded "permanent" closures, which he defined as an office remaining out of operation for at least ten years. More fleeting post office closures and reopenings are not represented on the maps. If anything, then, the maps understate the western postal system's instability—one of the book's core arguments.

I relied on several additional datasets to generate the maps and charts in this book. Claudio Saunt generously provided spatial data that tracks the changing boundaries of unceded Native land and government reservations over the nineteenth century. I then made some minor corrections to the shapefiles in this dataset. State and territory boundaries come from Lincoln Mullen and Jordan Brett's invaluable "USABoundaries" R library, based on shapefiles produced by the National Historic Geographical Information Systems. Any other sources of data used in a specific map or chart have been noted in its caption. Finally, unless otherwise stated, all the maps and charts in this book were generated using the R language for statistical computing, with a particular reliance on the "tidyverse" and "sf" libraries.[3]

# Paper Trails

# Introduction

## The Gossamer Network

"I had forgotten where I had left my overcoat," wrote Clark Thompson on January 20, 1864. A regional supervisor for the federal government's Office of Indian Affairs, Thompson had been visiting the Yankton Indian Reservation in Dakota Territory on official business when he lost his coat. Unwilling to delay his trip, Thompson found a replacement and pressed on with his winter journey. When he eventually reached his office in Saint Paul, Minnesota, he wrote a letter to one of his acquaintances back at the Yankton reservation telling him that his old coat was up for grabs. The entire letter was just four sentences long. There was no official business, no discussion of his trip, not even any complaints about the weather. It was just a few lines about an overcoat. Clark Thompson did not go on to alter the course of American history. Neither, presumably, did his overcoat. Clark's letter was utterly unremarkable, the historical equivalent of a 21st-century text message. But it wasn't the 21st century. It was the dead of winter in 1864, in the midst of the US Civil War, and on the outskirts of the nation. Despite this, Thompson was able to dash off a few lines about a misplaced overcoat seemingly without a second thought. The significance of Thompson's letter has less to do with its contents than with the fact that he was able to send it at all.[1]

Roughly four hundred miles separated Clark Thompson's office in Saint Paul from the Yankton Reservation in Dakota Territory. Just 18 months earlier, this area had descended into all-out warfare. In the summer of 1862, Dakota fighters had launched an insurgency that plunged southwestern Minnesota into chaos. The US Army quickly dispatched troops to the area to pursue them, and in December of 1862 troops hanged 38 men at the town of Mankato, in what remains the largest mass execution in American history. The following summer, Minnesota's adjunct general organized volunteer squads to hunt down Dakota men, promising a $25 bounty for every scalp they brought to his office. Six months later, Thompson's letter would have passed directly through Mankato and its execution site before eventually winding its way into Dakota Territory. The recently created federal territory was home to just a few thousand white Americans, most of whom clustered in its southeastern corner along the Missouri River. Thompson's letter would have traversed this string of settlements before disembarking at the second-to-last stop on the stage line, at the Yankton Indian Reservation. Any farther west and Thompson's letter would have crossed into an ocean of grassland controlled by the Lakota and

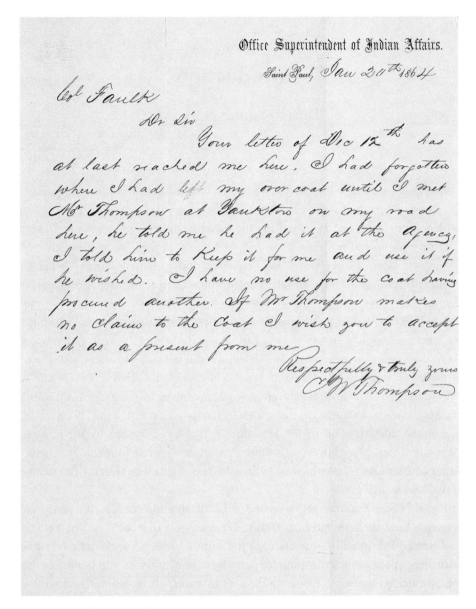

**Figure I.1.**  A Forgotten Coat

C. W. Thompson to Andrew Jackson Faulk, January 20, 1864, box 1, folder 1, Andrew Jackson Faulk
Papers, Yale Collection of Western Americana, Beinecke Rare Book and Manuscript Library, New Haven,
Connecticut.

Northern Cheyenne that unfurled across Dakota Territory and into present-day
Wyoming and Montana.[2]

How was a government official able to send an utterly inconsequential letter hundreds of miles through occupied territory, in the middle of winter, and at the height
of the Civil War? Clark Thompson's letter was made possible by a network of post
offices and mail routes that linked Saint Paul, Minnesota, to a remote government

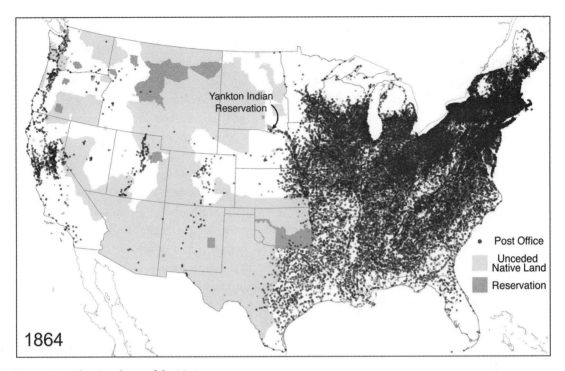

**Figure I.2**  The Outskirts of the Nation

Clark Thompson mailed his letter to the Yankton Indian Reservation, located at the end of a postal route and near the edge of Lakota territory. This map shows post offices, unceded Native land (light gray), and Indian reservations (dark gray) in 1864. For more information about the data used to create this map, refer to the Note on Methods.

outpost in Dakota Territory. Like Thompson's letter, this network is easy to over-look. And like Thompson's letter, it shouldn't be taken for granted. The infrastructure of the US Post is what allowed a half-page message about a misplaced overcoat to make its way to the very edge of the nation.

*Paper Trails* is a history of the US Post's expansion across the western United States. The spread of the nation's postal system during the second half of the 19th century shaped the history of the region, knitting the American West into a national system of communications. It kept western settlers connected to the people and communities they left behind, shuttling millions of letters between family and friends. It carried newspapers, magazines, petitions, and pamphlets that allowed westerners to engage with national politics, culture, and social movements. It circulated the legal and financial instruments—money orders, checks, drafts, mortgages, property deeds, receipts, and invoices—that kept the region's economy running. The US Post was the underlying spatial circuitry of western expansion.

When Clark Thompson mailed his letter to Dakota Territory in January of 1864, the future of the American West was very much up for debate. The United States may have laid claim to territory that stretched from coast to coast, but very little of this land was actually within its control. The western interior was still "Indian country," occupied by powerful groups like the Lakotas in the northern plains and the Comanches in the Southwest. In many places, Native people exercised much more on-the-ground authority than the US government itself. The West's rugged terrain was equally daunting for Americans—a remote and inhospitable landscape of treeless plains, deserts, and towering mountain ranges unlike anything in the eastern United States. Roads were few and far between, railroad construction was in its infancy, and navigable waterways were virtually nonexistent. Americans may have had grand visions for the West, but a healthy dose of caution was in order.[3]

It had taken Anglo-American settlers the better part of two hundred years to occupy the eastern half of the United States; they occupied the western half in the span of a single generation. Between the 1860s and 1890s the western United States was utterly transformed. Millions of people moved to the region, building homesteads, founding towns and cities, and incorporating new western states and territories. An influx of industry and capital poured westward into mines, mills, dams, and railroads, all of which accelerated the extraction of resources that fueled the nation's meteoric rise as the world's leading industrial economy. The mass movement of people and industry remade the western landscape, as new arrivals plowed farmland, raised herds, felled forests, redirected rivers, and blew apart mountains. All of these changes rested on a foundation of conquest and dispossession. Across the region, soldiers and settlers alike waged war against the West's Native inhabitants, forcing the survivors to give up legal title to their land and move onto reservations. Western expansion unfurled across plundered Native territory. When the dust finally settled by the end of the 19th century, a once remote region had been conquered, occupied, and integrated into the nation.[4]

How did western expansion unfold so quickly and in the face of such daunting conditions? Despite the popular "Wild West" narrative of self-reliant cowboys and pioneers, the real history of the region is one of big government: public land and national parks, farming subsidies and grazing permits, military bases and defense contracts. Arguably no other part of the United States has been so profoundly shaped by "the state"—a term for the government, institutions, and policies that govern a society. Decades of historical scholarship has dispelled the myth of rugged individualism and replaced it with a story about state power. Yet for all of the attention that historians have paid to the role of the federal government in the West, they have written remarkably little about its largest organization, the US Post.[5]

This lack of attention is especially strange given that no other government entity left behind such an extensive paper trail. The 19th-century postal system transmitted billions of pieces of mail each year.[6] Whether neatly filed away in the stacks of an archive or haphazardly piled up inside a shoebox in the corner of an attic, the historical record is littered with letters, newspapers, and postcards that traveled through the US Post. Historians spend countless hours riffling through these pieces of paper. So what explains the relative absence of the US Post in the annals of western history, despite its pervasive presence in the historical archive? When something is everywhere, it can start to become invisible. Historians read letters and quote them in their writings, but rarely pause to consider them as physical pieces of paper that had to travel from writer to recipient, from point A to point B. It is easy to take for granted both the journeys themselves and the infrastructure that made them possible. After all, large-scale networks, organizations, and institutions have a tendency to hide in plain sight, camouflaged by their own routine, ubiquitous presence. This book is an attempt to bring one of those networks into view.[7]

To see the postal network in its entirety requires a different approach: digital history, or the use of computational methods to study the past. The field of digital history first emerged in the 1990s and early 2000s as libraries and archives began to digitize historical sources and make them available online. A wealth of newly available electronic material enabled working with these sources in new ways, from curating virtual museum exhibits to applying statistical techniques to large collections of text.[8] Some have complained that digital history has been long on flash and short on substance, a fancy way of showing patterns that we already know.[9] This book is a rejoinder to that critique. Many of its core arguments and interpretations originate from a dataset created by the philatelist and postal historian Richard Helbock that contains information about every post office that ever existed in the United States—some 166,000 records in total. As detailed in the Note on Methods, Helbock's work laid the groundwork for this book. Processing, analyzing, and visualizing the dataset casts light on a subject that otherwise fades from view, uncovering new patterns and insights that would have otherwise gone unnoticed.[10] Mapping the expansion of the US Post on a year-by-year basis not only revealed the geography of this network but helped uncover how its machinery worked and the ways that it shaped the occupation and incorporation of western territory. Some of these findings were expected, while others were quite surprising. Four findings in particular about the US Post laid the foundation for this book's larger interpretations about the history of the western United States and the nature of state power: the US Post was big, expansive, fast moving, and unstable.[11]

*The US Post was big.* In 1889, John Wanamaker, the postmaster general of the United States, boasted that he managed "the largest business concern in the world."[12] He wasn't exaggerating. At that point, Wanamaker oversaw a network that encompassed some 59,000 post offices and 400,000 miles of mail routes. This was roughly two and a half times as many post offices and three times the mileage of mail routes as any other country in the world. The size of the US Post made it a global outlier during the 19th century. But numbers alone can be difficult to conceptualize. What, for instance, does 59,000 post offices actually mean? To put that figure in a modern context, it is roughly twice as many post offices as operate in the United States today. Fifty-nine thousand locations also dwarfs the number of Walmart retail stores (5,362), Wells Fargo banking branches (5,472), Walgreens pharmacies (9,560), and even McDonald's restaurants (13,914) in the United States in 2019. In fact, if McDonald's were to buy up every single Burger King, Wendy's, Starbucks, Pizza Hut, and Taco Bell restaurant in the country, this massive fast-food

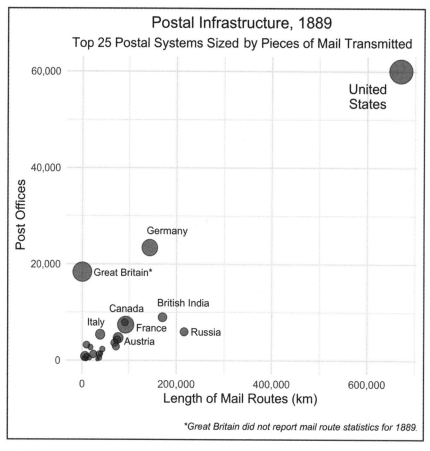

**Figure I.3** Global Outlier

The United States operated the largest postal infrastructure in the world, as measured by post offices, mail routes, and quantity of mail. Data was provided by John Gerring and Jon Rogowski and was transcribed from records of the Union Postale Universelle, *Statistique Générale du Service Postal Publieé par le Bureau International, Année 1889* (Berne: Imprimerie Suter & Lierow, 1891).

conglomerate would still have fewer combined locations than the number of post offices operating in 1889.[13]

*The US Post was geographically expansive.* The 19th-century postal network wasn't just big; it was everywhere. Postmaster General Wanamaker's 1889 report went on to proclaim that his department was "the only one that touches the local life, the social interests, and business concern of every neighborhood."[14] What seems like hyperbole starts to look much more literal when 59,000 post offices are laid out on a map like the one in Figure I.4. With some exceptions, there really was a post office in "every neighborhood" in the country, whether a mining camp in Idaho, a collection of homesteads in Nebraska, or a booming metropolis like New York City. The nation's postal geography stemmed from the US government's commitment to providing a universally accessible mail service. In an era before widespread residential mail delivery, Americans needed to have a post office nearby in order to send and receive their mail. And because Americans themselves were spread across a large

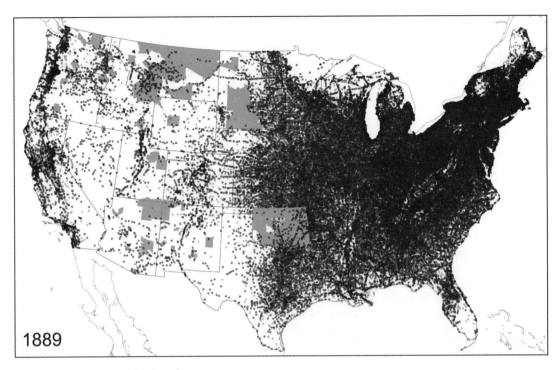

1889

**Figure I.4** Every Neighborhood

The Post Office Department operated around 59,000 post offices in 1889. Post offices are overlaid onto state and territory boundaries and Indian reservations (shaded in dark gray).

area, the federal government had to maintain a similarly widespread infrastructure of post offices and mail routes to serve them. The sprawling spatial coverage of the 19th-century postal network was in many ways its defining feature.[15]

This book is filled with maps like the one in Figure I.4. They are foundational for its arguments, interpretations, and larger narrative structure. But, like all maps, they are incomplete. As described in the Note on Methods, from a technical standpoint the locations of roughly one-third of the post offices in Richard Helbock's dataset are unknown. A smaller number of them may have been misidentified or placed in the wrong location.[16] More importantly, areas on the maps that are devoid of post offices were not uninhabited. In fact, for much of the 19th century the absence of post offices signaled the presence of Native peoples who effectively blocked the expansion of American settlers and the federal government. When Clark Thompson wrote his letter in 1864, the "blank" areas of the western postal system corresponded to the negative spaces of state power, or territory that the US government did not actually control. In Figure I.5, for instance, much of the land officially designated as Dakota Territory was in fact the domain of the Lakota people. Twenty-five years later, the meaning of those blank areas had changed. By the time Postmaster General Wanamaker wrote his report in 1889, the US government had succeeded in forcing western tribes to cede much of their territory and relocate onto reservations. Within their borders, the US Post's otherwise dense spatial

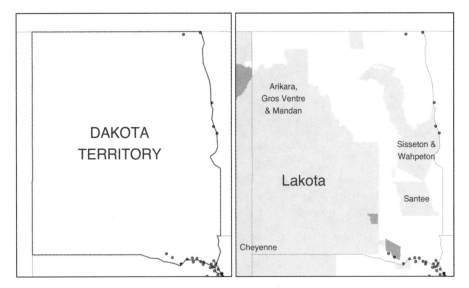

**Figure I.5** Network Boundaries in 1864

The left map shows the boundaries of Dakota Territory and post offices operating in 1864. The right map shows the same area overlaid with unceded Native land (light gray) and government reservations (dark gray). In 1864, much of Dakota Territory was controlled by Native groups, primarily the Lakota, who blocked postal expansion into the interior.

coverage all but withered away. Blank areas of postal coverage like the ones shown in Figure I.6 had come to reflect the unequal distribution of public services and the federal government's willful neglect of Native communities. These maps, then, must be approached with a healthy dose of caution.[17]

*The US Post was fast moving.* In the decades after the Civil War, the US Post spread like wildfire across the western United States. When Clark Thompson sat down to write his letter in 1864, there were just over 2,000 post offices operating in the region. When John Wanamaker sat down to write his report as postmaster general twenty-five years later, there were nearly 11,000 (see Figure I.7). The explosion of the western postal network was one of the most rapid and far-reaching spatial expansions of infrastructure in American history. For such a massive entity, the US Post was surprisingly nimble, capable of extending its infrastructure into remote places in a short period of time.[18]

*The US Post was unstable.* The US Post may have been capable of rapidly expanding its network, but not all of this new infrastructure was permanent. In his 1889 report, Postmaster General Wanamaker noted that in the past twelve months alone some 1,147 post offices across the country had shut down, and another 1,021 had changed names or locations. This was quite typical. Over the preceding twenty-five years a combined 48,000 US post offices had either closed, changed names, or moved locations—an average of roughly 1,900 of these changes every year (see Figure I.8). Instability was especially pronounced in the western half of the country, where post offices shut down at roughly two to three times the rate as their eastern

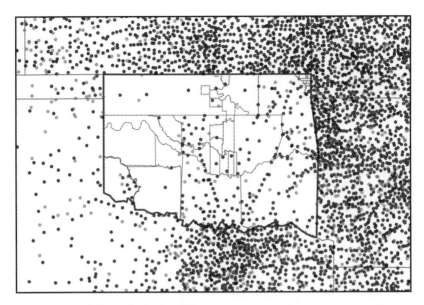

**Figure I.6** Network Boundaries in 1889

Indian Territory did not enjoy the same dense postal coverage as its neighboring states in 1889. Individual reservations are outlined in light gray, and Indian Territory is outlined in dark gray.

counterparts. In the American West, postal expansion and postal contraction went hand in hand.[19]

The nation's postal workforce was even more transitory than its infrastructure. In the late 19th century, roughly one out of every six postmasters was removed, resigned, or died in office each year.[20] This was partly due to the "spoils system" of electoral politics, in which the political party that controlled the executive branch doled out government jobs to party loyalists. Due to its size, the Post Office Department had more of these patronage positions than all other executive departments combined. Whenever the presidency changed between Republican and Democratic control, thousands of postmasters were swept out of office. In fact, when John Wanamaker took over as postmaster general in 1889, the Republican appointee immediately rescinded thousands of postmaster appointments made by his Democratic predecessor (see Figure I.9). New people constantly moved in and out of the nation's postal workforce.[21]

The composite portrait that emerges from the US Post is what I've termed a "gossamer network," a phrase that invokes the image of a gauzy web, rapidly spinning out new threads to distant locations. Its tendrils were light, even delicate, and apt to melt away at a moment's notice. These gossamer features weren't universally shared across the US Post. In more densely populated areas, the postal system was a much more stable entity. But across the American countryside the gossamer network reigned supreme, reaching a kind of apex in the western United States. There, the US Post was at its most sprawling, fast moving, and ephemeral. This might seem strange, given that words like "fast moving" and "ephemeral" aren't typically

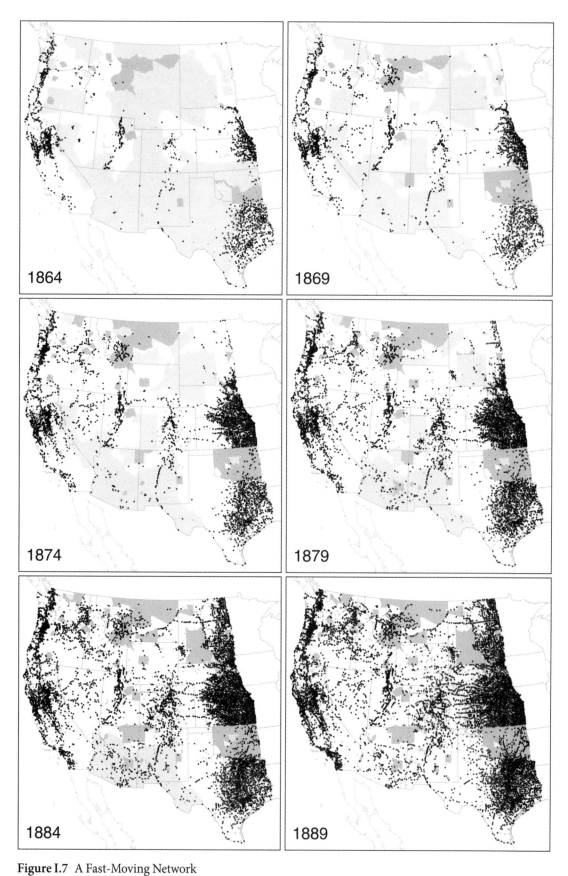

**Figure I.7** A Fast-Moving Network

These maps illustrate the rapid spread of the western postal network over a 25-year period. Each map shows post offices, unceded Native land in light gray, and reservations in dark gray for a given year.

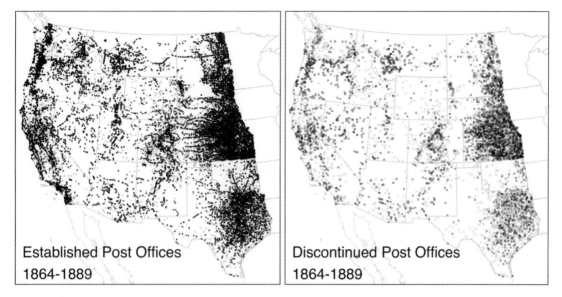

**Figure I.8** An Unstable Network

The map on the left shows western post offices that opened between 1864 and 1889. The map on the right shows western post offices that shut down or permanently changed names or locations during that same time period. Post offices for which exact locations could not be determined are randomly distributed within the county in which they operated and are displayed in a lighter, semi-transparent color to reflect their uncertainty (see the Note on Methods for more information).

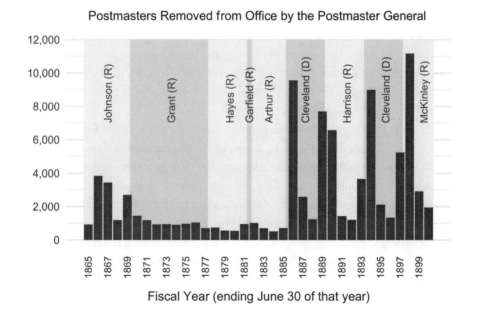

**Figure I.9** The Revolving Door

The authority to remove postmasters from office was often used by postmasters general for partisan purposes when the presidency changed from one political party to another. This chart displays the number of postmasters who were removed from office over the preceding fiscal year (July 1 to June 30) between 1865 and 1900. Numbers were transcribed from Annual Reports of the Postmaster General, 1865–1900.

associated with government institutions. Which raises the question: How did this federal network even work? How did it expand (and contract) so quickly and across such a large area?

The US Post forces a reconsideration of the American state and its history. Unlike today, most of the nation's postal infrastructure was not publicly owned or operated in the 19th century. Outside of big cities, the US Post did not erect its own stand-alone post office buildings, buy its own fleet of horse-drawn vehicles, or hire its own staff of salaried civil servants. Instead, it appointed local private agents to act on its behalf. It contracted with stagecoach companies to shuttle bags of mail between post offices and paid merchants or other business owners to sell stamps and distribute letters from inside their stores or homes. These responsibilities were rarely a full-time pursuit, so contractors and postmasters simply added their mail duties on top of their primary occupation. These temporary, flexible arrangements help to explain the gossamer network's rapid and unstable expansion across the western United States.

The rural postal system exemplified a larger organizational framework at the heart of *Paper Trails*: the agency model. Here, the term "agency" is not used as a synonym for "department" (as in "Environmental Protection Agency"), nor does it refer to an individual's ability to take action. Instead, it represents a specific kind of institutional arrangement. In the agency model, large organizations delegate local individuals (agents) to carry out specific tasks on its behalf, each of whom is responsible for a particular geographical territory. These agents act with minimal direct oversight and are typically far removed from administrative headquarters. They are often part-time, temporary positions, and in the 19th century they were largely paid through commissions, fees, and contracts rather than a regular salary. The agency model was widespread across the private sector, as local sales agents would peddle books on behalf of distant publishing houses or life insurance policies for large financial companies. But the agency model also powered large swathes of the public sector, including the US Post.[22]

In 21st-century terms, the agency model was like an algorithm for solving the problems of US geography. Even in an era of rapid urbanization, the majority of Americans lived in small towns and communities that were scattered across a huge area of land. How could the federal government provide mail service to all of these different places? Rather than starting from scratch, the Post Office Department grafted mail service onto a preexisting private infrastructure. This allowed it to extend its network to many more places and do so much more quickly than if it had built its own public infrastructure. It could then withdraw from those same distant places without having to dismantle or abandon anything in its wake. It simply terminated a storeowner's appointment as postmaster or allowed a mail contract with a staging company to expire. The agency model was the machinery behind the US Post's rural gossamer network.

The significance of the agency model within the American state has been overlooked, in part due to a different sort of organizational framework that has long defined government institutions: bureaucracy. Today, the words "government" and "bureaucracy" have become practically interchangeable. But a bureaucracy is a particular kind of government organization—a hierarchical institution marked by centralized oversight, organizational stability, and a workforce of professionalized, salaried civil servants. With its unstable infrastructure and part-time, semi-privatized workforce, the gossamer network was a far cry from a bureaucracy. It is tempting to see these contrasts with a bureaucracy as a sign of institutional weakness. But the rural mail system wasn't effective in spite of its lack of bureaucratic features; it was effective because of them. It was precisely the absence of so many traditional hallmarks of bureaucratic strength that made the gossamer network such a crucial part of the American state's efforts to incorporate the western United States.[23]

***

*Paper Trails* is a work of spatial history. Many of its findings started with a one-word question: Where? Where was the US Post actually located in the West? Where and when did it spread? How did that happen? You cannot understand the significance of the US Post and its gossamer network without understanding its underlying geography. Spatial history involves more than just locating things on a map (although there are many maps in this book). Stopping to consider questions of space and geography opens up a host of broader historical insights about the pace and character of western expansion and integration, the organizational machinery of the American state, and the connections that knit the nation together.[24]

*Paper Trails* begins with a conceptual overview of the US Post and the kind of power it exercised in the western United States. The first chapter situates the postal network and the agency model within the larger apparatus of the federal government, advancing a new framework for thinking about geography and state power. Chapter 2 concretizes how this power shaped everyday life in the West, following the story of a single family and the ways in which they relied on the US Post as they moved around the region. The remainder of the book presents a chronological narrative over five chapters about the network's expansion and operations in the West from the 1860s through the early 1900s. In order to understand such a large and complex system, each of the five chapters zooms in on a particular piece of its machinery. It begins with the US Post's breakneck expansion into new areas of the West in the 1860s and 1870s and chronicles the struggles of postal officials to oversee this growth, first through a new mapmaking initiative described in chapter 3 and then with the department's mismanagement of western mail routes, as detailed in chapter 4. The story then transitions into the 1880s and 1890s, during which the US Post "thickened" its coverage in the region and integrated local communities into larger orbits of governance, politics, and commerce. Chapter 5 uncovers the central role of post offices and postmasters within these towns during the 1880s, while chapter 6 recovers the financial flows that connected them through the rise of a new service, the postal money order system. Chapter 7 draws the story to a close in the early 1900s with the rise of Rural Free Delivery, which ushered in a new era for the US Post and the rural geography of the western United States.

Many of the same characteristics that made the US Post so important in the 19th century also make it an unwieldly subject to narrate today. Telling this history requires following a vast, ever-shifting network over five decades, thousands of different locations, hundreds of thousands of workers, and some one million square miles of land. Several narrative strategies are used to convey this history across different spatial scales.[25] At the largest scale, the book's maps, charts, and numbers help communicate the US Post and how it operated as a national and regional network, focusing on the area of the contiguous United States spanning from the Kansas-Missouri border in the east to California's Pacific coast in the west. Although the US Post's global connections were an important part of its history, *Paper Trails* stays mainly inside the nation's borders in order to focus on the American state's project of internal colonization and integration. For similar reasons, it excludes Alaska, Hawaii, and the United States' overseas colonies, all of which involved a much different, primarily ocean-based model of postal expansion.[26] Finally, given that the US Post was a national institution, this book focuses on the federal government rather than the administrative machinery of individual states.[27]

Even under these constraints, the static medium of the printed page makes it difficult to capture the full scope and dynamism of the postal network. To address this, I have created an online map-based visualization that charts the US Post's successive stages of western expansion: http://gossamernetwork.com.[28] The major arguments in this book stand on their own, but the online visualization makes it easier to understand the network's geography and its connections to other changes unfolding in the region. Of course, a digital medium comes with its own challenges. Websites from just 10 years ago already feel like relics from another era, and this visualization will doubtless show its age just as quickly. But in the meantime it allows readers to conceptualize the network's spread across the western United States in a new light.[29]

Maps of the postal network provide a bird's-eye view of the network as a whole, but most 19th-century Americans didn't interact with the US Post at thirty thousand feet. *Paper Trails* repeatedly descends to ground level in order to see the system through their eyes. Individuals make up the narrative heart of this book, and their stories unfold in two settings: at the Post Office Department's headquarters in Washington, DC, and in the small towns and stage roads of the rural West. At the system's center, government officials in the mapmaking (chapter 3), mail transportation (chapter 4), and money order divisions (chapter 6) attempted to administer the western postal network from their desks in Washington, often with uneven results. Their struggles tell a story about the enduring challenges to centralized administration during this period. On the postal system's periphery, a very different cast of characters takes center stage. Without the stagecoach operators who carried the mail (chapter 4) or the shopkeepers and businessowners who served as part-time postmasters (chapter 5), the nation's postal machinery would grind to a halt. These sorts of local private actors do not typically appear in histories of the

American state, but they drove much of the federal postal network's expansion and operations. Finally, even those westerners who weren't employed by the US Post still felt its effects. The experiences of a western governor (chapter 1), a migrating family (chapter 2), and the women and men of a California mining town (chapters 5 and 6) reveal the structural power of the US Post to shape the conditions of everyday life in the western United States.

*Paper Trails* is a history of large structures and processes. It is a story about the 19th century's most expansive communications network and the role it played within American society. It charts one of the most dramatic spatial reorganizations of people, land, capital, and resources in American history. And it reconsiders the history of the American state, how it functioned, and the ways in which it exercised power. *Paper Trails* is also filled with much smaller stories. A sister's decision to join her brother in California. A federal clerk tracing a line on a government map. The cluttered shelves of a local general store. A half-page note about a misplaced overcoat. Ultimately, this is history defined by the intersection between these two scales, the ways in which large forces shape individual lives and how human experience gives meaning to the structures that define our world.

# 1

# Geography and State Power

What is the state, and how does it exercise power? These seemingly abstract questions become much more concrete inside a 21st-century federal immigration courtroom. First-time observers of these proceedings tend to notice two features. For one, immigration hearings are overwhelmingly bureaucratic affairs. Judges and lawyers speak in an impenetrable legalese of I-589 forms, A-numbers, filing deadlines, and master calendars. As defendants wait for their names to be called, the proceedings look more like a trip to the Department of Motor Vehicles than a television courtroom drama. But unlike renewing a driver's license, the state's capacity for violence looms large in federal immigration court. Armed guards watch over shackled defendants dressed in prison jumpsuits. Judges decide whether and how the government will punish them through incarceration, fines, and deportation. This combination of mundane paperwork and muscular force captures two foundational characteristics of the state: bureaucracy and coercion.[1]

The early 20th-century sociologist Max Weber championed bureaucracy as one of the defining organizational models of modern social structures (and modern states in particular). He described the "ideal type" of bureaucracy as having certain features: a specialized and hierarchical organization that follows a set of internal rules and that employs a full-time, professionalized workforce that relies on written documents. Although bureaucracies exist across the private sector, they are most often associated with government institutions. Weber similarly emphasized coercion in his discussions of the state, which he defined as "a human community that (successfully) claims the monopoly on the legitimate use of violence within a given territory." Can the state wage war or put down insurrections? Can a government make people follow laws? Will they be punished if they don't? But this framework of bureaucracy and coercion is misleading. Government institutions aren't always organized as bureaucracies, and they don't always exercise power through coercion.[2]

A Weberian lens of bureaucracy and coercion produces a history of the American state divided into two acts. In act 1, a fear of monarchy led the founders to limit the authority of the national government in favor of state governments. By Weber's standards, the 19th-century federal government lacked both bureaucratic capacity and coercive power. It was, in a word, weak. In act 2, the 20th-century American state transformed into a powerful modern leviathan. Over the course of the Progressive Era, the New Deal, two world wars, the Cold War, and the Great Society, the American state built up new civilian agencies (bureaucracy) alongside the world's most powerful military force (coercion). Remove this Weberian lens, however, and the story changes. Rather than a sequential story about a weak state becoming a strong one, historians have uncovered a powerful federal apparatus stretching all the way back to the nation's founding.[3]

In the early years of the American republic, the federal government waged war, mapped territory, built infrastructure, collected tariffs, carried mail, provided disaster relief, and propped up the institution of chattel slavery.[4] The Civil War further expanded the state's capacity, as the federal government mobilized a vast military and civilian machinery to put down the Confederate rebellion. In the wake of that war it extended citizenship to millions of formerly enslaved people while launching new campaigns of conquest against Native groups in the West. By the end of the century, the federal government had seized, surveyed, and distributed vast tracts of western land and resources and begun to acquire an overseas empire.[5] Much of this was accomplished, paradoxically, by keeping federal authority "out of sight." Rather than establishing large civil-service bureaucracies or wielding nakedly coercive power, the federal government often delegated tasks to surrogates and intermediaries through a system of fees and bounties, including state and municipal governments, private corporations, entrepreneurs, voluntary associations, and religious organizations.[6]

Despite a surge of scholarship on the 19th-century American state, the topic is often discussed in abstract ways when it comes to geography. Otherwise sophisticated treatments of the state tend to use a spatial vocabulary—the "scales" of national, state, and local authority, the "sites" of governance, or the "boundaries" separating civil society, the market, and the state—without much spatial specificity. Little is known about the distribution of the state's infrastructure and workforce or when and how that geography changed over time. In concrete terms, where *was* the state? It is easy to take this question for granted. After all, states are inherently spatial things, with borders that appear on maps. In short, they have territory. This is what makes a state a state. But just because a state lays claim to a particular area of the globe does not mean that it actually controls that space evenly. Understanding where, when, and how a state extends authority over claimed territory is a crucial part of its history. And nowhere was this more true than in the western United States.[7]

Over the second half of the 19th century the American state incorporated the western United States into the nation. The speed and success of this project can lend it an air of inevitability, as the state takes on the appearance of a "weaponized filing cabinet" rolling across the region, violently displacing Native inhabitants in order to pave the way for farms and towns, mines and dams, railroad lines and telegraph wires. But there was nothing inevitable about the speed, success, or scope of western expansion.[8] At mid-century, the federal government's territorial claims may have stretched all the way to the Pacific Ocean, but its authority over this land was virtually nonexistent. It had little to no presence in the region outside of a handful of isolated army forts and some small footholds on the Pacific coast, and it lacked even basic knowledge about on-the-ground conditions in the region. In many places Native sovereignty trumped American law and governance. The state had to extend its authority across a vast and sparsely settled environment unlike anything it had faced in the eastern United States. It had to conduct long-distance military campaigns against powerful Indigenous groups while repeatedly facing down local challenges to federal authority across the region. It had to map land, catalog resources, and allocate them to settlers and private companies. It had to carve out federal territories, admit new states, and build an administrative apparatus to oversee the region. The American state's efforts to incorporate western territory faced daunting challenges of geography and distance. This would be a fundamentally spatial project, and the US Post would provide the underlying circuitry to complete it.[9]

## The Hidden Channel of Governance

"I had forgotten where I had left my overcoat," Clark Thompson wrote to the post trader at the Yankton Indian Agency in January of 1864.[10] While the fate of the overcoat has been lost to history, the fate of the post trader has not. The man in question, Andrew Jackson Faulk, was a successful lawyer and businessman in Pennsylvania before he moved to Dakota Territory in 1861 to take up the job of post trader at the newly created Yankton Indian Reservation. Faulk likely secured this position through his political connections within the Republican Party, which had recently taken control of the presidency. Faulk used those same connections in 1866 to catapult himself into a far more prestigious position: governor of Dakota Territory. From start to finish, Faulk's tenure in office was completely dependent on the mail.[11]

Andrew Faulk's appointment placed him quite literally on the periphery of the American state, far removed from the federal government's seat of power in Washington, DC. Unfortunately for Faulk, 19th-century governance was a never-ending exercise in long-distance communication. Legislators had to field grievances or requests from their constituents. Circuit judges needed to be able to disseminate decisions to courts across the country. Customs officials needed to collect tariffs and deposit them in the public treasury. The vast majority of these interactions unfolded at a distance rather than through face-to-face interactions. And as Thompson and Faulk could attest, in the United States those distances were quite large.

Even at the nation's founding the Constitution's framers worried whether a republican model of government could survive in a country as large as the United States. As historian Richard R. John has shown, the US Post held together the United States' fledgling political system. It carried newspapers and periodicals that kept citizens informed about politics and government. It provided common links to a dispersed population, cultivating a shared national sense of identity. And, crucially, it fostered connections between constituencies and their elected representatives. When officials convened in Washington, most of them were far removed from their constituents. Unable to regularly travel back to their districts, they instead relied on the so-called franking privilege. First instituted under the 1792 Post Office Act, the "franking privilege" allowed certain government officials to send and receive mail without paying any postage. Congressmen used this franking privilege with abandon, mailing not only letters home to their constituents but also pamphlets, copies of their speeches, printed government documents, and newspapers. This service gradually extended across the federal government, to postmasters, officers in the executive branch, soldiers during wartime, and even the widows of former presidents. These were the early long-distance links of the nation's representative democracy.[12]

As the United States seized more and more territory during the 19th century, the challenges of distance grew ever more urgent. In the western United States, the US Post was a prerequisite for even rudimentary functions of government. In fact, the first post office in what would later become Dakota Territory preceded its organization as a federal territory by a full decade. By the time the first territorial assembly met in Yankton in 1862, there were already 11 post offices up and running in Dakota. As elected officials started writing civil and criminal laws, drawing up a tax code, and establishing county boundaries, they used these nascent postal connections to collect and disseminate information. By comparison, the first telegraph line wouldn't reach Yankton until 1870, which meant that Dakota's early territorial politics and statecraft relied on letters rather than telegrams.[13]

Andrew Faulk's correspondence illustrates the extent to which the American state depended on the underlying federal infrastructure of the US Post. Appropriately enough, his tenure kicked off with a letter, an official notification from the Department of the Interior instructing him to fill out the required forms and forward them to Washington, DC.[14] Almost immediately, the new governor started using the mail to fulfill his new responsibilities. Government agencies like the Treasury Department's Bureau of Statistics sent him inquiries about Dakota and its population, with similar requests pouring in from private citizens who were considering moving there.[15] Faulk sent official letters appointing territorial officials, from a local probate judge to the paymaster of the Dakota militia.[16] He also corresponded with a US Treasury agent named Enos Stutsman who was stationed at Pembina on the far side of Dakota Territory along the northern border with Canada. Stutsman's letters to Faulk had to travel some seven hundred miles, detouring into neighboring Minnesota before winding their way back to Yankton. But this connection nevertheless allowed Stutsman to submit official election returns from a distant corner of Dakota to its seat of government on the opposite side of the territory.

Letters were part of a larger constellation of long-distance correspondence between government officials. All sorts of paperwork flowed across the US Post, including certificates, registries, forms, contracts, receipts, and commissions.[17] Take the case of Andrew Faulk's own appointment as governor. To make the position official, he had to fill out a bond and oath of office (including a "loyalty oath" to guard against ex-Confederates taking office) and then send those forms to his superiors in Washington, DC.[18] These pieces of paper made up the forgotten cogs of governance. Handwritten letters might make for more interesting reading material than a printed government form, but the latter is what kept the larger machinery of the state running. Without the postal network carrying those scraps of paper between distant places and seats of government, they would be just that: scraps of paper.

Faulk's appointment as governor came with the additional title of superintendent of Indian affairs for Dakota Territory, which made him the federal government's local proxy for dealing with the thousands of Native people who lived inside Dakota's borders. This put him at the frontlines of the state's larger project of Greater Reconstruction. Articulated by historian Elliott West, the era of Greater Reconstruction encompassed the 1840s through the 1870s, when the federal government consolidated its authority over both the southern and western United States, putting down the Confederate rebellion in the South while also waging war against Native groups in the West. Questions of race and citizenship loomed large as the nation debated whether and how to incorporate African American freed people, American Indians, former Mexican citizens, religious minorities, and new immigrants into the national polity.[19] Faulk used the mail to conduct Greater Reconstruction's on-the-ground operations. He sent letters coordinating peace envoys with the US Army and arranging for gifts to be sent from Yankton up the Missouri River to Dakota's northern tribes.[20] He used the mail to request an increase in federal troops to monitor these northern groups, appoint government agents to work on specific reservations, and ask for extra supplies for these reservations.[21] Indian agents in turn mailed him on-the-ground updates, including official letters that he forwarded on to the Commissioner of Indian Affairs to include in his annual report.[22]

Even in-person governance depended on long-distance communication. In early 1867, Andrew Faulk led a diplomatic envoy of 30 Yankton and Santee tribal leaders to Washington, DC, part of an effort to improve living conditions on Dakota's government reservations. The trip included a face-to-face audience with President Andrew Johnson, in which Johnson referred to himself as their "great father" and pledged "care and protection of [his] wards."[23] The language of the meeting reflected the federal government's pivot away from negotiating with western tribes as sovereign nations and toward a policy of removing them onto reservations where they could be assimilated into white "civilized" culture. Notably, the entire visit was coordinated through the mail. In the year leading up to the trip, Faulk and other government officials exchanged a series of letters hammering out the trip's details, down to what the delegates should wear on their visit, deciding between "full suits of [white] Citizen's clothing" or "Indian costumes" (they opted for both).[24] Faulk then added the cost of these clothes to a running tally of trip expenditures that included hotel accommodations, railroad tickets, and meals. He would later mail this handwritten expense report to his higher-ups in the Office of Indian Affairs for reimbursement.[25]

Andrew Faulk's dual position as both governor and superintendent of Indian affairs meant that he repeatedly played the role of peacemaker between his constituents and the US Army. [26] Many of Dakota's white residents wanted the federal government to annex the Black Hills, an area in western Dakota that the Lakota held as a sacred site called He Sapa.[27] The US Army, meanwhile, was battling the Lakota and their Northern Cheyenne and Northern Arapaho allies. Facing a string of defeats, a war-weary public, and spiraling costs, army officials increasingly looked toward peaceful negotiations. When word reached them that a group of private citizens were planning to march into the Black Hills, a general wrote to Faulk to warn him that "the military authorities will not protect them in an invasion of land still held unceded by the Indian tribes."[28] Although Faulk himself was an advocate for opening up the Black Hills to white settlement, he duly printed the general's letter in Yankton's *Union and Dakotaian* newspaper.[29] After Yankton's citizens disregarded the notice and continued to ready themselves for an expedition, a fed-up army officer finally warned Faulk in a letter that any such action would be "in violation of law" and instructed him to prevent it "using force if necessary."[30]

The correspondence between army officers and Andrew Faulk over federal Indian policy highlights the ways in which the American state's coercive power flowed through less obvious channels. The US Army supplied the violent force behind the state's project of Greater Reconstruction. But exercising this power required other kinds of administrative capacity, including the ability to coordinate actions from a distance. Again and again, the US Post provided the necessary infrastructure to do so. It shuttled communications up and down the military's chain of command, including directives about troop movements, accounts of skirmishes and battles, muster rolls, casualty lists, requests for more supplies or troops, and official reports. Soldiers themselves relied on the mail to bring them letters from friends and family, national newspapers and magazines, and even (depending on their home state) absentee ballots to vote in elections.

The army's reliance on the mail itself depended on the US Post's ability to extend its network into isolated places. During the mid-1860s, for example, the army built a string of forts along the Missouri River, deep in Dakota Territory's interior and hundreds of miles away from the nearest American settlements. This military infrastructure provided the state's coercive power. But the state's civilian infrastructure extended alongside it: by 1867, six of Dakota's forts also had post offices. This included the Fort Randall Post Office, which processed more mail that year than any other post office in Dakota Territory. The sheer quantity of correspondence and paperwork that passed through Dakota's military outposts underscores how the American state's violent campaigns were conducted with envelopes as well as rifles.[31]

In the end, Andrew Faulk's tenure in office drew to a close much as it began: through the mail. In April of 1869, Faulk opened up an envelope containing yet another sheet of government paper: a letter officially notifying him that he was being replaced as governor. As soon as his successor arrived in Yankton, Faulk was "to turn over all the records, books, correspondence, and general property of the Executive office." His removal likely stemmed from the changeover in administrations that had come with the inauguration of President Ulysses S. Grant the previous month. Although little comfort to Faulk himself, the letter was a testament to the postal connections that knit together the larger apparatus of the American state. From the headquarters of an executive department in Washington, the letter had traveled some twelve hundred miles to the desk of a western territorial official. Its journey had taken just one week.[32]

## Occupation

Eight hundred miles away from Yankton, government officials in Colorado Territory were wrestling with similar issues as Andrew Faulk. As in Dakota Territory, Native people still occupied much of Colorado when it became a federal territory in 1861. In particular, groups of Utes including the Mouache, Caputa, Parianuche, Sabuagan, Tabeguache, Weeminuche, and Yampa controlled large areas of western Colorado. Over the following years, officials attempted to carve out more and more land for white settlement. In 1868, a collection of Ute leaders signed an agreement with federal officials that shrank their land claims while establishing the western third of Colorado as Ute territory. As part of the agreement, non-Natives were forbidden "to pass over, settle upon, or reside in" this area. Americans promptly ignored this prohibition, trespassing on Ute land in search of gold and silver in the San Juan Mountains. In 1873, federal officials renegotiated with several Ute leaders and reached the so-called Brunot Agreement, which ceded an additional chunk of mineral-rich Ute land to the federal government. Congress officially ratified the agreement in 1874, opening up an additional 3.7 million acres to white settlers.[33]

The seizure of Ute land in southwestern Colorado was part of a larger process of settler colonialism, in which a colonizing society attempts to exterminate or remove Indigenous peoples and replace them with its own population. This was a project steeped in violence and explicitly backed by the coercive power of the American state.[34] However, while violence and coercion explain the seizure of western land, they do not explain the speed with which Americans then occupied this plundered territory. As historian Virginia Scharff emphasizes, colonization in the West wasn't just about removing Native peoples and taking their land; it also required Americans to move to places that "were unpromising, to say the least."[35] The mountainous corner of southwestern Colorado was one of those places. The area may have been promising in terms of its mineral wealth, but it was also one of the least accessible places in the contiguous United States. One newspaper editor in the summer of 1874 called it the worst "of all the rough and rugged countries that it has been my fortune to travel over."[36] Earlier that year, a prospector named Alferd Packer had resorted to cannibalism when his winter expedition became lost and snowbound in the mountains.[37] The American state had officially laid claim to this tract of Native land, but that did not in and of itself guarantee that Americans would occupy it.

But occupy it they did. Thousands of prospectors and settlers poured into south-western Colorado in the wake of the Brunot Agreement, bringing the US Post with them. As shown in Figure 1.1, the first post office in the area opened shortly after Congress ratified the agreement in 1874, and within three years there were nearly 20 post offices up and running. By 1877, horseback riders and wagons were carrying the mail to small and otherwise remote mining camps like Mineral City, Tellurium, and Animas Forks.[38] These new lines of communication carried news about mining strikes to newspapers in eastern Colorado, helping further stoke the "San Juan Fever" that brought so many people swarming into southwestern Colorado during the 1870s. The US Post did not cause settlers to occupy this area; the lure of gold and silver would have brought them with or without the mail. But when they reached this otherwise distant and inhospitable place, an accessible postal service helped make it a little more livable. The US Post's ability to rapidly expand its gossamer net-work facilitated a larger process of colonization.[39]

The impact of the US Post comes into clearer focus when situated within the wider landscape of the American state. By 1877, the project of Greater Reconstruction had reached a kind of culmination in the West. The government's large-scale mil-itary mobilizations against western tribes were winding down, and the state was building up its civilian infrastructure in order to administer all of this conquered territory. Three institutions in particular—the US Army, the Office of Indian Affairs, and the General Land Office—were tasked with some of the state's central functions in the region: conquering and dispossessing Native peoples, confining them on reservations, and parceling out their land to white settlers. So where were these three main government actors located? How were their offices and personnel distributed? Several sources list the locations of government offices, forts, and outposts that were operated by the US Army, the Office of Indian Affairs, and the General Land Office in 1877. Together, they start to answer the seemingly basic question: Where was the state?[40]

The maps in Figure 1.2 have their limitations. They only capture the places where people were stationed according to official government records, but people didn't always stay put: soldiers on patrol might range hundreds of miles from a fort, or a government surveyor might lead a mapping expedition far away from his of-fice. Relatedly, the maps do not show other government agents who "resided" in Washington, DC, but may have nonetheless traveled or worked in the western United States. In short, they imply a degree of stasis that did not exist on the ground. Nevertheless, they are a starting point for excavating the spatial skeleton of Greater Reconstruction in the West. In some ways, the maps confirm suspicions. The three main government institutions of the US Army, the Office of Indian Affairs, and the General Land Office operated across a largely rural geography: think of General George Custer's cavalry galloping across the plains, a schoolhouse on a wind-swept Indian reservation, or the rectangular grid of a homestead survey. Despite the scholarly attention that has been paid to these three institutions, however, they

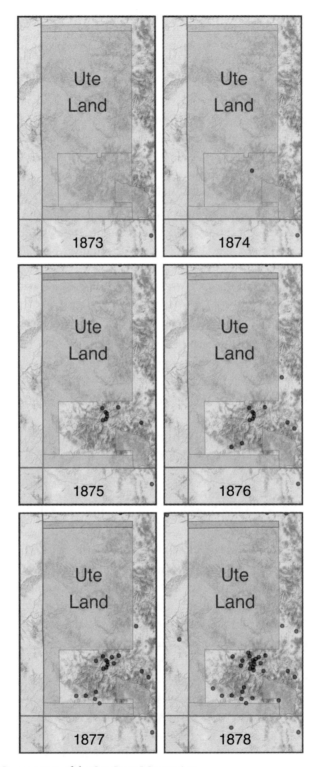

**Figure 1.1** Occupation of the San Juan Mountains

The seizure of Ute land (light gray) in southwestern Colorado was immediately followed by the rapid spread of US Post Offices between 1873 and 1878. Terrain imagery comes from Stamen Maps (http://maps.stamen.com/terrain/), downloaded September 27, 2019.

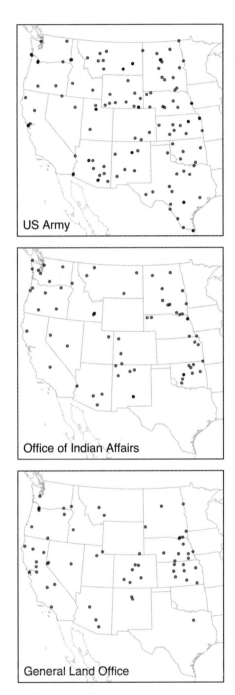

**Figure 1.2** The American State and Greater Reconstruction

These maps compare the locations of personnel working for the US Army, Office of Indian Affairs, and General Land Office in 1877. Data for the Office of Indian Affairs and General Land Office were collected from *The Official Register of the United States, 1877* (Washington, DC: Government Printing Office, 1877). Many thanks to Benjamin Brands for providing the locations of US Army forts.

weren't the only state actors in the West. The *Official Register of the United States*, a biennial directory of federal workers, reveals a much longer cast of characters.[41]

To take one example, the Treasury Department employed more people in the West in 1877 than the Department of the Interior, a classically "western" institution that housed both the Office of Indian Affairs and the General Land Office. Moreover, Figure 1.3 reveals that the Treasury Department operated a mainly urban and coastal geography rather than the better-known frontier geography of the rural western interior. This leads to a more complete picture of where the state was, who constituted it, and what those people did. "The state" wasn't just made up of people like James Craven, a government agent working at the Cheyenne River Indian reservation in Dakota Territory. It was also Maggie Cook weighing coins at the US Mint in Carson City, Nevada, and Julia Williams running the Santa Barbara lighthouse off the coast of California.[42] Government workers pursued a much wider range of state projects than just military campaigns, land surveys, or Indian reservations. Mapping the material presence of the federal government illustrates a more expansive state and its operations in the West.[43]

Finally, surveying the full landscape of the federal government in the West shows that no government institution had a more expansive spatial footprint than the US Post. In 1877, the Post Office Department operated more than five thousand offices in the West, or 10 times as many locations as all other government organizations (civilian and military) combined. Compared to army forts, Indian agencies, customs houses, land offices, courthouses, and lighthouses, the federal government's thousands of post offices blanketed the region. Small-town post offices popped up practically anywhere a group of people coalesced: in mining and timber camps, in

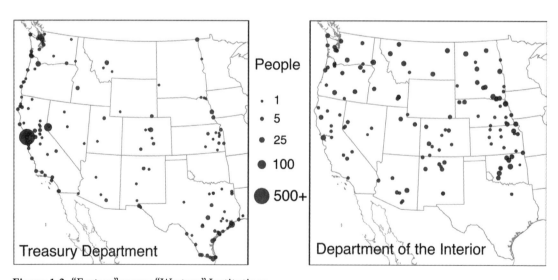

**Figure 1.3** "Eastern" versus "Western" Institutions

Despite its association with the eastern United States, the Treasury Department (*left*) employed more people in the western United States than the Department of the Interior (*right*), with its workforce concentrated largely in urban and coastal locations. Data collected from *The Official Register of the United States, 1877* (Washington, DC: Government Printing Office, 1877).

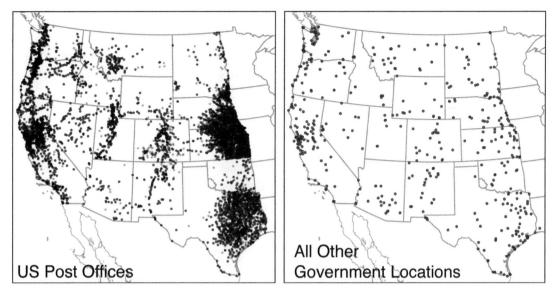

**Figure 1.4** The Most Expansive Arm of the State

The spatial distribution of post offices (*left*) dwarfed that of all other federal institutions (*right*) in the western United States 1877. All other government locations include personnel for the Department of the Interior, the Federal Judiciary, the Treasury Department, the War Department, and the US Army. Data for civilian institutions was collected from *The Official Register of the United States, 1877* (Washington, DC: Government Printing Office, 1877). Benjamin Brands provided the locations of US Army forts.

farming and ranching communities, at stage stations, railway stops, health resorts, and mill towns. No other government entity was capable of moving as quickly and operating in as many different places. Its expansive network extended the reach of the state into thousands of "in-between" places in which the federal government had no other institutional presence. The US Post was the lowest common spatial denominator of the state; this was the source of its power and the starting point from which all else flowed.[44]

## The Agency Model

How did the US Post operate such a spatially expansive network? Studying the inner machinery of the 19th century's largest public institution leads to a deeper understanding of how states are organized and the broader relationship between territory, geography, and state power. Once again, southwestern Colorado provides a useful example. The post offices that sprouted up in the 1870s on recently seized Ute land were not the kind of freestanding post office buildings that operate today. Not a single one of these offices was run by a full-time, salaried government employee. Instead, most Colorado postmasters worked part-time for small commissions and fees, typically housing their post offices in private residences or businesses. In 1877, the post office at Eureka, Colorado, was run by a hotel and restaurant owner named Thomas G. Andrews. Four and a half miles up the road, a mine and mill owner named Edwin M. Brown was in charge of the Animas Forks Post Office. Neither Andrews nor Brown was paid very much ($86.83 and $76.50, respectively), and neither of them held onto the position for very long. Two year later, both of them had lost their appointments.[45] The two may seem like unlikely candidates to illuminate the American state and its history. After all, they were not bureaucrats. They didn't have any particular technical expertise when it came to handling the mail, didn't work in a government building, didn't draw a regular salary, and weren't dedicated to a career in the public sector. They were just two local businessmen who occasionally sorted and distributed mail for their neighbors. These localized, semi-privatized, and temporary positions are difficult to square with the typical impression of a government job. Andrews and Brown were instead part of a less familiar structure of governance: the agency model.

The agency model was one of the principal organizational frameworks of the 19th-century United States. In basic terms, it was a solution to the challenges of distance and geography. An organization would delegate tasks to local representatives who were responsible for a surrounding geographical area. This allowed the organization to provide services to a dispersed populace scattered across thousands of different places. In the private sector, sales agents received commissions for peddling books, newspapers, and magazine subscriptions on behalf of companies like Scribner and Company. Life insurance companies like New York Life enlisted local agents to sell policies and vet the long-term health prospects of applicants. The credit rating company R.G. Dun, & Co. relied on local agents to file on-the-ground reports. So too did the Pinkerton National Detective Agency.[46]

The agency model was the engine behind the nation's rural mail service. Roughly 95 percent of all post offices operated according to this model. Small-town postmasters who ran these offices had more in common with sales agents than civil servants, offering services to their "clients" in exchange for small payments. The bulk of these payments came through a commission system that was calculated as a sliding-scale percentage of the outgoing mail from their office. Postmasters also received fixed fees for extra services, such as processing postal money orders or renting out letterboxes. Once a postmaster's annual combined compensation of commissions and fees reached one thousand dollars, their post office was reclassified from a "fourth-class" office to a "Presidential" office. This new designation meant that the postmaster's appointment had to be approved by the Senate and that they began receiving a fixed annual salary from the government.[47] The vast majority of postmasters, however, never came anywhere close to that level: at the end of the 19th century, roughly half received less than one hundred dollars a year.[48]

Rural postmasters worked with a second kind of local agent: contractors who carried mail along thousands of so-called star routes, or any form of transportation that was not a railroad or steamship. The Post Office Department awarded temporary contracts to companies or individuals to transport the mail along these star routes, most often via stagecoach or on horseback. For the majority of Americans who didn't live directly on a railway or major river, this was how they got their mail.[49] Like rural postmasters, the public responsibility of transporting the mail was largely a part-time task grafted onto an existing private business. Transportation companies that won a mail contract often simply added a few extra mail bags alongside their passengers, freight, or other cargo. Like postmaster appointments, postal contracts were impermanent: they lasted for a maximum of four years (many were shorter), and postal officials could alter the routes at any time.

The US Post used the agency model to rapidly expand into areas like Colorado's San Juan Mountains during the 1870s. The federal government didn't have to construct buildings, buy vehicles, or dispatch employees. It just appointed a local resident to work part-time as a postmaster and contracted with a staging company to carry the mail. The government's equipment costs were minimal. New postmasters received postage stamps, stamped envelopes, postal cards, and a book of rules and regulations from department headquarters. Small-town postmasters were responsible for supplying everything else, including letterboxes and keys, pens and pencils, rubber stamps, scales, money drawers, and bookkeeping forms—and of course the physical space of the post office itself. Mail contractors, meanwhile, were similarly expected to furnish nearly all of their own equipment, including vehicles, draft animals, barns, and waystations. The only physical equipment provided by the Post Office Department consisted of official sacks, pouches, and canvas bags to carry the mail.[50]

The agency model has been overshadowed by a bureaucratic model of the state. But in the 19th century, large swathes of the US federal government did not function at all like the idealized bureaucracy championed by Max Weber. The US Post's rural mail service highlights this neglected machinery of governance in action and provides a lens for recognizing the agency model in other contexts. Postal officials were not the only ones facing the challenge of American geography. Again and again, government institutions turned to the agency model to provide public services in far-off places. Returning to southwestern Colorado in 1877, two other federal institutions in addition to the US Post were operating on recently seized Ute land: the General Land Office and the federal judiciary. Both of them relied on the agency model. The surveyor general of the United States created the San Juan Land District and located its headquarters in the booming mining town of Lake City in early 1877. As with all of its field offices, the Lake City land office was staffed by two people, a receiver and a register, who were responsible for processing land applications. Although they received a modest base salary from the government, most of their public income came from a 1 percent commission on each land sale. Neither of the workers were full-time civil servants; one was a storeowner and assayer, the other a newspaper editor. They are a reminder that despite the trained, technocratic expertise of the General Land Office's surveyors and cartographers, the task of actually transferring public land into private hands was conducted by a scattered workforce of local agents doing minor clerical work on behalf of the federal government.[51]

The federal judiciary had also staked out a presence in southwestern Colorado by 1877, and much like the Post Office Department and the General Land Office, it had done so using the agency model. The federal court system relied on US commissioners, or local agents who performed minor judicial functions on its behalf. The position of commissioner was first established in 1793, when Congress passed a piece of minor legislation allowing a court to authorize a local person "learned in the law" to take bail in remote parts of a judicial district.[52] The responsibilities of commissioners gradually expanded to include tasks such as taking affidavits, administering oaths, or issuing search warrants. By 1877, more than 1,800 commissioners were scattered across the United States—including Colorado's San Juan Mountains, where John L. Pennington acted as both the private supervisor of a local mine and as a publicly appointed US commissioner in the town of Silverton. Like postmasters, commissioners did not receive a salary, instead receiving fees for part-time work. They also worked with little administrative oversight; anybody could be appointed as US commissioner (there were no requirements that they had received legal training), and they did not have to report the fees they earned for their work. And, like postmasters, the position of commissioner was also a contingent one. John Pennington, for instance, had left or lost his job as US commissioner in Silverton within two years of taking the position.[53]

Mapping the federal judiciary underscores the agency model's role within the larger apparatus of the American state. As shown in Figure 1.5, the federal judiciary had two distinct workforces with two distinct spatial patterns. The first consisted of circuit judges, district attorneys, court clerks, and bankruptcy registers. This workforce tended to function more like a bureaucracy, with salaried, professionalized

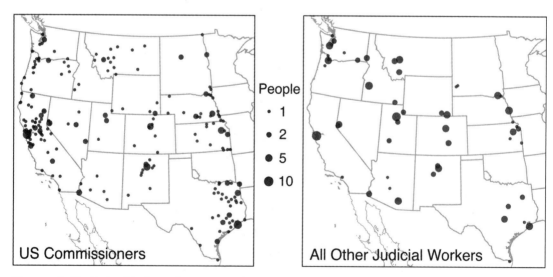

**Figure 1.5** The Federal Judiciary's Two Spatial Footprints

Locations of US Commissioners (*left*) versus all other workers in the federal judiciary (*right*) in 1877, sized according to the number of people working in that location. Data collected from *The Official Register of the United States, 1877* (Washington, DC: Government Printing Office, 1877).

employees who worked in official government buildings located in major population centers like Denver and Pueblo. The second workforce consisted of US commissioners like John Pennington. These part-time local agents outnumbered all other federal judicial employees combined and worked in many more locations, including smaller towns and cities like Silverton, Colorado. The difference was especially clear in California, where 67 US commissioners were spread over 54 different locations—compared to eleven other judicial employees stationed in just two cities, San Francisco and Los Angeles. Of course, size and geography did not directly translate into influence and power. A federal circuit judge in San Francisco wielded far more power than all of California's US commissioners combined. But part-time commissioners allowed the judicial branch of the federal government to function over a much wider area than it would have otherwise. Administrative structure and institutional geography went hand in hand, as the agency model's flexible administrative arrangements produced a much more expansive spatial footprint than more bureaucratic organizational corners of the American state.[54]

Some of the 19th century's most important government institutions used the agency model to function over long distances and large areas. The Pension Bureau, for instance, faced many of the same geographical challenges as other federal institutions. This organization was tasked with distributing payments for injured veterans along with the widows and dependents of soldiers who had died in service, an undertaking that became vastly more complex after the mass casualties of the Civil War. In order to establish who did and did not qualify for a pension, it first had to conduct in-person medical exams of hundreds of thousands of veterans. Rather than hire a full-time workforce of trained government doctors and dispatch them out across the country, the Pension Bureau grafted the medical examination process onto the existing private practices of local physicians. These "neighborhood practitioners" were tasked with evaluating pension claimants in the surrounding area. Instead of a full-time salary, they received a small fee for each exam. The Pension Bureau's physicians were not unlike the Post Office Department's postmasters or the federal judiciary's commissioners: private local agents responsible for providing services on behalf of the federal government within a given area.[55]

The US Census also used the agency model to fulfill its responsibilities. Each decade the federal government had to collect information about millions of households and individuals, in an attempt to make its populace legible to central planners, officials, and other government actors. This was no easy task in the United States, especially as Americans occupied more and more territory during the 19th century. From 1790 through 1870, US marshals were in charge of collecting information within their particular judicial district. Each marshal appointed "assistants" to act as enumerators—private residents who collected information about households in a given area. In 1879, Congress transferred responsibilities from the US marshals to an official Census Office. But the agency model didn't disappear with more specialized administrative oversight; if anything, it grew more entrenched. In June of 1880, 31,382 enumerators fanned out across their districts, going door to door to collect information about the nation's roughly fifty million inhabitants. This group looked a lot like postmasters: local agents responsible for a particular territory who were paid through commissions for part-time labor. Some postmasters, in fact, moonlighted as census enumerators. Moreover, their commissions were calculated based on geography, as sparsely settled parts of the country garnered a higher commission than urban districts because enumerators had to travel longer distances to count the same number of people. Despite advances in tabulating technology, statistical methods, and technocratic specialization within the Census Office, the success of its operations ultimately depended on an army of temporary, semi-privatized local agents acting on its behalf.[56]

The presence of the agency model did not preclude bureaucracy. "The state," after all, is not a singular entity. Even within the same institution, elements of the localized agency model often worked in conjunction with more centralized, bureaucratic arrangements. In the case of the US Post, the Railway Mail Service was an early beachhead of bureaucracy within the federal government, using salaried, full-time employees to transport and process mail along railway routes. These employees were subject to tightly managed, top-down oversight and were some of the first postal workers to take civil-service exams.[57] But once the mail was unloaded from the nation's railway cars, this bureaucracy bled into the agency model of the countryside. Railway mail agents would hand off mail bags to a stagecoach driver who would then deliver them to the doorstep of a local storeowner. The agency model could and did work in tandem with bureaucratic models of governance.[58]

## State Power

The western operations of the US Post challenges longstanding frameworks of state power. Rather than acting through coercion and force, as emphasized by Max Weber, its influence came from structural power, or the ability to define the conditions under which people take actions and make decisions.[59] Although the US Post's structural power is less visible than the American state's more muscular capacity for war and policing, it is just as crucial for understanding the federal government's efforts in the western United States. This structural power was on full display in Andrew Faulk's office in Yankton and the mining towns of the San Juan Mountains. There, the gossamer network's distinctive geography helped define the conditions under which government officials worked and settlers migrated. Its rapid extension and expansive coverage made it the underlying circuitry for the state's larger project of territorial conquest and occupation.[60]

The diffuse administrative structure of the agency model challenges a second assumption about state power: that the state is an inherently centralized entity. Under this framework, power flows from the top down and the center outward. Heads of state declare war, legislators pass laws, judges issue legal decisions, and administrators implement policies, and all of this gets transmitted through the rest of the government and across civil society. Some of the most influential theoretical models of the state define it in these terms. These models of the state often conflate organizational centralization with spatial centralization, assuming that leaders take actions from seats of governance and then implement them outward over a state's physical territory, like an earthquake's aftershocks reverberating from its epicenter.[61] Sociologist Michael Mann, for instance, defines the state as "a territorially centralized form of organization" that wields both "despotic" (or coercive) power and "infrastructural" power, or the ability to penetrate civil society and implement decisions throughout a territory.[62] Under this kind of framework, the state is powerful if the center can exercise control over the periphery, and a state is weak if the periphery can circumvent this control. Regardless of the outcome, the action largely flows in one direction.[63]

This book reverses the traditional direction of state power. The western postal system was dominated by local demands, local conditions, local politics, and local actors. By and large, officials in Washington did not decide when or where to expand the nation's rural postal infrastructure. Instead, local business owners and civic leaders would write petitions, gather signatures, and send their requests for new mail service to Washington, DC. Often these requests went directly to Congress, which had authority over designating new mail routes. Loath to deny their constituents' requests, Congress would duly rubber-stamp hundreds or thousands of new mail routes each year and send them on to the Post Office Department. Postal officials were then tasked with evaluating whether and how to establish service on the requested route. The department had no official guidelines for approving or denying these requests. There was, for instance, no requirement that a new post office serve a certain number of people. As postal officials readily admitted, requests for more mail facilities were rarely rejected.[64] Given the sheer size of the network, officials in Washington relied on local politicians and intermediaries to advise them on where to establish new post offices or who to appoint as postmasters to run them. Once an office was up and running, it was subject to minimal administrative oversight: in the words of one postmaster general when describing the nation's rural post offices: "The touch of the Department upon them is very slight . . . The machinery is set up and then let alone."[65] The periphery, rather than the center, drove the western postal network's growth and managed its on-the-ground operations.[66]

Centralized models of state power risk attributing a false sense of purpose, coherence, and intentionality to the state. After all, "the state" is not a pseudo-person who calculatingly compels people to act in a certain way, and not every state action can be chalked up to the rational decision-making of policymakers and officials.[67] Take the case of the agency model. It is tempting to see the US Post's reliance on this framework as some carefully planned tactic to extend the state's "infrastructural power" across the periphery. In reality, postal administrators found themselves barely hanging on to the reins of a regional expansion project that careened forward ahead of them.[68] The expansion of the western postal network lacked intentionality, top-down planning, and centralized coordination. But that didn't make it any less influential. In fact, its decentralized structure had a profound impact on the western United States.[69]

The US Post's embrace of the agency model directly shaped the network's geography and, by extension, its impact on the region. For one, a lack of centralized coordination contributed to its status as the world's most expansive postal network. Generally speaking, postal officials in other countries exercised more top-down oversight than their counterparts in the United States, which in turn led to a more cautious and limited expansion of new infrastructure. The Canadian Post, for instance, dispatched an inspector to personally visit each proposed mail route or post office in order to decide whether to grant the request. In Japan, the Meiji imperial government treated the national post as a vehicle for its modernization campaign, which subsequently made it one of the most closely regulated and centralized postal systems in the world. The Russian government exercised tight control over its post offices, requiring local communities to fund new post offices themselves and shutting down any offices that failed to turn a profit within three years.[70] There were no equivalent regulations in the United States, which meant that the US Post expanded far more capaciously: by 1878, the United States had seven times as many post offices as Canada and roughly 10 times as many as Japan and Russia. The agency model was what allowed the US Post to dwarf every other postal system on earth.[71]

In the western United States, the decentralized administrative structure of the US Post facilitated a breakneck brand of expansion. Again and again, westerners were able to mobilize postal infrastructure to serve their needs. Although settlers depended on a range of federal institutions, from the General Land Office to the US Army, the US Post proved most responsive to their demands. Westerners often saw the federal government as slow, unresponsive, or even downright opposed to their interests, such as when officials tried to keep squatters from illegally trespassing onto Native land or reservations. By comparison, westerners themselves were often in the driver's seat when it came to the region's postal system. The decentralized agency model meant that no matter where they moved, they could generally count on the postal network to follow them. Historian Gary Gerstle writes, "How the United States managed expansion without a large centralized state is . . . among the most significant stories of American history."[72] In some ways, Gerstle has it backwards. A better question might be: Would a centralized state have managed this kind of expansion at all?

Had the US Post followed the more centralized models of postal administration in countries like Canada, Japan, or Russia, it would have constrained its geography and slowed its expansion into rugged, sparsely populated areas such as the San Juan Mountains. Prospectors would have trespassed onto Ute land with or without the US Post. Mining companies would have constructed mills and sluices, and settlers would have built cabins and surveyed townsites. But without reliable mail service they would have struggled to maintain social ties, conduct business, join civic organizations, or participate in national politics. Some might have given up, while others might have never decided to relocate to a distant mountain range in the first place. Without the US Post's expansive network, the pace of settler colonization would have been slower, its reach more limited, and its prosecution more difficult.[73]

Instead, the US Post helped accelerate the seizure of Native territory and its transformation into a colonized landscape of settlements, mining claims, and post offices. The structural power of the western postal system to shape this process was far from the only way in which the American state exercised power. But it remains one of the least appreciated. Even today, large-scale, indirect forces like the US Post are difficult to pin down. They function in the realm of the everyday, the routine, even the mundane. Studying the sprawling geography of the US Post and placing it within the wider landscape of the federal government paints a new picture of the American state and its western operations. But fully understanding this larger system requires shrinking the scale of analysis. The US Post's structural power comes into focus when seen through the eyes of individual people.

# 2

# Stories and Structures

Benjamin Curtis gazed at his three-week-old daughter as she squirmed on the sofa, his wife Mary sewing in a rocking chair beside them. Benjamin was smitten with the newborn, who had her mother's blue eyes along with tiny ears that were, in his words, "just too pretty for anything." Although the baby had come down with a cold and Mary was still weak from her labor, both of them were steadily recovering. The hot Arizona air had even started to cool off in the evenings now that it was late September. Sitting with his family in the fall of 1886, Benjamin should have been at peace, but a quiet worry gnawed away at him. Since moving to the Arizona backcountry two years earlier, Benjamin had struggled with money. He had spent most of his savings trying to get his ranch off the ground, and while he was fond of the animals, they had yet to bring him any profit. Grass and feed were scarce, and irrigating his property had proven far more challenging than he had anticipated. There was precious little currency in circulation, and local merchants were wary of extending him credit. He couldn't even buy the cloth Mary needed to sew a hood for their daughter that would shield her face from the sun. If only they could find a buyer for their land and livestock, Benjamin and Mary were ready to leave this harsh, dry corner of the country behind them.[1]

The story of how Benjamin Curtis ended up as a penniless new father on a ranch in central Arizona winds its way across 40 years and thousands of miles. This story begins with four orphans in a small town in Ohio and ends in the crashing surf of a California beach. It follows Benjamin and his three siblings, Sarah, Delia, and Jamie, as they joined a migratory wave of people that washed across the western United States during the late 19th century. It is a story about the Curtis family's migrations along with the larger forces—colonial conquest, resource extraction, industrial capitalism—that propelled them. It is also a story about letters. On that warm September day in 1886, Benjamin Curtis was sitting at a table writing a letter to his two older sisters. It was one of several dozen surviving pieces of correspondence that the four Curtis siblings exchanged between the 1840s and the 1890s. Their letters offer intimate, if fleeting, snapshots of particular moments in time: what kind of chair Mary was sitting in, the state of Benjamin's receding hairline, and the color of their newborn daughter's eyes. But the letters also provide a window onto the era's largest communications network and the ways in which it influenced how individual American lived, worked, and made decisions.

In a more literary style that departs from the rest of *Paper Trails*, this chapter tells the story of the Curtis family over four decades, showing the different ways, both big and small, in which the four siblings relied on the nation's postal network.

Although they rarely wrote about the postal system directly, their correspondence itself hints at how important it was in keeping them connected. The Curtis family was in constant motion, moving to dozens of combined locations over half a century. No matter where they moved and what they did, the US Post was always there, quietly humming away in the background. Shrinking the narrative scale to the level of individual people gives meaning to how the US Post's institutional arrangements shaped everyday experiences and conditions in the 19th-century West. The story of the Curtis family, told through their letters, is a lens through which to glimpse the structural power of the US Post.

## Orphans

On April 3, 1847, 38-year-old Clarisa Curtis gave birth to an infant boy in the small town of Rossville, Ohio. Three years earlier she and her husband Henry had lost newborn twins, so it came as a relief when their new baby, who they named Benjamin, proved to be a "fine stout boy."[2] Relief was short-lived, however, as just three months later their oldest daughter Mary passed away at the age of fourteen. This left them with four surviving children: 12-year-old Sarah, the oldest, nine-year-old Jamie, six-year-old Delia, and Benjamin. Death would continue to stalk the Curtis family. Clarisa herself died in the summer of 1849, and three years later Henry followed his wife to the grave. In an especially cruel twist of fate, he died on Benjamin's fifth birthday. Sarah, Jamie, Delia, and Benjamin were now orphans.[3] The Curtis children suffered unimaginable loss, but they were fortunate to be part of a comfortably well-off extended family. A number of relatives volunteered to take them in, with each child going to a different family member. This was the moment at which the US Post entered their lives.

Rocked by the loss of their parents and scattered across Massachusetts, Tennessee, Ohio, and Illinois, the four orphans used the US Post to stay connected to each other as they grew up during the 1850s. The mail allowed the teenage Delia to write her brother Jamie in Tennessee with stories about their Massachusetts relatives, and Jamie to reply with descriptions of the girls in Memphis and to ask her how she was liking school in Boston.[4] Delia and Jamie were paying just three cents per letter, the result of postage reforms passed in 1845 and 1851 that had dramatically lowered the cost of sending mail and fueled a flourishing national epistolary culture.[5] The mail also helped Sarah, Jamie, and Delia to engage in their most common form of long-distance sibling bonding: worrying about Benjamin. A bright but troubled child, he had tried to run away from his uncle in Illinois at the age of nine and was apparently "rather backward in his studies."[6] Sarah, an aspiring schoolteacher, found this last part especially galling. She and Jamie hatched a plan to remove Benjamin from his caretakers and install Sarah as his guardian. Their plan apparently worked, because a year later Benjamin wrote his very first letter from his new home in Tennessee with Sarah.[7] It was addressed to his sister Delia, and the letter itself was short, formal, and rather stiff—understandable, given that the 11-year-old Benjamin had not actually seen his older sister for several years. Over time, the two would develop a palpable affection and easy intimacy that Benjamin would never quite manage with either Sarah or Jamie. Notably, over the course of Benjamin and Delia's lives their tight-knit bond would be an entirely long-distance one made possible by the US Post.

In April of 1861, fourteen-year-old Benjamin wrote a two-page letter to Delia telling her about his recent move back to Illinois and his new school. He closed with an ominous sentence: "We heard that Fort Sumtrie [Sumter] was taken today."[8] The US Civil War had officially begun. The Curtises, like so many American families, could not escape the reach of the war. One month after Benjamin's letter, Jamie, then living in Tennessee, confessed to Delia that his loyalties were divided between "tender feelings" for friends and family members in the north and strong southern sympathies for his adopted state. With Tennessee on the brink of secession, Jamie wasn't sure what to do. He was even more worried, however, about their brother: "I wish I could be satisfied that Ben will not take any part in the war. He is young, thoughtless, and easily led into almost anything."[9] Jamie's worries were well founded. Shortly afterwards, Benjamin ran away from his guardians to enlist in the US Navy. Two years later, in 1863, his siblings learned that Benjamin's ship, the *Indianola*, had been taken by Confederate forces. Their sixteen-year-old brother was either dead or a prisoner of war.[10]

While the Civil War raged, the US Post became the main vehicle that carried life-and-death information to millions of Americans, shuttling news about the fate of loved ones between battlefields and the home front.[11] Sarah, Jamie, and Delia spent two anxious months awaiting word of Benjamin's fate before a letter finally arrived, confirming that he had been captured after the battle but was alive and uninjured. Jamie quickly forwarded the letter to Delia, asking her to send it on to Sarah. One month later, in May of 1863, Benjamin sent a second brief letter to Jamie, informing his brother that he had been released from a military prison and was now in Washington, DC.[12] Upon receiving the news, Jamie immediately sent letters to Delia and Sarah to share the good news and then mailed Benjamin paper and ink so that he could keep them updated on his condition. Benjamin was eventually discharged from the Navy, and for the remainder of the Civil War he would stay well way from the fighting. A few months later, Sarah wrote from Pennsylvania to her sister in Massachusetts with an orphan's lament: "How pleasant it would be if we could all have a home together."[13] Scattered across three different states, the four of them had to rely on the next best thing to a shared home—the expansive coverage of the US Post.

## Migrations

As the Civil War wound down in 1865, a bloodied nation turned westward. Millions of people moved to western states and territories during the postwar years, fueling a demographic boom in the region. By 1880, the West's population had increased fourfold in the span of just two decades.[14] All four of the Curtis siblings would eventually join this westward surge of people during the 1860s and 1870s. Like so many migrations to the region during these years, theirs was made possible by the American state. Wartime mobilization had brought an unprecedented expansion of both the military arm of the American state and its civilian workforce. The Post Office Department, for instance, launched several new initiatives during the war. One of these, the Railway Mail Service, hired postal employees to sort mail inside dedicated railway cars while they were in transit, significantly cutting down travel time for the nation's long-distance mail.[15] This initiative continued after the war's conclusion, and in the spring of 1865 the Railway Mail Service hired Benjamin Curtis to work as a mail agent. The new government job triggered the first of several westward moves for the Curtis family.

By the fall of 1868, Benjamin was working for the Railway Mail Service on a section of the transcontinental railroad that ran across the central plains from Omaha, Nebraska, to Green River in southwestern Wyoming. Although Benjamin found the work a little dull, he fell in love with the western landscape, writing to Delia about the "wild and rough looking mountains and valleys in every direction." He confessed that he hoped to move even farther west, to either California or Mexico.[16] Benjamin eventually left his job with the Railway Mail Service and by September of 1871 was making his way up California's northern coast. From there, he traveled by wagon some three hundred miles to the rugged upper reaches of the state, less than 60 miles from the Oregon border. Benjamin had managed to purchase a tract of public land from the federal government and had grand plans for starting a ranch.[17] In what would become a common theme for Benjamin, his ambitions ran ahead of his savings. In an attempt to cobble together enough money to purchase some livestock, he bounced between the towns of Burgettville and Adin working as a sales clerk.[18]

Benjamin's experience in the small California towns of Burgettville and Adin offers a vantage point into what the agency model looked like along the postal network's outer edges. In both places, he clerked for a store owner who doubled as the town's postmaster. This meant that in addition to balancing the account books, answering correspondence, and peddling wares to customers, Benjamin also sorted, distributed, and processed the mail. A few years after leaving the Railway Mail Service, he had rejoined the US Post in a much less official capacity. Neither of his two employers were sticklers for following the Post Office Department's rules, which were distributed to postmasters in a thick manual that ran to more than four hundred pages. One of these regulations stipulated that no person could handle the mail who had not submitted an official oath of office, while another required postmasters to actually live in the town in which they were appointed.[19] Both of Benjamin's employers ignored these regulations, leaving mail duties entirely in Benjamin's hands despite the fact that he had not submitted an official oath to the department. The Adin postmaster, meanwhile, openly flaunted the department's restriction on absentee officeholding, spending most of his time with his family in Yreka (125 miles away) or trying to open a branch store in Hot Spring Valley (50 miles away). This is how the agency model worked on the periphery: localized, informal affairs conducted with little administrative oversight.[20]

Benjamin would soon transition into a more official role within the US Post. In the fall of 1873, a banking panic plunged the nation into depression that reverberated all the way to northern California, where Benjamin's boss in Burgettville watched sales plummet at his store. Benjamin decided to strike out on his own, relocating to the nearby mill town of Fall River Mills and opening up a merchandising store.[21] It's unclear how he managed to raise enough money to start this new venture, but it helped him secure an additional job as postmaster of Fall River Mills. When he filed his paperwork in the spring of 1875, Benjamin officially joined some 35,500 postmasters across the country.[22] His tenure was typical, as he held this part-time and semi-privatized public position for just seven months, receiving a grand total of $36.09 in commissions before losing the job to a local hotel owner. Benjamin's temporary forays into the postal workforce—both official and unofficial—are a reminder of just how many 19th-century Americans ended up working within the nation's postal machinery.[23]

Benjamin's move to northern California coincided with the end of a decades-long genocidal campaign against the state's Indigenous peoples. Since the discovery of gold in 1848, roving mobs of white settlers attacked Indian camps and villages to drive them out and seize their land. California's state militia led similarly brutal expeditions against Native groups, often supported with funds from the federal government. Finally, the US Army launched its own official campaigns of violence and dispossession. Shortly after Benjamin's arrival in northern California, American soldiers embarked on what became known as the Modoc War. Just 50 miles away from his new home, a group of several hundred Modocs fled a government reservation in southern Oregon and returned to their homelands along the California border. Over several months in 1872–73, federal troops pursued and eventually captured them, executing two Modoc leaders, imprisoning several others, and forcibly transporting the remainder of the group some two thousand miles away to a reservation in Indian Territory. Through a harrowing combination of violence, removal, and disease, California's Indigenous population plunged from roughly 150,000 in 1846 to some 30,000 people by 1870.[24]

Benjamin Curtis was not a direct participant in this process. He did not appear to call for the removal of Native peoples, join a local militia, or engage in vigilante attacks. But he was a colonizer, part of a wave of American settlers who were happy to move onto plundered Native land. His experience highlights some of the subtler ways in which the American state facilitated this process beyond its use of direct violence.[25] Over the preceding years, government officials had forced the Achumawi and Atsugewi peoples to give up their claims to this part of California and move to a government-run reservation located hundreds of miles away.[26] Another federal agency, the General Land Office, then surveyed and parceled out their newly seized land, including a tract of property that Benjamin purchased in 1874.[27] Finally, Benjamin's colonization of this remote area depended on the US Post's ability to rapidly expand into distant western locales. As late as 1867, there wasn't a single post office operating in the northeastern corner of California. If Benjamin Curtis had moved to the same location even a few years earlier, he would have had to travel some 70 miles to the nearest post office to mail a letter. By the time he found work in 1872, there were no fewer than three weekly postal routes shuttling sacks of mail between roughly a dozen new post offices.[28]

The decision to move to a distant location like Fall River Mills was as much an emotional process as it was a rational calculation of costs and incentives. For Benjamin and for many others settlers, the move westward was wrapped up with hopes, dreams, and ambitions but also loneliness, homesickness, and guilt. In Benjamin's case, he repeatedly used the mail to process these emotions. In one letter to Sarah, he wrote, "I sometimes blame myself for straying so far away from all friends and going among strangers. . . . I can not think that either you or Jamie would attribute my actions to selfishness, although I sometimes think it must look like it to you if your love for me was not so great."[29] After he moved to the other side of the continent from his siblings, these kinds of letters were the only channel that Benjamin had to reaffirm his love for his family. From Massachusetts, Sarah and Delia Curtis were able to send their youngest brother letters, copies of Boston newspapers, and issues of *Harper's Weekly*. Sarah even used the mail to send him a pair of wristlets as a Christmas present in late 1872. In reply, Benjamin thanked her for the present, recounted a recent wedding he had attended, and discussed his plans to develop his ranch before asking Sarah to give his love to Delia and Jamie. Benjamin Curtis may have sat down to his holiday dinner by himself in 1872, but the expansive reach of the US Post meant that he wasn't truly alone.[30]

In the most common migration pattern of the 19th century, family members and neighbors from a particular location would move to the same destination in staggered waves. The earliest arrivals would then report back on their experiences, answer questions from family and friends, and arrange for travel, lodging, and employment for those who wished to follow them. In short, the era's long-distance migrations depended on long-distance communications, the vast majority of which unfolded through the mail.[31] The Curtis family followed this pattern. Benjamin was the first of his siblings to move west. Almost immediately he began trying to persuade the others to join him. His letters from California detailed exactly what property was available and where it was located, the prices of different goods, precisely how they should ship their belongings, and the best way to travel from San Francisco to Fall River Mills.[32] His efforts were at least partially successful, as Sarah moved to California sometime in the late 1870s. By 1878, she was working as an assistant at a school in San Rafael, just north of San Francisco, and by the following year she was running her own private school. The oldest of the Curtis siblings soon

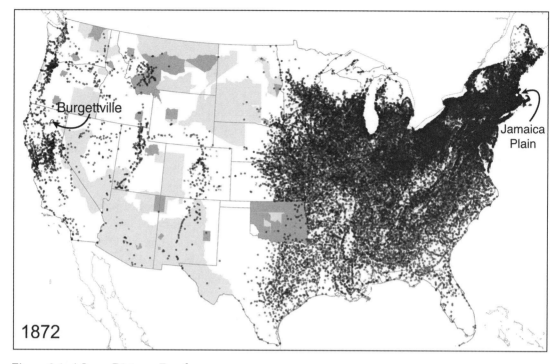

**Figure 2.1** A Long-Distance Family

Benjamin and Sarah Curtis were able to exchange letters and gifts from opposite sides of the country. This map shows their locations, along with post offices, unceded Native land (light gray), and reservations (dark gray) in 1872.

convinced Delia to leave her schoolteacher position in Massachusetts to join Sarah's new business venture in San Rafael. From start to finish, the Curtis siblings coordinated their migrations using the US Post.[33]

A few years after Sarah and Delia's move to California, Benjamin moved on to Arizona Territory. It's unclear what spurred his move, but whatever it was had gone well. In 1881, he mailed his sisters a letter that included several postal money orders totaling $250, which he urged his sisters to spend on a vacation "somewhere where they will make you laugh every hour in the day."[34] Benjamin's remittance joined 24 million dollars' worth of money orders that were sent by westerners that year—yet another reminder of the range of material that traveled through the US Post.[35] These financial flows facilitated the movement of both capital and settlers across the West, allowing someone like Benjamin to abandon his store near the California-Oregon border, pop up in southern Arizona Territory, and remit money to his sisters in San Rafael, California. A few months later, Benjamin himself returned to California, using some of his new earnings to buy an orange grove in San Diego. By the end of 1881, Sarah and Delia had sold their school in San Rafael and joined him in southern California. Within a few months, their brother Jamie had moved westward to join his siblings. Orphaned three decades earlier in Ohio, the four Curtis siblings had finally reunited as adults in the far southwestern corner of the country.[36]

## Transitions

The family reunion didn't last long. Jamie was the last to arrive and the first to leave, retracing his younger brother's footsteps to northeastern California and going into a joint business venture with one of his brother's previous employers in Fall River Mills. Benjamin, meanwhile, struggled to turn a profit on his orange grove, so in 1884 he sold his California property and moved back to Arizona to try his luck at ranching.[37] Sarah and Delia decided to stay in San Diego to work as schoolteachers, which proved to be a smart decision. When a new railroad line reached the city in 1885, its population more than doubled, and the two sisters found themselves awash with new clients. By 1886, they were buying and selling thousands of dollars' worth of property in southern California, part a frenzied burst of land speculation that swept across Los Angeles and San Diego in the mid- to late 1880s. Delia and Sarah Curtis, ever the entrepreneurs, were at the forefront of this real-estate boom.[38] Benjamin wasn't nearly as successful. Hundreds of miles away, he was leading a lonely existence as he tried to start up his ranch in the Salt River Valley in Arizona's rugged interior. Traveling to the nearest major town required a 60-mile roundtrip journey, which (as he ruefully noted to his sisters) left him with little more than his cows and horses for company.[39]

Yet even there, in the Arizona backcountry, Benjamin could still rely on the US Post. His experience in the Salt River Valley illustrates the importance of the network's geographic coverage for westerners. Even though he lived in physical isolation, the mail remained surprisingly accessible to him. The very same year that Benjamin moved to Arizona, the Post Office Department opened a new post office just two miles away from his homestead in the ranch home of its newly minted postmaster, Lucinda Armer.[40] Tiny as it was, the Armer Post Office immediately became the nexus point that linked Benjamin across deserts, mesas, mountains, and scrubland to his sisters in San Diego. Delia and Sarah not only wrote letters to their brother but also took advantage of discounted postage rates for periodicals to forward him "bundles" of California newspapers. In return, he penned them affectionate replies, asking about San Diego's booming property market or teasing Delia that she should find herself a husband from Dakota to make her "Queen of a cattle ranch."[41]

Less than a year after Sarah and Delia had bid farewell to their younger brother, an announcement appeared in their letterbox at the San Diego Post Office: Benjamin was engaged. He had been courting his neighbor's 20-year-old-daughter, and the two were to be married the following month.[42] The announcement kicked off a flurry of new correspondence between the Curtis siblings in the spring of 1885. Delia and Sarah wrote letters welcoming Mary Hocker, Benjamin's fiancée, to the Curtis family. Benjamin, in turn, sent them a photograph of his betrothed along with requests for books to read on their honeymoon ("Fiction, but good. Send by mail").[43] In the weeks leading up to the wedding, registered letters and packages continued to pour into the Armer Post Office from San Diego—such a deluge that

Benjamin joked it would overwhelm poor Lucinda Armer. When the wedding day arrived in June 1885, Mary said her vows while wearing a brooch that Sarah and Delia had mailed to her in the preceding weeks, delivered to the tiny post office on the Armer family ranch.[44]

The US Post's extension into Arizona's Salt River Valley exemplifies how it was able to expand in lockstep with the West's growing settler population. The same year that Benjamin and Mary exchanged their vows, a man named P. C. Robertson bought land near them and began farming, raising livestock, and selling goods out of a small general store. In December of 1885, Robertson was appointed an official United States postmaster, and his storefront became the brand-new Catalpa Post Office. Given that the new office served such a small population and was located just three miles away from the Armer family's post office, it's hard to see how the expansion was warranted. But Benjamin and Mary weren't complaining. Sitting between Robertson's and Armer's homesteads, they could choose between two post offices within a roughly two-mile radius of their home.[45]

From the vantage point of Benjamin and Mary's front porch, the US Post really did seem to be everywhere. But its coverage was not universal. If either of them were to ride due east from their ranch, they would soon run up against the limits of this coverage at the border of the White Mountain Indian Reservation, just sixteen miles away. Also known as the San Carlos Reservation, it had been established in 1872 as part of a broader attempt by the federal government to conquer and subjugate Apache groups in Arizona and New Mexico. By the time Benjamin moved to the Salt River Valley the following decade, there were around three thousand Apache people living on the reservation.[46] Despite this, there were just two post offices operating within the entire reservation—an area that was roughly the size of Delaware. As it did across the region, the US Post's ubiquitous coverage withered away at the borders of the reservation.[47] Moreover, the two post offices operating within the White Mountain Reservation were meant to serve the needs of government officials, not Native peoples. One was located at the government's administrative headquarters at the San Carlos Agency, the other at Fort Apache, a US Army garrison of more than two hundred federal troops who were tasked with violently suppressing Apache resistance. If Native residents wanted to use the mail, they had to visit one of these two locations run by state actors who were tasked with surveilling, policing, and, if necessary, killing them.[48]

Despite the US Post's limited coverage within the borders of Indian reservations, Native peoples across the western United States actively used the mail. During the 1880s the federal government expanded schools on western Indian reservations as a means of eradicating Indigenous languages and customs and replacing them with the values of a white, Christian society. This produced a boom in literacy rates that Native peoples then deployed as a weapon of resistance, all through the long-distance channel of the US Post. Tribal leaders sent petitions to federal officials to try and address a range of issues, such as inadequate rations, shoddy buildings, or settlers illegally grazing on their land. By the end of the 1880s, the commissioner of

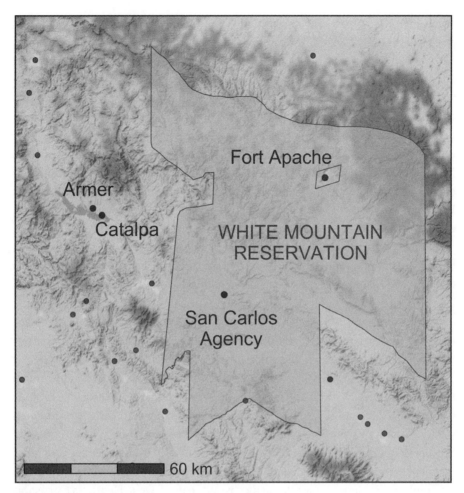

**Figure 2.2**  Benjamin and Mary Curtis's Neighbors

Benjamin and Mary Curtis could access two post offices (Armer and Catalpa) within a short walk from their homestead, compared to the two post offices (Fort Apache and the San Carlos Agency) that served the entire White Mountain Indian Reservation. Terrain imagery comes from Stamen Maps (http://maps.stamen.com/terrain/), downloaded September 27, 2019.

Indian affairs in Washington, DC, was receiving hundreds upon hundreds of these petitions from reservations across the country. Native peoples also used the mail to maintain ties of family and kinship, exchanging letters with relatives or friends who had been split up across multiple reservations or forcibly sent to live in eastern boarding schools. They used the mail to foster political and cultural alliances across different tribes and in 1889 exchanged letters that helped spread the Ghost Dance, one of the era's most influential pan-tribal movements. The expansion of the US Post may have facilitated Native dispossession and settler colonial expansion in the West, but Indigenous peoples across the region also marshaled its connective power to suit their own needs.[49]

Benjamin and Mary Curtis, meanwhile, were settling into married life on their ranch. Like many newlyweds, they seemed content to spend most of their time with each other. Apart from Mary's nearby parents, Benjamin rarely mentioned other people in his letters, writing more about Tip, Nellie, and Colonel—their dog, mare, and new colt, respectively—than any of their friends or neighbors. Working on a remote ranch in the sparsely settled Arizona backcountry, Benjamin and Mary were living in physical isolation. But thanks to the US Post, they were not isolated. Between the two of them they subscribed to some half dozen periodicals, including the *Delineator* (a women's magazine), the *American Agriculturalist* (a farming periodical), one regional paper from the nearby town of Globe, and national newspapers from San Francisco, Chicago, and New York.[50] And, of course, they continued to correspond with Sarah and Delia in San Diego. Stacks of letters flowed between Benjamin and his two sister, filled with business advice and encouragement, stories about weather and excursions, and updates about friends and relatives. The Curtis sisters also sent small gifts with their letters, including a silk kerchief for Mary and a decades-old photograph of their deceased parents. A short walk to the Catalpa Post Office linked them to a dense web of connections that stretched far beyond the Salt River Valley.[51]

In the summer of 1886, the flow of mail arriving in the Catalpa Post Office ramped up considerably, as Delia and Sarah began sending their brother and sister-in-law packages of cloth, household supplies, and, finally, some "little shirts."[52] Those "little shirts" arrived just in time. In early September of 1886, Mary gave birth to a nine-pound baby girl in the midst of Arizona's stifling hundred-degree heat. As his newborn daughter slept next to him, Benjamin sat down to write two letters—a separate one for each of his sisters. He recounted Mary's labor, noted the infant's healthy weight, and joked that the baby "doesn't take after its father because it has plenty of hair on the top of its head." Finally, he got around to her name. "Mary says she thinks Delia Henrietta would do nicely, and so do I." Delia Henrietta Curtis was named after her two aunts, Delia Augusta and Sarah Henrietta. Benjamin dropped the two letters off at P. C. Robertson's store on a Saturday, and they reached his sisters in San Diego just four days later. The orphaned Curtis siblings had spent the better part of three decades spinning together the threads of their family across the gossamer network of the US Post. It was here, in the euphoric scrawl of an exhausted new father, that those filaments wound their way through the next generation.[53]

## Contractions

The Curtis family's correspondence offers a personalized glimpse into how the American state facilitated western occupation. The US Post's expansionary network was part of a larger mosaic of federal policies attempting to direct the flow of settlers, capital, and industry westward during the 19th century. Arguably the most famous of these was the Homestead Act. Under this legislation, individual settlers moved onto plots of public land (typically 160 acres) and then had five years to plant crops, build a home, and otherwise "improve" the land. If they accomplished this, they received full title to the property.[54] Other public land laws worked through similar mechanisms. When Benjamin Curtis had first moved to the Salt River Valley, for instance, he filed for his property under the Desert Land Act. This piece of legislation allowed people to buy public land from the federal government at a steep discount, so long as they managed to irrigate the land within three years. Benjamin's particular tract of Arizona property had gone unclaimed because nobody thought it could be irrigated. Benjamin disagreed, claiming when he first moved to Arizona, "It will be an easy matter to get water onto it."[55] Yet after years of stalled schemes to build dams and ditches, he was unable to meet the Desert Land Act's requirements to irrigate the property. Undeterred, Benjamin turned to yet another public land policy, the Timber Culture Act, which promised discounted land to settlers who successfully planted at least 10 new acres of trees on their property.[56]

Government policies like the Desert Land Act and Timber Culture Act helped produce a pattern of quixotic overexpansion into places like Arizona's Salt River Valley. Benjamin's initial and shortsighted claim about his land—"It will be an easy matter to get water onto it"—could have been a mantra for the region as a whole. Across the western United States, optimistic Americans rushed headlong into harsh environments that could not support them. Their decisions to move to these areas were facilitated by government policies aimed at encouraging exactly this kind of settlement. Nineteenth-century western boosters and policymakers believed that settlers like Benjamin could fundamentally transform the region's underlying climate and environment. As Americans planted crops and set up homesteads, the thinking went, they would bring more rain and change the West's arid and semi-arid landscapes into bountiful, productive farmland.[57]

Compared to the Desert Land and Timber Culture Acts, the US Post was a much less explicit channel through which the American state facilitated the overexpansion of settlers westward. But the ability of the gossamer network to rapidly expand and contract over unforgiving western environments was in many ways just as important. The agency model allowed the US Post to rapidly expand into the Salt River Valley, extending a new mail route through the valley and establishing new post offices at the Armer family ranch and P. C. Robertson's storefront. The nature of these arrangements made the gossamer network sensitive to any changes in local conditions. And in central Arizona, local conditions had grown quite bad by the late 1880s. In letter after letter to his sisters, Benjamin Curtis described how the area was crippled by a scarcity of cash and credit. By 1887, he had run out of money, and local businesses were wary of extending him credit. He was forced to leave his beloved pocket watch behind as security at a local store in order to make purchases on credit. The storeowner's generosity proved short-sighted, however, as later that year Benjamin reported that the man had sold too many goods to people who couldn't pay him back and had subsequently defaulted on his mortgage. The man in question was P. C. Robertson, Benjamin's neighbor and postmaster of the Catalpa Post Office.[58] By early 1888, the county tax collector was threatening to seize and auction Robertson's belongings for unpaid taxes.[59] Facing bankruptcy, Robertson shuttered his store and abandoned his ranch. The Post Office Department officially discontinued his post office shortly after.[60]

The Catalpa Post Office had been in operation for less than three years. From a system-wide perspective, the costs of adding the Catalpa Post Office had been minimal. The office was already located on an existing mail route that ran once a week through the Salt River Valley. P. C. Robertson acted as the department's local agent, distributing mail to Benjamin, Mary, and other local residents for a piddling annual commission of between $30 and 40 dollars a year.[61] When Robertson's luck turned, the larger network contracted with barely a ripple. The department simply rescinded the storeowner's appointment, removed his ranch from the local mail contractor's postal route, and diverted the small amount of mail he had been processing to surrounding offices. At Lucinda Armer's post office, her postmaster commission nearly doubled the following year after her office absorbed some of the Catalpa Post Office's rerouted mail.[62] This was what the US Post's gossamer network looked like on the ground: a fleeting entity capable of popping up and then quickly melting away along with the fortunes of a local business owner.

Benjamin and Mary Curtis weren't faring much better than P. C. Robertson. Five months after the birth of their daughter, they were still struggling to make ends meet. Benjamin had poured all of his money into buying livestock, building a house, and improving his property. Unable to sell any of his animals in a cash-starved economy, he was in dire financial straits. With his livestock venture floundering, at one point he even considered leaving his wife and infant daughter behind to find temporary work as a railroad laborer. Benjamin's sisters did what they could to help him. Delia sent several infusions of cash in 1887 (one of which quite literally reduced Benjamin to tears) along with a steady stream of hats, bibs, linen, shoes, and other small gifts to clothe her newborn niece.[63] All of this left a grateful Benjamin chuckling in one letter to his sisters, "What you and [Sarah] have sent will give her a wardrobe fit for a little Queen, and she is only a little Country Girl you know."[64] Delia, in particular, provided Benjamin with much-needed encouragement, humor, and affection to buoy his spirits. Both materially and emotionally, the mail gave Delia and Sarah Curtis the ability to extend a long-distance lifeline to their brother and his family.[65]

Like most Americans, Benjamin Curtis took the US Post for granted. Outside of the times in which he was directly employed by the Post Office Department, first as a mail agent and then as a postmaster, he rarely mentioned it in his letters. For him, the nation's postal network and its expansive coverage was simply a fact of life. Yet Benjamin's ability to access this network no matter where he lived was not some natural condition. It's worth imagining what his life would have looked like with a more geographically constrained postal system. In the Salt River Valley, for instance, the Post Office Department first established mail service sometime in late 1883 or early 1884, a year before Benjamin arrived. But none of the post offices along this new route processed very much mail.[66] What if the department had instead decided to wait a few more years before providing service to this location? Would Benjamin still have moved there when he did? Even if the Post Office Department had forged ahead with the new route, it might have operated fewer post offices along it. In this alternate scenario, it's unlikely that the tiny Catalpa and Armer post offices would have been established given the comparatively minuscule amount of mail that they processed. Instead of having two post offices within a two-mile radius of his front porch, Benjamin would have had to travel 20 miles to the Tonto Post Office or 30 miles back to the route's terminus in Globe every time he wanted to pick up his mail. Either one of these journeys would have taken the better part of a day or more to complete.[67]

What if, even more radically, the Post Office Department hadn't subsidized its rural mail service? After all, the two-cent postage it charged for letters did not cover the costs of transporting them to remote places like the Salt River Valley. Newspapers and periodicals traveled at an even steeper discount. What if settlers like Benjamin and Mary Curtis had to cover the true costs of maintaining all of their long-distance connections? In this case, they probably wouldn't have subscribed to a half dozen periodicals from across the country. Delia and Sarah wouldn't have sent them quite so many letters and gifts. In this alternate reality, life in the Salt River Valley would have been far more isolated and much more difficult. Under these circumstances, would Benjamin have been quite so willing to leave his sisters behind in San Diego in order to move to this harsh, remote location? The US Post's expansive rural coverage meant that he was able to make that decision with the confidence that he could stay connected to his family and the wider world. It was a decision that would ultimately end in disaster.

## Endings

In 1889, Mary Curtis gave birth to a second daughter, who she and Benjamin named Rena. Her birth coincided with the family's improving fortunes, as the local economy rebounded and they were able to sell some of their livestock. By February of 1891, their homestead was thriving, with horses, milk cows, chickens, and a fledgling orchard grove that Benjamin had raised to comply with the Timber Culture Act. Mary was looking forward to planting a new garden and even had plans to start raising silkworms.[68] The following month everything came crashing down around them. Heavy rains brought a massive flood through the Salt River Valley, uprooting all of their carefully planted trees and blanketing their entire property in one to two feet of sand that, in Benjamin's words, "left it in such a shape that I can never use it." With their property in ruins, they decided to sell what they could and leave Arizona for good. The family packed their meager belongings onto a wagon, appointed a local lawyer to try and sell their property on their behalf, and started on a journey northward to Boise, Idaho.[69]

Apart from his wife and children, Benjamin saw his time in the Salt River Valley as a series of personal failures: failure to irrigate his property, failure to raise livestock, failure to "prove up" his land claim, failure to provide for his family. A change of location failed to improve his luck. The Curtises arrived in Boise in October of 1891, one year after Idaho had gained statehood. Its capital city was bustling, but Benjamin couldn't find steady work. He briefly tried his hand as a laborer in a saw-mill before realizing that it was too taxing for his 44-year-old body. Two weeks after arriving, he was despondent. With a wife and two children to feed, he was facing down a long winter with no job and high rents, in an unfamiliar place where he felt like "a complete stranger." Temporary relief came through the familiar channel of the US Post, when his brother Jamie mailed Benjamin a $10 postal money order to help them "wiggle through the winter."[70]

Nine years Benjamin's senior, Jamie had followed his younger brother's footsteps by moving to northern California and going into business with one of Benjamin's former employers in Fall River Mills. After a few years of running a store, Jamie even managed to secure Benjamin's old job as the town's postmaster. His experience in this position exemplified the agency model's localized and ever-shifting adminis-trative structure. The post office in Fall River Mills was constantly changing hands. Between Benjamin's brief seven-month tenure as postmaster in 1875 and Jamie's appointment fifteen years later, the town had no fewer than nine different postmas-ters. Jamie managed to secure the position only after fending off a rival storeowner, who promptly began scheming to take control of the office. He first offered to pay Jamie to relocate the post office into his own store and then started lobbying politicians at the county convention to try and remove Jamie from the position. All of this left a fed-up Jamie to complain to his sisters, "I am getting more tired of this slow-pokey place. . . . I would gladly give up here altogether."[71]

In Boise, meanwhile, Benjamin was the one who was ready to "give up here al-together." Unable to find work, he and his family made their way to San Francisco and boarded a steamer for San Diego in January of 1892. When they arrived, Delia was waiting with open arms to welcome them into her home.[72] Aside from a brief period in the early 1880s, Benjamin and Delia had spent the entirety of their adult-hood living far from one another. They had forged their relationship by exchanging countless letters across thousands of miles. For the first time since they were chil-dren in Ohio, they were living together under the same roof. Delia had dreamed of reuniting with her siblings ever since she had been sent to live with relatives as an 11-year-old orphan, and 40 years later it appeared as if her dream might finally come true. Delia wrote to Jamie shortly after Benjamin's arrival: "Now if you will come down too, we will all be together and we can be very happy." The 50-year-old schoolteacher loved children, although she never had a family of her own. Delia lavished her three- and five-year-old nieces with attention, buying them a monthly subscription to *Babyland*, a Boston children's magazine, and recounting to Jamie all the new words she was teaching them. "It seems to put fresh life in us to have these little children around."[73]

On May 30, 1892, Benjamin left his sister's house and went for a morning walk on the beach in San Diego. He never came home. His body was found in the ocean surf several days later, drowned at the age of 45. Nobody knew for certain what happened that morning, but his ongoing financial struggles led some (including his wife) to suspect suicide.[74] We can only speculate on his state of mind. Benjamin had always shown a melancholy streak in his letters, and in retrospect there were some warning signs in Delia's letter to Jamie two months before. Benjamin was apparently finding it just as difficult to secure a job in San Diego as it had been in Boise. He had been making some half-hearted efforts to secure a veteran's pension from the government, reaching out to a lawyer in Washington, DC, to send him the necessary paperwork. However, as Delia reported to Jamie, he "kept putting off" completing the forms to provide evidence of his wartime service. Instead, Benjamin largely helped Delia with chores and fixed up her yard. He adored his wife and daughters, and the fact that he had to rely on his sister to put a roof over their heads must have been difficult. At this point, he was a middle-aged father with no job, no money, and no prospects of finding either anytime soon. His childhood had been defined by the death of his parents and separation from his siblings. The story of his adult life had been one of restless migration, failed business ventures, and financial misfortune. Suicide or not, one thing was clear: Benjamin Curtis's life had not gone the way he had hoped.

"I feel we have something to live for," Delia had written to Jamie in March of 1892. As heartbreaking as these words seem in light of Benjamin's death, the letter itself was an appropriate conclusion to some four decades of correspondence between the Curtis siblings. It had to travel roughly seven hundred miles between Delia and Jamie, departing from San Diego in a railway car and traveling almost the entire length of California before disembarking at Redding, near the border with Oregon. It covered the last 80 miles in the back of a stagecoach, up into the rugged northeastern corner of the state to Jamie's post office and general store in Fall River Mills. The entire trip would have taken around six days. At eight pages, the letter was longer than most of the family's surviving correspondence. But those pages contained a typical mix of news about family and friends interspersed with reminiscences about the past and speculation about the future. The letter also pointed to just how many different things traveled through the mail: a children's magazine, official paperwork for Benjamin to apply for a pension, cartoons that Jamie had mailed to his nieces, and, finally, a drawing by Rena, Benjamin's younger daughter. Just before Delia had sealed up the envelope, her niece had woken up from a nap and decided to make a picture for "Uncle Jamie." As Delia explained in a hastily scribbled postscript across the top of her letter, Rena's drawing was of a chair, a table, a lemon, and a pear, the last of which included a stem so that Jamie "could take hold of it." It was the last surviving piece of correspondence between the Curtis siblings.[75]

Studying and mapping the US Post from a system-wide vantage point has its advantages. But for people like the Curtises, the postal system was woven into their lives in much more intimate ways, the meanings of which cannot be truly calculated. How do you put a number on a lonely young store clerk receiving a family Christmas present from across the country? How do you quantify a letter to two sisters announcing the birth of their niece? How do you measure the significance of a three-year-old's drawing, sent through the mail to an uncle she'd never met? From the time they were orphaned as children, the postal network connected the Curtis siblings across space. For Benjamin in particular, the US Post was one of the few constants in an otherwise tumultuous life: an orphan in Ohio, an unhappy ward in Illinois, an underage navy sailor on the Mississippi River, a postal employee on the central plains, a store clerk in northern California, a merchant and postmaster in a new mill town, a fruit farmer in San Diego, a struggling rancher in Arizona, a migrant worker in Idaho, and, finally, an unemployed father walking alone on a beach. No matter where he moved, no matter his situation, he could always rely on the mail to stay connected to his siblings. Like so many Americans, the Curtises were a postal family.

The letters exchanged by Benjamin, Delia, Jamie, and Sarah were part of an ocean of correspondence that flowed between people and communities during the late 19th century. Those long-distance connections in turn depended on an underlying infrastructure of mail routes and post offices that, by Benjamin Curtis's death in 1892, had spread across the western United States with remarkable speed. The growth of the postal network in the West tells its own story about the history of the American state and its efforts to remake the region. And that larger story of the US Post and its western expansion begins in 1860, with the nation on the precipice of war.

# 3

# Postal Maps, 1860–83

In the fall of 1860, the United States was on the brink of fracture. The election of President Abraham Lincoln, an antislavery northerner, was seen by the slaveholding South as an existential threat. Over the coming months 11 states would secede from the United States, putting into motion the bloodiest war in the nation's history. Typically, the Civil War has been told from the perspective of the eastern United States, on battlefields like Antietam, Shiloh, and Gettysburg, while the western half of the country waits quietly offstage. But the American West didn't stand still during the Civil War. The 1860 election and the subsequent defection of southern Democratic congressmen left Lincoln's Republican Party with a commanding grip on both the executive and judicial branches of government. Republicans used their majority to radically expand the authority and capacity of the federal government. Even as this "Yankee Leviathan" mobilized to put down the Confederate rebellion in the South, it simultaneously took aim at Native sovereignty in the West. The Union Army repeatedly dispatched troops to western outposts to wage war against the Dakota in the northern prairies, the Cheyenne and Arapaho on the central plains, and the Apache and Navajo in the Southwest. Government officials orchestrated the seizure of millions of acres of Native land, while Congress crafted legislation explicitly aimed at promoting settlement, industry, and commerce in the West. The Homestead Act, Pacific Railway Acts, and Morrill Act—all passed during the Civil War—created a legal framework for transferring plundered Native land from the public domain into the private hands of individuals, railroad companies, and universities. During the war and its aftermath, the United States embarked on a new phase of aggressive colonial expansion in the West.[1]

The US Post's gossamer network facilitated the nation's westward turn during Civil War and its aftermath. In 1860, fewer than two thousand post offices were operating in the West, with most of them confined to the eastern and western edges of the region. Outside of a few isolated clusters of post offices in the interior, powerful groups like the Lakota, Ute, Cheyenne, Comanche, and Apache continued to block further postal expansion. Over the course of the next two decades, the conquest and forced removal of these groups opened up areas that had long been off-limits to permanent white settlement. American settlers occupied these areas in rapid succession, and the US Post opened thousands of new post offices alongside them. By 1880, there were some 6,700 post offices operating west of the Kansas/Missouri border—a more than threefold increase in the span of just two decades. The gossamer network's more ephemeral properties were also on full display during this period, as each year hundreds of western post offices disappeared from the network,

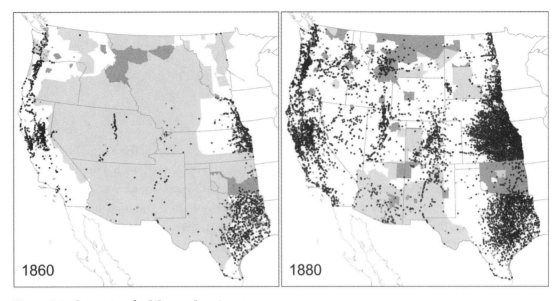

**Figure 3.1** Occupying the Western Interior

Between 1860 and 1880, the United States seized Native land (light gray), established new Indian reservations (dark gray), and extended its postal system across the interior of the western United States.

many of them just a few months or years after opening. Chaotic as it may have been, over the course of the 1860s and 1870s the US Post successfully extended its infrastructure across the western interior.[2]

The breakneck, unstable pattern of growth in the western United States posed fundamental challenges for the American state and its efforts at centralized administration. Officials across the federal government may have actively pursued the larger project of western expansion, but they also struggled to govern so much recently conquered and newly occupied territory. How were they supposed go about administering a region and a populace that refused to stand still? Information about the region was notoriously unreliable, as boosters spun tall tales about the region's riches. Boom towns sprouted up and then disappeared. Waves of seasonal labor led to fluctuating populations. Arguably no other institution witnessed the pace of these changes more acutely and regularly than the Post Office Department. To oversee its western periphery, postal officials turned to a particular division housed in the department's headquarters: the Topographer's Office, which was tasked with mapping the nation's post offices and mail routes.

Beginning in 1863, a cartographer named Walter Nicholson took over the Topographer's Office and embarked on a multi-decade campaign to produce a series of regional postal maps covering every state and territory in the country. These maps were, to borrow a phrase from historian Susan Schulten, "quiet yet necessary tools of governance."[3] Administering the western United States required a basic knowledge about the region's people and towns. Postal maps captured where these places were located and how they were connected to one another, and the

Topographer's Office did its best to keep these maps up to date. Nicholson's maps were in high demand amongst government officials. By the time Nicholson retired, his office was printing thousands of copies of them each year and distributing them to practically every organization in the federal government, from the General Land Office and the Treasury Department to the desks of senators and congressmen all the way to the president of the United States.[4]

The Topographer's Office and its postal maps would appear to fit within a larger narrative about the increasingly centralized capacity of the federal government. They were, after all, a top-down initiative to surveil and monitor the locations of tens of thousands of communities—a classic example of what sociologist James Scott terms "seeing like a state."[5] Moreover, the internal organization and workforce of the Topographer's Office had features of a modernizing bureaucracy: it was staffed by salaried, full-time employees and managed by Walter Nicholson, a professionalized civil servant with extensive technical training and expertise. A closer look at the Topographer's Office and its maps, however, reveals the ongoing challenges to centralized bureaucratic authority during this period. Again and again, the sprawling, unstable geography of the western United States and its gossamer network foiled the ability of government officials to administer the nation's periphery.

## Postal Cartography Takes Root

The clock had just struck midnight on a chilly December night in 1853 when Walter Nicholson began his shift at the Smithsonian Institution's telescope in Washington, DC. Over the next four hours he gazed up at the stars and recorded observations every five minutes. The 28-year-old Scotsman was born in 1825 in Edinburgh to an intellectual and artistic family, studying civil engineering in England before immigrating to the United States in 1851 to work as a railroad surveyor. In his spare time, he became increasingly involved in the city's growing scientific community that revolved around the Smithsonian Institution.[6] Nicholson's astronomical observations that winter night in 1853 were part of a multiyear scientific project overseen by Alexander D. Bache, director of the US Coast Survey and one of the era's most powerful government scientists.[7] Nicholson's participation in the Smithsonian's astronomy project endeared him to Bache, who then hired him for a permanent position as a cartographer.[8] By the time the Civil War broke out, Nicholson was heading up the Coast Survey's lithography division. In 1862, Nicholson drafted a map of Virginia as part of the Coast Survey's larger efforts to map the southern states for use by the Union Army. The map won Nicholson wide acclaim and helped secure him a new position in 1863 as topographer of the US Post Office Department.[9]

Postal cartography had a long history in the federal government. The first official map of the nation's post roads had been produced in 1796 under the direction of Abraham Bradley Jr., a cartographer, politician, and clerk in the Post Office Department. Bradley was subsequently promoted to assistant postmaster in 1799, a position he would occupy for the next three decades. He produced a handful of subsequent post road maps, but not until 1837 did Congress create a separate position of "topographer" within the Post Office Department. Henry A. Burr, a draftsman at the US Coast Survey, was appointed as the department's first official topographer. In 1863, Walter Nicholson became its second.[10] The move came with a salary bump and a top-ranking position at a major government bureau, but he had left one of the country's most powerful and well-funded scientific organizations to oversee a tiny, neglected corner of a giant institution.[11] In Nicholson's first year with the Post Office Department, he received $10,000 in funding for mapmaking, or less than the department spent each year on twine and string. Moreover, the new Topographer's Office was not even an officially designated division within the department, with its budget for salaries and supplies falling under the department's catch-all category of "miscellaneous expenses."[12]

Walter Nicholson nevertheless threw himself into his new position. He began by launching an initiative to produce a series of regional maps, much as he had done for the US Coast Survey.[13] Nicholson and his employees would first create a large-scale map of a single state or a handful of states. They would then chart the location of all existing post offices in that region and the mail routes that ran between them, with each route colored according to the frequency with which the mail was delivered along it. From the very start the western United States drew Nicholson's attention. Shortly after undertaking his new project, Walter Nicholson wrote a letter to the American Philosophical Society that described his interest in the West and "the opening out and clearing up of these terrae incognito."[14] He wasted little time in following through on that interest. The first regional postal map produced by his office was a two-sheet map of New England, published in 1866; its second was of the western United States, released the following year.

Western mail routes snaked along the emigrant trails on the Central Plains, the wagon roads in the Pacific Northwest, and the desert trails of New Mexico and Arizona Territories. Depicted with thick red lines on the 1867 postal map of the West, these routes resemble the arteries of a circulatory system of information knitting the region together. Look past the bold lines, however, and the map might as well have been labeled "Under Construction." A hatched line representing the transcontinental railroad unfurled from Sacramento before petering out at the Nevada border. Some of the region's post offices and mail routes had been erased, while others had been written over. A thin pencil line arced across northern Dakota Territory accompanied with the notation: "Probable course of mail route under contract." It was fortunate that the mapmaker had used a pencil, because the Post Office Department canceled the route less than two years later.[15]

In 1869, Walter Nicholson's office released an entirely new map of the western postal system. This meant that two out of the first five regional postal maps produced by the Topographer's Office were of the western United States when it had

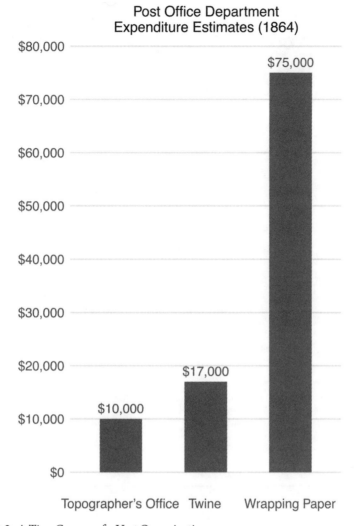

**Figure 3.2** A Tiny Corner of a Vast Organization

The Post Office Department's 1864 budget allocation for the Topographer's Office was less than it spent on office supplies such as twine and wrapping paper. *1864 Annual Report of the Postmaster General* (Washington, DC: Government Printing Office, 1864), 13, 27, 88.

yet to issue a single map of the Midwest or South, even though these regions were far more populous.[16] A close reading of the two maps offers some clues as to why Nicholson's office focused on the West. The first 1867 map of the region abandoned the department's standard color-coded schema for mail routes and instead printed only the largest transportation routes in the region. It also contained a handwritten notation reading "Presentation Copy of the Engineer Bureau," which was part of the War Department. The second map of the West had an even more anomalous cartographic style that prominently plotted and labeled every single Indian reservation in the region, going so far as to include the boundaries of a future reservation planned for northern Montana. In short, these maps were never intended to capture

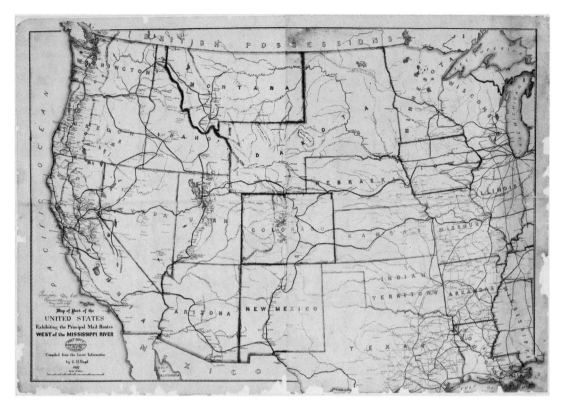

**Figure 3.3** Turning Westward

The Post Office Department Topographer's Office issued its first postal map of the western United States in 1867. E. D. Boyd and Walter L. Nicholson, "Map of Part of the United States Exhibiting the Principal Mail Routes West of the Mississippi River" (Washington, DC, 1867), National Archives II at College Park, Maryland, I, Record Group 77, Records of the War Department, Map 285.

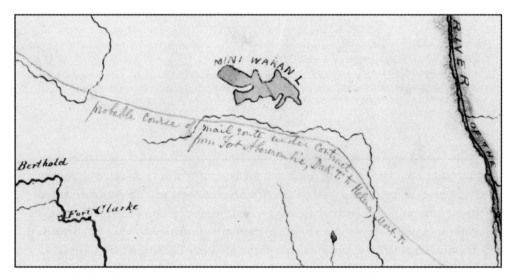

**Figure 3.4** Under Construction

The pencil annotation on this map reads: "Probable course of mail route under contract from Fort Abercrombie, Dak.[ota] T.[erritory] to Helena, Mont.[ana] T.[erritory]." Detail from E. D. Boyd and Walter L. Nicholson, "Map of Part of the United States Exhibiting the Principal Mail Routes West of the Mississippi River" (Washington, DC, 1867), National Archives II at College Park, Maryland, I, Record Group 77, Records of the War Department, Map 285.

solely the postal system but were tools for the state's larger project of conquest and governance in the West.[17]

## Spatial Administration in the West

Walter Nicholson's early postal maps of the western United States reflected some of the challenges facing the American state in the region. As the federal government turned its attention westward during the 1860s and 1870s, it wrestled with a recurring problem: its authority far outstripped its administrative capacity. The West's federal organizations were often understaffed and riddled with corruption. The General Land Office, for instance, was tasked with making accurate surveys and then parceling out a massive quantity of land in the West. Its overstretched workforce was vulnerable to speculators, squatters, and crooked officeholders, to the point where the government surveyor in the pocket of a local "land ring" was almost as familiar a western trope as the emigrant family in a covered wagon.[18] The Office of Indian Affairs—one of the other main federal agencies in the West—was similarly rocked by corruption scandals during the 1860s and 1870s. The US Army was arguably the most effective arm of the federal government in the region, but it too suffered from desertion and spasms of government retrenchment.[19]

The Post Office Department also suffered from a lack of administrative capacity in the West. Its Inspection Division was one of the principal vehicles for internally regulating the nation's mail service, dispatching postal inspectors to investigate fraud and theft conducted through the US Mail.[20] In the words of one postmaster general, they were the "fingers of my official hand." But in the West, those fingers didn't stretch very far.[21] In 1865, the Post Office Department appointed Quincy Brooks as its special agent to oversee the entire Pacific Northwest. At the time, Brooks was one of only 30 to 40 inspectors who were each responsible for monitoring different areas of the country. In that capacity, Brooks was expected to oversee the entirety of California, Oregon, and Washington Territory from his office in Portland. Brooks's letters to his superiors in Washington, DC, paint a picture of an overwhelmed and overextended government official. Among his many complaints, one in particular stands out: a lack of geographical information. Upon taking office, Brooks immediately wrote to his superiors in Washington, DC, begging for a post route map or, at the very least, a statement of the postal routes in his district. He didn't even wait for a reply before writing to Oregon's surveyor general requesting copies of any maps he might have of the region to help him with his work. A year after taking office, he was still waiting in vain for any kind of map and was struggling to evaluate incoming requests for new post roads or to address rumors of negligent postmasters. The harried inspector lacked even basic information about where post offices and mail routes were located within the vast area under his oversight.[22]

Quincy Brooks's repeated requests for western maps illustrate the challenges of administering a giant amount of territory during a time in which geographical knowledge about that territory was in such short supply. The region was undergoing such rapid changes that officials across the federal government were struggling to keep pace with on-the-ground conditions. The US Army was forced to conduct fast-moving and far-ranging military campaigns against enemies whose familiarity with local environments far outstripped their own. To try and close this knowledge deficit, army officers used both Indian scouts and topographical surveyors to help them navigate the region's canyons, rivers, and mountains. The Bureau of Indian Affairs and General Land Office faced similar deficits of geographical knowledge in trying to delineate the boundaries of Indian reservations or distribute public land to settlers. A shortfall of geographic knowledge explains why two out of the first five regional postal maps produced by the Post Office Department Topographer's Office were of the western United States.

Between the 1860s and early 1880s, Nicholson's office completed maps of every state and territory in the country.[23] As the coverage of these maps expanded, demand skyrocketed. In his annual report to Congress in 1868, the postmaster general reported that Nicholson's maps had "been found of great use in the several branches of this Department." Five years later, demand proved "beyond the capacity of the Department to satisfy." A decade later, by 1883, Nicholson's office reported a one-year backlog of requests.[24]

The Topographer's Office maps were vital instruments for administering the nation's gossamer postal network. They helped the first assistant postmaster general and his clerks establish new post offices and appoint postmasters to manage them. The Dead Letter Office used the maps to try and decipher the scrawled addresses of undeliverable letters. The second assistant postmaster general, in charge of mail transportation, used postal maps to draw up government contracts to carry the mail along different routes. The Railway Mail Service, however, proved to be the single largest consumer of Nicholson's maps within the department. As more and more material traveled by railroad, postal clerks started sorting long-distance mail in specially designated railway cars. The job required considerable knowledge and recall of geographical information, including railroad divisions and connections, the locations of thousands of post offices along railroad lines, and an ever-changing list of post office names.[25] Clerks started using Nicholson's maps as early as 1868, and by the early 1880s Nicholson's office was sending more than two thousand map sheets each year to the Railway Mail Service.[26] The Topographer's Office even started producing customized versions that only showed offices along railway lines. These handheld single sheets were designed to be portable so that they could be unfolded in the back of a clattering railway car rather than hung on the wall in a government office.[27] For clerks in the Railway Mail Service employees, the maps were "like the mariner's charts on the ocean."[28]

Congressmen paid regular visits to Nicholson's office asking for maps of their state or region, both for themselves and on behalf of their constituents.[29] The maps helped respond to local demands and requests even when they were removed from their states and districts. In the words of one congressman, "You save an hour's time frequently by a few minutes' observation of these maps."[30] Nearly every major executive agency also sought out Nicholson's maps, including the State Department, the Treasury Department, the US Mint, the Coast Survey, the War Department, the Navy Department, the General Land Office, the Census Bureau, the US Geological Survey, and even the president of the United States. By the end of the 1870s, Nicholson's office was distributing more than two thousand map sheets every year to government officials outside of the Post Office Department.[31]

Thousands of copies of postal maps also made their way outside of the federal government, appearing in libraries, historical societies, geographical associations, and museums across the country.[32] They even won the highest award for cartography at the 1881 International Congress of Geography in Venice, Italy.[33] In 1876, the Centennial International Exhibition in Philadelphia provided the US government with a prominent stage on which to project its postwar reunification and growing status as an international power. As part of the exhibition, Walter Nicholson was tasked with preparing a wall-sized map of the continent measuring 16.75 feet long and 15 feet tall. Six copies of the map went to the Smithsonian, five to the Agricultural Department, and one each to the Lighthouse Board, Census Bureau, Education Bureau, and Geological Survey of the Territories. These bureaus overlaid their own particular information onto Nicholson's map: the Agricultural Department, for instance, used the map to chart the value of different kinds of farmland or the wages paid to farm workers.[34] When the exhibition finally opened, Nicholson's handiwork literally covered the walls of the United States Government Building.[35] The American state trumpeted its mastery of territory on the back of its postal cartography. The irony was that this mastery of territory was largely an illusion.[36]

## "Bringing Up the Diagrams"

Walter Nicholson stepped into his position as post office topographer just as the federal government was entering a golden era of cartography focused on the American West. Between 1867 and 1879, the federal government launched four "great surveys" headed by Clarence King, George Wheeler, Ferdinand Hayden, and John Wesley Powell. Over roughly 10 years, these scientists led expeditions to explore and map the region's remote mountains, canyons, and deserts. The "great surveys" captured the imagination of the American public and future historians alike. Their feats have become the stuff of western mythology, as the teams of geologists, paleontologists, botanists, and ethnologists avoided river rapids and grizzly bears, braved lightning strikes and skirmishes with Native inhabitants, and surveyed the region's forbidding and previously unmapped landscape.[37] By quite literally filling in the blanks of contemporary maps of the West, Powell, Wheeler, King, and Hayden also fed into a longstanding triumphalist narrative that emphasizes increasingly comprehensive and accurate mapmaking.[38] Romanticized histories of the surveys have overshadowed more mundane kinds of cartography, including Walter Nicholson's postal maps. But postal maps were no less important for understanding the federal government's attempts to administer the space of the western United States during this era.

Compared to the "great surveys," mapmaking in the Post Office Department was about as romantic as actuarial accounting. While surveyors like John Wesley Powell trekked through western canyons with zenith telescopes and climbing axes, Nicholson and his employees wielded colored pencils at their office desks in Washington, DC. Mapmaking at the Topographer's Office was divided into two stages, one focused on capturing space, the second on capturing time. The first stage involved the traditional cartographic practice of locating topographical features on a two-dimensional surface. Draughtsmen first outlined state and county boundaries on the map along with major features such as lakes or rivers. They then had to add the location of post offices. This was no easy task, as a decade into Nicholson's tenure there were 34,000 post offices connected by nearly 270,000 miles of postal routes that ran along the country's roads, waterways, and railroad lines.[39] To locate them, draughtsmen tried to cobble together geographical information from existing maps, atlases, and state or county surveys.[40] If that failed, they would then ask individual postmasters for information about the locations of their offices in relation to nearby offices, mail routes, railroad lines, and other landmarks.

Once the draughtsmen finished placing post offices on their map, the second phase of postal cartography began. An engraver would print several hundred sheets of the regional map, which resembled an untouched page from a connect-the-dots book. It showed the names and locations of thousands of post office dots, but the routes connecting them were absent. Clerks still had to "connect the dots" by coloring in the routes that ran between each office. This second stage of the mapmaking process hinged on representing time as much as space.[41] Nicholson and his employees used a color-based schema to represent how frequently the mail traveled along different routes, ranging from six times a week (a black line) down to once a week (a red line). The colored lines infused these maps with an important temporal dimension, transforming a static map of unconnected dots into a diagram of how information traveled across the system.[42]

The two cartographic stages in the Topographer's Office, one capturing space and one capturing time, were divided into "gentlemen's work" and "ladies' work."[43] The first stage of laying out and drawing the postal maps was conducted largely by men whose salaries were based on their training and experience, ranging from $1,200 to $1,600 a year (the highest pay grade for a federal clerk).[44] The second stage, known as "ladies' work," consisted of keeping maps up to date and coloring in routes to "connect the dots" of the unfinished diagrams. These female "colorists" received only $900 annually and made up fully two-thirds of the office's employees by the end of the 1870s.[45] This put the Topographer's Office at the forefront of a larger movement by women into the federal workforce in Washington, DC, during the

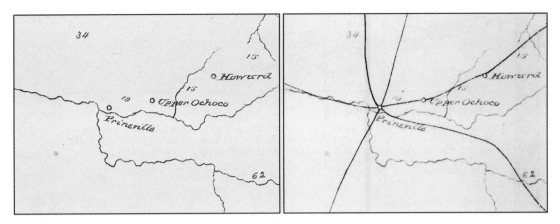

**Figure 3.5** Connecting the Dots

Postal maps were initially printed without their mail routes (*left*), which colorists would then fill in by hand (*right*). *Left*: W. L. Nicholson, *Post Route Map of the State of Oregon and Territory of Washington* (Washington, DC, 1877), 1:760,320 [unfinished]. From Beinecke Rare Book and Manuscript Library, New Haven, Connecticut, call number 846gmd 1877. Many thanks to Justin Gage for sharing this map with me. *Right*: A. F. Dinsmore and W. L. Nicholson, *Post Route Map of the State of Oregon and Territory of Washington* (Washington, DC, 1880), 1:760,320. Located in National Archives II, College Park, Maryland, RG28, Records of the Division of Topography, Regional Postal Route Maps before 1894, folder IV.

late 19th century—a process that preceded the private sector by several decades. Many of the women who worked in the Topographer's Office were unmarried or widowed, young, and from a middle-class background.[46]

Female colorists may have been paid less than their male counterparts, but they were the ones who made postal maps usable and supplied the bulk of the labor in the Topographer's Office. By coloring in routes according to the frequency of mail service, they captured the US Post's temporal dimensions. Even more importantly, their labor involved a much more challenging task: keeping postal maps up to date, or, in their own parlance, "bringing up the diagrams."[47] This was a never-ending battle, as every single day new post offices were established, old ones discontinued, and others changed locations or names. These women were, in effect, trying to paint a still life while someone kept rearranging the fruit. The Topographer's Office tried to convey the fleeting nature of their maps by including a blank space in their legend: "The service on this diagram brought up to date of _____." As in Figure 3.6, an employee would fill in this blank space at the last possible moment, often down to the specific day, before sending the map out. Postal maps were an exercise in capturing transience.

Whereas the "great surveys" of the era used sextants and hypsometers, Nicholson's employees relied on official Post Office Department stationery in order to map the nation. To keep pace with the nation's ever-shifting postal network, the Topographer's Office turned to other divisions within the Post Office Department. The mail contracting division sent them monthly reports with updated information about the nation's thousands of mail routes and their operations. The Railway Mail Service sent daily reports regarding any changes to the postal infrastructure along the nation's railroad routes. The Appointment Office, which oversaw the nation's

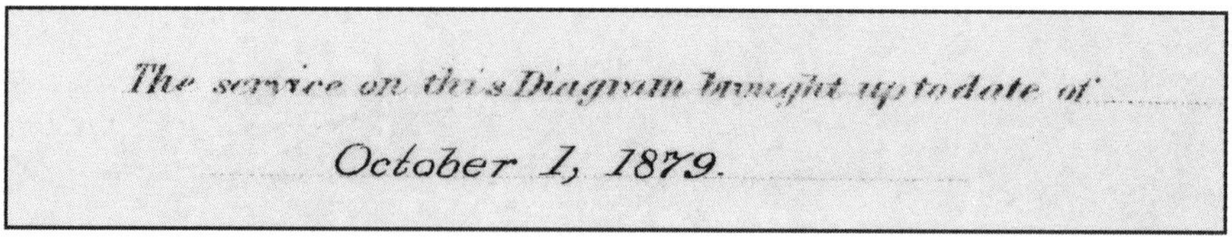

**Figure 3.6** A Snapshot in Time

Postal maps included a blank line to annotate the most recent date on which it was updated. Detail from W. L. Nicholson, *Post Route Map of the State of Colorado* (Washington, DC, 1879), 1:1,000,000. Located in National Archives II, College Park, Maryland, RG28, Records of the Division of Topography, Regional Postal Route Maps before 1894, folder III.

post offices and postmasters, sent weekly bulletins of new and discontinued post offices, along with any changes to their names or spellings.

The Post Office Department also solicited information about post offices from local communities themselves. In order to establish a new post office, a group of people would first petition postal officials or their congressmen. The Post Office Department's Appointment Division would then send a blank application form for the aspiring postmaster to fill out. The form included some 20 queries, including the proposed name of the post office and the approximate number of people it would serve. Almost all of its questions, however, were geared toward pinning down the precise location of the new post office: where it fell within public land surveys, the nearest mail route and railroad line, the locations of surrounding post offices, and the names of nearby rivers, streams, and other natural features. The form even included an empty half-page grid for the applicant to draw a small map of the office and the surrounding area. To supplement these post office applications and get more updated information for older post offices, the Topographer's Office would mail out additional "Site Report" circulars to postmasters asking many of the same geographical questions. By 1880, Nicholson's office was sending out some 1,800 of these circulars each year to postmasters across the country. From their office building in Washington, DC, Walter Nicholson and his employees reeled in filaments of information across a web of official correspondence.[48]

## The Gossamer Network and the Limits of Centralized Administration

On the surface, Walter Nicholson's Topographer's Office embodied an "ideal type" of bureaucracy. It was under the professional management of Walter Nicholson, an accomplished man of science and career technocrat who moved through the upper echelons of Washington, DC's intellectual elite. Nicholson oversaw a staff of salaried employees, some of whom had developed technical expertise through years of training as draftsmen and mapmakers. And if generating paperwork is one of the markers of a bureaucracy, then the Topographer's Office certainly fit the bill.

Its preprinted postmaster questionnaires were an attempt to impose internal rules that would standardize the department's operations. These are all classic markers of bureaucracy. But the process of mapmaking was far more chaotic and much less bureaucratic than it first appears.[49]

One of the hallmarks of an effective government bureaucracy is autonomy: the ability to implement policies independent of outside influence or political pressure.[50] Walter Nicholson's office largely failed this test of autonomy. The Topographer's Office was buffeted by the era's prevailing political winds. Congress's annual post office appropriations bill, for instance, loomed over Walter Nicholson's tenure in office. During his first decade in office, from 1864 to 1874, Nicholson's annual budget grew more than threefold, but he had to claw and scrap for every dollar.[51] In 1869, he was so worried about the impending postal appropriations bill that he sent a letter directly to the House Appropriations Committee, telling them that his office's mapmaking efforts would be "seriously crippled and delayed" if they decided to decrease his $20,000 appropriation.[52] The following year, Nicholson and his boss asked Congress to increase Nicholson's personal salary from $1,800 to $3,000 due to "his superior qualifications" in mapmaking that required "the highest order of artistic skill for its proper execution."[53] Congress promptly rejected the request. Things got much worse for Nicholson in 1875 when a Democratic majority assumed control of the House of Representatives for the first time since before the Civil War. In the midst of a devastating economic depression, Democrats rode a wave of public anger to a legislative majority and promptly slashed funding across the federal government—including the appropriation for Nicholson's office. Within a matter of months, all new mapmaking efforts in the Post Office Department had ground to a halt.[54] The office's funding was eventually restored, but Nicholson and the Topographer's Office continued to face pushback from Democratic congressmen during the annual debate over postal appropriations.[55]

Democrats intent on reining in the Republican-led executive branch convened a congressional committee in the spring of 1878 to look into allegations of wasteful spending and mismanagement in the Post Office Department. As part of the inquiry, the committee called Nicholson and several employees to testify. Although some of the questions focused on exorbitant expenses, the investigation got more and more personal with each new witness. When Nicholson's chief assistant took the stand, Democrat John W. Caldwell from Kentucky asked him: "Have you ever seen Mr. Nicholson intoxicated?"[56] It was the start of a two-week-long character assassination, during which the committee called every one of Nicholson's employees to pepper them with questions such as: "Do you know of his drinking during office hours?"—"State what Mr. Nicholson's habits are to sobriety"—"Do you know of his using liquors to excess?"[57] Several affirmed that their boss did, in fact, drink on the job, while others alluded to a hair-trigger temper, his "nervous" or "peculiar" character, and, in the delicate words of one employee, "a very artistic way of speaking."[58] Having already endured years of trying to fend off attempts in Congress to defund his office, Nicholson now faced personal humiliation at the hands of Democratic legislators.

Setting aside questions about his personal habits, Walter Nicholson's management of the Topographer's Office did not epitomize some lofty bureaucratic ideal. He oversaw a workforce that was defined by personal and political patronage as much as technical meritocracy. Nicholson himself owed his position almost entirely to the influence of his own former patron at the US Coast Survey, Alexander Bache. Once in office, Nicholson reported directly to the postmaster general, whose control over the nation's deepest well of patronage positions made it one of the most politicized positions in the entire federal government.[59] The Topographer's Office was part and parcel of this patronage regime. In 1872, Congressman James Garfield happily noted in his diary that he had managed to secure a position in the Topographer's Office for a family friend named Elizabeth Ladd who had been living with Garfield's family in Washington.[60]

That same year, Nicholson hired an ailing widow and mother of two named Sarah Cushing at the behest of the postmaster general and Senator Thomas Ferry, a powerful Republican legislator from Cushing's home state of Michigan. The influence of these powerful "friends" secured Sarah Cushing not only a position in the Topographer's Office but also preferential treatment. Due to her ailing health, Nicholson allowed her to work entirely from her apartment rather than in the office. She barely showed her face inside the Post Office building throughout her entire time on the job, leaving other clerks to grumble as they corrected her mistakes. Nicholson proved either unwilling or unable to do anything about the situation, continuing to employ Cushing for six more years.[61] Entangled webs of personal and political connections left him with only limited autonomy to decide who actually worked for him.[62] Nicholson himself was not a paragon of technocratic management; the 1878 Congressional investigation found that he regularly kept both his wife and son on the office payroll.[63] For all of Walter Nicholson's professional expertise, his office embodied an administrative state during the 19th century in which politics and patronage outweighed bureaucratic autonomy.

Ultimately, politicization was not the biggest challenge for the Topographer's Office and its efforts at administering the nation's postal network. Rather, the greatest struggle came from trying to map the gossamer network's ever-shifting geography, especially in the western United States. As early as 1864, Walter Nicholson acknowledged the "choice bits of perplexity" that came with mapping the western states and territories.[64] To take one example, a western mining company might petition Congress to establish a mail route to its new mountain camp. Once approved and put into service, the route then had to be drawn on the department's postal maps. But when the mine wound down and its workforce trickled away, the department might curtail the route's service from three times a week to once a week. The Topographer's Office would then need to change the route's color from blue to red on all of its maps. And when the mine ultimately closed and the department discontinued its post office, the Topographer's Office would need to cross out the name of

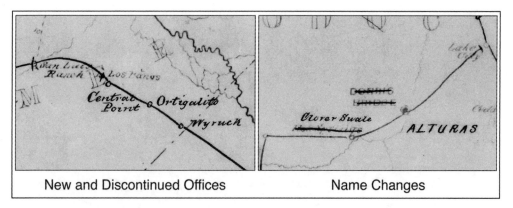

New and Discontinued Offices          Name Changes

**Figure 3.7** "Bringing Up the Diagrams"

Colorists in the Topographer's Office had to constantly add new post offices to their maps and cross out the locations of discontinued ones (*left*), along with updating existing post offices whose names had changed (*right*). Detail from Post Office Department, *Post Route Map of the States of California and Nevada*, Washington, DC, December 1, 1876. 1:760,320. Located in National Archives II, College Park, Maryland, RG 75, Bureau of Indian Affairs, Map 278.

the office on both existing and future editions of the map. Like Sisyphus pushing his boulder up a hill only to watch it roll down again, postal mapmakers were engaged in a never-ending fight to keep pace with the region.

In 1876, one of California's senators rose to make the case for maintaining funding for the Topographer's Office during the annual postal appropriations bill. After all, he pointed out, postal maps involved an enormous amount of upkeep, because "a map of the year before last would be entirely obsolete."[65] He was entirely correct. Even as he was speaking, Nicholson's mapmakers were busy drafting a postal map of California and Nevada, two states undergoing rapid changes. In California, for instance, laborers for the Southern Pacific Railroad were busy trying to complete the company's railway line between San Francisco and Los Angeles. Nicholson's mapmakers finished their work before the company finished its railroad, which left their postal map with a conspicuous gap in the route between Los Angeles and Bakersfield. When the railroad company completed this final section later that year, a colorist then had to connect the postal map's railway line by hand before reissuing this particular copy of the map on December 1, 1876.

Even with this correction, however, the map didn't stay up to date for long. Two days later, on December 3, a California post office changed its name from Prairie to Black's Station, and on December 7 a new post office opened in Nevada.[66] By the following summer, the department reported that more than 250 post offices had opened, closed, or changed names or locations in California and Nevada over the preceding year—joining some three thousand total changes nationwide.[67] Every single real-world alteration to the nation's postal system required a corresponding change to the nation's postal maps. As the postal network steadily grew during the late 19th century, so too did the challenges of trying to keep track of this expansion: by the late 1880s, the Topographer's Office was responsible for trying to capture some seven thousand changes to the nation's post offices in a single year.[68]

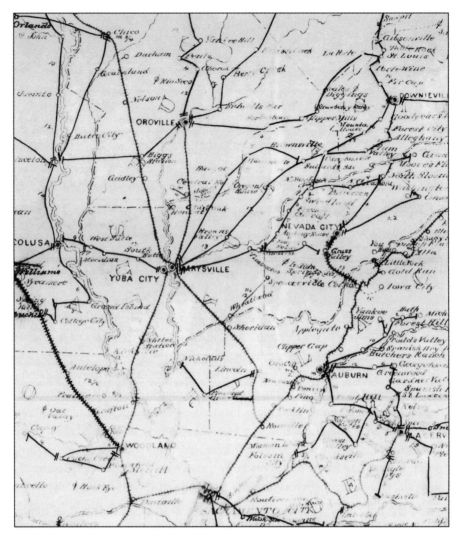

**Figure 3.8** Tracking the Gossamer Network

This section of a postal map of northern California shows the complexity that came with trying to map the nation's sprawling and ever-shifting collection of post offices and mail routes. Detail from Post Office Department, *Post Route Map of the States of California and Nevada* (Washington, DC, 1876). 1:760,320. Located in National Archives II, College Park, Maryland, RG 75, Bureau of Indian Affairs, Map 278.

In Walter Nicholson's words, "the changes [to the postal system] are so great that unless you see it directly in my office you have no idea of the extent of them; not even the Postmaster-General himself could realize the enormous changes that have occurred."[69] Updating maps constituted the bulk of labor in Nicholson's office. The Topographer's Office was responsible for supplying updated maps for all other divisions of the Post Office Department, including the Appointment Division, the Contracting Office, the Money Order Office, the Dead Letter Office, the Railway Mail Service, and the Postal Inspection Service. In the case of the Appointment Division and the Contracting Office in particular, Nicholson's office was expected to update every one of their maps on a daily basis. Demands for "bringing up the diagrams" went well beyond the Post Office Department. Congressmen often brought their own personal maps into his office roughly once a year to have them corrected, as did officials from other executive agencies.[70] As one of the few official cartographic initiatives that attempted to track changes to the nation's geography with any degree of regularity, the Topographer's Office found itself fielding requests for updates from across the federal government.

The instability of the nation's postal infrastructure wasn't the only way in which the gossamer network stymied attempts at centralized oversight. The US Post's reliance on the agency model to run its rural offices and mail routes created endless headaches for administrators like Walter Nicholson. The Topographer's Office may have used quintessential tools of centralized bureaucratic administration, including questionnaires, standardized forms, maps, and site reports. But much of that paperwork had to be filled out by a far-flung collection of part-time local agents, many of them political appointees who spent the bulk of their time and energy running their own private businesses. Meticulously filling out paperwork was not their forte. When the Topographer's Office mailed postmasters blank site reports to complete, many of the forms came back with entire sections blank.[71] The descriptions that postmasters did provide, meanwhile, could be frustratingly unhelpful. In the words of one mapmaker, these descriptions were "often very erratic . . . so it makes it a very difficult thing to put offices in the right places."[72] The Topographer's Office was lucky to receive even those "erratic" descriptions. In 1882, Nicholson reported that nearly one-quarter of the postmasters who were mailed blank forms by his office over the previous year— around one thousand in total—never even bothered to return them.[73]

Walter Nicholson wasn't the only federal official stymied by the decentralized sprawl the nation's postal workforce. In 1879, the compilers of the biennial *Official Register*, a directory of federal workers, decided to move the Post Office Department into its own volume to be printed separately from the rest of the federal government's workforce. It was taking so long to collect information about the nation's tens of thousands of postmasters, clerks, and contractors that it threatened to delay the entire project's publication by several months. The very same organizational arrangements that allowed the gossamer network to expand so easily across the western periphery also made that network fiendishly difficult to administer from its center.[74]

## Churn

Cartography has long been used as a tool of state power. The rectangular gridded land surveys conducted by the General Land Office, for instance, were a process of abstraction that allowed the American state to catalog and lay claim to its territory, resources, and people. By imposing spatial order on the landscape—regardless of how accurate those maps actually were—this kind of government cartography legitimated the state's own authority. Postal maps had no such pretense, offering an alternative perspective on what it meant to "see like a state" in the 19th century. Postal maps did not project mastery or control. With their connect-the-dots mail routes, crossed-out labels, and added-in features, they embodied a state that was squinting to make out what was actually happening on the ground. Walter Nicholson and other officials did their best to keep pace, but they were routinely frustrated by the postal network's ever-shifting geography and decentralized administrative structure. A decade and a half into his tenure at the Post Office Department, the pace of these changes reached frenetic new heights.[75]

The period straddling the late 1870s and early 1880s is not an obvious watershed moment in the history of the western United States. Outside of the Chinese Restriction Act of 1882, it can seem like a historical lull between the Indian Wars of the 1860s and the explosive agrarian populism of the late 1880s and early 1890s. But in important ways this period marked a turning point for the American West, a transition from an earlier phase of territorial expansion and toward a new era of consolidation and integration. By the late 1870s, as the national economy was recovering from a devastating financial depression, hundreds of thousands of Americans took the opportunity to move to distant corners of the West, often onto recently plundered Native land. The US Post moved alongside them, and its expansion between 1878 and 1883 offers a useful lens through which to understand this transitional moment and some of the challenges it posed to central administration.

The American West has become synonymous with a "boom-and-bust" style of growth. More so than any other region of the United States, the West's dependence on extractive industries and eastern capital meant that the region's economy experienced sudden shifts of fortune: new mineral discoveries followed by ecological collapse, or frenzied land speculation followed by a bursting financial bubble. This cyclical pattern has become central to narrating the region's history and, in particular, the ways that the West was shaped by capitalist expansion.[76] During the late 1870s, the region experienced one of these booms. A surge of eastern and European investment poured into western railroad construction and extractive industries. The Northern Pacific Railroad laid down tracks in Dakota, Montana, northern Idaho, and eastern Washington, helping to touch off a frenzied rush of settlers on the northern plains known as the "Great Dakota Boom."[77] Other railroad companies extended shorter lines from Salt Lake City to the Colorado Rockies, over Idaho, and across New Mexico and Arizona. These new lines went hand in hand with an acceleration of mining in the Mountain West. New mineral strikes in Butte, Montana, and in southwestern Colorado's San Juan Mountains set off a burst of mining camps, further aided by the passage of the Bland-Allison Act in 1878, which required the US Treasury to buy, mint, and circulate silver currency. Finally, new homesteaders and a "ranch rush" of cattle and sheep brought Americans farther and farther west over the plains.[78]

Not surprisingly, the western postal network underwent its own boom during this period. The US Post's expansionary gossamer network facilitated the frenetic expansion of settlers, railroads, mines, and ranches by opening more than 5,300 new post offices in the western United States between 1878 and 1883.[79] This boom posed challenges for the network's administrators in Washington. Every one of these new western post offices had to be added to the Topographer's Office's postal maps, along with the new mail routes that connected them. One can easily imagine the frustrations of Walter Nicholson's employees as they "brought up the diagrams" during these years. Postal growth was especially explosive in states and territories in the western interior over these years: Arizona Territory's postal network more than doubled in size, while Dakota Territory's more than tripled. A postal map of either of these territories would have been rendered virtually unusable in the span of just a few years.[80]

Boom and bust is, above all, a sequential model: first the bender, then the hangover. And the late 1870s and early 1880s had all the markings of a classic western boom. A closer look at the region's postal network, however, shows a different sort of pattern. Had the western postal network followed a boom-and-bust pattern, one

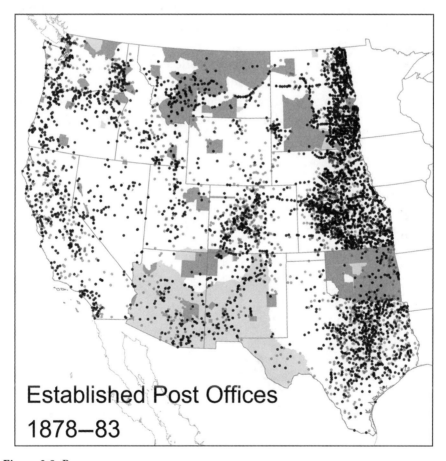

Established Post Offices
1878–83

**Figure 3.9** Boom

This map shows new post offices that opened between 1878 and 1883, along with unceded Native land (light gray) and reservations (dark gray) in 1883.

would expect to see two distinct phases. In the first "boom" phase, the annual tally of newly opened post offices would increase, while the number of discontinued post offices would decline. In the second "bust" phase, the number of new post offices would crater, while the number of discontinued post offices would rise. But this wasn't the case. Instead, during the late 1870s and early 1880s post office openings and post office closings moved in tandem, as the number of opened and closed post offices both rocketed upward. This was a pattern in which growth and contraction were not sequential but simultaneous. Instead of boom then bust, it was boom with bust. In a word: churn.

Many of the region's post offices that opened during the late 1870s and early 1880s only operated for a vanishingly short period of time. Across the region as a whole, roughly one out of every two post offices established between 1878 and 1883 would exist for less than 10 years before closing down or changing its name or location. More than four hundred of these new post offices shut down in the same calendar year in which they opened.[81] The West was littered with post offices like the one at Stone Cabin, Arizona, which opened its doors in December of 1880 before permanently closing less than two months later.[82] The geography of the western postal network reveals a regional landscape marked by explosive growth and spectacular failure, all unfolding in tandem.

The US Post's churning growth in the American West was part of a regional expansion project that galloped ahead of government officials in Washington, DC. Again and again, the federal government's administrative responsibilities outstripped its actual capacities in the West. When Congress passed legislation

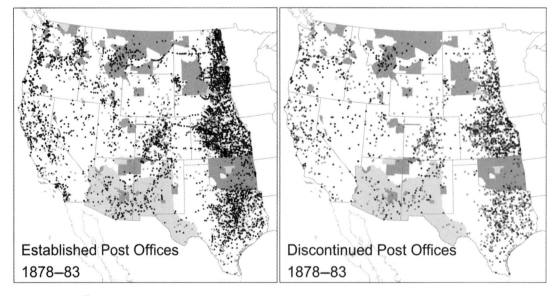

Established Post Offices 1878–83

Discontinued Post Offices 1878–83

**Figure 3.10** Churn

These two maps compare post offices that opened (*left*) and post offices that shut down or changed names or locations (*right*) between 1878 and 1883. Unceded Native land in 1883 is in light gray and reservations in 1883 are in dark gray on both maps.

restricting Chinese immigration, it fell to an overstretched government workforce to enforce it. At a loss for how to monitor thousands of miles of Pacific coastline, customs officials and US marshals enlisted ship captains, militia members, and other private citizens to help them. Border enforcement turned into an extralegal affair that soon spiraled into bouts of vigilantism and violence.[83] In the interior, the creation of Yellowstone National Park in 1872 set aside some two million acres of public land for protection. Congress neglected, however, to allocate funds to hire people to enforce these protections in one of the most remote parts in the continental United States. Even after hiring 10 assistant superintendents in 1883, this skeletal workforce failed to prevent encroachments onto park land by poachers, squatters, and Shoshone, Bannock, and Crow hunters. Ultimately, administrators had to call in the US Army to help police the park. Across the western United States, federal power ran aground against the realities of the region's sprawling and remote geography.[84]

Within the Post Office Department, employees in the Topographer's Office scrambled to locate and map the thousands of western post offices that opened and closed during the late 1870s and early 1880s. Other postal officials were similarly struggling to oversee the gossamer network's western periphery during this period. On a hot summer day in 1882, Walter Nicholson took the stand in a Washington, DC, courthouse to testify about the location of a particular western mail route. His testimony was part of an ongoing federal trial in which mail contractors and postal officials were accused of colluding to defraud the Post Office Department of millions of dollars' worth of ill-gotten government mail contracts. At the request of one of the government prosecutors, Nicholson's office had prepared a map of one of the mail routes that was under investigation. After winning the bid to carry the mail on this particular route, the mail contractor's annual compensation had been tripled by a high-ranking postal official. Prosecutors suspected fraud and wanted to use Nicholson's map to conclusively demonstrate that the route could not possibly have warranted such an extravagant increase in payment. Defense lawyers, however, honed in on the fact that the map only showed where the route was supposed to run according to departmental reports, not its actual, on-the-ground operations. As Nicholson admitted during cross-examination, "I cannot tell how the service is [actually] performed."[85]

Walter Nicholson's testimony reflected a federal apparatus that simply could not keep up with on-the-ground conditions. The postal maps produced by his office were one attempt to monitor and regulate the nation's western periphery. But these maps say just as much about the limits of centralized government oversight during these years. The American state may have actively bolstered the expansion of white settlers and industrial capitalism in the West—not least by extending a far-reaching regional communications network—but it was rarely, if ever, in the driver's seat. The churning, unstable growth of the gossamer network during the late 1870s and early 1880s was made possible in part by the decentralized administrative structure of the agency model. By grafting public mail functions onto local private businesses, the US Post could rapidly expand and contract across the region. But, as Nicholson's testimony hints at, these arrangements also came with considerable costs. By the late 1870s, the brightly colored mail routes on western postal maps represented the seams of a regional system that were starting to burst under the weight of collusion and fraud.

# 4

# Mail Routes and the Costs of Expansion, 1866–83

The Pony Express is one of the most recognizable brands in American history. It has been the subject of books, dime novels, comic books, movies, and television shows, capturing all of the drama and danger associated with the American West: the image of a young man galloping across a rugged western landscape, his satchel of precious letters at his side and with highwaymen or Indians in hot pursuit. Like so many western symbols, the Pony Express is based largely in myth. Established in 1860 by a large freighting firm, the horse relay was a private mail service that promised to carry letters from Missouri to California in under two weeks, during a time when the official US mail took the better part of a month to make the same trip. It was an expensive operation, requiring scores of riders, hundreds of horses, and more than 150 relay stations scattered across some 1,900 miles of prairies, plains, and mountains. The company subsequently charged its customers astronomical rates (the equivalent of roughly $60 to $160 per letter today). Even so, the company knew it would never be able to turn a profit without a key source of income: a government contract. The Pony Express was one giant publicity stunt aimed at trying to secure a lucrative contract from the Post Office Department to carry the mail. The government contract never came, and without it the company racked up massive losses. In the end, the vaunted Pony Express operated for a grand total of 19 months before selling off its operations to a rival firm in 1861. From a business perspective, it was an abject failure.[1]

The struggles of the Pony Express highlighted a broader challenge from this period: how should the United States transport mail to western states and territories? What was the best way to extend lines of communications across the region's sparsely settled and rugged terrain? Once again, the agency model provided the federal government with its answer. The vast majority of the nation's mail routes consisted of so-called star routes, or any form of transportation that was not via railroad or a steamship, most often using stagecoaches or on horseback. If star routes were the filaments of the gossamer network, government mail contracts were what wove them together. Unlike today, full-time, salaried mail carriers did not transport the mail along these routes. Instead, the Post Office Department paid private companies to carry the mail on its behalf. Fixed-term contracts, most often for four years or less, lent the federal government the ability to rapidly expand and withdraw mail service without having to build or maintain its own public infrastructure of roads, drivers, and vehicles. These arrangements underlay the breakneck expansion of the 1860s and 1870s, leading to some 70,000 combined miles worth of star routes crisscrossing the western United States by 1879 .[2]

The expansion of the western star route system came with a hefty price tag. As the proprietors of the Pony Express discovered, transportation in the sparsely settled West was often disastrously expensive. The difference between success and failure for a western staging company often hinged on whether or not it could win a government mail contract. This turned the US Post and its contracting division into an arena of fierce competition, one in which the stakes were high and not everyone played by the rules. Starting in the late 1860s, a small group of powerful businessmen began using an array of fraudulent tactics to win bloated government contracts. By the end of the 1870s, the situation had devolved into a full-fledged institutional crisis. This episode was not just another example of the era's notorious political corruption. It is a story about the American state and the ways it went about implementing a grand developmental vision for the western United States. The decentralized agency model allowed the US Post to rapidly extend across the western countryside. In some ways, this was a highly democratic project driven by local demands and a broader commitment to provide a universal public service. But the agency model and the churning style of expansion it produced also left the US Post vulnerable to abuse. It was in the deserts, mountains, and canyons of the West that the costs of territorial expansion came into focus.

## The "Postal Power" Moves West

Mail service was enshrined in the US Constitution through the "postal power," a clause that specifically granted the federal government the right "to establish post offices and post roads." The Post Office Act of 1792 subsequently formalized the position of postmaster general within the executive branch and gave them the authority to enter into contracts to carry the nation's mail. Congress, however, retained control over designating which routes qualified as "post roads." As Americans pushed into the nation's interior over the coming decades, a small army of stagecoaches and post riders carried the mail to them along congressionally approved routes. By the close of the 1830s, a transportation boom of canals, roads, turnpikes, and railroads had led to a web of post roads in the eastern United States, with a handful of tendrils snaking out past the Mississippi River and into Missouri, Arkansas, and Louisiana.[3]

The expansion of mail routes flowed through the channels of representative democracy. In order to get a new mail route established, a community would write a petition that detailed how far they currently had to travel to fetch their mail and then propose details for a new mail route, including all of the different places it should stop along with its total mileage.[4] After gathering signatures, petitioners would mail the letter to either the Post Office Department or one of their elected officials.[5] Postal administrators, however, could not establish new mail service along the route until Congress officially designated it as a "post road." So, during each legislative session, representatives and senators would duly submit a list of new routes in their district or state to each chamber's Committee on Post Offices and Post Roads, which would then roll them together into a single bill spelling out hundreds (and sometimes thousands) of newly established official mail routes.[6] After both houses passed the annual post route bill and the president signed it into law, the Post Office Department was free to start transporting the mail along the new routes.

To do so, the Post Office Department solicited bids each year from private companies to carry the mail for a different batch of new mail routes, advertising where the routes ran, which post offices were on them, the speed of the trips, and how many times a week the company was required to make them. Once they had collected bids, postal officials awarded a contract to the lowest bidder (usually for a term of four years), who would then start delivering mail along the route as an official contractor for the Post Office Department. This contracting system worked fairly well when most Americans lived in the eastern third of the country. Most mail routes were relatively short and could be operated at a low cost, especially after the transportation revolution of the 1820s and 1830s improved the density and quality of eastern routes.[7] Beginning in the mid-1840s, however, two new developments would radically change the geographical calculus of the nation's communications network: territorial expansion and universal postage.

The United States added an enormous amount of land in the span of just a few years through the annexation of Texas in 1845, the Oregon Treaty of 1846, and the Treaty of Guadalupe Hidalgo in 1848, which seized the northern third of Mexico. All of this new territory came with new challenges for the Post Office Department. How was it going to transport the mail across millions of acres of land, much of it occupied and controlled by Native people? What kind of service should it offer, and how much was it willing to pay for that service? To further complicate matters, the territorial seizures of the 1840s coincided with the rise of a postage reform movement that dramatically lowered the price that people had to pay to send the mail. Until the 1840s, the Post Office Department factored distance into its postage rates—the farther a piece of mail traveled, the more it cost. But beginning in 1845, Congress passed a series of laws that dramatically lowered postage rates while simultaneously severing the relationship between price and geography for an individual piece of mail. These policies culminated in 1863 when Congress instituted a universal postage rate of three cents for all letters, regardless of their origin or destination. Whether in Albany or Albuquerque, Peoria or Portland, every American could send mail for the same low price no matter where that mail traveled. The new universal postage rate had effectively abolished distance from the calculus of American letter writing.[8]

Postage reforms helped cement the US Post as a fundamentally progressive institution by making long-distance communications possible for many more Americans. They were part of the federal government's broader commitment to provide an accessible, reliable, and affordable public mail service to its citizens.[9] But these democratizing impulses ran headlong into the realities of territorial expansion. Making the mail accessible and affordable in the context of the western United States was no easy task. One solution was to take advantage of a rapidly expanding railway network by contracting with private railroad companies to carry mail. The completion of the transcontinental railroad in 1869 accelerated the growth of the region's railway mail system. By the end of the 1870s, the Post Office Department counted more than 11,000 combined miles of railroad mail routes in the West, a nearly fourfold increase in the span of a single decade. A cross-country letter that used to take the better part of a month to travel from New York to San Francisco could now reach its destination in a little more than six days.[10]

Much like the Pony Express, the symbolic power of the railroad—with its industrial muscle and steam-powered speed—obscures a basic fact: most places in the western United States weren't actually near a railroad line. Railroads made up the trunk lines of the western postal network, shuttling correspondence between east and west and linking together the region's urban centers. But across most of the western countryside, the mail had to reach its final destination in the back of a stagecoach, buggy, wagon, or other animal-drawn vehicle. This was the classic "last mile" problem of supply chain management, in which the final leg of a trip (such as a home delivery) is often the most costly. The 19th-century American West embodied the "last mile" problem writ large, with its relatively small population separated by long distances and daunting terrain. This geography shaped the region's postal network: in 1879, 10 years after the completion of the transcontinental railroad, there were still more than six times as many miles of star routes as railway routes. The spatial coverage of its star route service dwarfed that of its railway mail service.[11]

The combination of new territory, universal postage, and the "last mile" problem skewed the Post Office Department's balance sheet. Unlike most federal agencies, the Post Office Department was expected to generate revenue in order to offset the costs of its operations. The sale of stamps and postage made up most of this revenue, while its operational costs consisted mainly of paying its workforce, buying supplies, and contracting with companies to carry the mail. In 1871, the annual costs of mail service in the Far West outweighed its postal revenue by $1.5 million, and by the end of the decade that deficit had ballooned to $2.6 million. On a per capita basis, the numbers were especially stark: even as the northeastern United States generated a modest postal surplus of 22 cents per person in 1880, those Americans living in the Far West generated an average deficit of $1.43 per person. As Figure 4.1 makes clear, eastern letter writers ended up subsidizing their western peers.[12]

Transportation costs were the main culprit for the West's postal deficits. The more remote and sparsely settled the area, the higher these costs. In densely settled New England and mid-Atlantic states, mail transportation made up around 35 percent of total postal expenses in 1880, with the rest going toward things like renting post office buildings and paying the salaries of postmasters, clerks, and city letter carriers. In the western United States, that ratio was flipped, with 75 percent of the region's expenditures going toward mail transportation. The problem was not

## Postal Surplus/Deficit, Per Capita (1880)

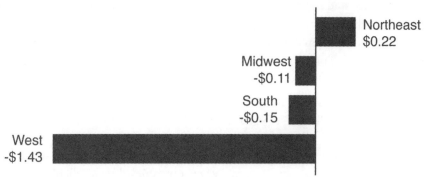

**Figure 4.1** The Costs of Mail Service in the West

Mail service was costlier in the western United States on a per capita basis than in any other region of the country. Data calculated from *1880 Annual Report of the Postmaster General* (Washington, DC: Government Printing Office, 1880), 558–59; "List of U.S. States by Historical Population," *Wikipedia, the Free Encyclopedia*, http://en.wikipedia.org/w/index.php?title=List_of_U.S._states_by_historical_population, accessed February 15, 2015.

that westerners didn't generate any revenue for the department. On the contrary, westerners were some of the nation's most prolific letter writers; residents of the Mountain West bought more stamps and postage, per person, than any other part of the country. The problem lay in the confluence of geography and universal postage. When a washerwoman mailed a letter from an Idaho lumber camp to her cousin in Pennsylvania, she paid the same three cents in postage as a Manhattan merchant sending a brank draft across the river to Brooklyn. No matter how many three-cent stamps westerners bought, they were not going to cover the true costs of bringing them their mail.[13]

Star route mail contracts made up the single largest annual expenditure for the western postal network, which in turn funneled millions of dollars each year into the region's stagecoach industry.[14] Stagecoaches played a vital part in the western economy, shuttling goods and freight for local merchants, currency and parcels on behalf of express companies, and passengers who wished to travel anywhere that was not directly on a railroad line. Western staging firms were expensive business ventures. Compared to the dense pattern of towns and cities that blanketed the eastern United States, western settlements were separated by longer distances and, in some parts of the region, dangerously arid deserts or towering mountain ranges that were virtually impassable during the winter months. The region's geography required mammoth start-up costs for staging companies. A new firm first needed to "stock the road" before it could begin carrying passengers or freight, which involved building or importing vehicles and assembling a herd of animals to pull them. Horses, mules, and oxen required loads of hay and grain, along with barns and stables to house the animals and their feed. A firm then had to hire new route agents, drivers, and hostlers and arrange for their room and board at hotels and way stations. Once a stage firm had set up the route, it required constant infusions of capital to cover salaries, repairs and maintenance, rent for buildings, room and board, feed and supplies, and local taxes and road tolls.[15] Then there was the chronic volatility that plagued the western economy. Along one long route, for instance, the price of grain doubled in the span of a single year.[16] The completion of a nearby railroad line or the shuttering of a local mine had the potential to render an entire route (along with its stations, barns, and stables) all but obsolete.[17] Capital-intensive western staging required ready access to cash and credit in a region where both were in short supply, especially given the West's skeletal banking system and steep interest rates.

In this context, a government mail contract acted like a lifeline for western stage-coach companies. Quarterly payments gave companies direct, reliable infusions of cash to cover their expenses. In 1866, for instance, Henry Corbett won a large contract to carry the mail from northern California to southern Oregon. Almost immediately, he began exhorting his employees to promptly fill out the paperwork that the department needed in order to disburse its quarterly payments. Corbett went so far as to instruct route managers to submit duplicates of these forms: one to the Post Office Department and a backup to the company's agent in Washington, DC, who acted as the company's liaison to the department.[18] One reason why he was so anxious to get paid on time was that he had recently drawn a $20,000 bank draft to temporarily cover costs "in anticipation of the mail money being paid promptly."[19] This underscores a less obvious benefit from winning a government contract: the public mail contract helped secure private lines of credit. There was

**Figure 4.2** Carrying the Mail

The staging firm Barlow, Sanderson & Co. was one of the largest mail contractors in the western United States. Detail from [G.?] Holderting, and Woodward, Tiernan, and Hale, "Overland Mail Company: Bradley Barlow & J. L. Sanderson, proprietors," print on paper: lithograph, [18--], BANC PIC 1963.002:1404--D, (The Robert B. Honeyman Jr. Collection of Early Californian and Western American Pictorial Material, UC Berkeley, Bancroft Library, Berkeley), available online at *Calisphere*, https://calisphere.org/item/ark:/13030/tf1q2nb4bs/, accessed May 5, 2020.

no better way to prove creditworthiness than to obtain a lucrative four-year mail contract from the US government. Unlike fickle passengers or other customers, the government guaranteed a staging company four years of guaranteed revenue. One Texas stage man explained that when his company first began operating, "We would have to show that we had the money ready to pay for anything we wanted, and would have to pay in advance, and all that sort of thing." Everything changed once they received a mail contract: "Texas now all over is our friend. We have established credit and have established a name, and my draft, or [my partner's] draft is good anywhere in any town in Texas."[20] The specific amount of a mail contract mattered less than the fact that it established the firm's financial soundness for lenders. As one experienced mail carrier succinctly explained, "The contract itself is credit."[21]

If stagecoach lines were the West's economic arteries, government mail contracts kept them pumping. This created a codependent relationship between the federal government and the stagecoach industry. The Post Office Department used contractors to solve the "last mile" problem in the West, grafting public functions onto their private infrastructure. Those same companies were no less dependent on the government for their survival. This entanglement between public and private was a defining feature of the agency model. It proved quite effective at extending the gossamer network's coverage over new territory during the 1860s and 1870s. But this codependency—and the decentralized, ever-changing geography of the network itself—began to collapse under the weight of fraud.

## Star Route Frauds: Act 1

Cries of conspiracy echoed down the halls of the US Capitol building during the late 1860s and early 1870s. Congressmen spoke darkly of a shadowy ring of powerful men known as the "Forty Thieves" who were perpetrating a "vicious system for the purposes of plunder and corruption" on the American government. The locus of this "monstrous robbery" was the Post Office Department, where western stagecoach companies stood accused of bribing officials and forging documents in order to win hundreds of thousands of dollars of government mail contracts.[22] By 1872, a handful of businessmen had managed to gain control over a number of high-paying western star routes. The most powerful of these was Bradley Barlow, proprietor of the staging firm Barlow, Sanderson & Co. who also held an interest in the Southern Overland Mail Company, the California Stage Company, and the Northwestern Stage Company. His combined star routes crisscrossed every state and territory in the Far West and paid out more than one million dollars a year in government mail contracts.[23] Barlow didn't fit the profile of a bare-knuckle western stage man from a dime novel. He was an eastern patrician, a banker who hailed from St. Albans, Vermont, and reportedly never set foot on any of his mail routes.[24] Just how did a New England banker become the West's wealthiest mail contractor?

Each year the Post Office Department solicited bids from private companies to carry the mail on specified routes, at which point it awarded the contract the lowest bidder. Postal officials received bids on thousands of routes every year. Most bids were quite small, perhaps a few hundred dollars to carry the mail along a few miles of road. But in the western states and territories, the longest post routes could stretch for hundreds of miles and command an annual mail contract of more than one hundred thousand dollars. By the 1860s and early 1870s, a fraudulent system of "straw bidding" upended the bidding process for these lucrative western mail contracts. A "straw bid" was an artificially low bid submitted by someone who colluded with a higher bidder and had no intention of ever providing service on the mail route. The only goal of a straw bidder was to disrupt the normal bidding process by winning the contract at any price. They would then either withdraw their bid or renege on their contract just before service was scheduled to commence. Soliciting a new round of bidding might take many weeks or even months, during which the mail would go undelivered. This left postal officials scrambling to find a temporary replacement. At this point the straw bidder's backer stepped in. Freed from the official procedure of the bidding process, a mail contractor like Bradley Barlow would lobby and outright bribe officials to award them the contract at an exorbitant price.

Straw bidding was in full bloom when the department solicited bids for hundreds of western mail routes in the spring of 1870. One of the longer routes was a 356-mile thoroughfare running along the Rio Grande Valley from El Paso, Texas, to Santa Fe, New Mexico. Contractors submitted 55 bids for the route, ranging from $9,000 to $100,000. The list of bidders included Bradley Barlow's daughter, son-in-law, two business partners, an employee, and the brother of one of his associates. These were his straw bidders. As required by law, the department awarded the contract to the lowest bidder, C. W. Lewis. Although Lewis's link to Barlow is unclear, one thing is certain: the Arizona politician had little experience with staging and even less intention of ever carrying the mail along the route. Two weeks before the scheduled start date for the contract, the department declared Lewis a failed bidder. Bradley Barlow promptly went to work. After some suspicious decisions, postal officials awarded the contract to a new bidder: Jared L. Sanderson, a partner in the staging firm Barlow, Sanderson & Co. Barlow had won by stacking the deck.[25]

Bradley Barlow wasn't alone. In the northwest, the Huntley Express Company relied on straw bidding to win routes that crisscrossed Montana, Wyoming, and Idaho.[26] A veteran mail contractor named Francis P. Sawyer used similar tactics to secure dozens of routes in Texas, Kansas, Indian Territory, and New Mexico that were worth more than four hundred thousand dollars a year in aggregate.[27] These western contractors spent surprisingly little time in the western United States. Charles Huntley of the Huntley Express Company bounced between hotels in Washington, DC, during bidding seasons and left his cousin Silas Huntley in Helena, Montana, to supervise their western stage routes.[28] Francis Sawyer bought a house in the Washington's Georgetown neighborhood and only rarely traveled back to his company's headquarters in Texas.[29] And Bradley Barlow—the most successful of the bunch—reportedly "never saw a horse or wheel owned by the company." He left the operations entirely to his partner, Jared L. Sanderson, and split his time between Washington, DC, and his official residence in Vermont.[30] For contractors like Huntley, Sawyer, and Barlow, the success of their firms depended less on the day-to-day management of the mail routes than on a shadowy world of lobbying, finance, and fraud in the nation's capital.

Ironically, face-to-face interactions played an outsized role in shaping the nation's largest long-distance communications network.[31] Mail contractors went out of their way to cultivate personal relationships with clerks and administrators in Washington, DC. Bradley Barlow proved to be especially adroit at this kind of maneuvering. In the late 1860s he hired a lobbyist named Thomas Hood, whose main qualification for the job seemed to be that he hailed from the same Wisconsin town as then–Postmaster General Alexander Randall.[32] Barlow invited other postal officials to dinner, shared wine and cigars with them, and distributed other gifts far and wide—even sending two packages of Vermont maple sugar to President Ulysses S. Grant.[33] These personal relationships gave contractors an edge on competitors who didn't have a presence in Washington. Mail contractors quite literally roamed the halls of the Post Office Department headquarters on a daily basis. When a winning bidder reneged on their contract, they were able to appear within the hour at the Postmaster General's office to offer up their company's services.[34] Even after they won a contract, mail contractors still wheedled postal clerks to try and expedite their quarterly payments or haggled with them over the docked pay that the department levied for lost letters, late deliveries, or missed trips.[35]

Bradley Barlow had one additional advantage over his rivals: he wasn't just a mail contractor; he was also the president of the Vermont National Bank. This turned the bank, in essence, into the financial arm of Barlow, Sanderson & Co.[36] Barlow used personal checks and drafts to channel money to his firm's agents from thousands of miles away. He also extended a "loan" to a man named Morgan L. Smith.[37] When pressed for details, Barlow admitted that he couldn't remember the exact amount of the loan, never recorded the transaction, couldn't specify what the money was in exchange for, and did not expect Smith to repay it. Smith's brother, of course, just happened to be in charge of the Post Office Department's mail contract division.[38] It was even alleged that Barlow had been behind a piece of congressional legislation that required bidders on large mail contracts to include a check or draft from a national bank for 5 percent of the value of their bid.[39] This was an ostensible attempt to halt the practice of straw bidding, but it also disqualified those contractors who weren't able to secure thousands of dollars' worth of checks or drafts from a national bank.[40] Barlow had no such problems as the president of a bank.[41]

Once a contractor secured a star route, they would then try to convince postal officials to increase their compensation by bumping up mail service along the route. Service increases could take the form of adding more trips each week (say, delivering the mail twice a week rather than once a week) or speeding up the rate of deliveries (taking 36 hours rather than 48 hours to traverse a route). The compensation for these increases were calculated on a linear basis: if mail service increased from once a week to twice a week, the department would pay a contractor twice as much. This calculation had little basis in reality. A stage line didn't suddenly have to build twice as many barns along a route just because it carried the mail twice as often. And the arrangements of the agency model meant that oftentimes contractors were already making these additional trips as they shuttled passengers and freight through their private stage business. By throwing a few bags of mail onto each departing stage-coach, they could double or even triple their annual compensation.[42]

Crooked western mail contractors took full advantage of the decentralized agency model that powered the gossamer network. The network's periphery drove its expansion with little administrative oversight from postal officials in Washington. The postal petition, a classic tool of representative democracy, became a tool that contractors wielded to inflate their profits. Montana contractor Charles Huntley, for instance, pressed his cousin in Helena to "send petitions at once to me to have service extended.... Have the postmaster at Missoula write a letter recommending the service [and] have all the county officers sign the letters" assuring him that "we will have a big thing . . . when all our routes are increased."[43] Another western contractor went even further by doctoring the content of a postal petition after he had already collected its signatures.[44] As one crooked contractor explained, "It was an easy thing to cook up petitions by the yard, to order, on any such subject."[45] These petitions were even more effective because of the murky administrative authority surrounding the nation's mail routes. Although the Post Office Department operated mail routes, it was Congress that established them. This split responsibility led to endless confusion. For one, even legitimate petitioners never seemed to know who had authority over what, as they addressed their requests to the post-master general, the second assistant postmaster general, their own representatives and senators, the chairman of the Committee on Post Offices and Post Roads, or "Members of Congress" generally. Some petitions even had to be hastily revised before mailing them: "To the ~~Post Master General~~ House of Representatives U.S."[46] With responsibility divided between two separate branches of government, it was easier for contractors to "cook up" falsified petitions in order to increase their pay.

Moreover, postal officials didn't have an effective system for evaluating whether or not these petitions were valid. Again and again, postal officials struggled even to gather basic information about the conditions along western star routes, much less regulate the contractors who operated them. One postal inspector based in Portland, Oregon, for instance, didn't even know how many post offices were on one route because it ran across multiple states and territories: "When the route got to Spokane Bridge it was out of my district, and I paid very little attention to it."[47] Without an effective regulatory apparatus, postal officials ended up relying on politicians to act as intermediaries to evaluate postal petitions that came from their districts.[48] Of course, Congressmen were only too happy to get new mail routes, faster mail service, and more frequent trips as a form of political pork to carry home to their constituents.[49]

Crooked mail contractors also benefited from instability and patronage appointees that dotted the Post Office Department's upper ranks, in particular the second assistant postmaster general, who oversaw the nation's mail transportation. In 1871, John L. Routt stepped into this position. Routt was a Republican partisan from Illinois who showed little interest in actually managing his division.[50] When called in front of a congressional committee, Routt struggled to recall basic details about how his office operated and spent most of his testimony complaining about his workload.[51] He did, however, enjoy one particular part of his job: receiving barrels of oranges, boxes of cigars, cases of wine and mineral water, and other gifts and favors from mail contractors.[52] By the end of his tenure, Routt was abandoning most of his responsibilities to his chief clerk, a man who moonlighted as a life insurance agent and used his position to sell insurance policies to the very contractors he was tasked with policing.[53]

Not surprisingly, mail contractor fraud grew bolder under Routt's administration (or lack thereof). A contractor named William D. Kittle exemplified the lack of regulatory oversight under Routt's division. Kittle engaged in the usual chicanery by plying officials with gifts and buying life insurance from the division's chief clerk. But he went even further by falsifying and intercepting what would have been damning official reports about his mail routes in Arkansas, Florida, and Texas.[54] Then, during a new round of bidding for mail contracts, Kittle bribed three clerks and a mentally handicapped messenger to show him the lowest bids for selected routes. He then composed lower bids, used a counterfeit seal to backdate them, and paid the clerks to refile them alongside the legitimate bids.[55] After postal officials noticed a single bidder winning so many routes by a narrow margin, they launched an investigation that was either incompetent or corrupt.[56] Government prosecutors inexplicably decided to grant Kittle and the bribed clerks immunity in exchange for testifying against another mail contractor (which ultimately failed to produce any conviction). The clerks who had accepted bribes were dismissed from office, but otherwise faced no criminal charges.[57] And Kittle, a man who admitted to colluding with postmasters, composing counterfeit documents, and bribing government officials, walked away cleanly. Months after his admission of guilt, William Kittle was once again bidding on a new round of mail contracts.[58]

As abuses in the contracting division piled up, Congress started looking into the star route frauds. In 1872 and 1874 the House of Representatives held two different investigations. Predictably, in both cases Republican majorities absolved the Republican appointees in the Post Office Department of any wrongdoing.[59] It wasn't until 1876, after Democrats won control of Congress, that legislators embarked on a real investigation. The postal committee called scores of witnesses, including Bradley Barlow, over the course of several months in 1876 and issued a blistering report that skewered the Post Office Department's management under Republican leadership.[60] President Ulysses S. Grant promptly removed the acting postmaster general and appointed his deputy to replace him. With a presidential election just four months away, reformers might have hoped for a fresh start for the federal government's largest executive department. Instead, the star route frauds began an audacious new chapter.

## Star Route Frauds: Act 2

During the late 1870s two new characters stepped onto center stage in the Post Office Department's star route saga: Stephen Dorsey and Thomas Brady. Dorsey was a caricature of a corrupt carpetbagger. He had moved from Ohio to Arkansas after the Civil War in order to head up the Arkansas Central Railroad Company, which he and his associates used to enrich themselves while doing little to build a functioning railroad. Amidst allegations of embezzlement and bribery, Dorsey managed to win (or buy) enough votes from the Arkansas legislature to elect him as the state's US senator in 1872. Dorsey spent much of his time in Washington figuring out how to get rich from his position. Many of his schemes focused on the American West, such as when he used his new political connections to purchase land in New Mexico or invest in Colorado mines. Near the end of his time in office, the West provided him with one more opportunity for profit: star route mail contracts. When the Post Office Department solicited bids for western mail routes in 1877, Dorsey marshalled a group of business associates and family members to bid on them (as a sitting congressman, Dorsey himself could not participate in the bidding). He then used his influence to secure certificates, bonds, and sureties on behalf of the cabal of bidders. Dorsey's group submitted thousands of bids, many illegally, and won some two dozen lengthy western mail routes. At this point, Dorsey crossed paths with the second character in this drama, Thomas Brady.[61]

Brady was a deep-pocketed Republican businessman who had been appointed second assistant postmaster general in July of 1876 as part of President Grant's shake-up of the Post Office Department. When Republican Rutherford B. Hayes narrowly won the presidential election a few months later, Hayes decided to keep Brady in office. This put Brady in position to oversee the nation's star route contracts. Whereas his predecessors had been indifferent or incompetent, Brady was actively corrupt. Western star route frauds took different forms under his administration. Whereas earlier contractors like Bradley Barlow had used straw bidding to win their routes, a growing number of contractors (the Dorsey ring included) focused on winning a route with a laughably low bid and then extracting extravagant payment increases on their contract. The strategy itself wasn't new, but it reached new heights under Brady's management.

Over the course of 1878–79, Thomas Brady approved two million dollars in payment increases for just 93 western star routes—at a time when the nation's entire star route service had a budget of less than six million dollars to cover some nine thousand routes. The most egregious of these payment increases was for a route that ran more than seven hundred miles across Indian Territory and the Texas Panhandle and into New Mexico Territory. When the route was first advertised, the lowest bidder agreed to carry the mail once a week and complete the journey in 10 days, all in exchange for a minuscule $6,330. Over the following months, Brady approved a series of changes to the route: extending the route to include new post offices, shortening each trip from 10 to seven days, and increasing the frequency of those trips from once a week to twice a week, then three times a week, and eventually to seven times a week. Altogether, the contractor's pay on the route leapt from his initial bid of $6,330 to more than $150,000 a year. By the time Brady was finished, the route was providing daily mail service across some of the most sparsely settled land in the nation.[62]

Ballooning star route contracts took their toll on the Post Office Department's finances. In December of 1879, Thomas Brady asked Congress for a temporary appropriation to cover the two-million-dollar deficiency in his division. Instead of showing contrition, he went on the offensive. Brady threatened that if he didn't receive the extra funds, he would be forced to curtail mail service on every star route in the country (and in every congressman's district). It was an audacious strategy. It was also an effective one. Any interruptions to the nation's mail service would have infuriated constituents from both parties. With a presidential election just a few months away, Congress capitulated by passing a stopgap funding measure for $1.1 million in the spring of 1880.

At this point, Stephen Dorsey had left the Senate with his own version of a golden parachute. Dorsey's ring of family members and business associates had managed to secure more than four hundred thousand dollars in extra compensation from Thomas Brady on just 19 western mail routes.[63] Despite a cloud of allegations that followed Dorsey like a swarm of mosquitos, he continued to stay active in Republican politics and was nominated as the secretary of the Republican National Convention in the summer of 1880 to help with the upcoming presidential election. Dorsey was a clever and unscrupulous campaign strategist. He poured campaign funds into the swing state of Indiana, which was widely expected to vote for the Democratic candidate. Dorsey's gamble paid off, as the Republican candidate, James Garfield, eked out a victory in Indiana and then went on to win one of the closest presidential elections in American history. Indiana had made the difference, which made Dorsey the savior of the Republican Party. In February of 1881, a month before Garfield's inauguration, party luminaries held a banquet in Dorsey's honor in New York City. None other than Ulysses S. Grant introduced Dorsey to an audience that included John Jacob Astor, J. Pierpont Morgan, and Vice President Elect Chester A. Arthur. At one point, attendees made a veiled reference to the "soap" (bribes, vote buying, and other shenanigans) that had tipped Indiana in their favor. It's not clear where the money had come from, but newspapers speculated that Dorsey and Brady—himself an Indianan—had funneled profits from the fraudulent star route contracts into the state's presidential campaign.[64]

The New York banquet for Stephen Dorsey was the high point in a political career that was about to fall to pieces. Newly inaugurated President Garfield installed a reformer as the new postmaster general and instructed him to begin looking into the star route frauds. In April of 1881, Thomas Brady was removed from office—the government's opening salvo against Stephen Dorsey and other crooked mail contractors. The investigation was abruptly put on hold in July of 1881 when an assassin shot President Garfield. Two months later he succumbed to his wounds. His successor, Chester Arthur, was widely seen as a partisan hack, but to everyone's surprise he promptly took up the mantle of reform and resumed the star route investigations. By early 1882, government investigators felt they had enough evidence to charge Stephen Dorsey, Thomas Brady, and seven others with conspiracy to defraud the government.

Lawyers called more than one hundred witnesses to testify over three summer months in 1882. Newspapers splashed details from the "star route trial" across their front pages as more and more evidence piled up against Dorsey, Brady, and the rest of the ring.[65] In September the jury issued a surprise verdict. They convicted two of the defendants, acquitted two others, and were unable to reach a consensus on the remaining defendants (including Dorsey and Brady). Several of the jurors admitted that they had been approached with offers of bribes, leading the flabbergasted judge to order a retrial for all the defendants. The second "star route trial" took place in 1883 and was largely a rerun of the first. Despite overwhelming evidence, the jury returned an even more shocking verdict: not guilty for every single defendant. Accusations of bribery flew fast and thick, but the verdict was final. The major perpetrators of the star route frauds walked away unpunished. Thomas Brady and Stephen Dorsey may have avoided jail, but the star route trials effectively ended their political careers. Brady retired and moved to Virginia, while Dorsey retreated to a ranch in New Mexico and spent the remainder of his life battling financial troubles, alcoholism, and legal suits over fraudulent land dealings.[66]

## The Costs of Western Expansion

Despite receiving extensive news coverage at the time, the star route frauds have since faded into obscurity. The machinations of Thomas Brady, Stephen Dorsey, and other crooked postal officials and mail contractors have become simply one minor episode in a litany of government corruption scandals during the post–Civil War years such as the Credit Mobilier affair and the graft machine of William "Boss" Tweed's Tammany Hall.[67] But framing the star route frauds as a purely political story about corruption misses an important point: they were, at their core, a story about western expansion. In 1881, the *New York Times* published damning details from ninety-three star route contracts that Thomas Brady had approved for extravagant payment increases. Every single one of these routes was located west of the Mississippi River. The political drama of these route frauds may have unfolded in Washington, DC, but they were made possible by the American state's larger developmental project in the western United States.[68]

During the 1860s and 1870s the federal government took an interventionist role within the national economy. Under the Republican Party, the federal government used tariffs and subsidies to bolster manufacturers, financiers, and transportation companies. This activist vision for the American state flourished in the western half of the country, where mail contracts were part of a larger constellation of federal policies that funneled public resources toward the private sector. The Republican Party's state-backed developmental agenda didn't stop at the shores of the Pacific. With enough government support, the West would also become a commercial gateway to international markets in Asia and the Pacific, turning the United States into a global imperial power through the expansion of shipping, commerce, and trade. Once again, the US Post provided officials with an ideal vehicle for this expansion.[69]

In 1865, a Republican Congress passed an appropriation to establish the country's first transpacific mail service. The following year, the Post Office Department awarded a giant contract to the Pacific Mail Steamship Company to inaugurate this service. Beginning in 1867, the company's steamers started carrying the mail once a month between San Francisco and ports in China and Japan. Although the transpacific mail route unfolded in a different physical environment than western star routes, the two types of mail service shared similarities. Like stagecoach companies, the Pacific Mail Steamship Company wasn't starting from scratch. It was already operating a fleet of steamers that plied the waters between ports in Valparaiso, Callao (present-day Lima), Guayaquil, Canton, Shanghai, Manila, and

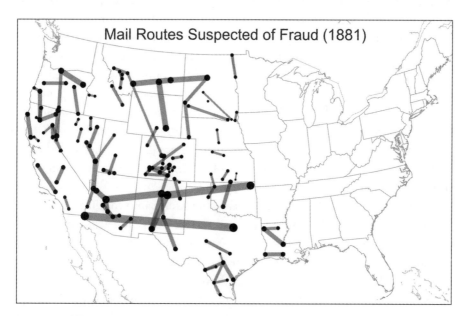

**Figure 4.3** The Costs of Western Expansion

This map shows the start and end points of 93 star routes where mail contractors were suspected of fraud in 1881. Each route is sized according to how much the contract increased from its original terms. Data transcribed from "Star Service Corruption," *New York Times*, April 25, 1881, 1, available online at https://timesmachine.nytimes.com/timesmachine/1881/04/25/98553855.html?pageNumber=1.

Honolulu. When the company won the department's transpacific mail contract, it simply grafted the public service of carrying the mail onto its existing passenger and freight business.[70]

And like western mail contractors, the Pacific Mail Steamship Company also drained the government's coffers. At five hundred thousand dollars a year, the company held the nation's largest single mail contract, even though the service generated a paltry amount of postal revenue for the department (just $15,000 over 12 months).[71] And, like western mail contractors, the company inflated its profits through fraud. In 1872 postal officials approved an increase in service that doubled the company's pay, bringing its compensation to a tidy sum of one million dollars a year. Subsequent investigations found that the company had engineered this increase through illegal lobbying and bribes that totaled hundreds of thousands of dollars. One can imagine Bradley Barlow and other crooked western mail contractors tipping their caps to the Pacific Mail Steamship Company's lobbyists as they passed each other in the halls of the Post Office Department's headquarters in Washington, DC.[72]

The Pacific Mail Steamship Company's million-dollar mail contract in the early 1870s represented the high-water (or low-water) mark for a Republican-led vision of state-backed commercial expansion in the Pacific. Its defenders argued that the Pacific Mail Steamship Company's mail contract wasn't some corporate handout; it was simply a means of putting American shipping on a more competitive footing with its international rivals. After all, the letters that Americans sent overseas largely traveled in the holds of European ships, like the ones operated by the British-owned Cunard steamship company. Most of these foreign companies were subsidized by their home governments, so why shouldn't the United States do the same?[73] As details continued to surface regarding the Pacific Mail Steamship Company's bribery campaign, however, this imperial commercial project fell apart. In early 1875, Congress voted to repeal the Pacific Mail Steamship Company's recent five-hundred-thousand-dollar increase in compensation. The following year, it declined to renew the company's 10-year mail contract. By 1878, the Post Office Department's expenditures for transpacific mail service had dwindled to just a few thousand dollars a year. Republican dreams of a state-backed commercial empire in the Pacific were in full-scale retreat.[74]

The timeline of the Pacific Mail Steamship Company's decline presents a puzzle: why did the US Post withdraw mail service from the Pacific in the mid-1870s, just as it was ramping up its star route service in the western interior to dizzying new heights? Why did one state-backed expansion project wither away even as the other accelerated? After all, both were marred by ballooning costs and corruption, providing juicy targets for pro-retrenchment Democrats seeking to rein in the excesses of the Republican-controlled presidency. The difference between transpacific mail contracts and star route contracts revolved around who benefited from these arrangements. The transpacific mail subsidy served the interests of a core constituency within the Republican Party: merchants and other businessmen interested in gaining a foothold in Asian markets. Star routes had a wider base of support. After all, Republicans and Democrats alike had an interest in expanding mail service within their districts. In one of the most partisan eras in American history, the annual post route bill was arguably Congress's least controversial piece of legislation, typically passing with widespread support and minimal debate.[75]

When it came to the nation's star routes, sectionalism trumped partisan loyalties.[76] In one 1876 debate over postal appropriations, for instance, a Republican senator from Vermont delicately questioned whether just because "I choose to go and set up a camp for fishing or shooting in some vastness of the mountains . . . that all other people of the United States are to be taxed forthwith in order that I may get my daily papers every morning." A member of his own party from California immediately retorted, "The old States and the overgrown cities enjoy all the luxury of the Post-Office Department. . . . I think they are not the ones to complain and to begrudge the service which is for the benefit of the more sparsely settled States and Territories." Three years later, even as the full extent of the star route frauds started to come to light, a western bloc of politicians from both sides of the aisle repeatedly closed ranks to defend them.[77]

One of the most loquacious defenders of the star route service was Christopher Columbus Upson, a Democratic congressman from Texas. In the midst of one appropriations debate, he harangued "if, in the line of 'economy and reform,' we are to strike at the mail privileges of the sun-bronzed cheek, labor-calloused hand, and brave heart of the frontiersman, in the name of common justice let the blow fall with equal severity upon the kid-gloved gentry, codfish aristocracy, chicken-hearted millionaire, and bloated gormandizer of the populous cities."[78] Upson then handed the baton across the aisle to Dudley Haskell, a Republican from Kansas: "You eastern men, with your railway lines by almost every farm, have no use for star service. . . . My friend from Connecticut has not a post-route in his State twenty-five miles long."[79] In the Senate, meanwhile, Texas Democrat Samuel B. Maxey was the primary champion of the star route service. Maxey even defended the notorious route on which Thomas Brady had approved an increase in compensation from $6,330 to more than $150,000 a year. In fact, Maxey had been one of the people most responsible for the route's increase when he marshalled petitions and testimonials from postmasters, politicians, businessmen, and army officers – even obtaining a letter from the famed western general Tecumseh Sherman that described western star routes as "the skirmish line of civilization."[80] Two years later, Maxey would take the witness stand in order to defend Brady, Dorsey, and other prominent Republicans during the star route trials, despite ongoing rumors that their fraudulent gains may have swung the 1880 election against Maxey's own party.[81]

One Congressman tried to justify the breakneck expansion of western star routes as simply the byproduct of "the 'boom,' as we have been pleased to call it in this country."[82] He wasn't wrong, at least not entirely. The most egregious of the star route frauds under Thomas Brady and Stephen Dorsey *did* coincide with the western postal network's frenetic, churning expansion during the late 1870s. Between 1878 and 1880, for instance, the annual tally of new post offices in the West jumped from 447 to 1,139. It was the largest two-year jump in the history of the western postal network. This larger pattern of postal growth may have been reckless, but it wasn't necessarily fraudulent.[83] When Congress called in Thomas Brady to explain the two-million-dollar deficiency in his division's star route service, he pointed out that it was Congress, not the Post Office Department, that had established some two thousand new mail routes over the preceding years through their annual post road bills. He was just putting these routes into operation and trying to meet the needs of a rapidly growing region.[84] Although Brady's reasoning was disingenuous, it points to a fundamental truth: fraudulent and corrupt mail contractors were not responsible for the churning overexpansion in the West during the 1870s; they simply took advantage of it.

The American state's larger project of colonizing and occupying the West came with high costs. Some of these costs came from corruption, but others were simply the result of ideology crashing headlong into western geography. The federal government had committed itself to making the mail accessible for all of its citizens, even when those citizens moved to a distant region with sky-high transportation costs. The corrupt machinations of contractors may have cost the federal government millions of dollars, but so too did westerners who demanded mail service no matter how remote their location. The federal government had committed itself to making the mail affordable for all of its citizens through universal postage, which meant that the rest of the country ended up covering the costs of that service for western residents. Rural mail was—and remains—a subsidized public service. Finally, the federal government's use of the agency model meant that it relied on private companies operating in an unstable regional economy. In the West, the line separating fraudulent from legitimate costs was often a blurry one.

Other costs extended beyond the Post Office Department's balance sheet. Western mail routes were entangled with the federal government's larger campaign of conquest, extermination, and dispossession against the West's Native peoples. Again and again, the protection of transportation corridors provided a pretext for military action. Western newspapers printed blood-soaked reports of Indian attacks on mail stages to call for military escorts along these routes.[85] Already beset by disease, desertion, and low morale, soldiers resented having to relocate to remote garrisons and risk their lives in order to protect the property of private stagecoach companies and their passengers. As one western officer grumbled: "Except to guard the El Paso Mail I am unable to discover the necessity for a single soldier at this post."[86] The expansion of western star routes did not cause the era's violent wars of conquest, but the two federal initiatives often went hand in hand.[87]

As the mail contract frauds came to light, they contributed to a wider loss of faith in the federal government in the 1870s. Faced with high-profile corruption scandals, Americans grew disenchanted with an activist national state they saw as serving the interests of private companies rather than the general public. Although politicians and newspaper editors expressed moral outrage over the frauds sweeping through the Post Office Department and its contracting division, they just as often harped on waste, bemoaning the "extravagance of expenditures" or "schemes against the public Treasury."[88] In this context, fraudulent western mail contracts were part of a larger "corruption issue" that Democrats wielded as a cudgel to beat back the gains made under Republicans during the Civil War and its aftermath. This spasm of retrenchment proved disastrous for the millions of freedpeople in the former Confederacy who depended on the federal government to safeguard the gains that had been made during Reconstruction.[89] The corrosive effects of government corruption rippled far and wide.

In November of 1881, Postmaster General Thomas James penned his annual report to Congress, detailing his first year at the helm of the Post Office Department. In it, James offered his own take on who was to blame for the star route frauds that were then under investigation. In addition to corrupt mail contractors, he pointed the finger at a different kind of culprit: western expansion. "The extension of the mail service was unquestionably far in advance of the actual needs of the country. . . . It is questionable whether the good accomplished in the remote regions of the West compensated for the positive evil which resulted."[90] James was highlighting a larger tension at the heart of the US Post and its history. In some ways the US Post was a progressive force in the 19th century, a democratic institution committed to providing an accessible and affordable public service to all of its citizens, no matter where they lived. Nowhere was this commitment to universal mail service clearer than in the western United States, where the US Post used the agency model to rapidly extend its gossamer network in order to meet the needs of an expanding population. But this solution created new problems. Western star routes expanded faster than the department's own administrative capacity to oversee them, giving rise to a morass of mismanagement and fraud during the 1870s. The ability to rapidly extend new lines of communication, regardless of their expense, facilitated a particularly unstable and churning settler colonial occupation of the western interior. In the end, westerners got their mail. But at what cost?[91]

# 5

# The Post Office Window, 1880–92

The western United States entered a new chapter in the 1880s. The preceding decades had been marked by wars of removal and dispossession against the region's Native peoples and the rapid occupation of their land by American settlers. During the 1880s, the emphasis shifted from expansion to integration, from occupying the West to bringing the region more tightly within the national orbits of politics, economy, and culture. Once again, the US Post and its gossamer network provided the spatial circuitry for this process. The Post Office Department established some nine thousand new western post offices across the region during the 1880s. Although the US Post continued to extend its tendrils into distant corners of the West, the dominant pattern of growth in this decade, visible in Figure 5.1, was a thickening and filling in of existing areas of postal coverage as the department added new nodes to what was already the most expansive communications infrastructure in the world. Understanding how the system functioned and its integrative power in the western United States, however, requires zooming in on some of the individual nodes that made up the larger network.[1]

Two post offices in California serve as a useful starting point. In the state capital of Sacramento, a newly remodeled post office building reopened in September of 1881. It had been under construction for three months and was a welcome upgrade for the city's residents. Although modestly sized, Sacramento was a hive of postal activity: the previous year, residents had sent some 3.4 million pieces of mail, an average of nearly 160 items for every woman, man, and child.[2] The city's postmaster, William C. Hopping, had managed the office for the past six years and oversaw a full-time staff of 15 employees.[3] Ten postal clerks sorted mail, sold stamps, and provided other routine services, while five letter carriers delivered mail directly to residents' homes. Fortunately for the city's municipal coffers, the federal government paid these employees' salaries while also covering the building's rent, lighting, and upkeep. In short, it had many of the classic features of a government bureaucracy.

Seventy-five miles away from Sacramento, a very different kind of post office operated in the mining town of North Bloomfield. Located in the foothills of the Sierra Nevada Mountains, the North Bloomfield Post Office was little more than a windowed partition in the corner of the town's general store. If not for a painted sign hanging outside the building, a customer might have been completely unaware that there was a post office on its premises, nestled as it was among overflowing shelves of merchandise.[4] There were no salaried letter carriers or mail clerks in North Bloomfield. The town's storeowner, T. P. Crandall, simply handed out mail to the town's residents as they came into his store and received a few

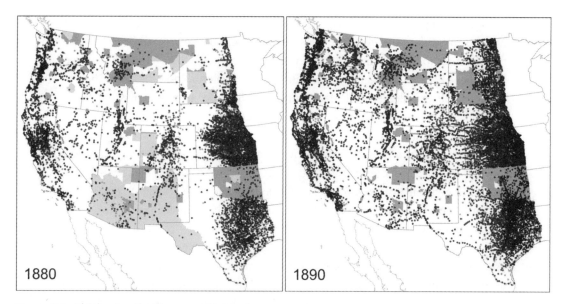

**Figure 5.1** Thickening the Gossamer Network
These two maps compare post offices, unceded Native land (light gray), and reservations (dark gray) in 1880 (*left*) versus 1890 (*right*).

**Figure 5.2** The Post Office Window
The North Bloomfield Post Office, part of the historical reconstruction of the McKillican and Mobley General Store in Malakoff Diggins State Park. Photograph by the author, August 31, 2014.

hundred dollars each year in commissions and fees for this part-time work. Unlike the Sacramento postmaster, Crandall was a private businessman, not a full-time civil servant. The North Bloomfield Post Office exemplified the agency model of administration.[5]

It's tempting to trace the lineage of the modern American administrative state back to the ordered, bureaucratic operations of the Sacramento Post Office. It's much harder to trace the roots of American governance to the chaotic, shared-use space of T. P. Crandall's general store. But the Sacramento Post Office was the exception, not the rule, in the 19th century. In 1881, only 4 percent of the nation's post offices did enough business to employ a full-time salaried postal clerk.[6] The rest of the nation's tens of thousands of post offices looked like the one in North Bloomfield, run by a local businessowner who worked part-time for commissions and fees. These two administrative structures produced the divergent geographical pattern visible in Figure 5.3: post offices that were large enough to qualify for a salaried government clerk were confined mainly to cities; those that followed the agency model were, broadly speaking, everywhere else.

The North Bloomfield Post Office can look like an antiquated relic from a bygone era.[7] Perhaps not surprisingly, scholars of the American state have devoted far more attention to bureaucrats like William C. Hopping and more recognizable institutional contexts like the Sacramento Post Office.[8] In doing so, they have missed a constellation of 19th-century governance that was far more widespread and just as consequential. To understand the full history of the American state means turning away from Sacramento's municipal post office building and peering through the window of T. P. Crandall's general store. What did these small-town post offices look like? Who ran them, how did they operate, and what roles did they play in their communities? How did post offices and postmasters link these places to larger systems of politics and governance, gender and race, commerce and capitalism? All of

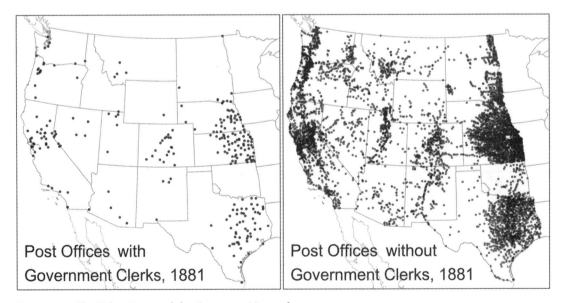

Post Offices with
Government Clerks, 1881

Post Offices without
Government Clerks, 1881

**Figure 5.3** The Urban Post and the Gossamer Network

Far fewer post offices were large enough to employ salaried government clerks (*left*) compared to post offices without salaried government clerks (*right*) in 1881. Data on clerks was collected from *Official Register of the United States, 1881*, vol. 2 (Washington, DC: Government Printing Office, 1881), 610–78.

these questions revolve around the issue of scale. It is impossible to understand the significance of the US Post's gossamer network without understanding the unique position of post offices as connection points between local and national geography. More so than any other feature of the network, this was where the different spatial scales of 19th-century society came together.

## "Post Office Rows"

Nineteenth-century Americans cared a little too much about post offices. That, at least, is a conclusion one might draw from surviving political correspondence. Congressmen and other politicians were constantly adjudicating "post office rows" over, say, the location of a post office or who would be appointed as its postmaster. Congressman James Garfield found himself wading into one such row in his Ohio district. A cascade of competing petitions and letters flooded his desk opining about the proposed location of a local post office and who should be appointed postmaster, leaving Garfield to complain in his diary about "the smallness of the material out of which men can get up a fight."[9] These "post office rows" erupted everywhere. In the biography *Old Jules*, Mari Sandoz chronicled her father's fleeting experience as a local postmaster in western Nebraska during the 1880s and 1890s. When Jules Sandoz was replaced as postmaster, he "took up his fight . . . with the local committeemen, the Congressman from his district, the fourth assistant Postmaster General, and the President." He continued battling for years, leaving one of his friends to sigh in his old age, "Why did you have to spend your whole life fighting over stupid things like post offices, Jules?"[10]

The standard explanation for the cause of "post office rows" can be boiled down to one word: politics. Nineteenth-century party politics hinged on the control of government patronage positions. This was the height of the "spoils system," in which the party that controlled the government used it to disburse jobs as a reward for party loyalists.[11] And outside of times of war, the Post Office Department had more of these jobs than the entire rest of the executive, judicial, and legislative branches combined.[12] One dataset collected by political scientist Scott James, for instance, contains information about 80,000 presidential-level appointments sent to the US Senate for confirmation between 1829 and 1917. As shown in Figure 5.4, more than three-quarters of these appointments were in the Post Office Department.[13] And presidential-level appointments were themselves only a fraction of the US Post's total patronage pie; the overwhelming majority (roughly 95 percent) of postmasters from this period didn't need Senate confirmation and therefore aren't captured in Figure 5.4.[14] Exact figures for the total number of postmaster appointments are hard to come by, but it is safe to assume that hundreds of thousands of people worked as postmasters at some point in their lives during the second half of the 19th century. In a purely quantitative sense, post offices and postmasters fueled the era's patronage machine.[15]

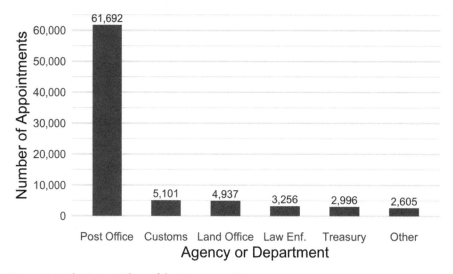

**Figure 5.4** The Fattest Slice of the Patronage Pie

This chart shows all executive branch appointments submitted by the president of the United States for confirmation by the US Senate between 1829 and 1917. Many thanks to Scott James for providing this dataset.

Controlling the Post Office Department provided political parties with a major electoral advantage. During the 19th century the United States did not provide public funding to run elections, instead leaving them in the hands of political parties themselves. Given their number, size, and frequency, American elections were often quite expensive. To help pay for them, the party that controlled the executive branch solicited campaign contributions or "assessments" from the nation's tens of thousands of postal workers.[16] Just as important as the size of the postal workforce was its spatial distribution. Post offices gave the ruling party a ready-made campaign office in every precinct in the country from which postmasters could distribute campaign literature, mobilize voters, hand out election ballots, and complete a variety of other electioneering tasks.[17]

Postmaster appointments brought clear advantages to political parties, but it is less obvious why people would actually want the position. Although some postal appointments paid well—a postmaster at one of the country's largest post offices could earn a salary of several thousand dollars a year—most of them did not.[18] Postmasters constantly complained about how little compensation they received for their work.[19] In 1887, more than half of all postmasters received less than one hundred dollars a year, the equivalent of just a few thousand dollars today.[20] The Post Office Department calculated postmaster compensation based on a percentage of the receipts from outgoing mail at their office, in addition to any fees a postmaster charged for renting out letterboxes or processing money orders. In 1889, for instance, the postmaster at North Bloomfield received just over five hundred dollars from his position. Of this, a small amount ($66) came from letter-box rental fees, while the bulk ($446.15) came from a roughly 70 percent commission on stamps that were canceled on outgoing mail from his office.[21] Compensation was directly tied to the size of the surrounding community and how much mail they sent; as one postmaster put it, "There was no money in a post office where nobody lived."[22] And there were a lot of places where nobody lived, especially in the rural United States. In fact, the term "twelve dollar post office" became a recognizable turn of phrase during this period to describe the country's tiny post offices where postmasters earned $12 a year, the department's minimum annual commission.[23]

Not only did a postmaster appointment pay poorly, but it was also a precarious position. In one observer's words, "In every Hamlet, at every cross-roads, each man asks his neighbor: How long will it be after the new President comes in before the old postmaster goes out?"[24] Whenever the presidency's electoral pendulum swung between Republican and Democratic control, thousands of postmasters lost their jobs. This revolving door of postmaster appointments reflected a wider pattern: tenures in public office were much shorter in the 19th century than they would be in the 20th and 21st centuries. Famous career politicians from this era such as John Quincy Adams, William Seward, or James Blaine were the exceptions rather than the rule. During the 19th century, the average career of a representative in Congress was never more than four years. Senate tenures were slightly longer, but even in that chamber the average time in office hovered between three and six years.[25] Local postmasters occupied their office for even shorter periods of time. A dataset of some 21,500 19th-century postmasters from Texas reveals that the median time in office was a little over two years.[26] Between their modest compensation and short tenures, postmaster positions hardly look like plum patronage jobs. Small rural post offices may have been at the front lines of partisan warfare, but this doesn't explain why Americans fought so fiercely over them. To understand why "post office rows" carried the weight that they did requires dropping down to the level of local communities.

## The Crossroads Post Office

Post offices stood at the crossroads of American towns, often quite literally.[27] If you unfold a 19th-century map of a specific town and look for Main Street, you will likely see a building labeled with two simple letters: "P.O." This building was the center of a community's social orbit. Prior to the launch of Rural Free Delivery at the turn of the 20th century, most rural Americans had to travel to the nearest post office to send and receive their mail. This meant that the local post office became the principal gathering place for communities, frequented by a wider swath of its residents on a more regular basis than arguably any other local institution, including churches, schools, or saloons.[28] The clattering arrival of the mail stagecoach drew neighbors together at regular intervals to a central location in order to pick up their mail, read newspapers, trade gossip, buy stamps, and send letters. Arguably no other institution was so embedded in the everyday lives of so many different people.

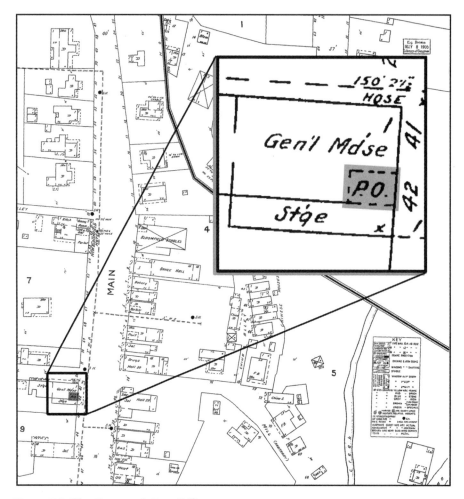

**Figure 5.5** The Crossroads Post Office

Like many small-town post offices, the North Bloomfield Post Office was located on Main Street and housed inside a general store. Sanborn Map Company, North Bloomfield, California, 1905, scale not given, 1905, *Digital Sanborn Maps, 1867–1970*, http://sanborn.umi.com.

Post office locations defined the spatial practices of millions of 19th-century Americans on a daily or weekly basis. Consequently, the politicized battles over post-master appointments were as much about where a post office would be located as they were about who would occupy the position. Congressman James Garfield's political lieutenant, for instance, wrote to him about two such disputes, "one at Wickliffe, where the P.M. [postmaster] is charged with drunkenness, and the other at East Claridon, where the P.M. is charged with being dead. The latter charge is true, but there is a trouble about location [of the post office]."[29] Many "post office rows" were, in effect, battles over local space. Since most post offices were housed inside the postmaster's own private business or residence, operating a post office guaranteed a regular flow of potential customers for its proprietor. This made postmaster appointments espe-cially valuable for a particular kind of businessowner: storeowners.

One business directory from 1884 contained listings for more than eight hundred postmasters in Arizona, Colorado, Nevada, New Mexico, and Utah. Only one-quarter of them listed "postmaster" as their sole occupation, while the rest had at least one other private business in addition to their public position. "General Store" was far and away the most common occupation, occurring roughly two and a half times more frequently than the next most frequently listed occupation of "Livestock." These postmasters were joined by more specialized sorts of retailers, including stores that sold medicine and drugs, groceries, stationery, hardware, or tobacco. In aggregate, all of these different kinds of stores made up more than half of the private businesses operated by this set of western postmasters.[30]

The prevalence of storeowners as postmasters is not surprising. A post office was the single most reliable way to drive steady foot traffic into their store. A person who went to pick up mail or buy stamps might also leave with a piece of merchandise under their arm. Especially for retailers with relatively low margins, a post office

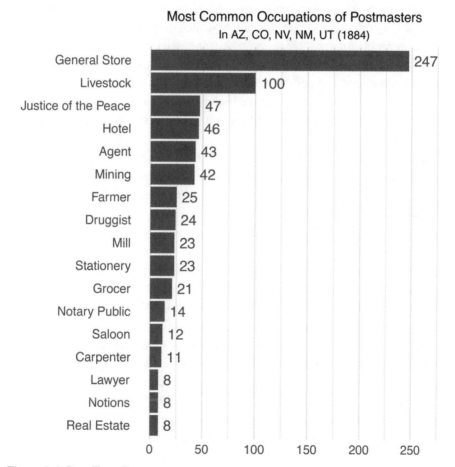

**Figure 5.6**  Part-Time Postmasters

This chart list the most common alternate occupations for postmasters that were listed in *Colorado, New Mexico, Utah, Nevada, Wyoming and Arizona Gazetteer and Business Directory, 1884–1885* (Chicago: R. L. Polk & Co. and A. C. Danser, 1884).

acted as a kind of insurance policy against fluctuating demand and a competitive edge against local rivals. Wholesale prices might rise or fall, consumer tastes could change, a competing store might open across the street, but people never stopped needing their mail.[31]

Although a majority of western post offices were housed in stores, they also appeared in other sorts of businesses. The same 1884 directory lists a total of 90 different occupations for western postmasters, from bakers and butchers to physicians and photographers. In one Utah town, the post office was even run by a professional organist. But another kind of organ was surprisingly scarce in this business directory: the partisan organs of local newspapers. Nineteenth-century newspaper editors were some the most politically active members of a community. In standard accounts of the era, political parties appointed droves of these partisan editors as postmasters.[32] Yet the evidence simply does not support the connection between postmasters and newspaper editors, at least in the Mountain West. Of the six hundred postmasters with other occupations listed in the 1884 business directory, only seven of them were newspaper editors. In fact, a western postmaster was more likely to operate a saloon than a newspaper, despite an explicit department regulation prohibiting post offices from being housed on the premises of drinking establishments. The dearth of western newspaper editors does not necessarily translate into a dearth of politics within the US Post—a saloonkeeper could be as partisan as a newspaper editor—but it does imply that too much attention has been paid to postmasters as political operatives and not enough to their role as commercial actors.[33]

There were less obvious financial reasons to fight for a postmaster appointment. The position's commissions and fees, no matter how small, offered a dependable revenue stream during an especially volatile economic period.[34] Some postmasters were also exempt from militia and jury duty, freeing up more time to run their own businesses. And for much of the 19th century, postmasters could take advantage of the "franking privilege" to send their own mail free of charge. The department gradually restricted this privilege to cover only "official" government business, but postmasters nevertheless had little chance of repercussion if they decided to send personal correspondence under official envelopes.[35] A postmaster appointment could also help secure loans, as agents for the Dun & Bradstreet Co. credit agency would frequently include the shorthand of "P.M." (postmaster) or "P.O." (post office) in their reports about local business owners as a proxy for judging their trustworthiness. Although not enough to guarantee creditworthiness on its own, the position of postmaster was nevertheless an indicator to these insurance agents about a person's honesty, industry, and good character.[36]

Finally, postal appointments weren't just about money. Postmasters were often civic leaders, on par with constables, school superintendents, and other local notables. In fact, "Justice of the Peace" was the third most common occupation for postmasters in the Mountain West behind "General Store" and "Livestock."[37] Postmasters were also some of the era's most prolific information brokers. Arguably nobody knew more about the affairs of a town than the local postmaster, who had an intimate glimpse into the lives of their neighbors' reading preferences, political allegiances, family news, and business connections. Companies solicited postmasters to provide information about a town and its residents. Government agencies relied on postmasters to collect information about everything from population statistics to veteran pensions to weather data.[38] And families even turned to postmasters to track down wayward loved ones.[39]

Located at the crossroads of American communities, the nation's tens of thousands of post offices were where all sorts of people came together. This meant that larger fault lines of gender and race left their imprint on the local space of post offices. Just two months after the renovated Sacramento post office opened its doors to the public in 1881, for instance, the postmaster printed his usual notice in the city's newspaper listing the names of people who had letters waiting for them. He divided these letters into a "Ladies' List" and a "Gentlemen's List"—a gendered division that had become common practice across the nation's urban post offices by the late 19th century.[40] As more and more people adopted letter-writing practices, contemporaries fretted about women having to brave the crowds of rowdy men who congregated in urban post offices.[41] The Post Office Department itself even felt the need to remind each postmaster to "keep his post-office in such a clean and orderly condition that it may be visited by women and children and others without impropriety or embarrassment."[42] To do so, urban postmasters like the one in Sacramento would segregate the interior space of post offices by requiring women and men to use two separate windows to send or receive their mail.[43] Unlike in eastern cities, the Sacramento postmaster included one additional category of letters awaiting pickup at the post office: "Chinese."[44]

Immigrants from China had first traveled in large numbers to the American West beginning with the California Gold Rush in the late 1840s and 1850s. Almost immediately, white westerners mobilized political campaigns against them. By the 1870s, California politicians were lobbying for national restrictions on Chinese immigrants and Congress passed a series of laws that culminated in 1882 with legislation that barred Chinese labors from immigrating to the United States—a watershed moment in the history of American immigration law. By the early 1880s, these racial tensions and exclusionary policies were inscribing the local space of western post offices, as illustrated by the Sacramento Post Office segregating its "Chinese" letters from the rest of the mail. [45] Of course, the farther one moved into the countryside and the chaotic, mixed-use spaces of rural post offices, the harder it was to maintain the strict segregated boundaries of urban post offices. This was especially true for places that relied on extractive industries such as mining and timber that employed large numbers of Chinese workers.[46] Places exactly like North Bloomfield, California. The North Bloomfield Mining and Gravel Company employed hundreds of Chinese workers as part of California's largest hydraulic mining operation, and as the company boomed during the 1870s, a local "Chinese Quarter" sprouted up in downtown North Bloomfield. The town's Chinese residents quickly became part of the social fabric of the town, selling fresh produce to its residents and frequenting local businesses. One of these businesses was T. P. Crandall's general store and post office on Main Street, less than one hundred yards away from China Alley.[47]

Debates over race and immigration did not take place solely on a regional or national level. They also played out at a local scale through thousands of daily, mundane interactions between individual people. Inside the crowded confines of T. P. Crandall's general store, a Chinese miner might stand next to a teamster's wife as they waited to receive their mail through the store's tiny corner post office window. One can imagine how fraught these interactions must have been during the 1880s. In May of 1882, Congress passed the Chinese Restriction Act. In December, a local newspaper printed an editorial claiming, "A Chinese merchant's wife becomes a Chinese prostitute within twenty-four hours after her debarkation."[48] The following month, night watchmen at the North Bloomfield Mining and Gravel Company shot and killed a Chinese laborer who they claimed was trying to skim off amalgam from the mine's sluices.[49] One year later, the postmaster in the neighboring town of North San Juan was arrested for stealing a package containing $950 that was in transit to a Chinese businessman.[50] Over 1885 to 1887, roughly a dozen counties in California forcibly expelled all of their Chinese residents, and in other towns white residents boycotted Chinese businesses, destroyed Chinese homes, and assaulted Chinese workers.[51] For Sue Kee, Ah Lie, and other residents of North Bloomfield's "China Quarter," all of these developments were probably at the front of their minds as they stood in line to pick up their mail.[52]

## Officeholding

Post offices were inseparable from the people who ran them. By housing the post office in their business or home, a postmaster imprinted their personal identity onto a public entity—sometimes quite literally when they named the post office after themselves. In Colorado, for instance, the post offices of Allen, Bland, Bristol, Bush, Cockrell, Deane, Farnham, Gwillimville, Hardin, Hawxhurst, Hillsborough, Kuhn's Crossing, Littleton, Lyons, Madrid, Mitchell, Parlin, Powell, Selak, Semper, and Wheeler all shared a name with their postmaster.[53] The highly personalized nature of the position meant that, rather than a tool for making citizens legible to the state, a local post office made the state legible to its citizens. Post offices were not run by some far-off bureaucrat but by a nearby resident who temporarily took on the role of an official state actor.[54] Which raises the question: Who could and could not act in this capacity as an agent of the state? Technically speaking, the Post Office Department had only a handful of qualifications to be a postmaster. The person had to live in the surrounding community, swear an oath of office, execute a bond, and secure two sureties to back that bond. Legal minors were barred from office, but married women and foreign-born residents were not (provided the latter had declared their intention to become citizens).[55] All of this meant that a relatively wide swath of the population were able to serve as postmasters.

Women had long taken on prominent leadership roles in temperance societies, sanitation leagues, antislavery organizations, and religious movements. By the end of the century, they could add post offices to that list.[56] No single source systematically records the number of women who served as postmasters in the Post Office Department on a year-by-year basis, but a number of quantitative indicators point to an upward trajectory. Between the 1860s and 1890s US presidents submitted the names of at least 1,200 women for the Senate's approval to serve as postmasters in the nation's presidential post offices. Although women made up a small percentage all presidential postmaster appointments, their relative annual share roughly tripled over the course of four decades.[57] State-level datasets paint a similar picture. In Oregon, the proportion of female postmasters increased roughly fivefold between the 1870s and the 1890s.[58] In Texas, only around 6.5 percent of all postmaster appointments went to women in the 1870s. By the 1890s that figure had nearly doubled to 12.5 percent, and 20 years later it doubled again. By the 1920s, more than one-third of Texas post offices were operated by women.[59] Finally, historical newspapers from the database *Chronicling America* and the digital libraries of HathiTrust and Google Books show a meteoric rise in the phrase "postmistress" (a female postmaster) during the 1870s and 1880s.[60] On their own, each of these measurements is incomplete. Together, they point to the same phenomenon: more and more women served as postmasters during the final decades of the 19th century.

**Figure 5.7**  The Rise of Women in the US Post

The phrase "postmistress" began to appear in published material much more frequently during the last three decades of the 19th century. This chart uses a three-year smoothing function to compensate for year-to-year fluctuations. Data from Google Books Ngram Viewer of American English Books between 1800–1900, https://books.google.com/ngrams/graph?content=postmistress&year_start=1800&year_end=1900&corpus =17&smoothing=3&share=&direct_url=t1%3B%2Cpostmistress%3B%2Cc0, downloaded on April 5, 2017.

Although Americans became increasingly accustomed to women working behind the counters of post offices, their entry into these public positions was far
from smooth. Female postmasters could elicit a good deal of derision, as when
journalists and writers lampooned postmistresses as gossiping busybodies or made
puns about their ability to handle both "the mails" and "the males."[61] In Colorado
Springs, the postmaster fired his female clerk after he found out she was hoping to
succeed him in office, declaring he "would take great delight in turning out into the
world and in search of husbands every woman now in the employ of government."[62]
But the Colorado Springs postmaster was fighting a losing battle. Just 15 miles away,
a woman named Elvina Hutchins was appointed that same year as the postmaster
at Fountain, Colorado. She was joined by a large cohort of western women such as
Emily S. Hoyt in Summit County, Utah, and Isabella Howe, who ran the post office
out of her general store in Ellsworth, Nevada.[63] By 1891, a nationwide survey by
the Post Office Department found 6,335 postmistresses serving across the United
States, in roughly 10 percent of all post offices.[64]

The position of postmaster—and the larger agency model that underlay it—
held several advantages for women seeking office. As a hybrid private and public
space, post offices gave women an opening through which to step into public office
without representing a wholesale transgression of traditional gendered boundaries.
This was especially true if the office itself was housed within the postmaster's home,
a space over which women held traditional authority.[65] The nature of the work
helped as well. Postmasters did not wield regulatory or coercive power. They were
not tax collectors or constables. They instead acted as vendors who provided a popular public service, a much more familiar position for women who were already
running stores, laundromats, and boarding houses. Moreover, some women were
already acting as postmasters in an unofficial capacity. Across the country, male
postmasters would leave the day-to-day operations of mail service in the hands of
their wives or daughters.[66] Finally, the sheer ubiquity of postmasters, both numeri-
cally and geographically, along with the era's ever-revolving carousel of partisan patronage, gave women many more opportunities to serve in federal office. The local
post office was one of the likeliest places an American would first catch glimpse of
a woman in an official government position, paving the way for them to take on
larger roles in the federal government.[67]

Yet the US Post's decentralized agency model also tested the boundaries of
officeholding within the department. In Indian Territory (present-day Oklahoma),
for instance, postal officials were tasked with operating a skeletal postal system to
connect its federally administered Indian reservations. Although most of these
post offices were run by white government agents, the localized nature of the US
Post meant that occasionally Indians would act as a postmaster. In 1882, an Eastern
Shawnee minister named Charles Bluejacket was appointed postmaster of a new
post office within the Cherokee Nation. In many ways, Bluejacket embodied a typical postmaster working through the agency model: he named the post office after
himself, operated it on a part-time basis, and earned less than one hundred dollars a

year in government commissions. But Bluejacket and other members of American Indian tribes were not technically American citizens. The question of whether they could legally serve as postmasters eventually made its way up to the attorney general for the United States, who in 1885 ruled that "an Indian citizen . . . is not eligible to the office of postmaster." As was often the case in rural areas, the new regulation proved difficult to enforce. Charles Bluejacket continued to serve as his town's postmaster and receive a government commission for at least two more years after the new rule was adopted.[68]

In neighboring Kansas, tens of thousands of Black southern migrants had resettled during the "Exoduster" movement of the late 1870s. The town of Nicodemus, in the northwestern part of the state, was at the forefront of this migration. In the spring of 1877, a group of Black ministers and promoters had chartered the Nicodemus town site. A few months later the first group of 60 or so Black settlers arrived, mainly from Tennessee and Kentucky. A few of them expressed dismay at the barren and windswept landscape, especially given that the promoters had distributed circulars promising rich soil, abundant water, and plenty of timber. Included in this list was an additional amenity that the town actually did have: a post office. In September of 1877, a storeowner named Zachary Fletcher was named postmaster of the brand-new Nicodemus Post Office, part of a small cohort of Black officeholders who worked as postmasters during this era.[69]

The end of the Civil War in 1865 and the emancipation of millions of freedpeople ushered in a new era of political mobilization for African Americans, who streamed to the polls to vote members of their communities into office as constables, state legislators, and even US senators.[70] In 1867, James W. Mason of Arkansas was appointed the nation's first Black postmaster. Both Mason in Arkansas and Fletcher in Kansas embodied a larger trend during Reconstruction. Black postmasters and other local officeholders came mainly from majority-Black "plantation counties" like Mason's Chicot County or all-Black towns like Fletcher's Nicodemus, Kansas.[71] This was partly due to the localized agency model in which postmasters were drawn from a post office's surrounding community.[72] A postmaster was different, however, from a constable or other local elected office, in that it was a federal appointment made by the Post Office Department itself. An aspiring Black postmaster needed to have not only the backing of their community but also the backing of politicians and postal officials in Washington, DC. In practice, this tied the fortunes of Black federal officeholders like Mason and Fletcher to the ongoing electoral success of the Republican Party. If the pro-southern Democratic Party were to win the presidency, they would almost assuredly be kicked out of office.

A large swath of the American populace may have served as postmasters during the 19th century, but the Post Office Department erected subtle institutional barriers to officeholding. Perhaps chief among these for aspiring Black officeholders was the "bond question."[73] Like other government agencies, the Post Office Department required an officeholder to provide a bond as security against any losses incurred by negligence or theft while in office. A postmaster bond could range from five hundred to thousands of dollars at the nation's largest post offices. On top of that, two local sureties needed to own enough property to back the bond for at least twice its total amount.[74] For formerly enslaved people without wealth or property, these seemingly benign institutional requirements effectively barred them from office. Black postmasters like Zachary Fletcher in Nicodemus were thus relatively rare during this period. One investigation found a total of 142 Black postmasters appointed in the postwar decades, over a period in which literally hundreds of thousands of white Americans filled the same position.[75]

National debates over gender, race, and citizenship set the backdrop for who could and could not serve in federal office. Women like Elvina Hutchins might have been barred from the federal ballot box, but they were nonetheless able to serve as postmasters in ever-growing numbers. African American men like Zachary Fletcher could cast votes, but the Post Office Department's regulations erected institutional barriers to their holding federal office. American Indians like Charles Bluejacket weren't allowed to be postmasters, but sometimes they were anyway. As personalized and localized institutions that were nevertheless closely linked to federal administration, post offices were sites where many of the larger tensions and contradictions in American society came into collision.

## Public and Private Space

The agency model wove together public and private space within small-town post offices like North Bloomfield, and it did so in ways that made these two threads all but impossible to disentangle. In the Nevada town of Sodaville, for instance, M. L. Stanfield ran a post office, railroad depot, telegraph station, and express company office, all inside the same building. In 1885, Stanfield received an annual commission of $139.60 from the Post Office Department. The rest of his income came from working for the Carson and Colorado railroad company, the Western Union telegraph company, and the express company Wells, Fargo & Co. The Sodaville Post Office was a one-stop location for a suite of different services, as Stanfield could check their luggage, deliver them a telegram, send a package, and then add their postcards to a pile of outgoing mail. In practical terms, customers who walked into the Sodaville Post Office wouldn't have noticed much of a difference between the private operations of these companies and the taxpayer-funded, publicly administered system of the US Post.[76]

The agency model was not a one-way street. Even as the US post grafted itself onto an existing business infrastructure, some of those same private companies grafted their operations onto the public space of a local post office. After all, the benefits of managing a post office weren't confined to local storeowners. Being at the crossroads of a community conferred similar advantages on any business, local or national, that wanted to sell goods and services to that community. National retailers, for instance, recognized postmasters as ideal sales agents. For one, a postmasters was a trusted figure drawn from a community's own ranks. They were already well versed in clerical duties such as collecting payments, processing items, and distributing them to customers, and unlike a traveling salesman or saleswoman, a postmaster's potential clients had to come to them rather than the other way around. Finally, the nature of the position gave a postmaster an intimate glimpse into townspeople's interests and spending habits.[77] National sales companies recruited postmasters by advertising to them directly in the Post Office Department's monthly postal guide. Publishers offered to send discounted books to postmasters to sell at a markup, while others agencies promised free gifts or raffle tickets for each new client a postmaster secured. Other postmasters hawked subscriptions to magazines like *Harper's Weekly* and *Frank Leslie's Lady Magazine*.[78] Postmasters sold everything from farm equipment to hair-loss gadgets to pocket knives on behalf of national retailers. One company summarized its strategy this way: "Every Postmaster an Agent. Every Post Office a Centre of Distribution."[79] This captured the essence of the agency model: a larger organization delegating a local agent to act on its behalf. This time, however, the public appointment of a postmaster provided the infrastructure for private services rather than the other way around.

In the 19th century there was wasn't a clear division between the public sector and the private sector—even when it seemed like there should be. This blurriness was especially prevalent in the relationship between the US Post and private carriers of parcels and packages. Congress had granted the US Post a public monopoly over the nation's mail. The reason for this was simple: the US Post had a mandate to provide a universal service to all Americans, even in places where it wasn't profitable to do so (such as the rural West). Without this mandate, private letter carriers could undercut the US Post by only operating along the most densely populated, profitable routes while leaving the federal government to provide service to costlier parts of the country.[80] The postal monopoly did allow private companies to provide some kinds of mail services, most notably in transporting packages and parcels. The US Post's weight limit of four pounds on mail material meant that anything heavier had to be transported via private express companies. In the western United States, the largest of these express companies was Wells, Fargo & Co.[81] First established in the early 1850s, the company originally transported freight, money, and gold dust for miners during the California Gold Rush. It also provided a shadow mail service, taking advantage of a loophole that allowed private carriers to transport letters provided they did so using prepaid stamped postal envelopes. During these early years, Wells, Fargo & Co. provided a faster, more reliable (albeit more expensive) alternative to the US Post, which initially struggled to operate on the Pacific Coast.[82] This early history, combined with a romanticized iconography of swashbuckling stagecoach drivers fending off bloodthirsty Indians and highwaymen, has turned Wells, Fargo & Co. into a totemic example for those who trumpet the virtues of the private sector over government bureaucracy.[83] It is also more myth than reality.

Wells, Fargo & Co. was never a viable competitor to the US Post and its letter-carrying service. After some initial stumbles during the California Gold Rush, the

US Post rapidly caught up to, and then surpassed, the express company. By 1880, the US Post was carrying approximately 10 times the number of letters that Wells, Fargo & Co. carried "outside the mails" in the West.[84] Moreover, as shown in Figure 5.8, the US Post's coverage dwarfed that of the regional express company. Even within the western states where Wells, Fargo & Co. was active, the US Post still operated close to four times as many offices as the private express company.[85] This was the direct outgrowth of offering a universal public service versus a profit-generating private one. In the words of one writer, "Express companies extend their business wherever it promises to pay. The Post-office extends its operations wherever there are settlers."[86]

Comparing the spatial coverage of the US Post to Wells, Fargo & Co. shows that anywhere the express company operated, so too did the nation's postal system. In fact, the two networks sometimes shared the same infrastructure and workforce. One postal official estimated that postmasters made up fully one-fifth of the Wells, Fargo & Co.'s California agents.[87] At the local scale this overlap between private company and government institution is clearly visible. In Guerneville, California, for instance, a jeweler named Gerhard Dietz was appointed the town's postmaster

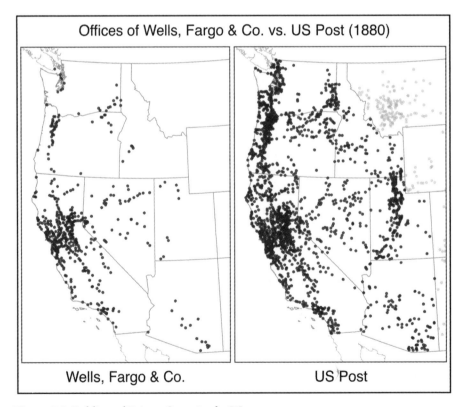

**Figure 5.8**  Public and Private Space in the West

These maps compare office locations of Wells, Fargo & Co. (*left*) versus post offices (*right*) in 1880. Wells, Fargo & Co. data was transcribed from Wells, Fargo & Co., "List of Offices, Agents, and Correspondents," July 1, 1880, in *Pamphlets on California*, Bancroft Library, F858.C18 v.3x.

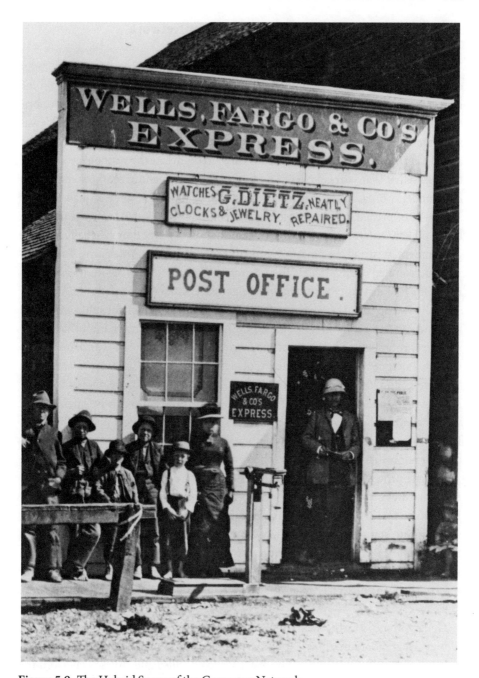

**Figure 5.9**  The Hybrid Space of the Gossamer Network

*Wells, Fargo & Co.'s Express*, 1880, black-and-white photograph, Sonoma County Library Photograph Collection, Sonoma County Library, ANNEX PHOTO 6084, https://digital.sonomalibrary.org/digital/collection/p15763coll2/id/14282/rec/4, accessed April 19, 2020.

in the spring of 1880. Soon after he started working as an agent for Wells, Fargo & Co.[88] This was a case of the private company grafting its services onto the public infrastructure of the US Post. Public and private were endlessly entangled inside Gerhard Dietz's jewelry store and across the US Post's wider network.

## Reform and the Gossamer Network

The entanglement of public and private space within the US Post spoke to larger debates during the late 19th century about the proper role of government within the nation's economy. This period has long been characterized as a "Gilded Age" of unbridled laissez-faire capitalism dominated by corporations and robber barons, but it was simultaneously an age of reform. As corporations like the Southern Pacific Railroad and Western Union Telegraph Company came to dominate the national economy in the post–Civil War years, a coalition of small producers and wage workers pushed back under a broad movement known as antimonopolism. They argued that the sheer size of private monopolies allowed them to buy politicians, control information, and levy unfair price and wage discrimination. Antimonopolists called for the government to curtail the power of companies over ordinary Americans. The movement accelerated during the 1880s and crested in the mid-1890s with the dramatic rise of the Populist Party within national electoral politics.[89]

In one sense, the US Post should have been a bogeyman for antimonopolist reformers. After all, its monopolistic power was more extensive than that of any private corporation. It was one of the largest institutions in the world, an organizational octopus whose tentacles touched more people in more places than Western Union, the Southern Pacific Railroad, or any other company. And its payment system funneled millions of dollars of public funds into private pockets each year, including the very railroad companies loathed by so many antimonopolists. Despite all of this, antimonopolists embraced the US Post as an exemplar of a "natural monopoly"—a service that was so central to the public good that it should be managed by the government rather than left in private hands. For them, the US Post epitomized effective public enterprise so much that they repeatedly called for the Post Office Department to radically expand its functions into gathering weather and farming statistics, setting up a system of postal savings banks, and, perhaps most dramatically, taking over the nation's private telegraph network. The US Post was so popular with antimonopolists that the People's Party, the populist agrarian reform party, included its expansion as a core plank of its official party platform in 1892.[90]

Geography was at the heart of antimonopolists' admiration for the US Post. Unlike telegraph, railroad, or express companies, the US Post did not discriminate on the basis of distance. Even if a westerner lived miles and miles away from the nearest railroad station or telegraph office, there was still likely to be a post office nearby. Even more radically, that same westerner paid a single, uniform postage regardless of where they lived or how far their mail was traveling—in sharp contrast to railroad freight rates or telegram prices. In a political economy that increasingly left the western and southern United States beholden to corporate and financial interests in the East, the US Post reversed this sectional power dynamic. The US Post was one of the largest 19th-century institutions explicitly tilted in favor of rural parts of the country. Finally, unlike the private "monied interests" that seemed to have captured politicians on both sides of the aisle, the nation's postal system was a public institution that was unequivocally tied to the democratic process. Through petitions to their elected officials, constituents in large part determined where post offices were located and who operated them. Although the postal machinery was influenced by partisanship, every four-year election cycle brought a fresh chance to seize control over the nation's postal affairs. The agency model meant that local communities had a say in public services.[91]

In other respects, the US Post's reliance on the agency model made it a target for reform. During the 1870s and 1880s, a growing cadre of professionals and social elites became fed up with the "spoils system" of officeholding that defined so much of 19th-century governance. These so-called civil-service reformers pushed for a more meritocratic system of appointing and promoting public officials, one in which effective management would take precedence over partisan affiliation. In 1883, the movement secured the passage of the landmark piece of legislation known as the Pendleton Civil Service Reform Act. This set up a framework for bringing government positions under new civil-service rules and regulations, including entrance exams for appointment and promotion and instituting curbs on partisan electioneering while in office. During the presidential election the following year, both national parties adopted a civil-service plank at their conventions. The Democrats, however, were able to paint the incumbent Republican Party and their candidate, James Blaine, as corrupt "spoilsmen," helping their candidate, Grover Cleveland, eke out a narrow victory.[92] Once in office, Cleveland installed William F. Vilas as his new postmaster general. A lawyer and professor from Wisconsin, Vilas embodied the kind of professional, elite administration championed by organizations like the Civil Service League. Vilas subsequently tried to move the Post Office Department in the direction of bureaucratic reform. In his annual reports to Congress, he called for increased efficiency and greater uniformity across the nation's tens of thousands of local post offices, warning of the need for "disengaging private interests from the public business" in these offices and lobbying for an administrative overhaul that would bring them under greater centralized oversight.[93] In short, Vilas was calling for a stronger bureaucratic structure under the purposeful guidance of professional civil servants.

To implement his push for administrative reform, Postmaster General William Vilas turned to the Post Office Department's Inspection Division, which was responsible for investigating violations, frauds, and outright criminal activity in the nation's mail service. Postal inspectors were hailed by both postal officials and the general public for their tenacity in hunting down criminals and fraudsters across the country. Scholars have since pointed to the Inspection Division as a paragon of professionalism and effective administration during an era of rampant partisan appointments and high turnover in office.[94] Small wonder, then, that Vilas entrusted the Inspection Division to bring the nation's sprawling network of local post offices under a more systematic, orderly, and centralized administrative

system. Vilas suspected that thousands of postmasters were falsifying their quarterly reports in order to inflate their government commissions and ordered postal
inspectors to ramp up their visits to post offices in order to review their account
books. Between 1886 and 1887, inspectors reviewed all of the country's larger presidential post offices and several thousand fourth-class post offices. The following
year Vilas managed to secure a temporary hundred-thousand-dollar appropriation
from Congress to expand this system-wide review, which helped postal inspectors
visit nearly 25,000 post offices between 1887 and 1888. The system-wide inspection
represented an unprecedented effort to extend centralized oversight across one of
the federal government's least centralized institutions—exactly the sort of administrative overhaul that one might expect from a reform-minded civil servant.[95]

From the Pendleton Civil Service Reform Act to Vilas's push for oversight and
accountability, government reform appeared to be ascendant during the 1880s.
A closer look shows a more muddled trajectory. Despite Grover Cleveland's public
embrace of civil-service reform during the 1884 presidential campaign, his administration quickly reversed course once in office. One month into his presidency,
newspapers printed a leaked, confidential circular that had been distributed to
Democratic congressmen promising to remove thousands of incumbent postmasters installed by the previous Republican administration. In the subsequent two
years, some 12,000 fourth-class postmasters were kicked out of office, with another
16,000 incumbent postmasters "resigning" over that same span. One of the most
drastic partisan purges in the Post Office Department's history was overseen by
none other than Postmaster General William Vilas, the very same reformer who issued such vocal calls for bureaucratic efficiency, uniformity, and oversight.[96]

William Vilas's management of the Post Office Department underscores the
limits and contradictions of reform movements during the late 1880s. Vilas was
not a technocrat. He was a leading partisan operative for the Democratic Party who
had chaired its national convention during the 1884 election. Shut out of the executive branch for the past quarter century, Democrats took control of the presidency and immediately followed a decades-long tradition in American politics by
installing one of its most prominent partisan figures as postmaster general.[97] Vilas
had a relatively free hand to revamp the department along partisan lines. After all,
the Pendleton Act had only imposed civil-service regulations on a small fraction of
government positions. In the Post Office Department, that grand bastion of partisanship and patronage appointments, the legislation caused barely a ripple. Civil-
service rules did not apply to most of its workers, including the tens of thousands of
fourth-class postmasters. The purge under Grover Cleveland became the blueprint
for subsequent administrations. As the presidency seesawed between Democratic
and Republican control during the subsequent elections of 1888, 1892, and 1896,
each new administration in the Post Office Department embarked on similar waves
of removals. Not until the 1910s—three decades after the Pendleton Act—were
all of the nation's postmasters finally brought under civil-service regulations. The
sheer size of the US Post and its deep well of patronage positions shielded it from

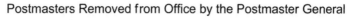
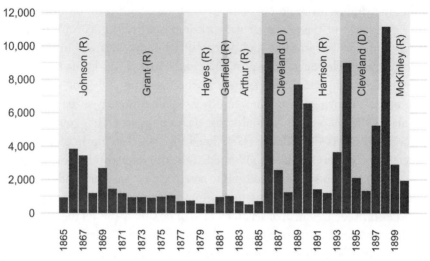

**Figure 5.10** The Spoils System

This chart displays the number of postmasters who were removed from office over the preceding fiscal year (July 1 to June 30) between 1865 and 1900. These numbers were transcribed from the Annual Reports of the Postmaster General, 1865–1900.

civil-service reform, and in an era of razor-thin electoral margins, political parties were loath to give up such a powerful partisan tool.[98]

William Vilas was better at appointing Democrats as postmasters than he was at regulating their behavior once they were in office. His campaign to standardize the operations of the nation's fourth-class post offices met with limited success. When Vilas reported that postal inspectors had visited 24,889 post offices during this campaign, he neglected to mention the fact that this still left around 30,000 post offices unaccounted for. Even armed with an extra hundred-thousand-dollar appropriation, the vaunted Inspection Division still failed to visit more than half of the nation's post offices. The reason was simple: there were too few officials tasked with overseeing far too many post offices. At the outset of the 1887–88 regulatory campaign, the Post Office Department had 75 postal inspectors on its payroll and 55,000 post offices. To review the operations of all these offices, each inspector would have had to visit roughly two offices every single day of the year. This would have been a full-time job in and of itself, but this was only one part of their responsibilities. The main function of the Inspection Division was to investigate mail theft and fraud: stolen letters, illegal lottery schemes, and the era's notorious "Comstock laws," which banned the transmission of obscene material. Over the course of the 1887–88 fiscal year, the Inspection Division ended up investigating nearly 94,000 total "cases," or an average of more than 1,200 per inspector.[99] No degree of professionalization could overcome basic arithmetic. Fewer than one hundred government officials were supposed to police a system that transmitted several billion pieces of mail each year.[100] Making site visitations to every post office in the country was simply infeasible.

The geography of the gossamer network imposed real limits on institutional reform. With such a sprawling and decentralized network, it was in many ways easier to change who operated a post office and where it was located than it was to change *how* that office was operated. As the Inspection Division could attest, postal officials struggled to monitor, much less police, the day-to-day operations of so many different places scattered across such a huge area. They could, however, replace officeholders with relative ease. After all, fourth-class postmasters were not protected by civil-service rules and served at the discretion of the postmaster general, who in turn outsourced decisions to congressmen, senators, and other party operatives. In order to revoke an acting postmaster's appointment and install his or her successor, a congressman or senator would often simply submit the name of one of their constituents to postal officials. After the appointee secured a bond, swore an oath of office, and filled out a few forms, they could then step into the position within a matter of weeks. This arrangements benefited both politicians and postal officials.[101] Although some members of Congress complained about the burdens of having to adjudicate "post office rows," these conflicts still gave them a form of political pork to dole out to constituents.[102] The Post Office Department, meanwhile, benefited from a national network of politicians who were far more familiar with local affairs than officials in Washington. This allowed them to maintain a massive workforce of part-time agents scattered across the countryside with a comparatively small workforce of centralized administrators.

## The Scales of the US Post

There is a general consensus that government officials should act according to the public good rather than their own private gain. For scholars of the state, this perspective dovetails with a tendency to privilege certain kinds of organizational structures and state actors—namely, centralized bureaucracies and reform-minded administrators. By these standards, it is easy to see the gossamer network's post offices as a failure of governance, riven as they were with partisanship, profit-seeking, and squabbling local interests. In fact, one political scientist's influential account of the 19th-century postal system argues that by the 1880s it was teetering on the brink of institutional collapse. In this narrative, the US Post was saved by a cadre of forward-thinking reformers who carved out "bureaucratic autonomy" and instituted much-needed administrative overhauls. But this perspective leads to a kind of circular reasoning: the US Post's agency model was ineffective and flailing precisely because it was not a centralized, civil-service bureaucracy.[103]

The decentralized, non-bureaucratic nature of the rural postal network in the 19th century was not some glitch in the system; it was what allowed the system to work. A diffuse and ever-shifting network of agents was the mechanism by which the state extended a public service to tens of thousands of far-flung communities. Without the agency model, the nation's mail service would have slowed to a crawl. Once again, the California town of North Bloomfield underscores the importance of these local private actors. In the early winter months of 1892, the North Bloomfield found itself without a postmaster. Donald McKillican had suddenly passed away while in office, leaving behind a widow, a general store, several mining claims, and a vacant postmaster position that needed to be filled. The town turned to Walter L. Mobley, McKillican's 27-year-old store clerk, to replace him. A familiar face for the town, Mobley had been born in nearby Sweetland before moving to North Bloomfield with his parents after they opened a boarding house for miners. Following a short stint in San Francisco, Mobley moved back to North Bloomfield and began working at Donald McKillican's general store in the 1880s. Social ties defined young Mobley's career. The store's co-owner was married to a relative of Mobley's, which likely helped him secure the position. When McKillican passed away, his widow and brother served as sureties on Mobley's official bond to the Post Office Department, despite the fact that the brother lived hundreds of miles away in Oakland.[104] After Mobley became the town's new postmaster in 1892, he purchased a one-third stake in the North Bloomfield general store from McKillican's widow for $1,000.[105]

Walter Mobley's appointment as postmaster exemplified the way in which the nation's most expansive national network flowed through webs of local social ties. North Bloomfield's former postmaster may have passed away, but the office remained in the same corner window of the town's general store, where it had operated for the past two decades. The man who replaced him had been working in the store for years, and his bond to the government was backed by the former postmaster's family. These were the types of relationships that wove the nation's gargantuan national postal system into the intimate scales of 19th-century society. In an age of growing anxiety over corporate behemoths and market forces running roughshod over the public good, the localized nature of the US Post cast the institution in an entirely different light. The face of Western Union was Jay Gould, the millionaire financier and robber baron; the face of the US Post was Walter Mobley, the store clerk who weighed his neighbor's weekly pouch of tobacco.

Local agents like Walter Mobley did more than just put a familiar face on the US Post's expansive power. These men and women kept the system running. The driver who carried the mail to the North Bloomfield Post Office in the back of his stagecoach needed to know which bridges were washed out and what time Mobley opened up his general store. Mobley himself needed to know the identity of every person who received mail at his post office.[106] In fact, somewhat paradoxically, local actors often needed to act outside the Post Office Department's bureaucratic regulations to keep the system running smoothly. Take the case of the postal registry system, which allowed a sender to pay an extra fee to have their letter or package tracked while in transit, after which they would receive a signed receipt when it finally reached its recipient. The department insisted that registered mail had to be picked up and signed for by the recipient alone, and that "no exception can be made to this rule because of relationship of any nature between the addressee and the person claiming the matter."[107] But that wasn't how Americans actually picked up their mail. In practice, relatives and neighbors fetched each other's mail all the time. Despite the department's regulations, more than half of the registered letters that arrived at the North Bloomfield Post Office were handed over to people other than their addressee. Fathers regularly signed for registered letters addressed to their wives, and sons and daughters often fetched their parents' letters. As postmaster, Walter Mobley used his local knowledge of the town's residents to grease the wheels of the mail system: allowing Violet Rouner to sign for a parcel addressed to her mother, or forwarding a package to J. Pagliosoti after the miner had moved to neighboring Grass Valley. Without Mobley's intimate knowledge of North Bloomfield's residents and his willingness to bend the rules, the town's mail service would have been slower and less effective.[108]

Each "P.O." marked on a 19th-century town map was a node within a communications system that did far more than just transport the mail. A post office connected the different scales of society, enmeshing the local space of a community within larger commercial, political, and social systems. It was where bags of mail left in the back of a stagecoach, on their way to a neighboring village up the road or a distant city on the other side of the country. It was where the economic prospects of a small-town business owner were bound up with the political fortunes of the Republican Party. It was where Mrs. Elvina Hutchins in Colorado could serve as a postmaster but Charles Bluejacket in Indian Territory could not. It was where the American state operated at its smallest possible scale, in the form of a letter passing across the counter of a general store.

# 6

# Money Orders and National
# Integration, 1864–95

It was a wet and cold winter morning in 1895 when Walter L. Mobley opened up his general store, unlatching the doors that opened onto North Bloomfield's Main Street and trading pleasantries with a few of the early customers before walking back behind the counter. They may have remarked on the crippling blizzard that had shut down the east coast or, more likely, complained about their own gloomy rain that had started the previous day and continued through the night.[1] One of Mobley's customers that Tuesday morning was Mrs. J. B. McKinney. The longtime resident of North Bloomfield was hoping to buy something from a Sacramento department store and wanted to pay for it through a postal money order, which would allow her to safely make her payment without sending actual money through the mail. Perhaps she did some last-minute calculations as she filled out her paperwork at the small post office window in the corner of the store. When she finished, Walter Mobley collected her money, stamped the form, and added it to a short stack of similar orders behind the counter. The stack would grow throughout the day: McKinney's husband sent $35 to a fraternal lodge in a nearby town, the town butcher placed an order with a furniture store, and the owner of North Bloomfield's hotel remitted a payment to his wife in San Francisco. In total, 14 money orders passed through the small corner window into Walter Mobley's hands. Early the next morning a stagecoach picked up the town's mail, sending those same money orders on their way to destinations as far away as Chicago and New York.[2]

The postal money orders that left North Bloomfield that day in 1895 added a few more drops to a river of financial transactions that flowed through the US Post. Twenty-three million postal money orders in total would pass through the mail that year, in aggregate worth some $169 million (the equivalent of roughly $5.4 billion in 2019).[3] The money order system was one of the era's most popular postal services, providing an affordable public channel for conducting small-scale transactions. It allowed people like Mrs. J. B. McKinney to remit small sums of money—no more than one hundred dollars—without having to send actual currency that might get stolen or lost in transit. To do so, the sender would simply go her local post office, fill out a short form, and hand over the funds she wanted to transmit to the postmaster. Then, for a small fee, the postmaster would mail the completed form to its recipient in order for them to redeem it at their local post office for the specified amount. Despite their distance, westerners could use money orders to send personal remittances both domestically and abroad. Just as importantly, they could use money orders to purchase goods and products from distant suppliers, a key channel through which the region participated in the United States' growing consumer economy. Money orders, much like the larger US Post, quietly wove together the strands of national integration in the western United States.

The Post Office Department's money order system was more than just a popular public service; it was also an efficient one. Unlike most government services, the Money Order Division was fiscally self-sustaining, paying for itself from the fees it charged the public. This was due in large part to the efforts of a technocrat named Charles Macdonald who managed the division for the first three decades of its existence. Between the system's initial launch in 1864 and Macdonald's retirement in 1893, he expanded the service while maintaining a relentless drive for economy and thrift. The Money Order Division was an exemplary government enterprise and an early pocket of centralized, technocratic management within the larger US Post. The story of its expansion is in some ways a triumphant narrative about the growing bureaucratic capacity of the American state and its ability to connect people and communities into national financial orbits.

There is a flip side to this story. The money order system was the exception rather than the rule across the American countryside. The very efficiency of the service was, in fact, predicated on limiting its accessibility and geographic coverage. Money orders were not available at every post office. As valuable as the service may have been, it was far from a universal one. This was especially true in the western United States, where the money order system's cautious, constrained spread put it at odds with the wider expansionary ethos of the US Post. Finally, zooming down to the individual town of North Bloomfield provides a glimpse into a surprisingly regional pattern of where westerners were actually sending their money. Charting the geography of the money order system reveals the limits of both bureaucratization and national integration within the West's gossamer network.

## The Birth of a System

In May of 1864, Congress passed legislation establishing an experimental money order service, which the Post Office Department officially instituted in November. The architect behind this new initiative was Charles F. Macdonald, a former doctor and schoolteacher who was appointed the inaugural superintendent of the Money Order Division.[4] It proved to be immediately popular, especially for Union Army troops wanting to remit wages back to families on the home front. The money order system protected funds by making them non-fungible. Rather than send physical currency, a person would mail a form to its recipient for them to redeem for the funds. To ensure safety, the form was only redeemable if: (a) the sender had identified the recipient, and (b) the recipient was at the post office specified by the sender. In short, a money order's financial value was unlocked only once it reached its proper destination and its proper recipient; while in transit it was just a piece of paper. The service was meant to facilitate small and medium-sized remittances, with the maximum size of an order initially capped at $50.[5] Although money orders were originally intended to facilitate remittances to family members or friends, Americans quickly started using them for long-distance consumer purchases such as subscribing to the *San Francisco Chronicle*, ordering a patent medicine, or paying a Freemason membership fee.[6]

Charles Macdonald wasted little time expanding his division, both domestically and overseas. In 1869, just five years after the domestic money order service was inaugurated, Macdonald brokered an agreement with Switzerland to allow money orders to travel between the two countries. Two years later, in 1871, Macdonald traveled to London and Berlin to finalize similar agreements with Great Britain and Germany, followed in short order by Canada, Italy, and France.[7] Macdonald's negotiations placed him within a larger cohort of government bureaucrats who were launching postal reforms across the globe. In Japan, for instance, the postal system became a core part of the state's modernization efforts during the Meiji restoration that began in 1868. Its leading postal official, Maejima Hisoka, took a trip to the United States and Great Britain in 1870 in order to gather information before launching Japan's own postal system the following year. Maejima borrowed heavily from the British Post while simultaneously tailoring his country's postal system to meet the needs of the Meiji imperial government. A few years later, Maejima hired four US postal officials to help manage Japan's postal operations.[8] Maejima Hisoka and Charles Macdonald never met each other, but they were part of a growing transcontinental network of technocrats and civil servants.[9]

At home, Charles Macdonald's Money Order Division continued to grow during the 1870s as he extended money order facilities to thousands of new post offices. But what this expansion meant for Americans living in those places and how they ended up using the new service are surprisingly difficult questions to answer. Postal officials collected annual statistics about the postal system—the number of postmasters or the mileage of mail routes in each state, for example—but it was much harder to track the billions of pieces of mail that Americans sent each year. Money orders were an exception. Due to their financial value and Charles Macdonald's exacting bureaucratic oversight, postmasters had to keep detailed records about each money order that left their office, including the sender, the recipient, its destination, and the amount of money being transmitted. Macdonald's office then aggregated this information into annual snapshots of the number and amount of money orders that were issued in every state in the country. Surviving records from individual money order offices are even more valuable than these annual statistics, offering a detailed glimpse of where people were sending their money. One set of surviving money order records comes from the boom town of Hamilton, Nevada.

Following the discovery of silver in east-central Nevada in the mid-1860s, a community of miners successfully petitioned the government to establish the Hamilton Post Office in 1868. Just three years after it was established, the office was already the fifth busiest in the state, and by 1872 the Post Office Department had extended money order facilities to Hamilton.[10] A surviving registry book from the 1870s documenting every money order that left the office gives a snapshot of how the city's residents used the service to remit their money. Over the course of 1878, for instance, Hamilton's residents sent 865 money orders totaling $19,718 (half a million dollars in today's terms), part of more than four hundred thousand dollars that Nevadans remitted through the service that year. As shown in Figure 6.1, Hamilton's residents sent their money orders to nearly 130 different locations across the country. New York was far and away the most popular destination, with 30 percent of all of the town's orders going to the nation's leading commercial metropolis. San Francisco anchored Hamilton's remittances on the other side of the country, along with a handful of other western locales in Nevada, Utah, and California. The rest of the town's remittance network was scattered across an arc of towns and cities stretching from eastern Kansas and Nebraska through the Midwest and into New England.[11] The remittances that flowed out of Hamilton, Nevada, in 1878 reflected just how eagerly westerners embraced the money order service. By 1880, the average westerner was sending more than twice as much money as his or her eastern peers on a per capita basis. Western residents like those in Hamilton, Nevada, had become the system's "power users."[12]

By providing an affordable channel for small-scale personal remittances and consumer purchases, the money order system was a public counterweight to a private

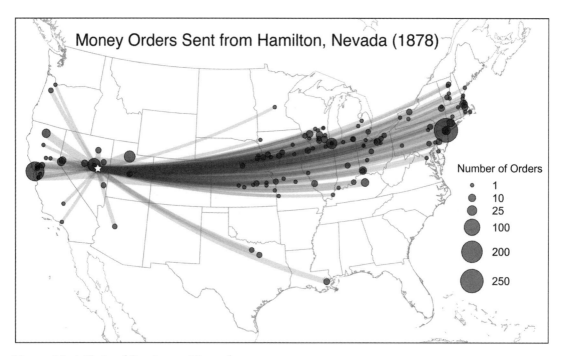

**Figure 6.1** A National Remittance Network

Destinations of money orders sent from Hamilton, Nevada, in 1878, sized by the number of orders. Data transcribed from Register of Money Orders Issued at the Post Office of Hamilton, White Pine County, Nevada, MSS 2011/175 v.1, Bancroft Library, University of Berkeley, California.

financial sector seen by many as exploitative and discriminatory. Wells, Fargo & Co., the region's largest express company, had been carrying gold and specie across the region for decades. But it charged high rates for this service, and, unlike the US Post, it pegged its rates to the distance that the money traveled.[13] Banks and other financial institutions, meanwhile, provided checks, drafts, and other financial instruments for westerners to transfer funds. But these services were often more expensive than an equivalent money order and were rarely available for sums less than five dollars. The money order system had no such constraints and was explicitly meant to facilitate these sorts of small-sized transactions.[14]

Postal money orders were not only cheaper than other financial services; they were also more widely available. In 1880, just a few dozen national bank branches operated in the entire Far West—compared to nearly three hundred in New York alone. The few banks that did operate in the West tended to be clustered in a small number of urban centers like San Francisco and Denver or second-tier cities like Sacramento and Boulder. Westerners who didn't live in or near these cities and their financial institutions faced higher interest rates, scarce currency, and a general lack of credit and liquidity to buffer the period's cyclical financial downswings. Not surprisingly, many of the region's residents resented a financial system that was stacked against them. Although postal money orders were not available at every post office, the service operated in many more locations than the region's banking infrastructure.[15]

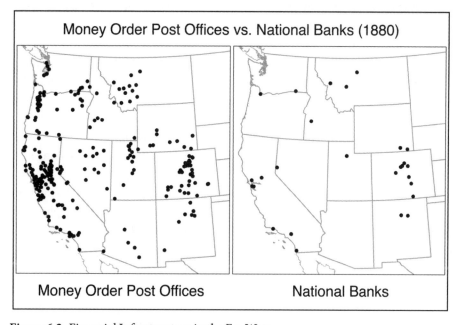

**Figure 6.2**  Financial Infrastructure in the Far West

Post offices offering money order services (*left*) were much widespread than national banks (*right*) in the Far West in 1880. Bank locations come from Scott L. Fulford, "Replication Data for: How Important Are Banks for Development? National Banks in the United States 1870–1900," V1 (July 1, 2015), distributed by Harvard Dataverse, http://doi.org/10.7910/DVN/PQ6ILM, accessed May 31, 2017.

During the late 19th century the US Post became involved in one of the era's most divisive political debates: the "currency issue." Prior to the Civil War, the United States did not have an official national currency, instead allowing state and local banks to print their own notes. When war broke out, the federal government issued so-called "greenbacks" as its first national paper currency. Over the following decades debate swirled around the nation's currency. So-called "hard money" advocates lobbied for the United States to peg its money supply to a gold standard and limit the number of greenbacks in circulation, which would benefit creditors, merchants, and financiers. "Soft money" advocates, drawn from the ranks of agrarian producers and debtors, thought that gold-backed currency unfairly benefited eastern financiers.[16] In 1876, meanwhile, the US Treasury began to limit the amount of silver coin in circulation, leading to a shortage of small-value currency. The US Post provided several alternatives.[17]

Postage stamps acted as a kind of shadow currency during the 19th century. After all, stamps had a universally recognized and stable value, could be purchased and "spent" at any post office in the country, and (unlike scarce silver coins) could be easily combined into fractional sums. Stamps were such a common alternative that many companies accepted them as a valid form of payment.[18] In 1880, officials proposed an idea for a more official kind of fractional currency: a "postal note." Capped at a maximum of five dollars, postal notes could be transferred from person to person and redeemed at post offices across the country. Three years later Congress signed off on this new bureaucratic innovation and put it in the hands of Charles Macdonald's Money Order Division. The department issued its first postal notes in September of 1883, and over the next nine months Americans sent nearly 3.7 million of them.[19]

The 19th-century US Post was one of the most admired, trusted, and popular public institutions in the country. This was doubly so for reformers who called for a more muscular state intervention in the national economy. As historian Charles Postel notes, "The striking success of the federal postal service in delivering the nation's mail fueled reformers' imaginations about the viability and necessity of state-run enterprise."[20] There were few more obvious examples of the "striking success" of the nation's postal service than the money order system. Under Charles Macdonald the money order system was one of the most cost-effective divisions in the entire organization, largely paying for itself or generating a modest surplus each year. This was especially notable given that the Post Office Department as a whole operated at a deficit in 26 out of Macdonald's 29 years in office. Set against this institutional backdrop, Macdonald's management was the bureaucratic equivalent of turning water into wine.[21]

In 1893, Charles Macdonald finally decided to retire. With his wife ailing, he requested a move to a cooler climate and was transferred to a consulate in Ontario, Canada.[22] Macdonald left behind a remarkable legacy. Over the course of three decades he had worked under no fewer than nine different presidential administrations and 17 postmasters general. From a wartime experiment the postal money order service had grown into an admired institution whose reach stretched both across the country and overseas. Fittingly, even during Macdonald's last year in office he managed to hammer out additional agreements for money order exchanges with the British colonies of Bermuda and South Australia, the Grand Duchy of Luxemburg, and the Republic of Salvador. After decades of bureaucratic diplomacy by Macdonald and other officials, Americans could remit money orders to scores of different nations and colonies across the globe. That same year, Macdonald proudly reported that out of the 14,365,734 money orders that were sent domestically and abroad, just 113 had been improperly paid out to the wrong recipient—a 99.9992 percent success rate.[23] Over Macdonald's three-decade tenure he earned a well-deserved reputation as one of the federal government's most competent and dedicated officials. In fact, his commitment to public service ran so deep that he later bequeathed two thousand dollars in his will to the Post Office Department to be used for "the improvement of the money-order system."[24]

Charles Macdonald was the platonic ideal of a civil servant, from his technocratic management to his relentless pursuit of efficiency to his decades-long tenure in office. The Money Order Division, meanwhile, was a harbinger of the sort of administrative agencies that would flourish in the 20th century. One could imagine Macdonald discussing the finer points of quarterly audits with New Deal bureaucrats in the Works Progress Administration or the Bureau of Labor Statistics. On first glance, then, the Money Order Division would appear to tell a story about a rising tide of bureaucratic reform. In reality, the money order system remained the exception rather than rule in the late 19th-century state.

## Efficiency versus Access

For all of its success, the Money Order Division was a small bureaucratic nook within the Post Office Department. When Charles Macdonald stepped down in 1893, his division was processing just over 22 million domestic and international money orders and postal notes each year. That might seem like a large number, but it made up less than 1 percent of all the mail that traveled through the US Post that year.[25] Newspapers and periodicals, by comparison, made up roughly 20-25% of the mail during the 1890s. And unlike money orders, periodicals traveled under heavily subsidized postage rates that wreaked havoc with the department's annual balance sheet.[26] From 1885 onwards, the department even carried local newspapers entirely free of charge, provided that they were delivered in the same county in which they were published.[27] These local papers joined other sorts of mail that the department carried for free, including correspondence between public officials, congressional documents, census material, bulletins and reports from executive agencies, and even seed samples sent through the Department of Agriculture. As shown in Figure 6.3, this "free matter" dwarfed the volume of money orders and postal notes that traveled through the mail. Charles Macdonald may have ensured that the money order service was self-sustaining, but this was far from typical within the 19th-century postal system.[28]

There is a fundamental tension between providing an efficient government service and providing an accessible government service. The money order system was efficient in part because it was not universally accessible. From the very beginning, Charles Macdonald's drive for bureaucratic efficiency trumped the extension of the service into new places. From Macdonald's perspective, a location needed to demonstrate that it could support the service. For example, it wasn't until February of 1866—some 15 months after the service was first launched—that the first money order facilities appeared in the western United States. By that point there were already hundreds of money order offices operating in the eastern United States.[29] The limited rollout in the West was due to the department's exacting regulations about which post offices qualified for the service. A money order office, like a miniature bank, needed to have a large amount of cash on hand to redeem incoming

Pieces of Mail Transmitted
by the US Post (1892–93)

469,386,883

22,118,944

Free Matter   Money Orders

**Figure 6.3**  A Drop in the Ocean

In the 12 months between July 1, 1892, and June 30, 1893, the Post Office Department transmitted more than 20 times as many pieces of mail free of charge than the combined number of money orders and postal notes sent through the mail. Data from *1893 Annual Report of the Postmaster General* (Washington, DC: Government Printing Office, 1893), xxxi, 688-91.

money orders. The service, then, was originally confined to post offices that both generated a requisite amount of revenue and whose postmaster could supply a four-thousand-dollar bond to safeguard against loss or theft of funds. These conditions were easier to meet at post offices that served larger, more prosperous, and more densely populated communities. Rural parts of the country struggled to meet these qualifications.[30]

By 1880, a decade and a half after the money order service was first launched, just 265 post offices in the Far West had money order facilities (roughly 10 percent of all post offices). The state of Illinois alone had more money order post offices than all of Arizona, California, Colorado, Idaho, Montana, New Mexico, Nevada, Oregon, Utah, Washington, and Wyoming combined.[31] But the fact that a local post office lacked money order facilities didn't mean the service was entirely unavailable to its community. After all, people could always travel to the nearest post office that did offer money order facilities. One way to evaluate the accessibility of the money order system is to combine post offices with money order facilities with other post offices that were within 10 miles of a money order office. Although not a perfect measurement, this offers a rough approximation of which communities could regularly access the money order system. This metric reveals a vast range of accessibility across the Far West. Residents of California and Colorado enjoyed the best "coverage" of money order facilities: 49 percent of post offices in California and 43 percent of post offices in Colorado either offered money order facilities or were within 10 miles of an office that did offer them. At the other end of the spectrum, just 8 percent of Arizona post offices either offered the service or fell within a 10-mile radius of a money order office.[32]

For a region accustomed to the capacious coverage of the US Post's larger gossamer network, the money order service's limited and cautious extension was both frustrating and unfamiliar. In 1867, one California correspondent grumbled about "the want of postal facilities for the transmission of money orders" in his particular town. It was a ridiculous complaint, given that his tiny local post office had nowhere near the necessary funds on hand to operate a money order service.[33] A decade later, westerners were still grumbling. In 1877, Charles Macdonald had to write a letter to Montana's outraged territorial delegate, Martin Maginnis, to explain why the paltry revenue at a small Montana post office disqualified it from becoming a money order office.[34] Rural and western congressmen from both sides of the aisle nevertheless continued to lobby for an expansion of the money order service into less settled parts of the country. One congressman from Arkansas spoke for this rural bloc when he complained that the money order system shouldn't just serve the "haughty dweller in the metropolitan city" but should also "follow the footsteps of the hardy pioneer wherever he may go in his brave and rugged march over our broad Western plains and distant mountains."[35]

Many of the Congressmen who called for extending the money order service into rural areas were the very same politicians who closed ranks to defend the rampant overexpansion of the star route service during the 1870s. In both cases, they argued

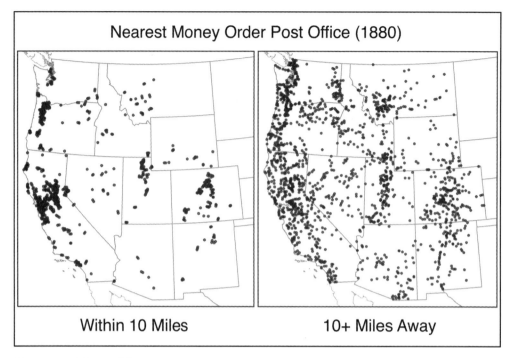

**Figure 6.4** A Limited Service

The map on the left shows which communities could access the money order system in 1880, as defined by: (a) post offices offering money order facilities, or (b) post offices that fell within 10 miles of a money order post office. The map on the right shows communities that could not easily access the money order system, as represented by post offices that were more than 10 miles away from the nearest money order post office. Dina Hassan collected and analyzed this data from United States Post Office Department, *1880 United States Official Postal Guide*, vol. 2, no. 1 (Washington, DC: Government Printing Office, 1880).

that the West's right to postal facilities trumped the department's desire for efficiency. The difference between the star route system and the money order system, however, was that Charles Macdonald's specialized division did not have a mandate to provide a universally accessible service. The US Post did. In the years after the US Civil War, it extended into all the "nooks and corners" of the western United States.[36] Even when the high costs of this expansion project became clear, department officials continued to reiterate their commitment to "providing adequate postal facilities for all communities, without regard to geographical location."[37] Charles Macdonald and his Money Order Division had no such commitments. He took geography into full account when it came to providing money order facilities, and many of the West's remote, lightly populated, and cash-strapped communities simply did not meet his exacting qualifications. The cost-conscious technocrat was dedicated to providing an efficient service rather than a universally accessible one, which left rural areas effectively outside of its reach.

The money order system underscores the relationship between geography and administrative structure. The decentralized agency model produced a spatially expansive but unstable infrastructure. The bureaucratic model of the Money Order Division produced a much more geographically constrained system. But the two didn't operate independently of one another. In many cases, Macdonald had to overlay the money order service onto the existing infrastructure of the gossamer network. This put his division's top-down, technocratic administration at odds with the localized arrangements of the agency model. The clerical labor involved with processing money orders was much more onerous than selling stamps or sorting letters. Money orders required postmasters to fill out and mail multiple blank forms for every transaction, issue receipts to customers, keep those transactions tabulated in three separate account books, and remit excess funds to postal depositories at regular intervals. Whereas most postmasters had to settle up their postal accounts with department headquarters every three months, postmasters at money order offices had to send in their accounts on a weekly basis. For those accustomed to the agency model and its part-time, lightly regulated postal duties, working under the bureaucratic Money Order Division would have been jarring.[38]

Macdonald kept down costs in the money order system in part by limiting how much money postmasters received for their work. In the 1880s, postmasters received just 3.5 cents for every money order and one cent for every postal note that they processed.[39] Postmasters complained that these fees were entirely insufficient. As one group of postmasters put it, money orders "consume one-third of the postmaster's entire time . . . yet [bring] him, as a rule, not one-twentieth part of the income which he derives from his office." Another postmaster noted that his post office had "recently been made a money order office which adds a very little to my income and a great deal to the responsibility and labor of the office."[40] The normal commissions and fees that came from a fourth-class post office might not have paid postmasters very well, but they also didn't ask very much of them. Money orders paid just as poorly but required them to do much more work.

Charles Macdonald spent much of his career successfully fending off demands to expand the money order service in ways that would align it with the gossamer network's more capacious coverage. During his last year in office, he finally relented. In 1892 the money order system underwent an unprecedented expansion to thousands of new places. The impetus for this expansion came from Macdonald's boss at the time, Postmaster General John Wanamaker. The department-store magnate was a wealthy Republican operative who had received his position as a reward for funding Benjamin Harrison's successful 1888 presidential campaign. Unexpectedly, Wanamaker became one the 19th century's most important postal reformers. While in office he called on Congress to set up postal savings banks, institute a parcel post to compete with express companies, and even take over the nation's telegraph and telephone network. These campaigns ultimately failed, but Wanamaker proved more successful in launching a series of quieter institutional reforms to reorganize and build up existing postal services. This included expanding residential mail delivery, bolstering the Railway Mail Service, and, finally, extending the money order system to thousands of new communities. In order to accomplish this last reform, the Post Office Department relaxed its longstanding regulations about which post offices qualified for the money order service by lowering the minimum revenue cutoff for a post office and reducing the bond a postmaster had to provide. Finally, it changed the previous "opt-in" mechanism for establishing a money order office in which a postmaster had to actively apply to become a money order post office. Moving forward, department officials in Washington would automatically enroll a post office in the system once it met the new qualifications. Seemingly minor administrative tweaks had a dramatic impact on the nation's money order system. Over 12 months spanning 1892–93, the number of money order offices in the United States exploded from 12,000 to more than 18,000 offices—by far the biggest annual jump in the history of the division.[41]

The sudden expansion of the Money Order Division marked an important administrative shift by melding Charles Macdonald's longstanding centralized bureaucratic management with the expansionary ethos of the larger gossamer network. Unlike the bottom-up expansion of post offices and mail routes driven by local communities, the sudden jump in money order facilities in 1892 was the result of a top-down initiative enacted through regulatory changes. With the stroke of a pen, thousands of communities across the country were suddenly able to access a valuable government service. But what did this newfound access mean for the people who lived in these places? How did they actually use this service and the nation-spanning financial connections it enabled? Answering these questions involves a familiar trip to the corner post office window of Walter Mobley's general store in North Bloomfield.[42]

## National Markets and Regional Streams

North Bloomfield could stand in for a number of western communities in the late 19th century. Located in the foothills of the Sierra Nevada Mountains, the town lay within the regional orbits of several neighboring urban centers. A stage road connected it to nearby Nevada City, which in turn was linked to Sacramento via a 60-mile railroad line. From Sacramento, one could ride 90 miles to San Francisco. North Bloomfield, like so many towns in the West, was dependent on extractive industries. Gold seekers had founded the town in the early 1850s during the California Gold Rush, but over the following decades large-scale mining companies had replaced individual prospectors. One of the largest of these companies was the North Bloomfield Gravel Mining Company. In the late 1870s the company became the object of a famous lawsuit over its hydraulic mining operations, as farmers who lived downriver accused the company of creating silted runoff that had ruined their farms. In 1884, the California Supreme Court banned the practice of hydraulic mining in the state. As the North Bloomfield Gravel Mining Company pared down its operations, the town went into a slow decline. In the 1890s, however, it was still home to roughly one thousand residents, two schools, a church, and a smattering of small businesses—including the McKillican and Mobley General Store and post office.[43]

North Bloomfield was one of thousands of towns that benefited from the Post Office Department's sweeping expansion of the money order service during the last year of Charles Macdonald's administration. On October 18, 1892, some 60 California towns were officially inaugurated into the money order system, including the North Bloomfield Post Office.[44] The new development was a welcome one for the town's residents. Previously, sending a money order would have required them to embark on a 28-mile roundtrip journey over mountain roads to either North San Juan or Nevada City. Now, they could simply walk to Walter Mobley's general store and immediately remit funds to some 18,000 different locations.[45] Fortunately for historians, Mobley saved the copious paperwork from his time as the town's postmaster, including individual records of the money orders that left his office. Much like the equivalent records saved by the postmaster in Hamilton, Nevada, the records from North Bloomfield capture each order's recipient, destination, and sender along with the amount of money remitted. Included in these records are some nine hundred money orders that left the North Bloomfield Post Office over the course of eight months in 1895.[46] These scraps of information offer a glimpse into a largely understudied corner of economic history and the commercial integration that was washing over the western United States.

Postal money orders present a bottom-up perspective on how individual people (albeit largely middle- and upper-class people) remitted money from a distance.[47] The data from eight months' worth of North Bloomfield money orders, fragmentary as they may be, show some surprising patterns. First, a majority of the town's money orders went to companies and organizations rather than people. A system that had originated as a personal remittance service for Union soldiers had increasingly turned into a channel for commercial transactions. A list of the most common recipients for North Bloomfield's money orders reads more like a business directory than a social network, littered with names like Weinstock Lubin & Co., Nolan Brothers Shoe Company, and Hale Brothers & Co. These money orders point to a larger economic transition unfolding in the late 19th century, as an older commercial system of regional markets gave way to a national consumer economy dominated by large companies, brand-name products, sophisticated advertising techniques, and large-scale distribution systems.[48]

The US Post provided some of the forgotten infrastructure of an expanding consumer culture, and no sector of this new economy was more dependent on the postal system than mail-order businesses.[49] By the end of the 19th century, two companies had come to dominate the market. The Chicago-based firms of Montgomery Ward and Sears, Roebuck & Co. mailed hundreds of thousands of catalogs to rural households and shipped goods across the countryside. In the words of one South Dakotan, "When you live ninety miles from a town, a Montgomery Ward or Sears Roebuck catalogue gets read more than the Bible or Shakespeare."[50] The mail-order industry, with its ability to provide local customers with a standardized array of mass-produced goods, exemplified the growing reach of a national consumer market. The residents of North Bloomfield in 1895 were in many ways ideal

potential customers for money order companies. Constrained by the limited se-
lection at Walter Mobley's general store, they presumably pored over mail-order
catalogs and sent money orders to the Chicago headquarters of Montgomery Ward
and Sears, Roebuck & Co. Except for one problem: they didn't.[51]

Surprisingly, North Bloomfield's residents sent just 11 money orders combined
to Montgomery Ward and Sears, Roebuck & Co. over the course of eight months in
1895 (around one percent of all orders). If the two national mail-order behmoths had
come to dominate the long-distance retail market one would have expected them to
have a much larger foothold in a town like North Bloomfield. Instead, its residents
largely ignored them. Despite expectations about a rapidly nationalizing consumer
culture, major commercial centers in the eastern United States were eclipsed by a
regional network of retailers. San Francisco and Sacramento were far and away the
most popular destinations for North Bloomfield's money order purchases, towering
over the eastern metropolises of Chicago, New York, Philadelphia, and Boston. If
the money order system was like a network of streams and rivers running out of
North Bloomfield, most of its water stayed pooled in Northern California.

So if North Bloomfield's residents weren't sending money orders to the mail-
order giants of Montgomery Ward and Sears, Roebuck & Co., where were they
sending their money? The single most common recipient of their money orders
was a Sacramento department store that has long since faded into obscurity named
Weinstock, Lubin & Co. Over eight months in 1895, North Bloomfield's residents
sent 123 money orders there, more than 10 times the number they sent to the two
Chicago mail-order companies combined. Harris Weinstock and David Lubin,
Jewish half-brothers from Poland, had launched their store in 1874 as a one-room
dry goods shop. By the 1890s it had become one of the largest retail outfits in the
western United States, with a dozen different departments housed in a three-story
building that covered an entire city block in downtown Sacramento.[52] Department
stores like Weinstock, Lubin & Co. were part of the same consumer revolution that
had produced the mail-order industry. Whereas mail-order companies brought
rural Americans within the orbit of national markets, department stores performed
a similar function for urban consumers.[53] Weinstock, Lubin & Co., however,
blurred the boundary between these two types of businesses. The Sacramento department store was an urban retailer that simultaneously catered to a rural clientele.
And it did so through the US Post.

Harris Weinstock and David Lubin had long relied on the mail. In 1878, they took
out a front-page advertisement in the *Sacramento Daily Record-Union* announcing
a new retail division of their dry goods store. In it, they highlighted their burgeoning
mail-order department by assuring customers that "a person living hundreds of
miles away can obtain as much for their money as one who applies personally to
our store."[54] Three years later, the company's "Country Order" department was
processing hundreds of orders a day. And by 1891, the company claimed that
their annual catalog reached a quarter of a million readers "from New Mexico to
Washington."[55] Although certainly inflated, the claim testified to the importance of

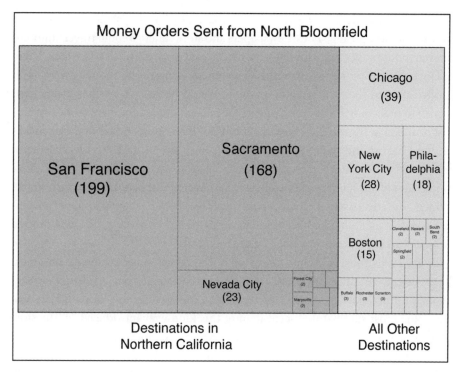

**Figure 6.5**  Regional Streams

This chart shows the number of money orders from North Bloomfield, California, that were sent to businesses located in different cities during February, March, April, June, August, September, October, and December of 1895. Destinations in northern California (dark gray) outnumber all other destinations (light gray) by a factor of three to one. Jenny Barin and Alex Ramsey transcribed data from Money Order Applications—January–December 1895, box 6, folders 12–16, Malakoff Diggins State Park Historical Collection, California Department of Parks and Recreation, Sacramento, California.

the US Post to the store's business model. Weinstock, Lubin & Co. wasn't unique in this regard, but its regional geography made it especially reliant on the mail. Large eastern department stores like Macy's in New York or Wanamaker's in Philadelphia also offered mail-order services, but Sacramento was not New York or Philadelphia. With fewer than 30,000 residents, Sacramento wasn't even Hoboken, New Jersey. Instead, Weinstock, Lubin & Co. had to cultivate a more dispersed clientele.[56]

The US Post gave Harris Weinstock and David Lubin the tools with which to build a far-reaching customer base. It did so in three ways: advertising in newspapers, mailing customers their catalogs, and collecting payments via money orders. First, the store's newspaper advertisements were heavily subsidized by the US Post. Newspapers and periodicals traveled under a second-class postage rate of one cent per pound, or 1/32nd the price of sending letters under first-class postage. This benefited not only the newspaper and magazine industry but also companies like Weinstock, Lubin & Co. that advertised in their pages.[57] Second, the store's catalogs traveled under third-class postage rates reserved for books and other printed material. Although not as steeply discounted as second-class mail, third-class postage was still less expensive than mailing an equivalent letter. Just as importantly for a company whose clientele was scattered across the Far West, distance did not factor into any of these postage rates: newspapers and store catalogs could travel hundreds or even thousands of miles for the same discounted price.[58] Third, Weinstock, Lubin & Co. collected payments from their customers using postal money orders. This service allowed their customers—many of whom had never set foot inside their store—to make purchases from long distances without fear of their money getting lost or stolen in transit.[59] Weinstock, Lubin & Co. were well aware of their reliance on the US Post and their remote customer base: one of its 1891 advertisements trumpeted, "We value to the utmost our out-of-town post office acquaintances. Uncle-Sam is our hard-working ally and we have no disposition to make his tasks lighter." The advertisement included an illustration of a particular kind of "post office acquaintance" that had become central to the store's success: two well-dressed women walking into a post office to place their orders.[60]

By the 1890s, most of Weinstock, Lubin & Co.'s retail items were aimed at women. Its catalogs were stuffed with items for female consumers, from "a splendid knock-about summer skirt" that sold for $1.25 to a best-selling line of petticoats that were "the most successful 50-cent item of this kind ever introduced."[61] The store offered gloves and hat pins, ribbons and sewing machines, shawls and parasols. Male customers were almost an afterthought in its catalogs; the first item exclusively targeted at men didn't appear until some 50 pages into one of its catalogs.[62] Consequently, women made up the bulk of the store's customers. In North Bloomfield, for instance, women sent 80 percent of the town's money orders to Weinstock, Lubin & Co.[63] Although it's unknown what women like Julia Hook or Maggie Watson were buying from the store, their purchases were part of an ascendant consumer culture. Women were a central part of this cultural and economic shift, but most of the attention paid to their roles as consumers has focused on urban spaces like retail shops, department stores, tearooms, dance halls, and restaurants.[64] Yet the same gendered consumption practices that were reshaping New York City were also penetrating homes in small towns like North Bloomfield. They just happened to take place at a distance. Catalogs from Weinstock, Lubin & Co. were marketed in part as fashion guides for women "who want to know 'what's going on' in the world of dress."[65] The company filled its catalogs with commentary such as: "Uwanta skirt lengths have gained an enviable reputation with California women" or "The kimono has taken the place of a dressing sacques to a great extent throughout the East."[66] The women of North Bloomfield may have lived along a dusty mountain stage road, 60 miles away from the nearest major city. They might not have been able to regularly browse the aisles of urban department stores. But they could still stay connected to national consumer shifts through the distance-shrinking medium of the US Post.

The postal connections that ran between North Bloomfield and Sacramento present something of a puzzle. In an age of national integration, why did so many of the town's consumer purchases never leave northern California? How did a Sacramento department store manage to keep mail-order behemoths like

Montgomery Ward at bay? After all, the Chicago company could use the US Post to reach North Bloomfield just as easily as a store in Sacramento. It too could advertise in newspapers, mail out catalogs, and collect money orders. The difference lay in how merchandise traveled compared to mail. Prior to the advent of parcel post in 1913, the Post Office Department only transported goods and products that weighed less than four pounds.[67] Its "fourth-class" postage rate for parcels and packages was also quite expensive, so most long-distance retailers turned to railroad and express companies to send the majority of goods. Unlike the US Post, private transportation companies factored distance into their rates. The farther an item traveled, the more they charged.[68] This meant that national mail-order houses headquartered two thousand miles away from California simply couldn't compete with Weinstock, Lubin & Co. on shipping costs to the region. Montgomery Ward and Sears, Roebuck & Co. may have captured the hearts and money of midwestern farmers in Iowa or Nebraska, but the challenges of distance and geography continued to limit its ability to make inroads in the Far West.[69] If the late 19th century was an age of expanding national connections and a growing consumer market, the spatial patterns that these connections produced could remain quite regional.

## The Geography of Integration

By nearly any measure, the American West of the 1890s was far more integrated into the rest of the country than it had been at any point in its history. Thousands of miles of new railroad tracks and telegraph lines connected the West and East to a degree that had been unthinkable just a few decades before. The incorporation of six new states between 1888 and 1890 gave westerners new clout in national politics. The region's mining, livestock, and other extractive industries linked it to distant manufacturers, markets, and financiers.[70] So how did these accelerating forces of national integration change the spatial practices of individual westerners? Postal money orders are one way to understand the changes that had unfolded in the region. Comparing North Bloomfield's money orders to earlier postal records from Hamilton, Nevada, provides a useful snapshot of where and how westerners remitted money at two different points in the region's history. The two mining towns were not perfectly analogous. In 1895, North Bloomfield had existed for some four decades but was in the midst of a steady if gradual decline. In 1878, Hamilton was still a new and booming population center. Nevertheless, money order records from the two communities capture some of the changes that had unfolded over the intervening two decades.

The nation's money order infrastructure had expanded considerably between 1878 and 1895. Whereas there were just over four thousand money order post offices in 1878, by 1895 that number had jumped nearly fivefold to some 20,000 locations.[71] Over that time the Post Office Department had increased the maximum size of an order from $50 to $100 while also lowering its fees; a money order that would have cost 15 cents in 1878 dropped in cost to just three cents in 1895.[72] Those same orders also covered ground faster than ever. Over the intervening years the time it took the mail to travel across the country from New York to San Francisco fell by more than two full days.[73] In short, North Bloomfield's residents in 1895 could remit funds to more places, more quickly, and more cheaply than Hamilton's residents in 1878. The money order system was the very embodiment of the national integration that had reshaped the West by the end of the 19th century.

Given all of this, one would expect North Bloomfield's remittance network to encompass a much more expansive geography in 1895 than Hamilton's network in 1878. Instead, a map comparing money orders from the two towns reveals precisely the opposite pattern. As seen in Figure 6.6, North Bloomfield's remittance network was much more geographically concentrated in 1895 than Hamilton's network was in 1878. Despite North Bloomfield sending around three hundred more remittances over the same eight months than Hamilton, all of those extra money orders went to fewer total locations.[74] They also didn't travel very far. Whereas most of Hamilton's money orders were sent more than one thousand miles away (many to the eastern United States), the majority of North Bloomfield's orders stayed firmly within a 150-mile radius. Rather than a national consumer economy pulling North Bloomfield into an ever more expansive commercial orbit, it was as if a giant magnet kept the town's remittances anchored to northern California. Integration, counter-intuitively, had produced a narrowing of spatial practices.

The remittance networks from North Bloomfield and Hamilton are based on fragmentary scraps of information—just eight months' worth of data from two western towns. The remittances from another town or from another year might look very different. But the differences between these two towns point to a larger lesson: national integration does not always unfold as expected. When historians and geographers talk about integration, they often conflate the capacity for connections with spatial practices themselves. Potential connections are not the same as realized ones. The fact that North Bloomfield's residents could send money orders to nearly five times as many locations as their predecessors in Hamilton didn't mean they actually did so.[75] The growth of a national mass market, the extension of transportation infrastructure, the rise of industry and capital, the spread of the US Post—all of these developments integrated the American West into the larger scale of the nation. But this did not necessarily produce a similar expansion of spatial practices. The maturation of the Anglo-American West, at least in northern California, meant that in certain respects the region had become more self-contained and self-reliant by the 1890s than it had been just two decades before. Why order a petticoat from a national mail-order catalog if one could buy it for a lower price from a Sacramento department store? Why pay for a subscription to the *Chicago Tribune* if the same standardized news content appeared in the regional *Sacramento Daily Union*? From the perspective of westerners, the need for individual connections with the rest of the country was not as pressing as it had once been.[76]

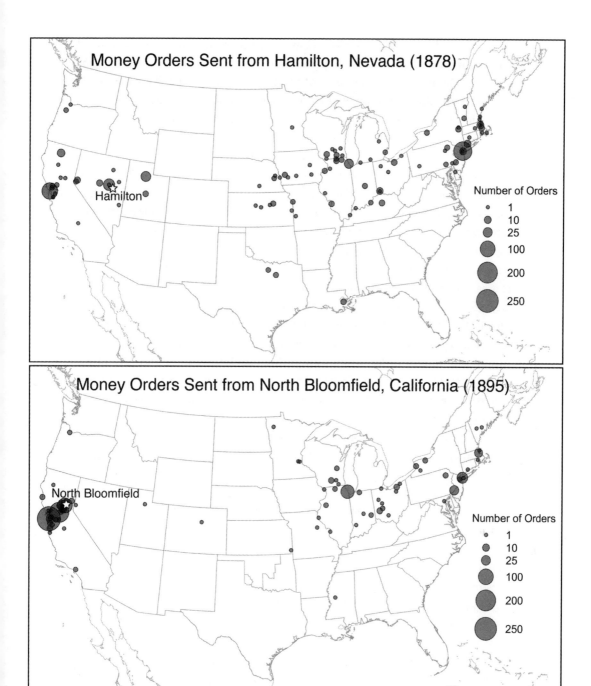

**Figure 6.6** National Integration and the Narrowing of Commercial Space

These two maps compare the 571 money orders sent from Hamilton, Nevada, during eight months in 1878 (top) versus the 876 money orders sent from North Bloomfield, California, during the same eight months in 1895 (bottom). Despite sending more orders and having access to many more potential destinations, North Bloomfield's residents sent their money orders to fewer distinct destinations. Both maps only display orders from the following months: February, March, April, June, August, September, October, and December. Hamilton data was transcribed from Register of Money Orders Issued at the Post Office of Hamilton, White Pine County, Nevada, Bancroft Library, University of Berkeley, California. North Bloomfield data was transcribed by Jenny Barin and Alex Ramsey from Money Order Applications, January–December 1895, box 6, folders 12–16, Malakoff Diggins State Park Historical Collection, California Department of Parks and Recreation, Sacramento, California.

Nor, too, did integration always follow a relentless upward trajectory toward more and more connections. Some parts of the West like California grew by leaps and bounds in the late 19th century, but other areas declined or collapsed entirely. This was especially true in the extraction-driven interior. And when people left, so too did the US Post and its gossamer network. Hamilton, Nevada, was one of those places. Between the 1870s and the 1890s the town underwent a precipitous decline. At its peak in 1875, the town's postmaster earned $2,100 a year as a full-time, salaried government official. Twenty years later, the town's post office had been downgraded to a fourth-class office, and its postmaster's compensation had dropped to less than $250 in part-time commissions. Whereas Hamilton had once been a hub for six different mail routes in the 1870s, by 1896 it was serviced by a single mail line. At least the Hamilton Post Office stayed operational, which is more than could be said of many nearby communities. Between the 1870s and the 1890s, the area surrounding Hamilton had turned into a graveyard of discontinued post offices: Eberhart, Treasure City, Mineral City, Duck Creek, Pinto, Diamond, Egan Canyon, Vanderbilt. In terms of its postal infrastructure, this particular corner of the West had grown less connected, not more, to the wider world.[77]

The postal money order system during the late 19th century was certainly a force for national integration, in both the public and private sectors. Its bureaucratic structure under Charles Macdonald was part of a small but growing movement for a more centralized kind of governance managed by professional civil servants and technocrats. It was a type of administration that diverted power away from local individuals and networks and into the hands of national administrators in Washington. The money order system itself concurrently facilitated a process of commercial integration in the private sector as well. Providing a public service for remitting small amounts of money allowed companies and consumers to conduct long-distance transactions cheaply, safely, and reliably. Yet for all of its distance-shrinking, integrative properties, the money order system was notable also for its geographical limits. Macdonald's technocratic commitment to cost-effective administration meant that for the first three decades of its existence, the money order service was constrained to a relatively small number of densely populated places. It operated a skeletal infrastructure compared to the sprawling coverage of the wider US Post.

Not until Postmaster General John Wanamaker launched a broader expansionary campaign in the early 1890s did the money order system extend its coverage into smaller, more rural places like North Bloomfield. This expansion was part of an important period of institutional reform under Wanamaker's administration that attempted to both modernize the US Post and expand its purview within the nation's political economy—exactly the kind of model offered by Charles Macdonald and the Money Order Division. But the history of the money order system is an important reminder about the limits of these types of reforms. Inside the federal government's largest organization, the reformist vision for a centralized

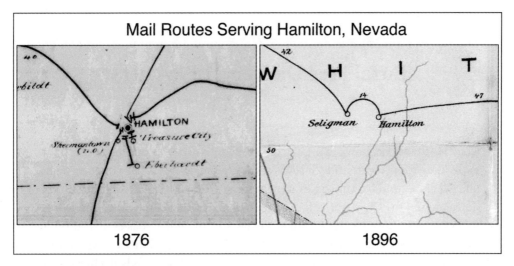

**Figure 6.7** Shrinking Connections

Postal service in Hamilton, Nevada, decreased from six mail routes in 1876 (*left*) to one mail route in 1896 (*right*). *Left*: Post Office Department, *Post Route Map of the States of California and Nevada* (Washington, DC, December 1, 1876). 1:760,320. Located in National Archives II, College Park, Maryland, RG 75, Bureau of Indian Affairs, Map 278. *Right*: United States Post Office Department, *Composite: Post Route Map of the States of California and Nevada* (Washington, DC, June 1, 1896). 1:696,960. Available online at the David Rumsey Map Collection, https://www.davidrumsey.com/luna/servlet/s/bkp613, accessed April 19, 2020.

administrative state faced fundamental challenges during the 1890s. Across the American countryside, the US Post's localized and decentralized structure still reigned supreme. In tens of thousands of rural places, the forces of institutional reform and national integration were shaped by the spatial and administrative arrangements of the 19th century's gossamer network. Change, however, was on the horizon. Ultimately, it would come in the form of a radical new kind of mail service that Postmaster General Wanamaker first proposed in 1891: Rural Free Delivery.

# 7

# Rural Free Delivery, 1896–1913

Charting the annual tally of post offices in the United States produces a pattern that looks like a roller coaster ride. It starts at the ground level in 1789 with just 75 post offices before steadily gaining elevation over the next 70 years. The ride briefly jolts down around the Civil War before resuming its dizzying climb up all the way up to 76,946 post offices in 1901. This is the peak of the roller coaster, that thrilling moment before the stomach-churning drop. The ride then plunges down over the following decade before embarking on a more gradual but steady decline for the remainder of the twentieth century. By 2000, there were fewer than 28,000 post offices operating in the United States, despite serving a population that had nearly quadrupled over the previous hundred years. What caused this precipitous drop from its 1901 peak? The answer hinges on a single three-letter acronym: RFD, or Rural Free Delivery.[1]

Today, door-to-door delivery defines the modern mail service. Carriers for the US Postal Service transport millions of pieces of mail each day directly to specific addresses where people live or work. In the 19th century, however, sending or receiving mail usually meant making a trip to the local post office. It wasn't until 1863 that the Post Office Department instituted its first experiment with residential mail delivery, first offering the service only in large cities with more than 50,000 people.[2] Over the following decades Congress gradually lowered this population cutoff to 10,000 people, so that by 1890 letter carriers were making door-to-door deliveries in some 450 cities across the country.[3] Limiting residential delivery to these urban areas allowed the postal system to keep down costs: the denser the population, the fewer letter carriers needed to be hired. But what about the tens of millions of people who didn't live in cities? Rural Americans were left to trek to the nearest post office in order to get their mail. The urban/rural gap in mail delivery first started to close under the administration of Postmaster General John Wanamaker in the early 1890s, as he argued that extending residential mail delivery into the countryside would bring "countless benefits for rural dwellers."[4] Although Wanamaker himself made little headway in securing funding from Congress, his administration planted the initial seeds for universal door-to-door mail service. Following successful experiments with the service during the late 1890s, Congress began to enlarge its operations and finally voted to establish Rural Free Delivery as a permanent service within the Post Office Department in 1902.[5]

Rural Free Delivery fundamentally altered the spatial structure of both the US Post and the rural United States by shifting the basic unit of delivery from a post office to an individual residence. Once people didn't have to travel to the nearest

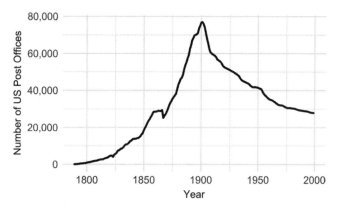

**Figure 7.1** The Rollercoaster

The number of post offices operating in the United States peaked on June 30, 1901, with 76,946 offices. United States Postal Service Historian, "Pieces of Mail Handled, Number of Post Offices, Income, and Expenses Since 1789," United States Postal Service, February 2020, https://about.usps.com/who-we-are/ postal-history/pieces-of-mail-since-1789.pdf, accessed April 23, 2020.

post office to get their mail, the Post Office Department was able to consolidate its network by shutting down thousands of rural post offices—hence the steady decline in the number of post offices over the twentieth century. The effects of Rural Free Delivery were profound. Residential mail delivery brought Americans within an expanding orbit of national markets, politics, and culture. Daily newspapers, rather than weekly editions, became a new possibility for those living on RFD routes, and they began to subscribe to many more periodicals than their peers who didn't have door-to-door delivery. Rural mail carriers also delivered mail-order catalogs directly to customers' homes, allowing them to order from national companies like Sears, Roebuck & Co. or from regional stores like Sacramento's Weinstock, Lubin & Co. By extending these connections to the doorstep of rural Americans, Rural Free Delivery stood poised to deliver a fatal blow to the isolation that had defined rural life for centuries.[6]

Perhaps not surprisingly, Rural Free Delivery has become a powerful symbol of the nation's transition from its agrarian past into a modern, interconnected society.[7] For more specialized scholars of the American state, Rural Free Delivery embodied a wider shift toward bureaucratic governance during the early twentieth century's Progressive Era. From the municipal level up to the federal government, reformers during this period extended the reach of government through the guiding hand of professional experts. As a top-down initiative launched by department administrators, Rural Free Delivery has become a canonical example of what one scholar describes as entrepreneurial civil servants carving out "bureaucratic autonomy" independent of politicians or special interests.[8]

At first glance, the rise of Rural Free Delivery in the 1890s and early 1900s should have sounded a death knell for both the gossamer network and the agency model that powered it. But the geography of this service and its expansion reveals a far messier story. The initial extension of Rural Free Delivery was not universal.

Instead, its rollout led to yawning disparities in the US Post's underlying geography. In some parts of the country Rural Free Delivery revolutionized mail service and postal administration. Other areas, especially the western United States, were left virtually untouched by this new system. There was no clean break with the past, no triumphant march into modernity for the western postal network and the American state.

## The Rise of Rural Free Delivery

The origins of Rural Free Delivery were closely connected to the rise of the People's Party (also known as the Populists) during the early 1890s, and both were the result of a decades-long wave of agrarian reform. During the late 19th century the United States rapidly transitioned into an industrial world power. As manufacturers, financiers, and corporations exercised more and more influence over the national economy, farmers and small producers increasingly called on the government to even the playing field. By the late 1880s, the movement had turned into a full-fledged political insurgency. The Populists championed an activist state to reign in the excesses and abuses of private markets and, more specifically, to work for the benefit of rural Americans. For Populist reformers, no other government institution embodied this ethos more than the Post Office Department. In 1892, the People's Party convened in Omaha, Nebraska, and drafted a party plank that explicitly allied it with the US Post: "We believe that the power of government—in other words, of the people—should be expanded (as in the case of the postal service) as rapidly and as far as the good sense of an intelligent people and the teachings of experience shall justify."[9]

Populist reformers found an unlikely ally in the postmaster general John Wanamaker, a fabulously wealthy Philadelphia businessman best known for founding one of the nation's largest department stores. Wanamaker seemed like exactly the sort of man who would represent the interests of eastern financiers and manufacturers. Instead, Wanamaker—who fashioned himself a "country boy"—became a vocal advocate for the rural United States. In 1890, Wanamaker convinced Congress to appropriate $10,000 in order to launch an experiment with Rural Free Delivery. Wanamaker used the funds to inaugurate a temporary door-to-door mail service along 46 rural mail routes in the spring of 1891. Just as importantly, Wanamaker began drumming up a widescale campaign to lobby for his new initiative. Agrarian organizations such as the Farmer's Alliance immediately embraced the cause, recognizing that residential mail delivery would directly benefit the nation's rural residents. A flood of petitions from farmers poured into Congress. These petitions painted residential mail delivery as a panacea for the ills of rural America: it would alleviate the boredom and isolation of country life, allow farmers to more easily sell their crops, link businessmen to distant markets, and stem the tide of people who were vacating the countryside for the nation's increasingly congested cities.[10]

John Wanamaker's early venture into Rural Free Delivery was a top-down initiative implemented by government officials in Washington, DC—a sharp departure from the typically decentralized pattern of rural postal expansion. It was part of a broader effort to bolster the power of postal administrators and bring the system's operations under greater centralized supervision. Although many of Wanamaker's boldest proposals never gained traction—such as nationalizing the telegraph industry and placing it under the control of the Post Office Department—he was more successful with quieter sorts of internal reforms. For instance, in 1891 Wanamaker launched an ambitious campaign to gather information about the nation's more than 60,000 post offices. The department distributed standardized questionnaires to several thousand postmasters located at county seats and then asked them to conduct on-site inspections of all of the post offices in their particular county. Within a year, these county-seat postmasters had conducted in-person surveys of around 70 percent of the nation's post offices. Although this still left some 20,000 post offices unaccounted for, it was nevertheless a notable surge in the administrative capacity of postal officials to monitor and regulate its dispersed communications network.[11] A 19th-century system that had long been defined by its decentralized structure and local autonomy was ever so slowly being brought under tighter centralized administration.

Unfortunately for John Wanamaker and his allies in the populist movement, the first foray of Rural Free Delivery in 1891 coincided with a new legislative session of Congress. In the previous fall elections the Democratic Party had won back control of the House of Representatives and its power over appropriations. The Democratic majority was not interested in helping John Wanamaker, a noted Republican partisan. Although the postmaster general may have been a bold reformer in certain respects, these impulses did not extend to civil service reform. One the era's most notorious "spoilsmen," Wanamaker oversaw the removal of tens of thousands of Democratic postmasters during his administration. Perhaps not surprisingly, his requests to extend Rural Free Delivery were largely ignored by the Democratic majority in the House of Representatives. The initial venture had been an important landmark for Rural Free Delivery, but it largely sputtered for the remainder of his administration.[12]

In 1892, the Democratic Party took back the presidency, and with it control of the Post Office Department. John Wanamaker was promptly replaced by Wilson Bissell. A reformer of a different sort, the new postmaster general focused on pruning back the department's costs rather than expanding its services. Bissell dismissed Rural Free Delivery as an extravagance, writing in his 1893 annual report that "the Department would not be warranted in burdening the people with such a great expense." The service languished until he was replaced by a new postmaster general in 1895 who proved more amenable to the initiative. The following year Congress granted new funds to extend Rural Free Delivery, allowing the department to institute 82 new door-to-door routes on a temporary basis in 1896.[13]

When Congress took up debate over Rural Free Delivery during the 1890s, it faced two options for how to operate these new rural mail routes. The US Post could continue to contract with private companies to carry the mail, or it could use salaried mail carriers who were subject to civil service regulations. Essentially, it could use the agency model or a civil service bureaucracy.[14] These two options mapped onto the two primary ways in which the nation's mail traveled by land, through the star route service and the Railway Mail Service. The Railway Mail Service was by all accounts the gold standard of professionalized administration within the Post Office Department.[15] It employed a full-time staff of postal clerks and agents who were subject to rigorous examinations. By the 1890s, these employees had developed a cohesive esprit de corps within the framework of an effective and hierarchical bureaucracy. In short, it was the polar opposite of the star route service and its scattered collection of lightly regulated private mail contractors. The Railway Mail Service and the star route service were also on different trajectories. After years of rampant growth, the star route service leveled off during the last two decades of the 19th century. Some of this was due to cleaning up the corruption in the contracting division, but the stagnation was also due to the ascendancy of the Railway Mail Service. Between 1880 and 1900, the US post's railway mileage more than doubled, while its star route mileage grew by only 14 percent. Although the star route system was still more geographically expansive than postal railway routes, it had nevertheless lost ground. By the end of the century the Post Office Department was spending more than seven times as much on its railroad service than its star routes.[16] Ultimately, lawmakers took their cues from the ascendant Railway Mail Service and decided to use salaried employees rather than private mail contractors to operate Rural Free Delivery routes.[17]

The growth of the Railway Mail Service was part of a slow shift toward more centralized administration within the Post Office Department. One can see these changes play out on the ground at Bell Ranch, a large cattle operation located in northeastern New Mexico Territory. The ranch's owner managed to obtain a post office in 1888 that was, in many ways, emblematic of the agency model and the gossamer network. It was a small-scale operation, one of New Mexico's smallest post offices, whose main clientele consisted of the ranch's employees.[18] It was also a privatized operation, with the ranch's on-site business manager doubling as its postmaster. And it was a remote post office, located dozens of miles away from the nearest settlement. Despite its tiny size and relative isolation, Bell Ranch was nevertheless connected to the rest of the postal system by a star route contractor who picked up and delivered its mail three times a week.[19]

For much of the 19th century, this kind of rural post office would have been largely left alone by Washington officials. Yet over 13 months spanning 1896 to 1897, postal officials in Washington, DC, repeatedly reprimanded the postmaster and manager of the Bell Ranch Post Office. The first salvo came from the auditor of the Post Office Department, who told him that his quarterly account paperwork was late and that he had 12 days to file it or he would be fined. The following year, postal officials chastised him for not accurately recording the departure and arrival times of the mail. "Be more careful in the future," admonished one official, or he would risk being removed from office. The postmaster's sloppiness wasn't particularly surprising, given that he was probably more concerned with managing Bell Ranch's livestock operations than its postal facilities. What was surprising was the fact that postal administrators actually caught these discrepancies. Just one decade earlier, Postmaster General William Vilas had tried, and failed, to dispatch inspectors to review the on-site operations of all of the nation's tens of thousands of post offices. Now, officials were successfully monitoring what time the mail left a tiny post office in rural New Mexico.[20] Of course, more centralized oversight brought some benefits for the nation's postmasters. A few weeks after his latest reprimand, the Bell Ranch postmaster received a brand-new map of surrounding post offices and mail routes from the Post Office Topographer's Office in Washington, DC. It had been mailed on October 7 and reached his post office just five days later. Walter Nicholson, the former director of the Topographer's Office, would have been astounded were he still alive. A mapmaking division that had once struggled to collect even basic geographical information about the western postal system was now providing up-to-date maps to a tiny post office on its western periphery.[21]

The Bell Ranch Post Office exemplified an institution that was extending centralized management not just over the network's operations but also over its expansion. Like so many westerners before him, the Bell Ranch postmaster had submitted a request to the department to establish a new, one-hundred-mail route that would better serve his office. In the spring of 1897, postal officials notified him that they were denying his request. They had solicited opinions about the proposed route from neighboring communities, weighed competing needs, and determined that an expansion of mail service was not warranted. Compared to the rampant and largely unchecked postal expansion of earlier decades, this unremarkable bit of bureaucratic administration was in fact a noteworthy departure. Local communities on the periphery had long determined the course and speed of the gossamer network's expansion, but by century's end that balance had started to shift.[22] By the end of the 1890s, administrators were exercising a degree of regulatory oversight over the day-to-day operations and growth of the nation's postal network that would have been inconceivable just a few decades earlier.

Rural Free Delivery followed a similarly exacting, top-down model of expansion. Unlike the approval process for new post offices and star routes, postal officials established explicit guidelines for establishing a new RFD route. Any community that wanted the service first had to petition its congressman, who would then send it on to the department with their own recommendation. The difference, however, was what came next. Once postal officials had received the request, they would send out a special agent to visit the area and collect information about local conditions, including literacy rates and the quality of roads.[23] A new RFD route had to meet very specific criteria: it had to be between 20 and 30 miles in length, run on roads that were passable during all seasons, and serve at least one hundred families who would otherwise have to travel between two and 12 miles to a post office.[24] If the postal agent decided that the area could indeed support an RFD route, he would then map the course of the route and hire a mail carrier to begin service. Compared to the decentralized, haphazard process by which the department had extended its gossamer network over the preceding decades, the extension of Rural Free Delivery was a top-down project managed by agents, inspectors, and other postal officials with an eye toward efficiency and cost-consciousness.[25] It was a remarkable transfer of power from local private agents on the periphery to bureaucrats at the system's center in Washington, DC.

The shift in administrative power over the nation's mail routes had been quietly underway for the better part of two decades. For most of its existence, the Post Office Department had to defer to Congress's "postal power," which meant that it couldn't legally provide mail service on any route that Congress had not officially designated as a post road.[26] By the 1880s, the sheer scope and breakneck pace of postal expansion had created an administrative bottleneck. Not only did Congress have to spell out the geography of every new mail route; it also had to approve alterations to existing ones—all of which were packed into the annual post road bill that could encompass thousands of different routes. Even then, the Post Office Department still had ultimate discretion over whether or not to actually provide mail service on these routes. By one legislator's estimate in 1883, he and his colleagues had established some 50,000 official post roads that the department had essentially ignored: "If there ever was a bill that is a farce year by year, it is this bill."[27] So in the spring of 1884, Congress relinquished its postal power by declaring all public roads and highways eligible for mail service. It marked a quiet handoff in administrative authority over the nation's mail routes from the legislative branch to the Post Office Department, helping to lay the groundwork for Rural Free Delivery's centralized rollout the following decade.[28]

By 1899 postal officials were launching a landmark experiment to provide an entire county in Maryland with RFD routes. The success of this venture prompted Postmaster General Charles Emory Smith to lobby Congress to make Rural Free Delivery a permanent and widespread feature of the US Post. In his annual report to Congress in 1900, he described the burgeoning service as "the most salient, significant, and far-reaching feature of postal development in recent times."[29] Plenty of people in the Post Office Department would have agreed with Smith's assessment, but not all of them saw this as a good thing. Rural Free Delivery was a direct challenge not only to mail contractors on existing star routes but also to the nation's legions of small-town postmasters. Door-to-door mail delivery disrupted the agency model that had fueled postal operations in the countryside. If people no longer had to travel as frequently to their local post office, this meant lower commissions and fees and less foot traffic into a postmaster's private store or business. As one postmaster from Utah complained in 1899, a recently established RFD route near his post office "seriously interferes with the patronage of this office, and it does not seem fair or just to me, as it passes my office, collecting over an extent of about 4 square miles of my patronage."[30] The postmaster saw the surrounding area as a kind of personal fiefdom within which residents paid tribute at his post office, and Rural Free Delivery threatened that territorial arrangement. For all of his complaints, the Utah postmaster was one of the luckier ones. At least he retained his position after the launch of a nearby RFD route. For other postmasters, the adoption of Rural Free Delivery ended their time in public office. Residential delivery meant that people no longer needed a post office in such close proximity to their homes, which meant that the department could in turn consolidate the number of post offices in the surrounding area.

In 1902, Congress officially institutionalized Rural Free Delivery and appropriated more than four million dollars for the department to launch the service, marking a turning point for both the spatial and administrative structure of the US Post. New RFD routes spread like wildfire in the subsequent years.[31] By 1910, there were more than 40,000 of these routes connecting millions of households across the countryside. The department's RFD budget that year was $37 million—a long way from the initial $10,000 appropriation Postmaster General John Wanamaker had been granted to start testing the service two decades earlier.[32] The explosion of RFD routes caused a corresponding contraction in the number of rural post offices: the nation's postal system shed some 18,000 post offices in the decade following Rural Free Delivery's 1902 launch. The spread of this new service didn't necessarily change the US Post's sprawling geographical coverage—if anything, it extended its reach all the way to the doorsteps of Americans—but it did change how that coverage was constituted. Residential mail delivery redefined the geography of the US Post and, in turn, the arrangements that defined daily life in the rural United States.[33]

By shifting the lowest common denominator in the nation's postal infrastructure from a post office to an individual residence, this network reconfiguration helped spur on a corresponding sea change in administration within the Post Office Department. The localized agency model gave way to more centralized administration during the early 1900s. Wielding more and more administrative capacity, reformers in the Post Office Department launched sweeping initiatives to expand the purview of the postal service within American society. The first postal savings banks opened in 1910, allowing people to receive interest from the government by depositing their money at their local post office. Three years later, the Post Office Department instituted a full-fledged parcel delivery service for the first time. In its first six months, the department delivered more than 300 million packages across the country. Much like Rural Free Delivery, these were top-down initiatives implemented and overseen by bureaucrats in Washington, DC, rather than the periphery-driven expansion of the gossamer network.[34]

The Post Office Department's move toward centralized bureaucracy and professionalized management was part of a wider shift in the American state during the Progressive Era of the early 1900s. This period witnessed a flourishing of reform movements aimed at expanding government's capacity to improve society, and while many of the progressive movement's most enduring successes took place at the municipal or state level, federal agencies also expanded their capacities during these years. The US Department of Agriculture was arguably the most successful. After its establishment in 1862, its leaders repeatedly carved out a larger and larger foothold for the agency by cultivating scientific expertise centered on resource management. By the early 1900s, it leveraged this expertise to successfully lobby for two major initiatives. In 1905, Congress granted the Department of Agriculture administrative authority over some 63 million acres of forest reserves, all to be overseen by the Forestry Service under the scientific management of conservationist Gifford Pinchot. The following year, the Pure Food and Drugs Act granted the Department of Agriculture new authority to inspect and regulate food and goods moving across state lines—a landmark precursor to the Food and Drug Administration. Like the US Forest Service, this new regulatory apparatus was to be overseen by civil servants with scientific training. Just as Rural Free Delivery was spreading across the American countryside during the early 1900s, technocratic bureaucracy were spreading across the landscape of the American state.[35]

## Left Behind

Rural Free Delivery embodied the Progressive Era's impulse to actively use the power of the state to improve the lives of American citizens, all under the professional guidance of trained experts. It extended an important public service that private companies were unable or unwilling to provide—a solution to the classic "last mile" problem endemic to transportation and communication networks. Residential mail delivery might be taken for granted today, but it marked an important new chapter for millions of Americans, mitigating long-standing challenges of distance and isolation. And no other part of the country was so defined by distance and isolation as the rural West. It was the nation's least densely populated region, with far-flung settlements separated by miles and miles of imposing terrain. If any group of Americans stood to benefit from the shift to residential mail delivery, it was the homesteaders, ranchers, and miners who lived in the western United States. One would expect, then, for Rural Free Delivery to have triggered a sea change across the American West. But it didn't. Or at least not initially.

By 1904, there were 24,556 RFD routes operating nationwide, the result of more than a decade's worth of administrative reform efforts. But only 3 percent of these routes were operating west of the Kansas/Colorado border. The lack of coverage was especially extreme in the western interior: just 11 routes in Montana, eight in Arizona, five in Wyoming, three in New Mexico, and one solitary route in the entire state of Nevada. The majority of RFD routes were concentrated in the Midwest and (to a lesser degree) the Northeast. In fact, in 1904 there more than four times as many RFD routes in the single state of Illinois (2,123) than in all of the states and territories of the Far West combined (480). The initial tidal wave of Rural Free Delivery barely touched the western half of the country.[36] Unlike the expansive geography of the gossamer network, Rural Free Delivery was strikingly limited during its early years. Much like the Post Office Department's money order system, its initial adoption made it a specialized service rather than a universal one. Two seemingly antithetical factors contributed to this uneven geography: partisanship and bureaucratization.[37]

Old-fashioned partisanship remained alive and well in the Post Office Department. Over the 1890s and early 1900s, civil service reformers had made inroads in bringing the federal government's largest civilian organization under more technocratic management. But an entrenched patronage-based system did not suddenly disappear during the Progressive Era. In fact, elements of both political patronage and technocratic administration didn't just coexist; they often worked in tandem. Take the case of Rural Free Delivery. Congress had voted to employ salaried mail carriers along these routes rather than private mail contractors, and these employees would be subject to civil service examinations and protections. Although this helped depoliticize how RFD routes were operated, it did not depoliticize how those routes were allocated. When postal officials received an application for a new RFD route, they would seek input from the congressman in that district in

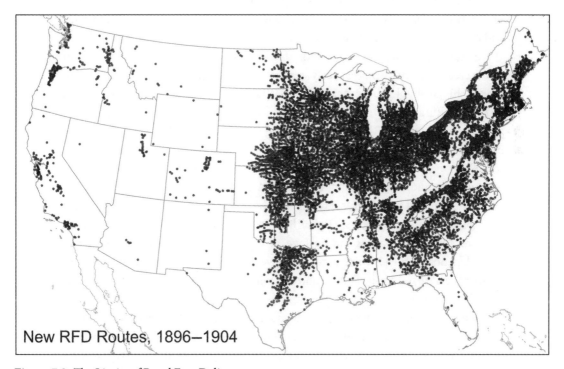

New RFD Routes, 1896–1904

**Figure 7.2** The Limits of Rural Free Delivery

Thousands of Rural Free Delivery routes were established between 1896 and 1904. This map locates each of those routes by its originating post office. Varun Vijay compiled the data from US Postal Service Historian, "First Rural Routes by State" (United States Postal Service, April 2008), https://about.usps.com/who-we-are/postal-history/first-rural-routes.htm.

deciding whether to approve the request. Much in the same way that postal officials had long relied on legislators to help appoint or dismiss postmasters, designate new post roads, or establish new post offices, the allocation of Rural Free Delivery routes was subject to political considerations as much as technocratic ones.[38]

Congress's influence over Rural Free Delivery had a predictable impact on where the Post Office Department established new RFD routes. During the late 1890s and early 1900s the Republican Party controlled the presidency and both chambers of Congress—an uninterrupted reign from 1897 to 1911 that happened to coincide with the initial expansion of Rural Free Delivery. RFD routes became a form of patronage for Republicans to strategically distribute based on their party's electoral needs. In one study, political scientists found that Republican incumbents from swing districts were more than ten times as likely to receive new RFD routes in their districts during the lead-up to the 1900 election than Democratic incumbents in swing districts.[39] The Midwest and Northeast—the electoral strongholds of the Republican Party—received the vast majority of the nation's new RFD routes. By 1903, one Democratic congressman from Georgia complained that while these Republican districts enjoyed a "dense forest" of RFD routes, Democratic districts had only "an occasional cottonwood on a bald prairie."[40] He was right. Iowa, which had voted Republican in the last presidential election, had 1,484 routes. The congressman's own state of Georgia, which had voted Democratic, had roughly the same number of residents as Iowa but less than one-third the number of RFD routes. The early geography of Rural Free Delivery followed familiar patterns of patronage and party politics that had long defined the 19th century's gossamer network.[41]

Partisanship wasn't the only factor that contributed to the uneven spread of Rural Free Delivery during its early years. A seemingly countervailing factor also shaped this geography: bureaucratization. When the Post Office Department began instituting Rural Free Delivery, it adopted standardized regulations about which places qualified for an RFD route, including certain thresholds for the number of people a route would serve, the literacy rates of those inhabitants, the distance of a route, and the quality of its roads. All of this was part of a turn toward technocratic management and organizational efficiency. After all, more densely settled routes allowed each mail carrier to serve more people and the Post Office Department to employ fewer mail carriers. Higher literacy rates meant more mail, bringing in more revenue from stamps and postage, and well-graded roads led to faster and more dependable travel. These regulations were put in place to ensure that the government service was both effective and efficient—hallmarks of the Progressive Era's push for governance by trained experts.

The department's bureaucratic management of Rural Free Delivery routes had an especially pronounced impact on the western United States. As much as southern Democrats may have protested the lack of RFD routes in their districts, their western colleagues—even Republican ones—had far more cause for complaint. If the landscape of Rural Free Delivery in Democratic districts looked like "an occasional cottonwood on a bald prairie," then most of the American West resembled the surface of Mars. This was because the department's regulations surrounding new RFD routes were much harder to meet in some places than others. Paloma, Illinois, for instance, was a much different place than Palomas, Arizona. The western Illinois farming community was located on a flat stretch of prairie just off the Chicago, Burlington, and Quincy Railroad. It was home to around six hundred surrounding residents and had narrowly voted Republican in the 1896 elections. In short, Paloma was an ideal location for a Rural Free Delivery route. So, in November of 1900, postal officials hired a mail carrier to begin operating a 24-mile RFD route in the community. Palomas, Arizona, on the other hand, was a small ranching and mining settlement on the Gila River in southwestern Arizona Territory. Unlike its Illinois counterpart, the Arizona town's rugged terrain, lack of graded roads, and sparse population disqualified it from receiving its own RFD route. So while the residents of Paloma, Illinois, began receiving mail at their doorsteps in 1900, the Arizona residents would continue to trek to their local post office until it eventually shut down in 1927. The two communities shared a name but little else when it came to how they fit within the new landscape of the US Post.[42]

The Post Office Department's most important regulation for Rural Free Delivery was that a new route must run along well-graded roads that were passable during the entire year. At first blush, this was a straightforward policy to ensure that mail carriers were able to do their jobs year round without getting mired in mud or snow. In practice, it linked the Post Office Department to another reform group: the good roads movement. Originally started by urban cyclists during the 1880s, the good roads movement called for the construction and maintenance of well-graded country roads that would allow them to go cycling outside of crowded cities. By the 1890s, the movement had grown to encompass farmers who wanted better means of travel and railroad companies that wanted to make their railway depots more accessible. This coalition of cyclists, farmers, and railroad companies found two main allies inside the federal government: the Department of Agriculture's Office of Road Inquiry and the Post Office Department's Rural Free Delivery division. The Office of Road Inquiry was first established in 1893 but was prohibited from actually constructing roads beyond small-scale experiments. Instead, the division acted as the technocratic research arm of the Good Roads Movement, gathering data about rural roads and disseminating reports free of charge under the Department of Agriculture's postal franking privilege.[43]

The US Post's Rural Free Delivery division had an even more direct impact on the nation's roads. The Post Office Department framed its regulations over RFD routes as straightforward bureaucratic measures: well-graded roads would allow their mail carriers to serve more households, more efficiently, and in more places. In practice, these criteria turned Rural Free Delivery into a policy wedge for federal officials to pressure state and local governments to improve their infrastructure. At the time, the federal government had little administrative authority over the nation's roads. It wasn't until 1916 that members of Congress—many of whom were suspicious of federal overreach into state and local affairs—managed to pass the first major federal legislation that granted funds for road development through the Federal Highway Act. Prior to that, officials instead turned to what historian Gary Gerstle describes as a "surrogacy strategy" in which policymakers used existing areas of federal jurisdiction to make policy in areas where they did not have explicitly enumerated powers. The Post Office Department's sweeping authority over the nation's mail system had long made it an ideal match for this surrogacy strategy. When it came to road policy, Rural Free Delivery gave the federal government a means of enacting changes to local and state roads despite the fact that it did not have the power to do so directly. In short, if a rural community wanted residential mail delivery, it would have to spend money to improve its roads.[44]

Rural Free Delivery followed a long tradition of the US Post reconfiguring rural space in the American countryside. But Rural Free Delivery only reconfigured certain kinds of rural space, namely, places that were able to build and maintain an infrastructure of public roads. This effectively shut out large sections of the western United States. Road construction and maintenance were difficult and expensive in the rugged and sparsely populated western interior. One government survey in 1904, for instance, found that Nevada had only around 12,000 total miles of public roads. This was less than Connecticut, New Hampshire, or Vermont, despite the fact that Nevada was several times the size of all three states combined. The reason for this stunted infrastructure was a familiar cocktail of demographic and environmental challenges that plagued the western United States. Roads in the West had to cover much longer distances and much rougher terrain than in the East, which made any sort of public infrastructure difficult to build and maintain. Moreover, very little of the public road infrastructure that did exist in the West was "improved," or surfaced with stone or gravel. As of 1904, for instance, there were exactly two miles of improved roads in the entire territory of New Mexico. The same was true across much of the mountainous western interior, where Utah was the only state or territory that had improved even 5 percent of its public roads.[45]

As it had done so many times before, western geography imposed real limits on institutional reform within the Post Office Department. What had changed, however, was who benefited from these limitations. For much of the 19th century, an expansionary postal policy meant that the federal government extended its gossamer network across the West without westerners themselves having to bear the costs of that development. Rural Free Delivery flipped this arrangement on its head. If western states and territories wanted access to this new service, they would have to build the necessary infrastructure to support it. The problem, of course, was that there were far fewer people in the West to fund road construction and maintenance. There were, for instance, only three residents for every mile of public roads in Nevada in 1904—compared to 164 residents per mile of public road in Massachusetts, or 181 per mile in Rhode Island. The story was similar across the West: of the 15 states and territories with the fewest people per mile of public roads, all of them lay west of the Mississippi River. It wasn't that westerners were unwilling to fund road improvements; on a per capita basis, western states and territories were actually spending more on public roads than their eastern counterparts. It was that this funding didn't go nearly as far. There were simply too few people spread across too rugged an environment to meet the Post Office Department's new bureaucratic regulations.[46]

## Echoes

Rural Free Delivery's rollout led to a paradox. Its bureaucratic management helped unleash a wider shift toward centralized administration in the Post Office Department, but that same impulse simultaneously limited its impact in the western United States. In the characterization of one scholar, the decline in rural postmasters and mail contractors helped sweep out an "old regime" of patronage-laden postal administration and inaugurated a new age of centralized, bureaucratic management.[47] But that characterization was only true in the eastern half of the country. With so many western communities unable to meet the department's technocratic criteria for new routes, Rural Free Delivery simply did not extend across most of western United States during its early years. And without this new spatial framework for mail delivery, the administrative framework of the agency model remained entrenched. The region's small-town post offices did not undergo the same wrenching consolidation of small fourth-class post offices as other parts of the country. Nationwide, the Post Office Department shed 13,490 fourth-class post offices between 1898 and 1908 in order to accommodate nearly 39,000 new RFD routes. Ohio and Indiana, two of the states on the frontlines of Rural Free Delivery's rollout, lost nearly half of their fourth-class post offices in this single decade. West of the Kansas/Colorado border, however, the number of fourth-class post offices didn't decline at all between 1898 and 1908. In fact, the total number of fourth-class offices in the Far West actually increased by 14 percent over that period, and in some states and territories in the western interior that figure climbed above 30 percent. The spatial and administrative transformations unleashed by Rural Free Delivery largely petered out at the hundredth meridian.[48]

The survival of the gossamer network and its localized agency model meant that bitterly partisan "post office rows" would continue to rage unabated in the West, even in the face of efforts to depoliticize the Post Office Department. In December of 1908, near the end of his final term, President Theodore Roosevelt issued an executive order that brought roughly 15,000 fourth-class postmasters under civil service regulations. This was a landmark policy for the federal workforce. Notably, however, Roosevelt's executive order only applied to postmasters in the northeastern United States.[49] For thousands of small-town postmasters in the West and South, partisanship would continue to define their appointments and tenures in office. New Mexico provides a useful example. In January of 1912, New Mexico was admitted as a state after more than 60 years as a federally administered territory. One of its two new senators, Republican Thomas B. Catron, promptly took

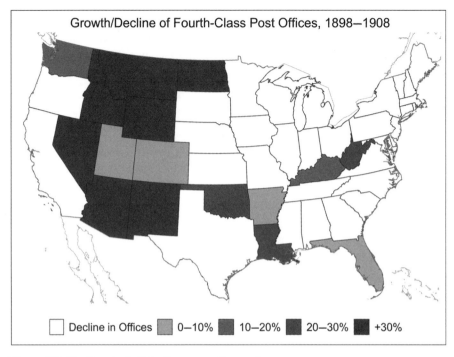

**Figure 7.3** The Survival of the Gossamer Network

Rural Free Delivery's uneven expansion resulted in post office closures in some parts of the country even as the number of post offices in other parts of the country continued to grow. This map shows the percentage change in the number of fourth-class post offices operating in each state or territory between 1898 and 1908. United States Post Office Department, *United States Official Postal Guide, 1898* (New York: Metropolitan Job Print, 1898), 1037, available online at https://babel.hathitrust.org/cgi/pt?id=pst.000003071618; United States Post Office Department, *United States Official Postal Guide, 1908* (Albany, NY: J. B. Lyon, 1908), 707, available online at https://babel.hathitrust.org/cgi/pt?id=uc1.b2919443.

up the pressing issue of postmaster appointments. President William Howard Taft (a fellow Republican) had informed Catron and other New Mexico Republicans that any postmasters who had been appointed before statehood were fair game for removal. Less than two weeks after being sworn into office, Catron was already scheming to install local allies and party operatives as postmasters in his home state.[50]

One of Senator Catron's exchanges highlights the degree to which postal administration remained an intensely localized affair in many western communities. During New Mexico's constitutional convention, a postmaster in the town of Santa Cruz had drawn the ire of fellow Republicans. One of these local politicians wrote to Catron "to see if you cannot do something to get him out of there."[51] Catron replied five days later from Washington, DC, assuring his colleague, "We can easily have that post-office changed" and asked for the name of a replacement postmaster.[52] He was then put in touch with a Santa Cruz businessman who made the following proposition: appoint one of his young employees, Ignacio Madrid, to replace the incumbent postmaster at Santa Cruz. The storeowner would house the post office on his premises, and Madrid would operate it. Catron acquiesced, forwarding Ignacio

Madrid's name to the Post Office Department. Five days later, he received word that Madrid had been appointed the new postmaster of Santa Cruz.[53]

As the new appointee started filling out paperwork, however, there were rumblings that Madrid would not be able to meet certain departmental requirements to take office. Anticipating trouble, a different storeowner from the town wrote to Catron nominating himself for the position in the event that Madrid's nomination fell through.[54] He was proven correct, when three weeks later the Post Office Department tersely notified Catron "that Mr. Madrid is not of legal age, that he can neither read nor write and does not speak English, and that the father and other members of the Madrid family made an assault upon the post office last November detaining the mail and breaking the glass in a window."[55] This left Catron scrambling to find a replacement until Ignacio Madrid's employer eventually put his own name forward: "Anything to take [the incumbent postmaster] Morris out of the way."[56] In the end, a member of the United States Senate who was in the midst of overseeing New Mexico's transition to statehood had exchanged no fewer than 19 different communications to try and replace a small-town postmaster whose position paid him a grand total of $140 a year.[57]

The correspondence from New Mexico may give the impression that little had changed in the previous four decades, when a similar "post office row" back in 1873 had left an exasperated congressman to write in his diary about "the smallness of the material out of which men can get up a fight."[58] But change was coming. In October of 1912, several months after Thomas Catron had resolved the post office row in Santa Cruz, outgoing president William Howard Taft issued an executive order strengthening civil service protections for the vast majority of the nation's fourth-class postmasters (not just those in the Northeast). Although civil service reformers lauded him, his opponents accused the president of fighting a rearguard action to make it harder to remove Taft's own Republican appointees from office. His successor, Democrat Woodrow Wilson, promptly passed his own executive order in May of 1913 that made incumbent postmasters—not just new applicants— subject to competitive civil service exams.[59] The decentralized agency model that had so long defined the rural postal system was being brought under increasingly centralized oversight. Although localized patronage and politics would never disappear from the US Post, they were nevertheless on the retreat.

The history of Rural Free Delivery underscores the need to think more materially about the relationship between the American state and its geography. Spatial factors influence the administrative arrangements of institutions, which in turn shape the space over which they administer. But there is nothing deterministic or comprehensive about that relationship. Faced with newly seized and sparsely settled western territory, the US Post's decentralized agency model extended the network's reach into remote locations and fueled the world's most geographically expansive postal system. Rural Free Delivery marked a departure from this model and a turn toward centralized, technocratic management that would have been inconceivable just a few decades before. In doing so, it extended the US Post's geographic reach all the way to the doorsteps of millions of Americans, fundamentally altering the space of the rural United States. But the uneven spread of Rural Free Delivery underscores how particular kinds of rural space posed stubborn challenges to bureaucratic administration. Although the coming decades would bring new changes to the American state's organizational structure, none of these changes were tidy or complete. Like musical notes lingering long after a musician has put down her instrument, both the decentralized agency model and the spatial challenges of governance would continue to echo down through the twentieth century and into the present.

# Conclusion

## The Modern American State

"The United States Post Office stands to-day with all American institutions at the threshold of a new era," the high-ranking postal administrator Daniel Roper declared in 1917. Over the preceding half century, the Post Office Department had become what Roper called a "modern postal system." When Abraham Lincoln was elected president in 1860, much of the nation's mail was sorted by hand and traveled by stagecoach and horseback. By 1917, the US Post had become an industrialized organization, deploying automobiles, conveyor belts, punch card readers, electric letter openers, and folding machines in order to process and transport billions of pieces of mail each year. Over that same period, the US Post had grown from a largely eastern institution into a continent-spanning network boasting a range of new services—money orders, postcards, parcel delivery, postal savings banks, and Rural Free Delivery—that wove the mail system deep into the fabric of American society. Roper attributed these developments to "modern principles of efficient control" deployed by technocrats like himself.[1]

But the modernization process was not yet complete, Roper lamented, for the nation's thousands of local post offices still lacked uniformity and had yet to comply with the "centralized authority" of professional administrators in Washington. In order to step fully into this "new era," Roper wrote, the institution would have to make a final and decisive break with the 19th century's haphazard and localized operations. As he grandly put it, "The barnacles of the dead past must be stript from the institution."[2]

What Roper considered "barnacles" were the very same features that had enabled the US Post to become such an important institutional force in the western United States in the first place. The decentralized agency model was at odds with Roper's vision of centralized bureaucratic management, but it had nevertheless allowed the US Post and the wider federal government to incorporate a massive amount of western territory over the preceding half century. By delegating mail duties to thousands of local business owners and stagecoach companies, the US Post had spread with remarkable speed, shaping the pace and character of colonization in the West. Its ephemeral infrastructure facilitated a chaotic, unstable, and occasionally fraudulent brand of regional expansion that culminated in the late 1870s and early 1880s. Extending lines of communication into remote places helped Americans like the Curtis siblings occupy distant corners of the region, cementing the state's hold over recently seized Native territory. The US Post's expansive spatial coverage acted as a channel for political and commercial integration as well as territorial occupation, connecting the region's far-flung towns like North Bloomfield to national patronage systems and a growing consumer economy during the 1880s and 1890s. By the early 20th century, the gossamer network had helped transform the western United States from a sprawling and remote territory over which the state had only a tenuous hold into an integrated region occupied by American settlers, industry, and government.

Writing in 1917, Roper believed that the agency model and the gossamer network would soon be washed away by a rising tide of modernization and bureaucratization. His confidence was understandable. Whether in private firms or government institutions, organizations were growing larger and more hierarchical during the early 20th century, overseen by a rising professional class of managers. Technocrats and civil servants in the federal government were taking on more administrative functions, from regulatory commissions to a newly instituted federal income tax. Technology, meanwhile, promised to extend central administrators' reach, as federal officials could use telephones, radios, automobiles, and airplanes to coordinate their bureaus from a distance, receive updates from subordinates, and conduct in-person inspections of remote places.

The kind of governance championed by Roper and other Progressive Era reformers has come to define to the emergence of the "modern" state: the pursuit of efficiency and reform, faith in expertise and professionalized management, and the triumphant march into a more rational age of industry and innovation. Few, if any, of these benchmarks of modernity would have applied to the 19th-century western postal network. It is tempting, then, to follow Roper's lead in dismissing the operations of the 19th-century postal system as "barnacles of the dead past," an anachronistic set of arrangements waiting to be displaced by the emergence of more recognizably bureaucratic structures. Yet many of the characteristics that defined the 19th-century postal system—including the decentralized agency model and the stubborn challenges of American geography—would continue to shape the US Post and the wider federal government throughout the 20th century and into the present.[3]

Even as the US Post adopted new technology and modes of transportation in the 20th century, it often ended up applying the older agency model to these initiatives. During the 1920s, for instance, the Post Office Department started experimenting with carrying mail via airplanes. At first, it turned to salaried government employees rather than private companies to conduct this service. But in 1926, it turned back to the familiar contracting system, paying private aviation companies to carry mail on the government's behalf. Much as it had done with stagecoach and steamship businesses in the 19th century, the US Post ended up subsidizing the burgeoning aviation industry through its mail contracts. And, in echoes of the star route frauds of the 1860s and 1870s, this culminated in scandal during the early 1930s as some companies manipulated the bidding process to win ill-gotten government contracts. The technology had changed, but much of the same decentralized, semi-privatized administrative structure survived.[4]

In the 19th century, the United States had faced the difficult task of extending a universally accessible mail service across the rugged and remote geography of the American West. Those spatial challenges did not go away in the 20th century. Even as Americans flocked to cities in ever-growing numbers, tens of millions of people remained in the countryside. In many rural areas, the costs of providing mail service would continue to outstrip postage revenue. By the 1960s, Congress was allocating more than one hundred million dollars each year towards a "Rural Allowance" to subsidize rural mail service, including payments to private star route contractors. Star routes steadily declined for the first half of the 20th century before making a dramatic comeback in the 1960s: buoyed by the construction of a federal highway system, star route mileage more than doubled over the course of this decade. At the same time, periodic attempts by postal officials to consolidate small-town post offices or rural mail routes met with fierce resistance from primarily western and southern congressmen. Much as it had in the 19th century, the network's rural periphery routinely stymied attempts at centralized reform.[5]

The mid-20th century brought a series of institutional crises for the Post Office Department. Aging government facilities buckled under the weight of a postwar boom in mail matter, even as the department suffered from lackluster leadership, a dearth of Congressional funding, and growing competition from long-distance telephone companies. The breaking point came in 1966, when a backlog of mail at the Chicago Post Office, then the largest postal facility in the world, sent delays and interruptions cascading through the country and paralyzed the national mail service for three weeks. The disruption spurred the creation of a government commission to reform the Post Office Department, which, after several months, came back with a radical call for change: to transform the US Post from a typical government agency into a "Postal Corporation" placed under "businesslike management."[6] In 1970, Congress followed the commission's recommendation and passed the Postal Reorganization Act. This created the modern US Postal Service as an "independent establishment of the executive branch," operated as a fiscally self-sustaining entity that was cut off from taxpayer funding.[7] The legislation marked a turning point for the nation's postal system, changing it from a flagging public institution to a more efficient business enterprise.

At least that was the hope. In reality, the Postal Reorganization Act of 1970 birthed what one historian has termed "a kind of government-business jackalope."[8] The already blurry line between public and private within the nation's postal system became even more muddled. Like a private business, the US Postal Service was expected to generate enough revenue to cover its costs without the help of taxpayers. Unlike a private business, it was legally required to operate in places where it was prohibitively expensive to do so, including rural communities. In fact, this was one of seven guiding principles for the new organization, enshrined into law on the very first page of a 69-page document: "The Postal Service shall provide a maximum degree of effective and regular postal services to rural areas, communities, and small towns where post offices are not self-sustaining."[9] As it had for so much of its existence, the organization would continue to struggle with the tension between providing a universal public service and operating a cost-effective system. But going forward, it was forced to provide that public service without the benefit of public funding.

The late 1990s and 2000s brought further financial challenges for the US Postal Service, as email and electronic communications caused letter writing to plummet. By 2019, the volume of first-class mail carried by the US Postal Service had been cut nearly in half from its peak in 2001.[10] At the same time, the growth of online shopping during the 2010s led to a boom in parcel transportation that has become one of the few bright spots on the US Postal Service's otherwise dire balance sheet. Private carriers lacked an established infrastructure in rural areas that they had long deemed unprofitable. The US Postal Service, with its mandate to provide universal service regardless of location, already had this infrastructure in place. Private companies subcontracted with the US Postal Service to carry their packages over the "last mile" to rural parts of the country. Much like the residents of North Bloomfield making long-distance department store purchases in the 1890s, 21st-century online shoppers similarly rely on the US Postal Service's expansive geographical coverage.[11]

Despite the 1970 Postal Reorganization Act's attempt to reorganize the institution under "businesslike management," its public-private status has created obstacles that few private businesses have had to face, including having its operations subject to direct congressional intervention. In 2006, for instance, Congress passed a law requiring the US Postal Service to prefund future retiree health benefits, forcing it to set aside an average of $5.5 billion annually over the span of 10 years to cover future pension costs. One economist described this aggressive pre-payment schedule as having "no obvious economic logic" and "little precedent in the private sector."[12] Weighed down with this fiscal albatross and in the face of steadily declining postage revenue, the US Postal Service has run an annual budget deficit for 13 years and counting.[13]

The institution's ongoing 21st-century fiscal struggles have triggered a resurgence of some of the very features that defined the 19th century's rural postal system. In 2011, the postmaster general announced plans to shut down some 3,700 post offices whose operating costs far exceeded their revenue, many of them in rural areas.[14] Communities and elected officials rallied to try and save their post offices. One Montana senator issued a statement that could have been written by one of his 19th-century predecessors: "In Montana and across rural America, post offices define communities and serve as lifelines to the rest of the world. . . . We must put sideboards on the Postal Service to prevent closures from disproportionately hurting rural and frontier America."[15] The bipartisan effort succeeded and the closure plans were abandoned. Once again, reformers in Washington, DC, found themselves stymied by communities on the periphery who demanded an accessible public service regardless of their location and the costs that came with providing that service. The nation's star routes, meanwhile, have been renamed Highway

Contract Routes but are still operated by private transportation companies paid through government contracts. In 2016 the US Postal Service disbursed some three billion dollars per year to roughly 8,300 contractors to carry mail along its Highway Contract Routes. That same year, the Office of the Inspector General conducted an audit of the nation's Highway Contract Routes and discovered a familiar lack of centralized oversight. In language that might as well have been describing the 19th century's rural star routes, the report described "limited management and oversight," a "decentralized . . . reporting process," and "no centralized method to manage performance irregularities."[16]

In an effort to cut operating costs, the US Postal Service now operates some 3,400 combined "contract postal units," "community post offices," and "village post offices," many of which bear a striking resemblance to 19th-century post offices.[17] Under these arrangements, the US Postal Service contracts with local business owners to offer a limited range of postal services inside a gas station, store, or other private business. The first Village Post Office in the country opened in August 2011 inside Red's Hop N' Market, a convenience store in the tiny town of Malone, Washington. The storeowners, Cheryl and Johnny Kim, received around two thousand dollars a year from the government to rent out mailboxes and sell stamps alongside their usual offerings of coffee, cigarettes, milk, and beer. Aside from the merchandise on its shelves, this rural western post office didn't look all that different from the one housed by Walter Mobley in his North Bloomfield general store during the 1890s.[18]

The village post office established inside Red's Hop N' Market in 2011 is a reminder that the "barnacles of the dead past" criticized by Daniel Roper in 1917 have not been scraped away by the forces of modernity. Indeed, the US Post is illustrative of a larger pattern: the decentralized agency model has continued to play an important and underappreciated role within the modern American state for the past century. Even during the period spanning the 1930s to the 1960s, a four-decade golden age of bureaucratic management and top-down statism, the federal government continued to rely on a web of "associational" arrangements with state and local governments, private companies, special interest groups, and nongovernment organizations in order to enact policies and provide services.[19] New Deal agencies were often administered at state and local levels and drew widely on the private sector. The Homeowner's Loan Corporation, established in 1933 to help homeowners who were hard hit by the Great Depression, was "a widely distributed and decentralized system" that relied on "local real estate brokers, fee attorneys, and appraisers."[20] Mobilization for World War II and the Cold War further expanded the federal government's centralized bureaucratic apparatus, but many of the federal agencies established during these years, including the Department of the Defense, the Joint Chiefs of Staff, the National Security Council, and the Central Intelligence Agency, continued to use a system of contracts and grants, including procurement contracts to industrial manufacturers and research grants for universities.[21] Great Society reforms during the 1960s, such as Medicare and Medicaid, seemed to mark a culmination of the federal government's top-down, technocratic management. Yet these federal initiatives were often implemented through block grants to state governments, municipal-level agencies, and nonprofit organizations, along with payments and contracts to private firms.[22] The federal leviathan of the mid-20th century was not a bureaucratic monolith. Its capacity had radically expanded, but much of that power flowed through far more decentralized administrative structures.

The modern American state was never able to fully surmount the administrative challenges posed by the nation's expansive rural geography. Instead, it continued to rely on the organizational precedents set by the 19th-century US Post. The clearest example lies in the western United States, where the Bureau of Land Management (BLM) administers some 245 million acres of federal land on which it oversees a dizzying "multiple-use" mandate of activities such as grazing, mining, conservation, and recreation.[23] Since its founding in 1946, the BLM has resembled the 19th century's rural postal network: a decentralized organization vulnerable to political meddling and entangled with local private interests. Powerful western politicians exerted pressure on administrators in Washington, DC, while its dispersed field managers were often accused of acquiescing to local interests. In particular, the BLM's generous allocation of permits and leases to private mining and grazing companies led to the derisive nickname of the "Bureau of Livestock and Mines." Today, each of the agency's roughly two hundred rangers are responsible for monitoring, on average, one million acres of land. This means that the actual enforcement of laws and regulations on federal land often falls on state police departments, county sheriffs, or other local law enforcement officials. In the words of one historian, the BLM "has always been a highly decentralized and fragmented agency."[24]

The US Post's reliance on stagecoach companies and local storeowners during the 19th century foreshadowed a swell of privatization and contracting that came to fruition in the late 20th century. The presidency of Ronald Reagan during the 1980s marked an ideological shift towards free-market, antigovernment policies, perhaps most clearly articulated in Reagan's inaugural address: "It is time to check and reverse the growth of government, which shows signs of having grown beyond the consent of the governed." He then moved to institute a hiring freeze for civilian agencies while slashing the budgets for the Departments of Labor, Commerce, Education, and Energy. Although the Reagan administration may have sought to shrink the federal government, its main impact had less to do with the size of the state than with how it operated and what its workforce looked like.[25] The 1980s witnessed a substantial growth in the number of "indirect" government workers, or employees who were paid through contracts and grants rather than "direct" salaried employees. This rebalancing was especially pronounced in the nondefense sector of the federal government: between 1984 and 1990, the federal government's workforce of nondefense contract employees nearly doubled from 835,000 to 1.6 million people. By 2017, the federal government's total indirect workforce, both military and nonmilitary, had expanded to 5.3 million people, outnumbering direct government employees and active-duty military personnel by nearly one and a half million people.[26]

The sheer size of the government's indirect workforce is a reminder of the need to think more expansively about how the state exercises power. Contractors and grant employees currently perform a dizzying range of functions on behalf of the federal government. In 2018, for instance, the US Immigration and Customs Enforcement (ICE) deported 256,085 people from the United States, using a large bureaucratic apparatus of roughly 20,000 full-time employees. Yet even this display of coercive power and bureaucratic capacity depended on the agency disbursing some five billion dollars' worth of government contracts, or approximately two-thirds of it's 2018 budget. Rather than building and operating an entirely public infrastructure, ICE contracted with private security firms to run detention centers, chartered flights to transport detainees, and paid technology companies for data hosting and analytics. Large state projects—whether conquering and colonizing Native land in the 19th-century US West or detaining, incarcerating, and deporting immigrants today—depend on a much wider constellation of channels than simply coercion and bureaucracy.[27]

The American state's capacity for centralized oversight may have improved since the 19th century, but its reliance on private contractors continues to outstrip its ability to effectively regulate them. In 2019, the Department of Homeland Security's Office of the Inspector General found that "ICE does not adequately hold detention facility contractors accountable for not meeting performance standards." Failure to impose those standards on private contractors had led to overcrowding, inadequate medical care, and the use of solitary confinement. To make matters worse, ICE outsourced the task of actually monitoring these facilities to yet another private company, which was itself faulted for lax inspection practices.[28] The growth of private contracting has further exacerbated geographical challenges of administration facing the American state. With millions of people scattered across the country and the globe, one high-ranking government official acknowledged in 2018 that nobody knew precisely how many people were part of the federal government's indirect workforce.[29] One can imagine Walter Nicholson, the 19th-century mapmaker who struggled to keep pace with the West's ever-shifting postal system, nodding along in sympathy.

At its broadest level, *Paper Trails* is about the large-scale structures, systems, and networks that quietly shape our world. Today, the state is not the only entity that wields this kind of structural power. Technology companies like Google and Facebook have become enmeshed in modern life and exercise enormous influence over society. They define the conditions under which people make decisions and take actions, including the videos we watch, the news we read, the people we date, the clothes we purchase, and the routes we drive. Seemingly minor design changes implemented by Facebook's developers can quietly alter the behavior and attitudes of millions of people. We are living in an "algorithm age," in which the structural power of digital platforms and online networks defines everyday life.[30] Even more so than the US Post, the machinery that underlies these systems quietly whirrs away in the background. Most users have little understanding of how these platforms work or the labor arrangements and regulatory frameworks that underlie them.

Studying the machinery of the 19th-century western postal network holds lessons for thinking about large-scale structural forces today. For one, the arrangements and structures of organizations can exercise just as much influence as their consciously implemented policies. The expansive, semi-privatized, and ever-shifting western postal network may have helped 19th-century settlers colonize plundered Native land, but its breakneck growth was not centrally coordinated by officials in Washington, DC. Western communities, businesses, and politicians drove its expansion on the periphery. If anything, the network's decentralized geography repeatedly short-circuited attempts at top-down reforms. Today's digital networks can similarly gallop ahead of the people tasked with administering them. Indeed, Postmaster General John Wanamaker's 1889 characterization of the postal system—"the machinery is set up and then let alone"—is an apt description of many of the platforms that have come to define modern life. A host of unintended consequences, including the spread of misinformation through social media, racially biased criminal sentencing software, and massive security breaches of consumer data, has led to calls for greater transparency and regulations around how today's algorithms are made, the data they use, and the contexts in which they are implemented.[31]

Structural forces tend to fade from view. This book has attempted to bring one of these structural forces into focus by asking the seemingly straightforward question of: Where? Where were post offices and mail routes located in the American West? Where and when did they spread? How did this geography compare to other government institutions? The pattern that emerged of a sprawling, fast-moving and unstable network opened up a window into the organizational model behind it and the impact these arrangements had on the 19th-century United States. A similar accounting is needed for the networks, systems, and structures shaping our world today, whether government institutions or private technology platforms. We need a fuller grasp of what, exactly, these forces are, what they do, and how they work. Only then can we start to tackle larger questions about what they *should* be. What are their responsibilities? How should they operate? What are their limits? What are their possibilities? These are not new questions; Americans have been wrestling with them for centuries. But they have never been more urgent.

# Notes

## Note on Methods

1. The dataset was based on eight printed volumes produced by Richard Helbock: Richard W. Helbock, *United States Post Offices*, vol. 1, *The West* (Scappoose, OR: La Posta , 1998); Richard W. Helbock, *United States Post Offices*, vol. 2, *The Great Plains* (Scappoose, OR: La Posta, 1998); Richard W. Helbock, *United States Post Offices*, vol. 3, *The Upper Midwest* (Lake Oswego, OR: La Posta, 2001); Richard W. Helbock, *United States Post Offices*, vol. 4, *The Northeast* (Scappoose, OR: La Posta, 2001); Richard W. Helbock, *United States Post Offices*, vol. 5, *The Ohio Valley* (Scappoose, OR: La Posta, 2002); Richard W. Helbock, *United States Post Offices*, vol. 6, *The Mid Atlantic* (Scappoose, OR: La Posta, 2004); Richard W. Helbock, *United States Post Offices*, vol. 7, *The Lower Mississippi Valley* (Scappoose, OR: La Posta, 2005); Richard W. Helbock, *United States Post Offices*, vol. 8, *The Southeast* (Scappoose, OR: La Posta, 2007).
2. U.S. Geological Survey, "U.S. Geographic Names Information System (GNIS)" (Reston, VA: U.S. Geological Survey), http://geonames.usgs.gov/, accessed March 3, 2020.
3. Lincoln A. Mullen and Jordan Bratt, "USAboundaries: Historical and Contemporary Boundaries of the United States of America," *Journal of Open Source Software* 3, no. 23 (2018): 314, https://doi.org/10.21105/joss.00314; Claudio Saunt et al., "The Invasion of America: How the United States Took Over an Eighth of the World," eHistory.org, http://invasionofamerica.ehistory.org/, accessed November 21, 2016; R Core Team, *R: A Language and Environment for Statistical Computing* (Vienna,: R Foundation for Statistical Computing, 2020), https://www.r-project.org/; Hadley Wickham et al., "Welcome to the Tidyverse," *Journal of Open Source Software* 4, no. 43 (2019): 1686, https://doi.org/10.21105/joss.01686; Edzer Pebesma, "Simple Features for R: Standardized Support for Spatial Vector Data," *The R Journal* 10, no. 1 (2018): 439–46, https://doi.org/10.32614/RJ-2018-009.

## Introduction

1. C. W. Thompson to Andrew Jackson Faulk, January 20, 1864, box 1, folder 1, in Andrew Jackson Faulk Papers, Yale Collection of Western Americana, Beinecke Rare Book and Manuscript Library, New Haven, CT.
2. For the Dakota War, see Anne F. Hyde, *Empires, Nations, and Families: A History of the North American West, 1800–1860* (Lincoln: University of Nebraska Press, 2011), 488–92; Carol Chomsky, "The United States-Dakota War Trials: A Study in Military Injustice," *Stanford Law Review* 43, no. 1 (1990): 13–98. For Minnesota's bounty on scalps, see Colette Routel, "Minnesota Bounties on Dakota Men during the US-Dakota War," *William Mitchell Law Review* 40 (2013): 1–77. For Dakota Territory's geography and mail service, see US General Land Office, *Dakota Territory*, 1:1,250,000 (Washington, DC: Major & Knapp Eng. Mfg. & Lith. Co., 1866), https://www.davidrumsey.com/luna/servlet/s/33ohal. E. D. Boyd and Walter L. Nicholson, *Map of Part of the United States Exhibiting the Principal Mail Routes West of the Mississippi River* (Washington, DC, 1867), National Archives II at College Park, Maryland, I, Record Group 77, Records of the War Department, Map 285.

3. For the challenges that the western United States posed for national expansion, see Susan Schulten, "The Civil War and the Origins of the Colorado Territory," *Western Historical Quarterly* 44, no. 1 (2013): 21–46, https://doi.org/10.2307/westhistquar.44.1.0021; Rachel St. John, "Contingent Continent: Spatial and Geographic Arguments in the Shaping of the Nineteenth-Century United States," *Pacific Historical Review* 86, no. 1 (February 2017): 18–49, https://doi.org/10.1525/phr.2017.86.1.18.

4. For industrialization, see William G. Robbins, *Colony and Empire: The Capitalist Transformation of the American West* (Lawrence: University Press of Kansas, 1994); Richard White, *"It's Your Misfortune and None of My Own": A New History of the American West* (Norman: University of Oklahoma Press, 1991), 236–97; Richard White, *Railroaded: The Transcontinentals and the Making of Modern America* (New York: W. W. Norton, 2011); Noam Maggor, *Brahmin Capitalism: Frontiers of Wealth and Populism in America's First Gilded Age* (Cambridge, MA: Harvard University Press, 2017), 96–106, 158–79; Sven Beckert, "American Danger: United States Empire, Eurafrica, and the Territorialization of Industrial Capitalism, 1870–1950," *American Historical Review* 122, no. 4 (October 2017): 1149, https://doi.org/10.1093/ahr/122.4.1137. For the environment, see Mark Fiege, *Irrigated Eden: The Making of an Agricultural Landscape in the American West* (Seattle: University of Washington Press, 1999); Sara Dant, *Losing Eden: An Environmental History of the American West* (Chichester, UK: Wiley-Blackwell, 2016), 1–101. For the theme of conquest and war against Native peoples, see Patricia Nelson Limerick, *The Legacy of Conquest: The Unbroken Past of the American West* (W. W. Norton, 1987), 45–46, 91–96; Jeffrey Ostler, *The Plains Sioux and U.S. Colonialism from Lewis and Clark to Wounded Knee* (New York: Cambridge University Press, 2004), 13–106; C. Joseph Genetin-Pilawa, *Crooked Paths to Allotment: The Fight over Federal Indian Policy after the Civil War* (Chapel Hill: University of North Carolina Press, 2014); Roxanne Dunbar-Ortiz, *An Indigenous Peoples' History of the United States* (Boston: Beacon, 2014), 133–61.

5. The West as a region of federal power was a central tenet of the "new western history" literature of the 1980s and 1990s. See Limerick, *Legacy of Conquest*, 58–60, 138–40, 191–96; White, *It's Your Misfortune*, 87–93, 130, 137–54. For an alternative viewpoint on the role of the federal government in the West, see Karen R. Merrill, "In Search of the 'Federal Presence' in the American West," *Western Historical Quarterly* 30, no. 4 (Winter 1999): 449–73. Major historical works on the 19th-century US Post include Richard B. Kielbowicz, *News in the Mail: The Press, Post Office, and Public Information, 1700–1860s* (Westport, CT: Greenwood Press, 1989); Richard R. John, *Spreading the News: The American Postal System from Franklin to Morse* (Cambridge, MA: Harvard University Press, 1995); David M. Henkin, *The Postal Age: The Emergence of Modern Communications in Nineteenth-Century America* (Chicago: University of Chicago Press, 2006); Winifred Gallagher, *How the Post Office Created America: A History* (New York: Penguin, 2016).

6. John Joseph Wallis, "Table Dg181–189—U.S. Postal Service—Post Offices, Finances, Pieces Handled, and Items Issued: 1789–1999," in *Historical Statistics of the United States, Earliest Times to the Present*, ed. Susan B. Carter et al. (New York: Cambridge University Press, 2006).

7. For the invisibility of infrastructure see Shannon Mattern, "Infrastructural Tourism," *Places Journal*, July 2013, https://doi.org/10.22269/130701; Paul N. Edwards, "Infrastructure and Modernity: Force, Time, and Social Organization in the History of Sociotechnical Systems," in *Modernity and Technology*, ed. Thomas J. Misa, Philip Brey, and Andrew Feenberg (Cambridge, MA: MIT Press, 2003), 185–224. For discussions of information infrastructure specifically, see Paul N. Edwards et al., "AHR Conversation: Historical Perspectives on the Circulation of Information," *American Historical Review* 116, no. 5 (December 2011): 1393–1435; Heidi J. S. Tworek, "Communicable Disease: Information, Health, and Globalization in the Interwar Period," *American Historical Review* 124, no. 3 (June 1, 2019): 813–42, https://doi.org/10.1093/ahr/rhz577. For the visibility of government institutions, see Suzanne Mettler, *The Submerged State: How Invisible Government Policies Undermine American Democracy* (Chicago: University of Chicago Press, 2011); Damon Maryl and Sarah Quinn, "Beyond

the Hidden American State: Classification Struggles and the Politics of Recognition," in *The Many Hands of the State: Theorizing Political Authority and Social Control*, ed. Kimberly J. Morgan and Ann Shola Orloff (New York, NY: Cambridge University Press, 2017), 58–80.

8. For an introduction to digital history and its origins, see Sheila Brennan, "Digital History," *The Inclusive Historian's Handbook* (blog), June 4, 2019, https://inclusivehistorian.com/digital-history/; Sharon M. Leon, "Complicating a 'Great Man' Narrative of Digital History in the United States," in *Bodies of Information: Intersectional Feminism and the Digital Humanities*, ed. Elizabeth Losh and Jacqueline Wernimont (Minneapolis: University of Minnesota Press, 2018), https://dhdebates.gc.cuny.edu/read/untitled-4e08b137-aec5-49a4-83c0-38258425f145/section/466311ae-d3dc-4d50-b616-8b5d1555d231; Stephen Robertson, "The Differences between Digital Humanities and Digital History," in *Debates in Digital Humanities*, ed. Matthew K. Gold and Lauren F. Klein (Minneapolis: University of Minnesota Press, 2016), http://dhdebates.gc.cuny.edu/debates/text/76.

9. Joshua Sternfeld, "Harlem Crime, Soapbox Speeches, and Beauty Parlors: Digital Historical Context and the Challenge of Preserving Source Integrity," *American Historical Review* 121, no. 1 (February 1, 2016): 143–55, https://doi.org/10.1093/ahr/121.1.143; Timothy Brennan, "The Digital-Humanities Bust," *Chronicle of Higher Education*, October 15, 2017, http://www.chronicle.com/article/The-Digital-Humanities-Bust/241424.

10. For more information about Richard Helbock's dataset, see the Notes on Methods. I purchased a CD-ROM of Richard Helbock's dataset that was available for sale online, containing digitized versions of eight volumes that he had published on post offices in different regions of the country: Richard W. Helbock, *United States Post Offices*, vol. 1, *The West* (Scappoose, OR: La Posta, 1998); Richard W. Helbock, *United States Post Offices*, vol. 2, *The Great Plains* (Scappoose, OR: La Posta, 1998); Richard W. Helbock, *United States Post Offices*, vol. 3, *The Upper Midwest* (Lake Oswego, OR: La Posta, 2001); Richard W. Helbock, *United States Post Offices*, vol. 4, *The Northeast* (Scappoose, OR: La Posta, 2001); Richard W. Helbock, *United States Post Offices*, vol. 5, *The Ohio Valley* (Scappoose, OR: La Posta, 2002); Richard W. Helbock, *United States Post Offices*, vol. 6, *The Mid Atlantic* (Scappoose, OR: La Posta, 2004); Richard W. Helbock, *United States Post Offices*, vol. 7, *The Lower Mississippi Valley* (Scappoose, OR: La Posta, 2005); Richard W. Helbock, *United States Post Offices*, vol. 8, *The Southeast* (Scappoose, OR: La Posta, 2007).

11. Several projects have taken similar approaches to mapping post offices, but most of them have focused on relatively small areas. See John A. Alwin, "Post Office Locations and the Historical Geographer: A Montana Example," *Professional Geographer* 26, no. 2 (1974): 183–86, https://doi.org/10.1111/j.0033-0124.1974.00183.x; James R. Shortridge, "The Post Office Frontier in Kansas," *Journal of the West* 13 (July 1974): 83–97; Morton D. Winsberg, "The Advance of Florida's Frontier as Determined from Post Office Openings," *Florida Historical Quarterly* 72, no. 2 (October 1993): 189–99; Kenneth E. Lewis, "Mapping Antebellum Euro-American Settlement Spread in Southern Lower Michigan," *Michigan Historical Review* 30, no. 2 (Fall 2004): 105–34; Andrew Allen, "Post Offices as a Measure of Nebraska's Settlement Frontier" (master's thesis, University of Nebraska–Lincoln, 2011), http://kuscholarworks.ku.edu/bitstream/handle/1808/7835/Allen_ku_0099M_11532_DATA_1.pdf. Gustavo Velasco has conducted a similar study of the role of postal infrastructure in the context of western Canada in Gustavo Velasco, "Natural Resources, State Formation and the Institutions of Settler Capitalism: The Case of Western Canada, 1850–1914" (PhD diss., London School of Economics and Political Science, 2016), 149–221, http://etheses.lse.ac.uk/3437/; Gustavo Velasco, "The Post, the Railroad, and the State: An HGIS Approach to Study Western Canada Settlement, 1850–1900," in *The Routledge Companion to Spatial History*, ed. Ian Gregory, Don DeBats, and Don Lafreniere (London: Routledge, 2018), 375–94. Other examples of mapping postal systems include Zef Segal, "Communication and State Construction: The

Postal Service in German States, 1815–1866," *Journal of Interdisciplinary History* 44, no. 4 (2014): 453–73, https://doi.org/10.1162/JINH_a_00610; Florian Ploeckl, "It's All in the Mail: The Economic Geography of the German Empire," School of Economics Working Paper (University of Adelaide, School of Economics, April 2015), https://ideas.repec.org/p/adl/wpaper/2015-12.html; Nicolas Verdier and Ludovic Chalonge, "The Issue of Scales in Geohistory. Post Offices from the 18th Century to the Present Day," *Cybergeo: European Journal of Geography*, July 25, 2018, https://doi.org/10.4000/cybergeo.29197.

12. *1889 Annual Report of the Postmaster General* (Washington, DC: Government Printing Office, 1889), 3.

13. Many thanks to John Gerring and Jon Rogowski for supplying international postal data from the Universal Postal Union. Gerring and Rogowski's team transcribed data from Union Postale Universelle, *Statistique Générale du Service Postal Publieé par le Bureau International: Année 1889* (Berne: Imprimerie Suter & Lierow, 1891). See also *1889 Annual Report of the Postmaster General*, 231, 254. There were 26,385 US post offices operating in 2018. United States Postal Service Historian, "Pieces of Mail Handled, Number of Post Offices, Income, and Expenses Since 1789," United States Postal Service, February 2019, https://about.usps.com/who-we-are/postal-history/pieces-of-mail-since-1789.pdf. Comparisons to private companies reflect numbers from 2019. "Location Facts: United States," Walmart corporate website, https://corporate.walmart.com/our-story/locations/united-states, accessed September 15, 2019; Wells Fargo, "Wells Fargo Reports $6.2 Billion in Quarterly Net Income; Diluted EPS of $1.30," July 16, 2019, https://newsroom.wf.com/press-release/corporate-and-financial/wells-fargo-reports-62-billion-quarterly-net-income-diluted; Walgreens Newsroom, "Facts & FAQs," https://news.walgreens.com/fact-sheets/frequently-asked-questions.htm, accessed September 15, 2019; "Ranking the Top 50 Fast-Food Chains in America," *QSR Magazine*, August 5, 2019, https://www.qsrmagazine.com/content/qsr50-2019-top-50-chart, accessed September 15, 2019.

14. *1889 Annual Report of the Postmaster General*, 3.

15. Door-to-door mail delivery was first inaugurated in 1863, but through the end of the 19th century was only offered in large cities. 37th Congress, 3rd Session, "Ch. 71: An Act to Amend the Laws Relating to the Post-Office Department," Statutes at Large, March 3, 1863.

16. The note on methods provides more documentation about the technical challenges of mapping post offices using this dataset.

17. As Alejandra Dubcovsky notes, communication networks are as much "about limits, boundaries, and exclusions" as they are about connections. Alejandra Dubcovsky, "Communication in Colonial North America," *History Compass* 15, no. 9 (September 2017): 4, https://doi.org/10.1111/hic3.12408.

18. In 1864 there were 2,084 post offices west of the Kansas/Missouri border. In 1889, there were 10,777 post offices. *1864 Annual Report of the Postmaster General* (Washington, DC: Government Printing Office, 1864), 57; *1889 Annual Report of the Postmaster General*, 231.

19. *1889 Annual Report of the Postmaster General*, 230–31. Figures calculated from the *Annual Report of the Postmaster General* between 1865–1889.

20. Calculated from yearly tallies of the *Annual Report of the Postmaster General*, 1865–1900. Between 1865 and 1900, the median percentage of postmasters who were removed, resigned, or died in office each year was 18.3 percent. The lowest annual percentage was 13.2 percent, and the highest was 36.9 percent. Over that same time there were some 325,000 combined changes to the nation's workforce of postmasters.

21. William Dudley Foulke, *Fighting the Spoilsmen: Reminiscences of the Civil Service Reform Movement* (G. P. Putnam's Sons, 1919), 54–64; Dorothy G. Fowler, *The Cabinet Politician: The Postmasters General, 1829–1909* (New York: Columbia University Press, 1943); Scott C.

James, "Patronage Regimes and American Party Development from 'The Age of Jackson' to the Progressive Era," *British Journal of Political Science* 36, no. 1 (2006): 39–60, https://doi.org/10.1017/S0007123406000032.

22. My thinking on the agency model has been influenced by the work of Natalie Marine-Street. Natalie Marine-Street, "Agents Wanted: Sales, Gender, and the Making of Consumer Markets in America, 1830–1930" (PhD diss., Stanford University, 2016), https://searchworks.stanford.edu/view/11616850. See also Sharon Ann Murphy, "Selecting Risks in an Anonymous World: The Agency System for Life Insurance in Antebellum America," *Business History Review* 82, no. 1 (April 2008): 1–30.

23. Max Weber, *Economy and Society*, ed. Guenther Roth and Claus Wittich (Berkeley: University of California Press, 1978), 956–58. For an overview of Weber's role in shaping conceptions of the state, see Ann Shola Orloff and Kimberly J. Morgan, "Introduction: The Many Hands of the State," in *The Many Hands of the State: Theorizing Political Authority and Social Control*, ed. Kimberly J. Morgan and Ann Shola Orloff (New York: Cambridge University Press, 2017), 5–7.

24. Richard White, "What Is Spatial History?," *The Spatial History Project*, 2010, 1–36; Jo Guldi, "What Is the Spatial Turn?," Spatial Humanities, Scholar's Lab, University of Virginia, 2011, http://spatial.scholarslab.org/spatial-turn/.

25. On the role of scale in history, see Sebouh David Aslanian et al., "AHR Conversation How Size Matters: The Question of Scale in History," *American Historical Review* 118, no. 5 (December 2013): 1431–72, https://doi.org/10.1093/ahr/118.5.1431; Bernhard Struck, Kate Ferris, and Jacques Revel, "Introduction: Space and Scale in Transnational History," *International History Review* 33, no. 4 (December 1, 2011): 573–84, https://doi.org/10.1080/07075332.2011.620735. On the relationship between structure and individuals: Anthony Giddens, *The Constitution of Society: Outline of the Theory of Structuration* (Berkeley: University of California Press, 1979), 1–40; William H. Sewell, "A Theory of Structure: Duality, Agency, and Transformation," *American Journal of Sociology* 98, no. 1 (July 1992): 1–29, https://doi.org/10.2307/2781191; William Roy, *Socializing Capital: The Rise of the Large Industrial Corporation in America* (Princeton, NJ: Princeton University Press, 1997), 13–14; Walter Johnson, "On Agency," *Journal of Social History* 37, no. 1 (Autumn 2003): 116–18.

26. For the Pacific world during this period, see Kornel Chang, *Pacific Connections: The Making of the U.S.-Canadian Borderlands* (Berkeley: University of California Press, 2012).

27. For the power of individual states during this period, see William J. Novak, *The People's Welfare: Law and Regulation in Nineteenth-Century America* (Chapel Hill: University of North Carolina Press, 1996); Gary Gerstle, *Liberty and Coercion: The Paradox of American Government from the Founding to the Present* (Princeton, NJ: Princeton University Press, 2015). On federalism, see Kimberley S. Johnson, *Governing the American State: Congress and the New Federalism, 1877–1929* (Princeton, NJ: Princeton University Press, 2006).

28. Cameron Blevins, Yan Wu, and Steven Braun, *Paper Trails* website, http://gossamernetwork.com.

29. For a discussion of digital history's contributions to narrative form, see Arguing with Digital History working group, "Digital History and Argument" (White paper, Roy Rosenzweig Center for History and New Media, November 13, 2017), https://rrchnm.org/wordpress/wp-content/uploads/2017/11/digital-history-and-argument.RRCHNM.pdf.

## Chapter 1

1. I draw these observations from visits to the federal immigration court in Boston, Massachusetts, in September 2018 and from reflection essays written by my students after

attending similar hearings. Nick Miroff and Maria Sacchetti, "Burgeoning Court Backlog of More than 850,000 Cases Undercuts Trump Immigration Agenda," *Washington Post*, May 1, 2019, available online at https://www.washingtonpost.com/immigration/burgeoning-court-backlog-of-more-than-850000-cases-undercuts-trump-immigration-agenda/2019/05/01/09c0b84a-6b69-11e9-a66d-a82d3f3d96d5_story.html.

2. Max Weber, *Economy and Society*, ed. Guenther Roth and Claus Wittich (Berkeley: University of California Press, 1978), 956–58; Max Weber, "Politics as a Vocation," in *From Max Weber: Essays in Sociology*, ed. H. H. Gerth and C. Wright Mills (New York: Oxford University Press, 1946), 78. For an overview of Weber's role in shaping conceptions of the state, see Ann Shola Orloff and Kimberly J. Morgan, "Introduction: The Many Hands of the State," in *The Many Hands of the State: Theorizing Political Authority and Social Control*, ed. Kimberly J. Morgan and Ann Shola Orloff (New York: Cambridge University Press, 2017), 5–7. Weber's ideal type of bureaucracy was based on the early 20th-century Prussian civil service with which he was most familiar, but has since become something like a universal framework of bureaucracy.

3. William J. Novak, "The Myth of the 'Weak' American State," *American Historical Review* 113, no. 3 (June 2008): 752–72, https://doi.org/10.1086/ahr.113.3.752.

4. For an overview of the state in the early republic, see Ariel Ron and Gautham Rao, "Introduction: Taking Stock of the State in Nineteenth-Century America," *Journal of the Early Republic* 38, no. 1 (March 2018): 61–66, https://doi.org/10.1353/jer.2018.0002. Max M. Edling, *A Hercules in the Cradle: War, Money, and the American State, 1783–1867* (Chicago: University of Chicago Press, 2014); Hannah Farber, "State-Building after War's End: A Government Financier Adjusts His Portfolio for Peace," *Journal of the Early Republic* 38, no. 1 (March 2018): 67–76, https://doi.org/10.1353/jer.2018.0003; Michele Landis Dauber, *The Sympathetic State: Disaster Relief and the Origins of the American Welfare State* (Chicago: University of Chicago Press, 2013); John Lauritz Larson, *Internal Improvement: National Public Works and the Promise of Popular Government in the Early United States* (Chapel Hill: University of North Carolina Press, 2001); Gautham Rao, *National Duties: Custom Houses and the Making of the American State* (Chicago: University of Chicago Press, 2016); Richard R. John, *Spreading the News: The American Postal System from Franklin to Morse* (Cambridge, MA: Harvard University Press, 1995); Robin L. Einhorn, *American Taxation, American Slavery* (Chicago: University of Chicago Press, 2008); David F. Ericson, *Slavery in the American Republic: Developing the Federal Government, 1791–1861* (Lawrence: University of Kansas Press, 2011).

5. Richard Franklin Bensel, *Yankee Leviathan: The Origins of Central State Authority in America, 1859–1877* (Cambridge: Cambridge University Press, 1990); Gregory P. Downs, *After Appomattox: Military Occupation and the Ends of War* (Cambridge, MA: Harvard University Press, 2015); Stephen J. Rockwell, *Indian Affairs and the Administrative State in the Nineteenth Century* (Cambridge: Cambridge University Press, 2010); C. Joseph Genetin-Pilawa, *Crooked Paths to Allotment: The Fight over Federal Indian Policy after the Civil War* (Chapel Hill: University of North Carolina Press, 2014); Richard Edwards, Jacob K. Friefeld, and Rebecca S. Wingo, *Homesteading the Plains: Toward a New History* (Lincoln, NE: University of Nebraska Press, 2017). For an overview of the American state during the postwar period, see Susan J. Pearson, "A New Birth of Regulation: The State of the State after the Civil War," *Journal of the Civil War Era* 5, no. 3 (2015): 422–39.

6. Nicholas R. Parrillo, *Against the Profit Motive: The Salary Revolution in American Government, 1780–1940* (New Haven, CT: Yale University Press, 2013); Brian Balogh, *A Government Out of Sight: The Mystery of National Authority in Nineteenth-Century America* (Cambridge: Cambridge University Press, 2009); Gary Gerstle, *Liberty and Coercion: The Paradox of American Government from the Founding to the Present* (Princeton, NJ: Princeton University Press, 2015); Bethel Saler, *The Settlers' Empire: Colonialism and State Formation*

*in America's Old Northwest* (Philadelphia: University of Pennsylvania Press, 2014); Lori J. Daggar, "The Mission Complex: Economic Development, 'Civilization,' and Empire in the Early Republic," *Journal of the Early Republic* 36, no. 3 (September 2016): 467–91, https://doi.org/10.1353/jer.2016.0044.

7. For the relationship between metaphorical versus material treatments of space, see Karen Halttunen, "Groundwork: American Studies in Place—Presidential Address to the American Studies Association, November 4, 2005," *American Quarterly* 58, no. 1 (April 2006): 2–3. Geographers, not surprisingly, have thought much more critically and materially about the spatial dimensions of the state. See, for instance, John Agnew, "The Territorial Trap: The Geographical Assumptions of International Relations Theory," *Review of International Political Economy* 1, no. 1 (1994): 53–80; Neil Brenner and Stuart Elden, "Henri Lefebvre on State, Space, Territory," *International Political Sociology* 3, no. 4 (December 2009): 353–77, https://doi.org/10.1111/j.1749-5687.2009.00081.x; Neil Brenner et al., "Introduction: State Space in Question," in *State/Space: A Reader*, ed. Neil Brenner et al. (Malden, MA: Blackwell, 2003), 1–26.; Stuart Elden, *The Birth of Territory* (Chicago: University of Chicago Press, 2013). Major historical works that discuss the relationship between space and state power include Thongchai Winichakul, *Siam Mapped: A History of the Geo-Body of a Nation* (Honolulu: University of Hawai'i Press, 1997); James C. Scott, *Seeing Like a State: How Certain Schemes to Improve the Human Condition Have Failed* (New Haven, CT: Yale University Press, 1999); Lauren Benton, *A Search for Sovereignty: Law and Geography in European Empires, 1400–1900* (Cambridge: Cambridge University Press, 2010); Charles S. Maier, *Once Within Borders: Territories of Power, Wealth, and Belonging since 1500* (Cambridge, MA: Belknap Press of Harvard University Press, 2016); Vanessa Ogle, "Archipelago Capitalism: Tax Havens, Offshore Money, and the State, 1950s–1970s," *American Historical Review* 122, no. 5 (December 2017): 1431–58, https://doi.org/10.1093/ahr/122.5.1431; Ruth Mostern, "The Spatial History of State Power: A View from Imperial China," in *The Routledge Companion to Spatial History*, ed. Ian Gregory, Don DeBats, and Don Lafreniere (London: Routledge, 2018), 462–78. Exceptions to the lack of attention to space and geography specifically in the context of the 19th-century American state include Rachel St. John, *Line in the Sand: A History of the Western U.S.-Mexico Border* (Princeton, NJ: Princeton University Press, 2011); Susan Schulten, *Mapping the Nation: History and Cartography in Nineteenth-Century America* (Chicago: University of Chicago Press, 2012); Downs, *After Appomattox*; Rao, *National Duties*; Paul Frymer, *Building an American Empire: The Era of Territorial and Political Expansion* (Princeton, NJ: Princeton University Press, 2017).

8. James T. Sparrow, William J. Novak, and Stephen W. Sawyer, introduction to *Boundaries of the State in US History*, ed. James T. Sparrow, William J. Novak, and Stephen W. Sawyer (Chicago: University of Chicago Press, 2015), 4.

9. For the geographical challenges posed by the US West, see Susan Schulten, "The Civil War and the Origins of the Colorado Territory," *Western Historical Quarterly* 44, no. 1 (2013): 21–46, https://doi.org/10.2307/westhistquar.44.1.0021; Rachel St. John, "Contingent Continent: Spatial and Geographic Arguments in the Shaping of the Nineteenth-Century United States," *Pacific Historical Review* 86, no. 1 (February 2017): 18–49, https://doi.org/10.1525/phr.2017.86.1.18.

10. C. W. Thompson to Andrew Jackson Faulk, January 20, 1864, box 1, folder 1, Andrew Jackson Faulk Papers, Yale Collection of Western Americana, Beinecke Rare Book and Manuscript Library, New Haven, Connecticut (henceforth AJFP).

11. *The National Cyclopaedia of American Biography*, vol. 7 (New York: James T. White, 1897), 220–21; George Washington Kingsbury, *History of Dakota Territory*, ed. George Martin Smith (Chicago: S. J. Clarke, 1915), 448–49, available online at http://archive.org/details/historyofdakotaterr01king.

12. Roman J. Hoyos, "The People's Privilege: The Franking Privilege, Constituent Correspondence, and Political Representation in Mid-Nineteenth Century America," *Law and History Review* 31, no. 1 (2013): 101–38, https://doi.org/10.1017/S0738248012000843; Matthew Glassman, *Franking Privilege: Historical Development and Options for Change* (Washington, DC: Congressional Research Service, Library of Congress, April 22, 2015), https://fas.org/sgp/crs/misc/RL34274.pdf; John, *Spreading the News*, 57–58, 240; Kathy J. Cooke, "Who Wants White Carrots?: Congressional Seed Distribution, 1862 to 1923," *Journal of the Gilded Age and Progressive Era* 17, no. 3 (July 2018): 475–500, https://doi.org/10.1017/S1537781418000075.

13. The Pembina Post Office, then in Minnesota Territory, opened in 1851. *1851 Official Register of the United States* (Washington, DC: Government Printing Office, 1851), 605. *1862 Annual Report of the Postmaster General* (Washington, DC: Government Printing Office, 1862), 155. Telegraph construction in Dakota was plagued by a lack of trees to use for poles. James Schwoch, *Wired into Nature: The Telegraph and the North American Frontier* (Urbana: University of Illinois Press, 2018), 28–29.

14. D. N. Cooley to Andrew Jackson Faulk, August 9, 1866, box 1, folder 2, AJFP.

15. Alexander Delmar to Andrew Jackson Faulk, December 5, 1867, box 1, folder 5; Department of the Interior, General Land Office to Andrew Jackson Faulk, August 10, 1868, box 1, folder 7; Department of the State, State of Texas to Andrew Jackson Faulk, December 8, 1868, box 1, folder 7, AJFP. John H. Brodhead to Andrew Jackson Faulk, October 26, 1866, box 1, folder 2; George H. Merrill to Andrew Jackson Faulk, November 20, 1868, box 1, folder 7, AJFP.

16. Charles E. Hedges to Andrew Jackson Faulk, October 23, 1867, and John L. Jolley to Andrew Jackson Faulk, October 18, 1867, box 1, folder 5, AJFP.

17. Andrew Jackson Faulk to C. E. M., Chief Clerk for Office Indian Affairs, March 23, 1867, box 1, folder 3; Charles E. Hedges to A. J. Faulk, October 23, 1867, box 1, folder 5, AJFP.

18. Andrew Faulk to William Seward, August 9, 1866, box 1, folder 2, Andrew Jackson Faulk Letters and Speeches, Newberry Library, Chicago, Illinois, Ayer.MS.3070. For the larger context of "loyalty oaths," see Anne Sarah Rubin, *A Shattered Nation: The Rise and Fall of the Confederacy, 1861–1868* (Chapel Hill: University of North Carolina Press, 2005), 164–71.

19. Elliott West, *The Last Indian War: The Nez Perce Story* (New York: Oxford University Press, 2009); Elliott West, "Reconstructing Race," *Western Historical Quarterly* 34, no. 1 (April 2003): 6–26. See also Stacey L. Smith, "Beyond North and South: Putting the West in the Civil War and Reconstruction," *Journal of the Civil War Era* 6, no. 4 (November 2016): 566–91, https://doi.org/10.1353/cwe.2016.0073.

20. Alfred Howe Terry to Andrew Faulk, June 3, 1868, box 1, folder 1, Andrew Jackson Faulk Letters and Speeches, Newberry Library, Chicago, Illinois, Ayer.MS.3070.

21. Andrew Jackson Faulk to N. G. Taylor, April 4, 1867, box 1, folder 4; S. L. Spink to Andrew Faulk, June 16, 1867, box 1, folder 4; Andrew Faulk to the Department of the Interior, Office of Indian Affairs, August 4, 1868, box 3, folder 41; Charles E. Mix to Andrew Faulk, June 5, 1868, box 3, folder 41, AJFP. See also Andrew Faulk to N. G. Taylor, August 15, 1868 in box 1, folder 2, Andrew Jackson Faulk Letters and Speeches, Newberry Library, Chicago, Illinois, Ayer.MS.3070.

22. P. H. Conger to Andrew Faulk, October 21, 1868, in box 1, folder 1, Andrew Jackson Faulk Letters and Speeches, Newberry Library, Chicago, Illinois, Ayer.MS.3070.

23. "Indians at the White House," *Washington (DC) Evening Star*, February 23, 1867, 2, available online at: https://chroniclingamerica.loc.gov/lccn/sn83045462/1867-02-23/ed-1/seq-2/.

24. D. P. Bradford to Andrew Jackson Faulk, March 4, 1869, box 1, folder 9; Andrew Jackson Faulk to N. G. Taylor, April 29, 1867, box 1, folder 4; W. A. Burleigh to Andrew Jackson Faulk, January 13, 1866, box 1, folder 2, AJFP. For "civilizing" initiatives, see Linda M. Clemmons, "'We Are Writing This Letter Seeking Your Help': Dakotas, ABCFM Missionaries, and Their Uses of

Literacy, 1863–1866," *Western Historical Quarterly* 47, no. 2 (May 2016): 183–209, https://doi.org/10.1093/whq/whw071; Stephen Kantrowitz, "'Citizen's Clothing': Reconstruction, Ho-Chunk Persistence, and the Politics of Dress," in *Civil War Wests: Testing the Limits of the United States*, ed. Adam Arenson and Andrew R. Graybill (Berkeley: University of California Press, 2015), 242–64.

25. Andrew Faulk to Charles E. Mix, March 23, 1867, box 1, folder 2, Andrew Jackson Faulk Letters and Speeches, Newberry Library, Chicago, Illinois, Ayer.MS.3070.

26. Andrew Jackson Faulk to Hon. D. M. Mills and Others, May 16, 1868, box 1, folder 6, AJFP.

27. Craig Howe, Lydia Whirlwind Soldier, and Lanniko L. Lee, eds., *He Sapa Woihanble: Black Hills Dream* (Saint Paul, MN: Living Justice, 2011).

28. General Alfred Howe Terry to Andrew Faulk, June 1, 1867, box 1, folder 1, Andrew Jackson Faulk Letters and Speeches, Newberry Library, Chicago, Illinois, Ayer.MS.3070.

29. "The Black Hills – Letters from Generals Sherman and Terry," *Union and Dakotaian*, June 15, 1867, box 1, folder 3, Andrew Jackson Faulk Letters and Speeches, Newberry Library, Chicago, Illinois, Ayer.MS.3070.

30. Charles H. Graves to Andrew Faulk, May 4, 1867, box 1, folder 1, Andrew Jackson Faulk Letters and Speeches, Newberry Library, Chicago, Illinois, Ayer.MS.3070.

31. *The Official Register of the United States, 1867* (Washington, DC: Government Printing Office, 1867), 709; *1867 Annual Report of the Secretary of War*, vol. 1 (Washington, DC: US Government Printing Office, 1867), 442–43.

32. R. W. Taylor, Office of the First Comptroller of the Treasury Department to Andrew Jackson Faulk, box 1, folder 9, AJFP.

33. "History of the Southern Ute Indian Tribe," Southern Ute Indian Tribe website, https://www.southernute-nsn.gov/history/, accessed September 10, 2019; Charles J. Kappler, ed., *Indian Affairs: Laws and Treaties*, vol. 2 (Washington, DC: Government Printing Office, 1904), 990–95, available online at http://hdl.handle.net/2027/uc1.31210003349790; Jonathon C. Horn, "Brunot Agreement," in *Colorado Encyclopedia*, May 18, 2016, https://coloradoencyclopedia.org/article/brunot-agreement.

34. Patrick Wolfe, "Settler Colonialism and the Elimination of the Native," *Journal of Genocide Research* 8, no. 4 (2006): 387–409; Lorenzo Veracini, "'Settler Colonialism': Career of a Concept," *Journal of Imperial and Commonwealth History* 41, no. 2 (2013): 313–33.

35. Virginia Scharff, "Broadening the Battlefield: Conflict, Contingency, and the Mystery of Women's Suffrage in Wyoming, 1869," in *Civil War Wests: Testing the Limits of the United States*, ed. Adam Arenson and Andrew R. Graybill (Berkeley: University of California Press, 2015), 206.

36. "SAN JUAN: Notes of a Georgetown Prospector," *Colorado Miner*, July 18, 1874, 1, available online at https://www.coloradohistoricnewspapers.org/?a=d&d=CLM18740718-01.2.3; "SAN JUAN: Something About its Mines," *Colorado Miner*, August 22, 1874, 1, available online at https://www.coloradohistoricnewspapers.org/?a=d&d=CLM18740822-01.2.2.

37. Andrew Gulliford, "Alferd Packer," in *Colorado Encyclopedia*, September 3, 2019, https://coloradoencyclopedia.org/article/alferd-packer. See also "A Horrible Story," *Colorado Springs Gazette*, June 6, 1874, 4, available online at https://www.coloradohistoricnewspapers.org/?a=d&d=CSG18740606.2.103.

38. *The Official Register of the United States, 1877* (Washington, DC: Government Printing Office, 1877), 545–46.

39. James Belich describes the postal system as one of the "vectors" that carried the "software" of settler expansion over the Anglo world. James Belich, *Replenishing the Earth: The Settler Revolution and the Rise of the Anglo-World, 1783–1939* (Oxford: Oxford University Press, 2009), 122–23, 184. Geographer Cole Harris similarly describes the underlying processes that underlay colonialism in the context of British Columbia in Cole Harris, "How Did

Colonialism Dispossess? Comments from an Edge of Empire," *Annals of the Association of American Geographers* 94, no. 1 (March 2004): 165–82, https://doi.org/10.1111/j.1467-8306.2004.09401009.x.

40. Two of the landmark books in the "new western history" emphasize these three organizations: Patricia Nelson Limerick, *The Legacy of Conquest: The Unbroken Past of the American West* (W. W. Norton, 1987), 58–60, 138–40, 191–96; White, *It's Your Misfortune and None of My Own*, 87–93, 130, 137–54.

41. Two sources were used to create Figure 1.2. Every two years, the US government published *The Official Register of the United States* for 1877, a directory listing the names and locations of every civilian who worked in the judicial, legislative, and executive branches of government. A separate dataset collected by historian Benjamin Brands provides additional data about the US Army and its personnel. Benjamin Brands, "Mapping the Army: Professionalization and 19th Century Army Posts," *Benjamin Brands Personal Website* (blog), December 11, 2014, http://benjamindbrands.net/uncategorized/mapping-the-army-professionalization-and-19th-century-army-posts-final-project-blog/. Many thanks to Benjamin for sharing this dataset.

42. *The Official Register of the United States, 1877* (Washington, DC: Government Printing Office, 1877), 123, 188, 283.

43. For discussions of the Treasury Department, see Parrillo, *Against the Profit Motive*, 221–88; Edling, *A Hercules in the Cradle*; Rao, *National Duties*. For the history of the Department of the Interior, see Megan Black, *The Global Interior: Mineral Frontiers and American Power* (Cambridge, MA: Harvard University Press, 2018), 16–50.

44. There were 5,096 postmasters, 440 clerks, and 47 letter carriers in the West in 1877. Figures compiled from *The Official Register of the United States, 1877*; *1877 Annual Report of the Postmaster General* (Washington, DC: Government Printing Office, 1877), 6–7.

45. *The Official Register of the United States, 1877*, 545–46; *The Official Register of the United States, 1879*, vol. 2 (Washington, DC: Government Printing Office, 1879), 164–65; Eric Twitty, *Historic Mining Resources of San Juan County, Colorado* (Denver: United States Department of the Interior, National Park Service, 2010), 49; Encyclopedia Staff, "Animas Forks," in *Colorado Encyclopedia*, August 31, 2017, https://coloradoencyclopedia.org/article/animas-forks.

46. Natalie Marine-Street, "Agents Wanted: Sales, Gender, and the Making of Consumer Markets in America, 1830–1930" (Ph.D. Dissertation, Stanford University, 2016), available online at https://searchworks.stanford.edu/view/11616850; Amy Sopcak-Joseph, "Reconstructing and Gendering the Distribution Networks of Godey's Lady's Book in the Nineteenth Century," *Book History* 22, no. 1 (2019): 161–95, https://doi.org/10.1353/bh.2019.0005; Sharon Ann Murphy, "Selecting Risks in an Anonymous World: The Agency System for Life Insurance in Antebellum America," *Business History Review* 82, no. 1 (April 2008): 1–30; James H. Madison, "The Evolution of Commercial Credit Reporting Agencies in Nineteenth-Century America," *Business History Review* 48, no. 2 (July 1974): 164–86.

47. 52nd Congress, 2d Session, "1893 Postal Laws and Regulations," 177–80. This salary ranged from $1,000 to $8,000 at New York City, the largest post office in the country. *1887 Annual Report of the Postmaster General* (Washington, DC: Government Printing Office, 1887), 98. Presidential postmasters oversaw offices that generated more than $1,900 in receipts each year, served four-year terms, and were appointed by the president of the United States and confirmed by the Senate. These postmasters were broken into first-, second-, and third-class categories depending on the size of their post office.

48. In 1871, 96 percent of the post offices were fourth-class offices. In 1889, that number was 95.4 percent, and in 1899, it was 94.4 percent. *1871 Annual Report of the Postmaster General* (Washington, DC: Government Printing Office, 1871), 85; *1889 Annual Report of the*

*Postmaster General* (Washington, DC: Government Printing Office, 1889), 230–31; *1889 Annual Report of the Postmaster General* (Washington, DC: Government Printing Office, 1899), 822–23. For postmasters earning less than one hundred dollars a year, see *1901 Annual Report of the Postmaster General* (Washington, DC: Government Printing Office, 1901), 983.

49. *1877 Annual Report of the Postmaster General* (Washington, DC: Government Printing Office, 1877), 8. In 1877, there were 8,178 star routes versus 958 railroad routes versus 98 steamboat routes.

50. Arthur Harry Bissell and Thomas B. Kirby, *The Postal Laws and Regulations of the United States of America, Published in Accordance with the Act of Congress Approved March 3, 1879* (Washington, DC: Government Printing Office, 1879), 55–63, 92–93, 135–43.

51. *The Official Register of the United States, 1877*, 280–81; *Colorado Business Directory and Annual Register for 1877* (Denver: J. A. Blake, 1877), 187, 190, 193, available on-line at http://archive.org/details/coloradostatebus00gaze. *Colorado Springs Gazette*, September 30, 1876, 2, available online at https://www.coloradohistoricnewspapers.org/?a=d&d=CSG18760930.2.29. For more details on the commission and fee system of the General Land Office, see Parrillo, *Against the Profit Motive*, 162–78. Settlers who lived far away from a federal land office could go to their county court, where a clerk could process the application for an additional fee.

52. Charles A. Lindquist, "The Origin and Development of the United States Commissioner System," *American Journal of Legal History* 14, no. 1 (January 1970): 1–16, https://doi.org/10.2307/844516.

53. *The Official Register of the United States, 1877*, 313. *Annual Report of the Attorney General of the United States* (Washington, DC: Government Printing Office, 1877), available online at https://catalog.hathitrust.org/Record/000521490. *The Official Register of the United States, 1879*, vol. 1 (Washington, DC: Government Printing Office, 1879), 405.

54. *The Official Register of the United States, 1877*, 310–42.

55. *Annual Report of the Commissioner of Pensions to the Secretary of the Interior* (Washington, DC: US Government Printing Office, 1877), 12–14; *The Official Register of the United States, 1877*, 292. For more on pensions, see Theda Skocpol, *Protecting Soldiers and Mothers: The Political Origins of Social Policy in United States* (Cambridge, MA: Belknap Press of Harvard University Press, 1992); Dale Kretz, "Pensions and Protest: Former Slaves and the Reconstructed American State," *Journal of the Civil War Era* 7, no. 3 (August 24, 2017): 425–45, https://doi.org/10.1353/cwe.2017.0061.

56. Margo J. Anderson, *The American Census: A Social History* (New Haven, CT: Yale University Press, 1988), 7–82. Much like postmasters, enumerators were patronage appointments. By the 1900 census, there were 53,000 of these enumerator positions to distribute to party operatives. See Anderson, *American Census*, 83–115. For postmasters as enumerators, see "The Next Census," *Sacramento Daily Union*, September 20, 1879, 6, available online at https://cdnc.ucr.edu/?a=d&d=SDU18790920.2.58&srpos=1.

57. For the Railway Mail Service, see Daniel Carpenter, *The Forging of Bureaucratic Autonomy: Reputations, Networks, and Policy Innovation in Executive Agencies, 1862–1928* (Princeton, NJ: Princeton University Press, 2001), 76–83, 96–102.

58. Other examples of the agency model at work in the federal government include contractors for the US Army and Office of Indian Affairs, overseas consuls, the Weather Bureau, and immigration agents. See Nicole Phelps, "Looking for the National Dream," *Researching the US Consular Service* (blog), August 17, 2017, https://blog.uvm.edu/nphelps/2017/08/07/looking-for-the-national-dream/; Jamie L. Pietruska, *Looking Forward: Prediction and Uncertainty in Modern America* (Chicago: University of Chicago Press, 2017), 108–55; Beth Lew-Williams, *The Chinese Must Go: Violence, Exclusion, and the Making of the Alien in America* (Cambridge, MA: Harvard University Press, 2018), 62–89.

59. Structural power has been extensively theorized across different disciplines, but I have found two approaches especially useful: Susan Strange, *States and Markets* (London: Pinter, 1988), 24–25; William Roy, *Socializing Capital: The Rise of the Large Industrial Corporation in America* (Princeton, NJ: Princeton University Press, 1997), 13–14.

60. Geographers such as Alan Lester and Cole Harris have articulated similar frameworks for understanding the relationship between spatial networks and imperial power. Alan Lester, "Imperial Circuits and Networks: Geographies of the British Empire," *History Compass* 4, no. 1 (January 2006): 124–41, https://doi.org/10.1111/j.1478-0542.2005.00189.x; Harris, "How Did Colonialism Dispossess?"

61. Charles Tilly, for instance, describes states as "centralized, differentiated, and autonomous structures," while Michael Mann defines the state as "a territorially centralized form of organization." Charles Tilly, *Coercion, Capital and European States, A.D. 990–1992* (Cambridge, MA: Wiley-Blackwell, 1990), 5; Michael Mann, "The Autonomous Power of the State: Its Origins, Mechanisms and Results," *European Journal of Sociology / Archives Européennes de Sociologie* 25, no. 2 (November 1984): 185, 189, https://doi.org/10.1017/S0003975600004239; Anthony Giddens, *The Nation-State and Violence*, A Contemporary Critique of Historical Materialism 2 (Berkeley: University of California Press, 1985), 5. For the way in which people conceive of states as vertical, top-down entities, see James Ferguson and Akhil Gupta, "Spatializing States: Toward an Ethnography of Neoliberal Governmentality," *American Ethnologist* 29, no. 4 (2002): 981–1002."

62. Mann, "The Autonomous Power of the State," 185.

63. Even some of the language used when discussing the state points toward an assumption of centralization, such as "central government" or "central state" being used as a synonym for "federal government" (rather than state or local governments). Prominent scholars of the state who actively employ Michael Mann's definition of central government and phrases such as "central government" or "central state" include Novak, "Myth of the 'Weak' American State," 763; Balogh, *A Government Out of Sight*, 3, 76, 155, 225; Gerstle, *Liberty and Coercion*, 314; Saler, *The Settlers' Empire*, 5, 7, 15; Kimberley S. Johnson, *Governing the American State: Congress and the New Federalism, 1877–1929* (Princeton, N.J.: Princeton University Press, 2007), 1–14; Charles S. Maier, "Consigning the Twentieth Century to History: Alternative Narratives for the Modern Era," *American Historical Review* 105, no. 3 (2000): 819–22, https://doi.org/10.2307/2651811.

64. Marshall Henry Cushing, *Story of Our Post Office* (A. M. Thayer, 1893), 277–81; *1882 Annual Report of the Postmaster General* (Washington, DC: Government Printing Office, 1882), xvi.

65. *1889 Annual Report of the Postmaster General*, 7.

66. An increasing number of historians of the American state are emphasizing the power of local state actors on the periphery rather than centralized administrators. These include Andrés Reséndez, *Changing National Identities at the Frontier: Texas and New Mexico, 1800–1850* (New York: Cambridge University Press, 2005); Peggy Pascoe, *What Comes Naturally: Miscegenation Law and the Making of Race in America* (New York: Oxford University Press, 2009), 131–59; Cathleen D. Cahill, *Federal Fathers and Mothers: A Social History of the United States Indian Service, 1869–1933* (Chapel Hill: University of North Carolina Press, 2013); Saler, *The Settlers' Empire*, 13–40; Alice L. Baumgartner, "The Line of Positive Safety: Borders and Boundaries in the Rio Grande Valley, 1848–1880," *Journal of American History* 101, no. 4 (March 2015): 1106–22; Benjamin Hoy, "Uncertain Counts: The Struggle to Enumerate First Nations in Canada and the United States, 1870–1911," *Ethnohistory* 62, no. 4 (October 2015): 729–50, https://doi.org/10.1215/00141801-3135322; Honor Sachs, *Home Rule: Households, Manhood, and National Expansion on the Eighteenth-Century Kentucky Frontier* (New Haven, CT: Yale University Press, 2015), 13–40; Tracy L. Steffes, "Governing the Child: The State, the Family, and the Compulsory School in the Early

Twentieth Century," in *Boundaries of the State in US History*, ed. James T. Sparrow, William
J. Novak, and Stephen W. Sawyer (Chicago: University of Chicago Press, 2015), 157–82;
Laura F. Edwards, "Reconstruction and the History of Governance," in *The World the Civil
War Made*, ed. Gregory Downs and Kate Masur (Chapel Hill: University of North Carolina
Press, 2015), 22–45; Hidetaka Hirota, "Exclusion on the Ground: Racism, Official Discretion,
and the Quotidian Enforcement of General Immigration Law in the Pacific Northwest
Borderland," *American Quarterly* 69, no. 2 (June 26, 2017): 347–70, https://doi.org/10.1353/
aq.2017.0031; Lew-Williams, *The Chinese Must Go*, 62–89; Stefan Link and Noam Maggor,
"The United States as a Developing Nation: Revisiting the Peculiarities of American History,"
*Past and Present* 246, no. 1 (February 2020): 31, https://doi.org/10.1093/pastj/gtz032.

67. William Novak makes this point in Novak, "The Concept of the State in American History,"
338–39.

68. For examples of postal administrator's frustrations and failures to regulate the periphery, see
*1868 Annual Report of the Postmaster General* (Washington, DC: Government Printing Office,
1868), 30; *1874 Annual Report of the Postmaster General* (Washington, DC: Government
Printing Office, 1874), 128; *1875 Annual Report of the Postmaster General* (Washington,
DC: Government Printing Office, 1875), xxxiii; *1876 Annual Report of the Postmaster
General* (Washington, DC: Government Printing Office, 1876), xxxii; *1877 Annual Report
of the Postmaster General*, 165; *1881 Annual Report of the Postmaster General* (Washington,
DC: Government Printing Office, 1881), 31; *1868 Annual Report of the Postmaster General*
(Washington, DC: Government Printing Office, 1868), 30; *1875 Annual Report of the
Postmaster General* (Washington, DC: Government Printing Office, 1875), xxxiii; *1876
Annual Report of the Postmaster General* (Washington, DC: Government Printing Office,
1876), xxxii.

69. Sociologist Theda Skocpol describes this as a "Tocquevillian" model of state power. Theda
Skocpol, "Bringing the State Back In: Strategies of Analysis in Current Research," in *Bringing
the State Back In*, ed. Peter B. Evans, Dietrich Rueschemeyer, and Theda Skocpol (Cambridge
University Press, 1985), 21.

70. For the Canadian Post, see Chantal Amyot and John Willis, *Country Post: Rural Postal Service
in Canada, 1880 to 1945* (Gatineau, QC: Canadian Postal Museum, 2003), 47–48, 57–59;
Velasco, "Natural Resources," 152–55, 168–69. For the Japanese postal system see Patricia
L. Maclachlan, "Post Office Politics in Modern Japan: The Postmasters, Iron Triangles, and
the Limits of Reform," *Journal of Japanese Studies* 30, no. 2 (July 30, 2004): 286, doi:10.1353/
jjs.2004.0044; Janet Hunter, "Technology Transfer and the Gendering of Communications
Work: Meiji Japan in Comparative Historical Perspective," *Social Science Japan Journal* 14,
no. 1 (January 2011): 1–12, doi:10.1093/ssjj/jyq005; Patricia L. Maclachlan, *The People's
Post Office: The History and Politics of the Japanese Postal System, 1871–2010* (Cambridge,
MA: Harvard University Asia Center, 2012), 46, 66–67. For the Russian Post, see K. V.
Bazilevich, *The Russian Posts in the XIX Century*, trans. David M. Skipton (n.p.: Rossica
Society of Russian Philately, 1987), 155.

71. State infrastructure does not follow deterministic rules of demography and geography. If it
did, the Russian postal system would have been more than twice as large as the US Post.
Instead, it was a fraction of the size. Statistics compiled by John Gerring and Jon Rogowski
from Union Postale Universelle, *Statistique Générale du Service Postal Publieé par le Bureau
International: Année 1889* (Berne: Imprimerie Suter & Lierow, 1891). See also *1889 Annual
Report of the Postmaster General*, 231, 254. A closer international state model to the gossamer network were the imperial networks of colonial powers. See Alan Lester, "Imperial
Circuits and Networks: Geographies of the British Empire," *History Compass* 4, no. 1 (January
2006): 124–41, doi:10.1111/j.1478-0542.2005.00189.x.

72. Gerstle, *Liberty and Coercion*, 345.

73. Manu Karuka makes a similar observation about the importance of railroad infrastructure in the settler colonial project. Manu Karuka, *Empire's Tracks: Indigenous Nations, Chinese Workers, and the Transcontinental Railroad* (Berkeley: University of California Press, 2019), 173. The Department of the Interior is another example of the less obvious ways in which federal organizations facilitated settler colonial expansion; see Black, *The Global Interior*, 5–6.

## Chapter 2

1. Benjamin Curtis to Delia Augusta Curtis, September 30, 1886; Benjamin Curtis to Sarah Henrietta Curtis, September 30, 1886, box 2, Curtis Family Correspondence, Huntington Library, San Marino, California (hereafter cited as CFC).
2. Henry J. Curtis to Mary Swift Tucker Curtis, April 7, 1847, box 1, CFC.
3. Philip A. Fisher, *The Fisher Genealogy: A Record of the Descendants of Joshua, Anthony, and Cornelius Fisher, of Dedham, Mass., 1636–1640* (Everett, MA: Massachusetts Publishing Company, 1898), 218, available online at https://books.google.com/books?id=8kNMAAAAMAAJ. For more on the Curtis family, see Annette Atkins, *We Grew Up Together: Brothers and Sisters in Nineteenth-Century America* (Urbana: University of Illinois Press, 2001), 103–15.
4. Jamie Curtis to Delia Augusta Curtis, April 3, 1857, box 1, CFC.
5. Richard R. John, *Spreading the News: The American Postal System from Franklin to Morse* (Cambridge, MA: Harvard University Press, 1995), 160–61; David M. Henkin, *The Postal Age: The Emergence of Modern Communications in Nineteenth-Century America* (Chicago: University of Chicago Press, 2006), 15–41.
6. Jamie Curtis to Delia Curtis, July 9, 1857, box 1, CFC.
7. Benjamin Curtis to Delia Augusta Curtis, August 14, 1858, box 1, CFC.
8. Benjamin Curtis to Delia Augusta Curtis, April 15, 1861, box 1, CFC
9. Jamie Curtis to Delia Augusta Curtis, May 10, 1861, box 1, CFC.
10. Jamie Curtis to Delia Augusta Curtis, March 8, 1863, box 1, Curtis Family Correspondence, Huntington Library, San Marino, California; Atkins, *We Grew Up Together*, 108–9.
11. For the context of letter writing during the Civil War, see Henkin, *The Postal Age*, 137–46; Long B. Bui, "'I Feel Impelled to Write': Male Intimacy, Epistolary Privacy, and the Culture of Letter Writing during the American Civil War" (PhD diss., University of Illinois at Urbana-Champaign, 2016), available online at http://hdl.handle.net/2142/90815.
12. Letter written on May 24, 1863, referenced in Jamie Curtis to Delia Augusta Curtis, June 1, 1863, box 1, CFC.
13. Sarah Henrietta Curtis to Delia Augusta Curtis, January 7, 1864, box 1, CFC.
14. The regional category of "West" consists of all states and territories west of the Kansas/Missouri border. This region went from 1,357,593 people in the 1860 census to 4,943,121 people in the 1880 census. United States Census Office, 8th Census, *Population of the United States in 1860; Compiled from the Original Returns of the Eighth Census under the Direction of the Secretary of the Interior by Joseph C. G. Kennedy* (Washington, DC: Government Printing Office, 1864), available online at http://archive.org/details/populationofusin00kennrich; Charles Williams Seaton and Francis Amasa Walker, *Statistics of the Population of the United States at the Tenth Census (June 1, 1880)* (Washington, DC: Government Printing Office, 1883).
15. *History of the Railway Mail Service: A Chapter in the History of Postal Affairs in the United States* (Washington, DC: Government Printing Office, 1885), available online at http://hdl.handle.net/2027/uiug.30112118440061; Fred J. Romanski, "The 'Fast Mail': A History of the US Railway Mail Service," *Prologue Quarterly* 37, no. 3 (2005): 12–21.

16. For Benjamin's work as a mail agent, see Benjamin Curtis to Delia Curtis, June 29, 1865, box 1, CFC; *The Official Register of the United States*, 1867 (Washington, DC: Government Printing Office, 1867), 757. See also Benjamin Curtis to Delia Curtis, August 15, 1867, box 1, CFC. For Benjamin's transfer West, see Benjamin Curtis to Delia Curtis, March 15, 1868, and Benjamin Curtis to Delia Curtis, October 31, 1868, CFC.

17. Bureau of Land Management, *General Land Office Records*, Accession No. AGS-0351-110, Document No. 1757, November 11, 1874, available online at https://glorecords.blm.gov/details/patent/default.aspx?accession=0351-110&docClass=AGS&sid=pegrp14u.zwm#patentDetailsTabIndex=1.

18. Benjamin Curtis to Delia Curtis, September 7, 1871; Benjamin Curtis to Sarah Curtis, July 25, 1872; Benjamin Curtis to Sarah Curtis, December 28, 1872, Benjamin Curtis to Sarah Curtis, December 28, 1872; Benjamin Curtis to Sarah Curtis, June 2, 1873; Benjamin Curtis to Sarah Curtis, October 24, 1873, box 1, CFC.

19. Sec. 441, "Who May Be Postmaster," in US Post Office Department, *The Postal Laws and Regulations of the United States of America, Comp., Rev., and Pub. in Accordance with the Act of Congress Approved March 30, 1886* (Washington, DC: Government Printing Office, 1887). See also Marshall Henry Cushing, *Story of Our Post Office* (Boston, Mass: A. M. Thayer, 1893), 198.

20. Benjamin Curtis to Sarah Curtis, December 28, 1872, box 1, CFC.

21. Benjamin Curtis to Sarah Curtis, October 24, 1873, box 1, CFC. A credit agent for R. G. Dun & Co. reported that Benjamin's boss was heavily in debt and making only $10–25 a day in sales. See entry for "J. E. Moore" in R.G. Dun & Co. Credit Report Volumes, Washington DC, vol. 24: Santa Cruz, Shasta, Sierra, Siskiyou, Page 185, Baker Library Historical Collections, Harvard Business School.

22. *1875 Annual Report of the Postmaster General* (Washington, DC: Government Printing Office, 1875), 210.

23. *The Official Register of the United States, 1875* (Washington, DC: Government Printing Office, 1875), 732. Benjamin was appointed on May 10, 1875, and replaced on December 27, 1875. United States Post Office Department, *Record of Appointment of Postmasters, 1832–September 30, 1871*, M841 (Washington, DC: National Archives Microfilm Publication, 1873), Shasta County, California, p. 1232; "Domestic News," *Marysville Daily Appeal*, May 18, 1875, 1, available online at http://cdnc.ucr.edu/cgi-bin/cdnc?a=d&d=MDA18750518.2.2. "Postal Changes," *Sacramento Daily Union*, January 3, 1876, 2, available online at http://cdnc.ucr.edu/cgi-bin/cdnc?a=d&d=SDU18760103.2.15.1. See also Henry G. Langley, *The Pacific Coast Business Directory for the Pacific States and Territories, 1876–1878* (San Francisco: Henry G. Langley, 1875), 143, available online at http://archive.org/details/pacificcoastbusi187678lang.

24. Benjamin Madley, *An American Genocide: The United States and the California Indian Catastrophe, 1846–1873* (New Haven, CT: Yale University Press, 2016); Brendan C. Lindsay, *Murder State: California's Native American Genocide, 1846–1873* (Lincoln: University of Nebraska Press, 2012).

25. Megan Black makes a similar point about the role of the Department of the Interior in Megan Black, *The Global Interior: Mineral Frontiers and American Power* (Cambridge, MA: Harvard University Press, 2018), 5–6.

26. "Tribal History," Official Home of the Pit River Tribe, http://pitrivertribe.org/tribal-history/, accessed September 15, 2019; Madley, *An American Genocide*, 243–76.

27. Bureau of Land Management, *General Land Office Records*, Accession No. AGS-0351-110, Document No. 1757, November 11, 1874, available online at https://glorecords.blm.gov/details/patent/default.aspx?accession=0351-110&docClass=AGS&sid=pegrp14u.zwm#patentDetailsTabIndex=1.

28. E. D. Boyd and Walter L. Nicholson, "Map of Part of the United States Exhibiting the Principal Mail Routes West of the Mississippi River" (Washington, DC, 1867), National Archives II, College Park, MD, I, Record Group 77, Records of the War Department, Map 285. For mail routes in 1872 see Benjamin Curtis to Sarah Curtis, December 27, 1872, box 1, CFC.

29. Benjamin Curtis to Sarah Curtis, October 24, 1873, box 1, CFC. Benjamin wrote Sarah from Burgettville, California, and addressed his letter to Jamaica Plain, Massachusetts, a suburb of Boston. For the broader context of homesickness during this period, see Susan J. Matt, "You Can't Go Home Again: Homesickness and Nostalgia in U.S. History," *Journal of American History* 94, no. 2 (2007): 469–97, doi:10.2307/25094961; Susan J. Matt, *Homesickness: An American History* (New York: Oxford University Press, 2011). The Curtis correspondence is part of what David Henkin describes as the rise of a "postal intimacy" during the middle of the 19th century. David M. Henkin, *The Postal Age: The Emergence of Modern Communications in Nineteenth-Century America* (Chicago: University of Chicago Press, 2006), 93–147.

30. Benjamin Curtis to Sarah Curtis, December 27, 1872, and Benjamin Curtis to Sarah Curtis, December 28, 1872, box 1, CFC.

31. Henry Yu and Stephanie Chan, "The Cantonese Pacific: Migration Networks and Mobility Across Space and Time," in *Trans-Pacific Mobilities: The Chinese and Canada*, ed. Lloyd L. Wong (Vancouver: University of British Columbia Press, 2017), 25–48; Elizabeth Sinn, "Pacific Ocean: Highway to Gold Mountain," *Pacific Historical Review* 83, no. 2 (May 1, 2014): 220–37, doi:10.1525/phr.2014.83.2.220; Richard White, *"It's Your Misfortune and None of My Own": A New History of the American West* (Norman: University of Oklahoma Press, 1991), 192–99.

32. Benjamin Curtis to Sarah Curtis, May 10, 1875, box 1, CFC.

33. "School Matters," *Marin Journal*, July 11, 1878, 3, available online at https://cdnc.ucr.edu/cgi-bin/cdnc?a=d&d=MJ18780711.2.25; "Our District Fair," *Marin Journal*, July 24, 1879, 3, available online at https://cdnc.ucr.edu/cgi-bin/cdnc?a=d&d=MJ18790724.2.24; "Miss Curtis' School," *Marin Journal*, 1 July 1880, page 3, available online at https://cdnc.ucr.edu/cgi-bin/cdnc?a=d&d=MJ18800701.2.12.1.

34. Benjamin Curtis to Delia Augusta Curtis, June 15, 1881, box 1, CFC.

35. People west of the Kansas/Missouri border sent $24,369,434.92 between July 1880 and June 1881. *1881 Annual Report of the Postmaster General* (Washington, DC: Government Printing Office, 1881), 678.

36. There are no surviving letters from the Curtis siblings documenting this move, but references appear in California newspapers. "Local Intelligence," *Marin Journal*, December 1, 1881, 3, available online at https://cdnc.ucr.edu/cgi-bin/cdnc?a=d&d=MJ18811201.2.24; "Local Intelligence," *Marin Journal*, May 18, 1882, 3, available online at https://cdnc.ucr.edu/cgi-bin/cdnc?a=d&d=MJ18820518.2.12.

37. For Benjamin's struggles raising an orchard, see Delia Augusta Curtis to Jamie Curtis, June 20, 1883, box 1, CFC; Sarah Henrietta Curtis to Jamie Curtis, November 27, 1884, box 1, CFC.

38. Douglas L. Lowell, "The California Southern Railroad and the Growth of San Diego," *Journal of San Diego History* 31, no. 4 (Fall 1985), available online at https://sandiegohistory.org/journal/1985/october/railroad-8/. Delia Curtis appears frequently as a buyer and seller of real estate in the *Los Angeles Daily Herald*. "Property Transfers," *Los Angeles Daily Herald*, December 3, 1886, 3, available online at http://chroniclingamerica.loc.gov/lccn/sn85042460/1886-12-03/ed-1/seq-3/; "Daily Real Estate Record," *Los Angeles Daily Herald*, January 22, 1887, 7, available online at http://chroniclingamerica.loc.gov/lccn/sn85042460/1887-01-22/ed-1/seq-7/; "Daily Real Estate Record," *Los Angeles Daily Herald*, August 10, 1887, 3, available online at http://chroniclingamerica.loc.gov/lccn/sn85042460/1887-08-10/ed-1/seq-3/.

39. Benjamin Curtis to Sarah Henrietta and Delia Augusta Curtis, February 12, 1885, box 2, CFC.

40. Alan H Patera and John S Gallagher, *Arizona Post Offices* (Lake Grove, OR: Depot, 1988), 63. The vast majority (96 percent) of Arizona's 141 post offices were operated in a similar fashion by non-salaried postmasters who earned less than one thousand dollars a year in fees and commissions. United States Post Office Department, *United States Official Postal Guide, January 1885*, vol. 7, no. 1, 2nd (New York: Houghton, Mifflin, 1885), 770, available online at https://babel.hathitrust.org/cgi/pt?id=coo.31924093025223.

41. Benjamin Curtis to Sarah Henrietta and Delia Augusta Curtis, April 21, 1885; Benjamin Curtis to Sarah Henrietta and Delia Augusta Curtis, August 10, 1886, box 2, CFC.

42. Benjamin Curtis to Sarah Henrietta and Delia Augusta Curtis, May 6, 1885, box 2, CFC.

43. Benjamin Curtis to Sarah Henrietta and Delia Augusta Curtis, May 20, 1885, box 2, CFC.

44. Benjamin Curtis to Sarah Henrietta and Delia Augusta Curtis, June 11, 1885, box 2, CFC.

45. Patera and Gallagher, *Arizona Post Offices*, 63. For details on Robertson, see *Portrait and Biographical Record of Arizona* (Chicago: Chapman, 1901), 183, available online at https://books.google.com/books?id=mgERAwAAQBAJ.

46. United States Office of Indian Affairs, *Annual Report of the Commissioner of Indian Affairs, for the Year 1886* (Washington, DC: Government Printing Office, 1886), 39–41, 381, available online at http://archive.org/details/usindianaffairs86usdorich.

47. Contemporaries remarked on the lack of postal coverage within reservations. One white re-former, for instance, criticized the fact that "the post office goes to the edge of [reservations] and stops" and called the mail a "Christianizing institution." *Proceedings of the Third Annual Meeting of the Lake Mohonk Conference of Friends of the Indian* (Philadelphia: Sherman, 1886), 52, available online at https://catalog.hathitrust.org/Record/100345799.

48. For a history of the reservation, see John Bret Harte, "The San Carlos Indian Reservation, 1872–1886: An Administrative History" (PhD diss., University of Arizona, 1972). For the broader treatment of spatiality and state power on reservations, see Matthew G. Hannah, "Space and Social Control in the Administration of the Oglala Lakota ('Sioux'), 1871–1879," *Journal of Historical Geography* 19, no. 4 (October 1993): 412–32, https://doi.org/10.1006/jhge.1993.1026.

49. Justin Randolph Gage, *We Do Not Want the Gates Closed Between Us* (Norman: University of Oklahoma Press, 2020), 17–51. ; United States Office of Indian Affairs, *Annual Report of the Commissioner of Indian Affairs, for the Year 1886* (Washington, DC: Government Printing Office, 1886), 392, available online at http://archive.org/details/usindianaffairs86usdorich. For other instances of Native peoples using the mail as a tool of resistance, see Linda M. Clemmons, "'We Are Writing This Letter Seeking Your Help': Dakotas, ABCFM Missionaries, and Their Uses of Literacy, 1863–1866," *Western Historical Quarterly* 47, no. 2 (May 1, 2016): 183–209, https://doi.org/10.1093/whq/whw071.

50. Benjamin Curtis to Sarah Curtis and Delia Curtis, April 10, 1885; Benjamin Curtis to Delia Curtis, February 2, 1887, box 2, CFC.

51. Benjamin Curtis to Sarah Curtis and Delia Curtis, April 22, 1886; Benjamin Curtis to Sarah Curtis and Delia Curtis, October 22, 1886, box 2, CFC.

52. Benjamin Curtis to Sarah Curtis and Delia Curtis, August 10, 1886; Benjamin Curtis to Sarah Curtis and Delia Curtis, September 3, 1886, box 2, CFC.

53. Benjamin Curtis to Delia Augusta Curtis, September 8, 1886; Benjamin Curtis to Sarah Henrietta Curtis, September 8, 1886, box 2, CFC.

54. Sara M. Gregg, "Imagining Opportunity: The 1909 Enlarged Homestead Act and the Promise of the Public Domain," *Western Historical Quarterly* 50, no. 3 (July 1, 2019): 257–79, https://doi.org/10.1093/whq/whz044; Richard Edwards, Jacob K. Friefeld, and Rebecca S. Wingo, *Homesteading the Plains: Toward a New History* (Lincoln: University of Nebraska Press, 2017).

55. Sarah Henrietta Curtis to Jamie Curtis, November 27, 1884, box 1, CFC.

56. Benjamin Curtis to Delia Augusta Curtis, May 31, 1889, box 2, CFC. For more on public land policies, see Paul W. Gates, "Public Land Issues in the United States," *Western Historical Quarterly* 2, no. 4 (1971): 363–76; Patricia Nelson Limerick, *The Legacy of Conquest: The Unbroken Past of the American West* (W. W. Norton, 1987), 61; Robert Lee and Tristan Ahtone, "Land-Grab Universities," *High Country News*, March 30, 2020, https://www.hcn.org/issues/52.4/indigenous-affairs-education-land-grab-universities.

57. Benjamin Curtis to Delia Augusta Curtis, May 31, 1889, box 2, CFC. For more on public land policies, see Gary D. Libecap and Zeynep Kocabiyik Hansen, "'Rain Follows the Plow' and Dryfarming Doctrine: The Climate Information Problem and Homestead Failure in the Upper Great Plains, 1890–1925," *Journal of Economic History* 62, no. 1 (March 2002): 86–120, https://doi.org/10.1017/S0022050702044042.

58. Benjamin Curtis to Delia Augusta Curtis, April 20, 1887, box 2, CFC.

59. "Delinquent Tax List of Gila County, Arizona, For The Year Ending December 31 1887," *Arizona Silver Belt*, March 24, 1888, 2, available online at http://azmemory.azlibrary.gov/cdm/ref/collection/sn84021913/id/810.

60. Patera and Gallagher, *Arizona Post Offices*, 63.

61. *The Official Register of the United States, 1887*, vol. 2 (Washington, DC: Government Printing Office, 1887), 413.

62. *The Official Register of the United States, 1889*, vol. 2 (Washington, DC: Government Printing Office, 1889), 465.

63. Benjamin Curtis to Delia Augusta Curtis, February 2, 1887; Benjamin Curtis to Delia Augusta Curtis, April 20, 1887, box 2, CFC.

64. Benjamin Curtis to Delia Augusta Curtis, October 28, 1886, box 2, CFC.

65. Benjamin Curtis to Delia Augusta Curtis, February 2, 1887; Benjamin Curtis to Delia Augusta Curtis, February 16–17, 1887, box 2, CFC.

66. *The Official Register of the United States, 1885*, vol. 2 (Washington, DC: Government Printing Office, 1885), 397–98.

67. Charles Roeser Jr., *Post Route Map of the Territories of New Mexico and Arizona: With Parts of Adjacent States and Territories, Showing Post Offices with the Intermediate Distances between Them and Mail Routes in Operation on 1st October 1883* (Washington, DC, 1883), 1:800,000, Beinecke Rare Book and Manuscript Library, New Haven, Connecticut, call number 842gmd 1883; W. L. Nicholson, *Post Route Map of the Territories of New Mexico and Arizona with Parts of Adjacent States and Territories* (Washington, DC, 1885), 1:760,320, National Archives II, College Park, Maryland, RG28, Records of the Division of Topography, Regional Postal Route Maps Before 1894, folder VIII.

68. Mary Curtis to Delia Augusta Curtis, February 13, 1891, CFC.

69. Benjamin Curtis to Delia Augusta Curtis, March 22, 1891; Benjamin Curtis to Jamie Curtis, June 21, 1891; Benjamin Curtis to Jamie Curtis, July 19, 1891, box 2, CFC.

70. Benjamin Curtis to Jamie Curtis, November 8, 1891, Benjamin Curtis to Jamie Curtis, November 16, 1891, box 2, CFC.

71. United States Post Office Department, *Record of Appointment of Postmasters, 1832–September 30, 1871*, M841 (Washington, DC: National Archives Microfilm Publication, 1873), Shasta County, California, 246–47. *The Official Register of the United States, 1889* (Washington, DC: Government Printing Office, 1889), 476; *The Official Register of the United States, 1891* (Washington, DC: Government Printing Office, 1891), 483. Jamie H. Curtis to Sarah Curtis and Delia Curtis, July 23, 1890; Jamie H. Curtis to Sarah Curtis and Delia Curtis, September 14, 1890, box 2, CFC.

72. Benjamin Curtis to Jamie Curtis, November 8, 1891; Benjamin Curtis to Jamie Curtis, November 16, 1891; Delia Augusta Curtis to Jamie Curtis, March 30, 1892; box 2, CFC.

73. Delia Augusta Curtis to Jamie Curtis, March 30, 1892; box 2, CFC.

74. For the suspicion of suicide, see Elizabeth MacPhail, "Ranching in Arizona, 1885–1891: Curtis Family Letters," *Mixed Brands*, 187, box 2, CFC; "He Was Out of Work" *San Francisco Call*, July 1, 1892, 1, available online at https://cdnc.ucr.edu/cgi-bin/cdnc?a=d&d=SFC18920701.2.29.

75. Delia Augusta Curtis to Jamie Curtis, March 30, 1892, box 2, CFC. For the route of the letter, see Charles Roeser Jr., *Post Route Map of the States of California and Nevada with Adjacent Parts of Oregon, Idaho, Utah, Arizona and of the Republic of Mexico: showing post offices with the intermediate distances and mail routes in operation on the 1st of October 1891* (Washington, DC, 1891), 1:750,000, Norman B. Leventhal Map Center Collection, Boston Public Library, Boston, Massachusetts, call number G4361.P8 1891.U55x, available online at https://collections.leventhalmap.org/search/commonwealth:cj82kj69r. For estimated travel times, see Jamie Curtis to Delia Augusta Curtis, October 19, 1890, and Jamie Curtis to Sarah and Delia Curtis, July 19, 1891, box 2, CFC.

# Chapter 3

1. For the importance of the American West during the Civil War, see Virginia Scharff, ed., *Empire and Liberty: The Civil War and the West* (Berkeley: University of California Press, 2015); Adam Arenson and Andrew R. Graybill, eds., *Civil War Wests: Testing the Limits of the United States* (Berkeley: University of California Press, 2015); Stacey L. Smith, "Beyond North and South: Putting the West in the Civil War and Reconstruction," *Journal of the Civil War Era* 6, no. 4 (November 3, 2016): 566–91, https://doi.org/10.1353/cwe.2016.0073; Margaret A. Nash, "Entangled Pasts: Land-Grant Colleges and American Indian Dispossession," *History of Education Quarterly* 59, no. 4 (November 2019): 437–67, https://doi.org/10.1017/heq.2019.31; Robert Lee and Tristan Ahtone, "Land-Grab Universities," *High Country News*, March 30, 2020, https://www.hcn.org/issues/52.4/indigenous-affairs-education-land-grab-universities. For more on the Republican Party and the West, see Heather Cox Richardson, *West from Appomattox: The Reconstruction of America after the Civil War* (New Haven, CT: Yale University Press, 2007), 73, 155–58; Steven Hahn, *A Nation without Borders: The United States and Its World in an Age of Civil Wars, 1830–1910* (New York: Viking, 2016), 6, 284–85, 359, 391–400. For "Yankee Leviathan" see Richard Franklin Bensel, *Yankee Leviathan: The Origins of Central State Authority in America, 1859–1877* (Cambridge: Cambridge University Press, 1990).

2. *1861 Annual Report of the Postmaster General* (Washington, DC: Government Printing Office, 1861), 38; *1880 Annual Report of the Postmaster General* (Washington, DC: Government Printing Office, 1880), 56–57. Figures calculated from *Annual Report of the Postmaster General*, 1860–1880.

3. Susan Schulten, *Mapping the Nation: History and Cartography in Nineteenth-Century America* (Chicago: University of Chicago Press, 2012), 7.

4. *1882 Annual Report of the Postmaster General* (Washington, DC: Government Printing Office, 1882), 539–40; *1884 Annual Report of the Postmaster General* (Washington, DC: Government Printing Office, 1884), 651–52.

5. James C. Scott, *Seeing Like a State: How Certain Schemes to Improve the Human Condition Have Failed* (New Haven, CT: Yale University Press, 1999).

6. 33rd Congress, 1st Session, "Ex. Doc. No. 121: The U.S. Naval Astronomical Expedition to the Southern Hemisphere, during the Years 1849-'50-'51–52. Volume VI. Magnetical and Meteorological Observations" (Washington, DC, July 13, 1854), 151; Edward Goodfellow, "Walter Lamb Nicholson, 1825–1895," *Bulletin of the Philosophical Society of Washington* 13 (1900): 407–9.

7. Hugh Richard Slotten, *Patronage, Practice, and the Culture of American Science: Alexander Dallas Bache and the U.S. Coast Survey* (Cambridge: Cambridge University Press, 1994), 145.

8. 34th Congress, 3rd Session, "Ex. Doc. No. 17: Persons Employed in the Coast Survey" (Washington, DC, December 23, 1856), 6.

9. Schulten, *Mapping the Nation*, 142, 277. For more on the immense size and impact of the Coast Survey under Bache, see Slotten, *Patronage, Practice, and the Culture of American Science*. For Nicholson's transfer, see Alexander Dallas Bache to W. L. Nicholson, May 1, 1863, Alexander Dallas Bache Collection, American Philosophical Society, box 1. Thanks to John Cloud and Albert E. Therberge at the National Oceanic and Atmospheric Administration for information about Nicholson's time at the Coast Survey.

10. See Arthur Hecht, "The District of Columbia Staff of the Post Office Department Topographer, 1830-1899," *Records of the Columbia Historical Society, Washington, D.C.* 50 (January 1980): 95-96, https://doi.org/10.2307/40067810; Arthur Hecht, "Postal Maps of the U.S. Postal Service in the 18th and 19th Century," *American Philatelist* 93 (November 1979): 981-86; Richard R. John, *Spreading the News: The American Postal System from Franklin to Morse* (Cambridge, MA: Harvard University Press, 1995), 69-71, 101, 221-23. For the broader significance of the Bradley map, see Brian Balogh, *A Government Out of Sight: The Mystery of National Authority in Nineteenth-Century America* (Cambridge: Cambridge University Press, 2009), 221-26.

11. 37th Congress, 2d Session, "H. Ex. Doc. No. 83: Names of Persons Employed in the Coast Survey. Letter from the Secretary of the Treasury, Transmitting a List of the Number and Names of Persons Employed in the Coast Survey, and Expenditures, during the Year Ending June 30, 1861" (Washington, DC, March 25, 1862).

12. For the Coast Survey budget, see Hugh Richard Slotten, "The Dilemmas of Science in the United States: Alexander Dallas Bache and the U.S. Coast Survey," *Isis* 84, no. 1 (March 1993): 26; *1864 Annual Report of the Postmaster General* (Washington, DC: Government Printing Office, 1864), 13, 27, 88.

13. For the launch of this new initiative, see *1864 Annual Report of the Postmaster General*, 13.

14. American Philosophical Society, "Stated Meeting, July 15, 1864," *Proceedings of the American Philosophical Society Held at Philadelphia for Promoting Useful Knowledge* 9, no. 71 (1865): 403-4.

15. The same route does not appear on the subsequent 1869 map of the western postal system: E. D. Boyd and Walter L. Nicholson, "Map of that Portion of the United States of America West of the 102nd Meridian Exhibiting the Post Offices and Mail Routes" (1869), NARA II, Record Group 75, Records of the Bureau of Indian Affairs, Map 277.

16. For a timeline of the Topographer's Office maps, see Finding Aid for Record Group 28, National Archives II at College Park, Maryland, RG28, Records of the Division of Topography, Appendix III: "Chronological List of Post Route Maps, 1866-1884. Filed in the Archives among Records of Agencies Other Than the Post Office Department."

17. To this day, the National Archives stores both maps separately from other Post Office Department maps, in the War Department and the Bureau of Indian Affairs, respectively. E. D. Boyd, "Map of Part of the United States Exhibiting the Principal Mail Routes West of the Mississippi River" (1867), NARA II, Record Group 77, Records of the War Department, Map 285; E. D. Boyd and Walter L. Nicholson, "Map of that Portion of the United States of America West of the 102nd Meridian Exhibiting the Post Offices and Mail Routes" (1869), NARA II, Record Group 75, Records of the Bureau of Indian Affairs, Map 277-79; "Post Route Map of the States of California and Nevada," (1876), NARA II, Record Group 75, Records of the Bureau of Indian Affairs, Map 278. A handful of non-western maps were similarly filed under the Bureau of Indian Affairs. See Finding Aid for Record Group 28, National Archives II at College Park, Maryland, RG 28, Records of the Division of Topography

Appendix III: "Chronological List of Post Route Maps, 1866–1884. Filed in the Archives Among Records of Agencies other than the Post Office Department."

18. Patricia Nelson Limerick, *The Legacy of Conquest: The Unbroken Past of the American West* (W. W. Norton, 1987), 59–60, 70; Malcolm J. Rohrbough, *Land Office Business: The Settlement and Administration of American Public Lands, 1789–1837* (New York: Oxford University Press, 1968); Mark W Summers, *The Era of Good Stealings* (New York: Oxford University Press, 1993), 49–50, 105. For the western trope of a corrupt surveyor, see William H. Goetzmann, *Exploration and Empire: The Explorer and the Scientist in the Winning of the America West* (New York: Alfred A. Knopf, 1966), 573.

19. Paul Stuart, *The Indian Office: Growth and Development of American Institution, 1865–1900* (Ann Arbor, MI: UMI Research Press, 1979), 17–20; Francis Paul Prucha, *The Great Father: The United States Government and the American Indians* (Lincoln: University of Nebraska Press, 1984), 586–89. Stephen Rockwell offers a different take on the Bureau of Indian Affairs, arguing that it was a far more effective agency if envisioned in terms of advancing a project of national expansion. Stephen J. Rockwell, *Indian Affairs and the Administrative State in the Nineteenth Century* (Cambridge: Cambridge University Press, 2010). For the US Army in the West, see Kevin Adams, *Class and Race in the Frontier Army: Military Life in the West, 1870–1890* (Norman: University of Oklahoma Press, 2009), 20–24, 156–58.

20. As roving detectives, postal inspectors gave rise to a cottage industry of memoirs written in the vein of crime fiction, like the series of sketches published by the chief of the division detailing "the many means and complicated contrivances of the wily and unscrupulous to defraud the public." Patrick Henry Woodward, *The Secret Service of the Post-Office Department, as Exhibited in the Wonderful Exploits of Special Agents or Inspectors in the Detection, Pursuit, and Capture of Depredators upon the Mails* (Columbus, OH: Estill, 1886). For other examples see James Holbrook, *Ten Years among the Mail Bags* (Philadelphia: H. Cowperthwait, 1855); Torrance Parker and David Bigelow Parker, *A Chautauqua Boy in '61 and Afterward Reminiscences by David B. Parker, Second Lieutenant, Seventy-Second New York, Detailed Superintendent of the Mails of the Army of the Potomac, United States Marshal, District of Virginia, Chief Post Office Inspector* (Boston: Small, Maynard, 1912); James Rees, *Foot-Prints of a Letter Carrier; Or, A History of the World's Correspondence: Containing Biographies, Tales, Sketches, Incidents, and Statistics Connected with Postal History* (Philadelphia: J. B. Lippincott, 1866). For a discussion of this genre, see John, *Spreading the News*, 77.

21. Postmaster General David M. Key to Hon. Stanley Matthews, June 30, 1876, Parker Letterbook, David Parker Collection, University of Delaware. Many thanks to Richard R. John for lending his notes on this source.

22. Quincy Brooks to Postmaster General Alexander Randall, December 26, 1865; Quincy Brooks to Elisha Applegate, December 30, 1865; Quincy Brooks to Second Assistant Postmaster General George W. McLellan, June 4, 1866, in Alan Patera, ed., *"Your Obedient Servant": The Letters of Quincy A. Brooks, Special Agent of the Post Office Department, 1865–1867* (Lake Oswego, OR: Raven, 1986), 23, 24, 110. Brooks seems to have left the Post Office Department in 1869. *Postal Railway-Car Service: Papers Relating to Postal Railway-Car Service* (Washington, DC: Government Printing Office, 1874), 40–41.

23. Letter from W. L. Nicholson to Henry H. Bingham on January 16, 1882, in HR 47A-F21.2, box 2, RG 233, National Archives.

24. *1868 Annual Report of the Postmaster General* (Washington, DC: Government Printing Office, 1868), 10–11; *1871 Annual Report of the Postmaster General* (Washington, DC: Government Printing Office, 1871), xi; *1873 Annual Report of the Postmaster General* (Washington, DC: Government Printing Office, 1873), xiii; *1883 Annual Report of the Postmaster General* (Washington, DC: Government Printing Office, 1883), 715.

25. Fred J. Romanski, "The 'Fast Mail': A History of the US Railway Mail Service," *Prologue Quarterly* 37, no. 3 (2005): 12–21; William Jefferson Dennis, *The Traveling Post Office: History and Incidents of the Railway Mail Service* (Des Moines: Homestead, 1916); Winifred Gallagher, *How the Post Office Created America: A History* (New York: Penguin, 2016), 159–80. The Railway Mail Service was also an early pocket of bureaucratic reform. In 1881, two years before the federal government even began to adopt limited civil service exams, the Railway Mail Service administered more than three thousand exams that tested clerks on their ability to sort 3.6 million postal cards. Test takers were graded on speed as well as accuracy, and, to add to the pressure, officials broadcast the exam scores for each of the service's nine geographic divisions in the Annual Report of the Postmaster General. See *1881 Annual Report of the Postmaster General* (Washington, DC: Government Printing Office, 1881), 325, 340; Daniel Carpenter, *The Forging of Bureaucratic Autonomy: Reputations, Networks, and Policy Innovation in Executive Agencies, 1862–1928.* (Princeton, NJ: Princeton University Press, 2001), 76–83.

26. As early as 1868 the postmaster general specifically highlighted the utility of postal maps "to the clerks of the traveling (railroad) post offices, in sorting and distributing letters." *1868 Annual Report of the Postmaster General*, 10–11; *1880 Annual Report of the Postmaster General* (Washington, DC: Government Printing Office, 1880), 294. *1881 Annual Report of the Postmaster General*, 454.

27. *1882 Annual Report of the Postmaster General*, 538. For an example of this map, see W. L. Nicholson, *Railway Postal Diagram of the State of Wisconsin Prepared for the Use of the Railway Mail Service*, 1882, 1:700,000, 1882, Library of Congress, http://www.loc.gov/item/98688570. Postal inspectors also started receiving maps upon their appointment in the early 1870s. See Charles Henry to James Garfield, December 27, 1873, in James D. Norris and Arthur H. Shaffer, eds., *Politics and Patronage in the Gilded Age: The Correspondence of James A. Garfield and Charles E. Henry* (Madison: State Historical Society of Wisconsin, 1970), 75.

28. Representative Garfield speaking on April 20, 1878, 45th Congress, 2nd Session, *Congressional Record* 7, part 3:2677.

29. Representative Dunnell on January 24, 1881, 46th Congress, 3rd Session, *Congressional Record* 11, part 1:894.

30. Representative Shallenberger on April 23, 1880, 46th Congress, 2nd Session, *Congressional Record* 10, part 3:2700.

31. *1880 Annual Report of the Postmaster General*, 294.

32. *1880 Annual Report of the Postmaster General*, 296.

33. Kansas State Historical Society, "First Biennial Report" 1 (1879): 29, available online at http://catalog.hathitrust.org/Record/000547922; "Additions to Library and Map-Rooms of the Society during the Year 1878," *Journal of the American Geographical Society of New York* 10 (January 1878): liii; "Accessions to the Map-Room, from May 27th, 1872, to May 26th, 1873," *Journal of the Royal Geographical Society of London* 43 (January 1873): cxxxvi; Peabody Museum of Archaeology and Ethnology, *Report of the Peabody Museum of Archaeology and Ethnology in Connection with Harvard University*, vol. 3 (Salem, MA: Salem Press, 1887), 38, available online at http://catalog.hathitrust.org/Record/000058910; *Catalogue of the State Library of the State of Louisiana, up to March 31, 1886* (New Orleans: E. A. Brandao, 1886), 126, available online at http://hdl.handle.net/2027/njp.32101073752741; *Finding List of Books in the Public Library of Cincinnati.* (Cincinnati: Board of Managers, 1882), 166, available online at http://hdl.handle.net/2027/mdp.39015033601561; *Finding List of the Chicago Public Library* (Chicago: Public Library Rooms, City Hall, 1887), 23, available online at http://hdl.handle.net/2027/uiug.30112084969226; State Historical Society of Wisconsin, "Wisconsin Historical Society Annual Meeting," no. 5 (1875): 12; George M. Wheeler, *Report upon the Third International Geographical Congress and Exhibition at Venice, Italy, 1881*

*Accompanied by Data Concerning the Principal Government Land and Marine Surveys of the World* (Washington, DC: Government Printing Office, 1885), 47–50; *1880 Annual Report of the Postmaster General*, 538–39; *1881 Annual Report of the Postmaster General* (Washington, DC: Government Printing Office, 1881), 4541880

34. 44th Congress, 2nd Session, "Ex. Doc. No. 20: Annual Report of the Board of Regents of the Smithsonian Institution, Showing the Operations, Expenditures, and Condition of the Institution for the Year 1876" (Washington, DC, 1877), 21–23.

35. United States Centennial Commission, *International Exhibition, 1876: Official Catalogue*, part 1, *Main Building and Annexes* (Cambridge, MA: John R. Nagle, 1876), available online at http://archive.org/details/internationalex00commgoog.

36. Bruno Giberti, *Designing the Centennial: A History of the 1876 International Exhibition in Philadelphia* (Lexington: University Press of Kentucky, 2002). I borrow "mastery of territory" from Matthew G Hannah, *Governmentality and the Mastery of Territory in Nineteenth-Century America* (New York: Cambridge University Press, 2000). See also Thongchai Winichakul, *Siam Mapped: A History of the Geo-Body of a Nation* (Honolulu: University of Hawai'i Press, 1997), 113–36.

37. Richard A Bartlett, *Great Surveys of the American West* (Norman: University of Oklahoma Press, 1962); Goetzmann, *Exploration and Empire*; Mike Foster, *Strange Genius: The Life of Ferdinand Vandeveer Hayden* (Niwot, CO: Roberts Rinehart, 1994); Donald Worster, *A River Running West: The Life of John Wesley Powell* (New York: Oxford University Press, 2001); Robert Wilson, *The Explorer King: Adventure, Science, and the Great Diamond Hoax— Clarence King in the Old West* (New York: Simon & Schuster, 2006).

38. On the linear narrative of progress in the history of cartography, see Matthew H. Edney, "Theory and the History of Cartography," *Imago Mundi* 48, no. 1 (1996): 185–91, https://doi. org/10.1080/03085699608592841; J. B. Harley, *The New Nature of Maps: Essays in the History of Cartography* (Baltimore: Johns Hopkins University Press, 2001).

39. *1874 Annual Report of the Postmaster General* (Washington, DC: Government Printing Office, 1874), 7, 265.

40. One map of Colorado from 1862 bears the stamp of the Post Office Topographer's Office, along with similar notations to other maps produced by the Walter Nicholson's office. It is likely that this map was used to prepare the department's early maps of the western United States. Many thanks to Susan Schulten for alerting me to this map. Frederick J. Ebert, *Map of Colorado Territory embracing the Central Gold Region drawn by Frederick J. Ebert, under direction of the Governor Wm. Gilpin*, Philadelphia: Jacob Monk, 1862. 1:760,320. Library of Congress Geography and Map Division, https://www.loc.gov/item/2003630493/, accessed May 20, 2015.

41. Daniel Rosenberg and Anthony Grafton, *Cartographies of Time* (New York: Princeton Architectural Press, 2010); Schulten, *Mapping the Nation*, 28–34.

42. The maps themselves were labeled as "diagrams," and employees in the Topographer's Office often used "map" and "diagram" interchangeably when describing their work. 45th Congress, 2st Session, "H. Mis. Doc. No. 65: Testimony Taken by the Committee on Expenditures in the Post Office Department" (Washington, DC, May 11, 1878), 15, 21.

43. 45th Congress, 2st Session, 15.

44. For salaries of the various employees of the office, see 45th Congress, 2st Session, 3–4. As the title "draughtsman" implies, mostly men performed this labor, although a few women eventually moved into their ranks. Two out of 14 draughtsmen listed in the 1885 Official Register were women: *The Official Register of the United States, 1885*, vol. 2 (Washington, DC: Government Printing Office, 1885), 9. At least two draughtsmen had started as engineers in the West employed on railroad surveys or for local municipal governments. E. D. Boyd served as Denver's city surveyor from 1859–1862, while Charles H. Poole was previously a

surveyor for San Diego County and had worked on a railroad survey in the 1850s. For Boyd, see Frank Hall and Rocky Mountain Historical Company, *History of the State of Colorado, Embracing Accounts of the Pre-Historic Races and Their Remains: The Earliest Spanish, French and American Explorations* (Chicago: Blakely, 1890), 523. For Poole, see Jean Louis Berlandier Papers, Smithsonian Institution Archives, box 5, folder 22, p. 5, 20–21.

45. 45th Congress, 2st Session, "Testimony Taken by the Committee on Expenditures in the Post Office Department," 3–4.

46. Data calculated from *The Official Register of the United States, 1879*, vol. 2 (Washington, DC: Government Printing Office, 1879), 8. Cindy Aron calculated that 16 percent of the Washington's government workforce was female in 1870, and 23 percent was female in 1880. Cindy Aron, *Ladies and Gentlemen of the Civil Service: Middle-Class Workers in Victorian America* (New York: Oxford University Press, 1987), 5, 40–62; Cameron Blevins, "Women and Federal Officeholding in the Late Nineteenth-Century U.S.," *Current Research in Digital History* 2 (2019), https://doi.org/10.31835/crdh.2019.08. The *Official Register* offers clues to the demographics of the Topographer's Office, in which 11 out of 15 of its female employees bear the title "Miss" rather than "Mrs." *The Official Register of the United States, 1879*, vol. 2, 8.

47. 45th Congress, 2st Session, "Testimony Taken by the Committee on Expenditures in the Post Office Department," 15.

48. *1880 Annual Report of the Postmaster General*, 297. For post office applications and site reports, see examples in *Post Office Department Records of Site Locations 1837–1950*, M1126 (Washington, DC: National Archives Microfilm Publication).

49. "Ideal type" is from Max Weber, *Economy and Society*, ed. Guenther Roth and Claus Wittich (Berkeley: University of California Press, 1978), 956–58.

50. Carpenter, *The Forging of Bureaucratic Autonomy*, 3–13.

51. Nicholson's budget was $10,000 in 1864 and $35,000 in 1874. *1864 Annual Report of the Postmaster General*, 13, 27, 88; *1874 Annual Report of the Postmaster General*, 31; *1870 Annual Report of the Postmaster General* (Washington, DC: Government Printing Office, 1870), 38.

52. Letter from W. L. Nicholson, October 1, 1869, House Committee on Appropriations, NARA I RG 233, 41A, F2.22, Papers Relating to the Post Office Department.

53. Letter from John Creswell, May 7, 1870, printed in *Congressional Globe*, 41st Congress, 2nd Session, May 23, 1870, 3710.

54. *1876 Annual Report of the Postmaster General* (Washington, DC: Government Printing Office, 1876), ix; *1877 Annual Report of the Postmaster General* (Washington, DC: Government Printing Office, 1877), x. For employee tenures during this period, see Hecht, "The District of Columbia Staff of the Post Office Department Topographer."

55. See, for instance: Senator Ingalls speaking on June 9, 1876, 44th Congress, 1st Session, *Congressional Record* 4, pt. 4:3710; Representative Blount on January 24, 1881, 46th Congress, 3rd Session, *Congressional Record* 11, Part 1:895.

56. 45th Congress, 2st Session, "Testimony Taken by the Committee on Expenditures in the Post Office Department," 5.

57. 45th Congress, 2st Session, 8, 10, 11.

58. 45th Congress, 2st Session, 16, 15, 5–6, 16. More cautious employees declined to comment, while a few others declared their outright support for Nicholson. See 45th Congress, 2st Session, 10, 11, 14, 23, 24.

59. Dorothy G. Fowler, *The Cabinet Politician: The Postmasters General, 1829–1909* (New York: Columbia University Press, 1943), 144–45.

60. Entries for June 19, 1872, May 15, 1873, June 7, 1873, in James A. Garfield, *The Diary of James A. Garfield*, ed. Brown Williams, vol. 2 (East Lansing: Michigan State University, 1967), 65, 180, 190.

61. 45th Congress, 2st Session, "Testimony Taken by the Committee on Expenditures in the Post Office Department," 3, 6, 9–11, 13, 16–18.

62. Later, a woman named Jessie Tannahill was appointed to the Topographer's Office specifically "by the Indiana delegation" of Congressmen. When she was eventually fired, she penned a letter to the postmaster general pleading with him to reinstate her and appealing to him both "as a kind-hearted gentleman" and as a fellow "Indianan." Jessie Tannahill to Walter Q. Gresham, June 21, 1883, in Walter Quintin Gresham Papers, Library of Congress Manuscript Division, MSS24117, box 10.

63. 45th Congress, 2st Session, "Testimony Taken by the Committee on Expenditures in the Post Office Department," 1–5, 21. For more on patronage during this period, see Aron, *Ladies and Gentlemen of the Civil Service*, 96–135; Sean M. Theriault, "Patronage, the Pendleton Act, and the Power of the People," *Journal of Politics* 65, no. 1 (2003): 50–68, https://doi.org/10.1111/1468-2508.t01-1-00003; Scott C. James, "Patronage Regimes and American Party Development from 'the Age of Jackson' to the Progressive Era," *British Journal of Political Science* 36, no. 1 (2006): 39–60, https://doi.org/10.1017/S0007123406000032; Kate Masur, "Patronage and Protest in Kate Brown's Washington," *Journal of American History* 99, no. 4 (March 2013): 1047–71, https://doi.org/10.1093/jahist/jas650.

64. American Philosophical Society, "Stated Meeting, July 15, 1864."

65. Senator Sargent speaking on June 9, 1876, 44th Congress, 1st Session, *Congressional Record* 4, pt. 4:3711.

66. See Prairie post office in microfilm reel for Yolo County, California, and Sonoma post office in microfilm reel for Humboldt County, Nevada, in United States Post Office Department, *Record of Appointment of Postmasters, 1832–September 30, 1971*, M841 (Washington, DC: National Archives Microfilm Publication, 1973).

67. *1877 Annual Report of the Postmaster General*, 7.

68. *1888 Annual Report of the Postmaster General* (Washington, DC: Government Printing Office, 1888), 94.

69. 45th Congress, 2st Session, "Testimony Taken by the Committee on Expenditures in the Post Office Department," 21.

70. Representative Garfield speaking on April 20, 1878, 45th Congress, 2nd Session, *Congressional Record* 7, part 3:2677.

71. For examples of postmasters leaving these forms blank, see site report for Graniteville Post Office (Nevada County) and post office application for Hot Spring Post Office (Mono County) in Roll 58, California, Mono—Nevada Counties, *Post Office Department Records of Site Locations 1837–1950*, M1126 (Washington, DC: National Archives Microfilm Publication).

72. Charles Burdett in 45th Congress, 2st Session, "Testimony Taken by the Committee on Expenditures in the Post Office Department," 19.

73. *1882 Annual Report of the Postmaster General*, 541.

74. *The Official Register of the United States, 1879*, vol. 1 (Washington, DC: Government Printing Office, 1879), iii.

75. Scott, *Seeing Like a State*; J. B. Harley, "Maps, Knowledge, and Power," in *The New Nature of Maps: Essays in the History of Cartography* (Baltimore: Johns Hopkins University Press, 2001), 51–81.

76. Historians who have emphasized the instability of the western economy include Limerick, *The Legacy of Conquest*, 147, 248; William Wyckoff, *How to Read the American West: A Field Guide* (Seattle: University of Washington Press, 2014), 398; Richard White, *"It's Your Misfortune and None of My Own": A New History of the American West* (Norman: University of Oklahoma Press, 1991), 285. For broader discussions of the unstable capitalist expansion in the West, see William G. Robbins, *Colony and Empire: The Capitalist Transformation of the American West* (University Press of Kansas, 1994), 148. James Belich argues that the

"settler revolution" across the Anglo world was fueled by a similarly cyclical pattern of boom, bust, and "export rescue" from a settler colony's metropole. James Belich, *Replenishing the Earth: The Settler Revolution and the Rise of the Anglo-World, 1783–1939* (Oxford: Oxford University Press, 2009), 5–8, 83–95, 182–209.

77. Jon K. Lauck, *Prairie Republic: The Political Culture of Dakota Territory, 1879–1889* (Norman: University of Oklahoma Press, 2010), 4–11.

78. Belich, *Replenishing the Earth*, 336–38; White, *It's Your Misfortune and None of My Own*, 222–23; Rodman Paul, *Mining Frontiers of the Far West, 1848–1880*, 2nd rd. (Albuquerque: University of New Mexico Press, 2001).

79. Figures calculated from annual reports of the postmaster general from 1878–1883.

80. For an overview of the historical geography of the western interior, see Donald W. Meinig, *The Shaping of America: A Geographical Perspective on 500 Years of History*, vol. 3, *Transcontinental America, 1850–1915* (New Haven, CT: Yale University Press, 1998), 89–167.

81. "Lifespan" figures for post offices were calculated from Richard Helbock dataset. From 1878 to 1883, 5,657 post offices were established west of the Kansas/Missouri border, with 2,657 of those offices shutting down or changing names in less than 10 years from when they were established. Of those western post offices, 438 of them either shut down or changed names in the same calendar year they were established.

82. Pima County, Arizona Territory, in United States Post Office Department, *Record of Appointment of Postmasters*.

83. Beth Lew-Williams, *The Chinese Must Go: Violence, Exclusion, and the Making of the Alien in America* (Cambridge, MA: Harvard University Press, 2018), 53–89; Hidetaka Hirota, "Exclusion on the Ground: Racism, Official Discretion, and the Quotidian Enforcement of General Immigration Law in the Pacific Northwest Borderland," *American Quarterly* 69, no. 2 (June 2017): 347–70, https://doi.org/10.1353/aq.2017.0031.

84. Karl Jacoby, *Crimes against Nature: Squatters, Poachers, Thieves, and the Hidden History of American Conservation* (Berkeley: University of California Press, 2014), 122–29.

85. *Proceedings in the Trial of the Case of the United States vs. John W. Dorsey, John R. Miner, John M. Peck, Stephen W. Dorsey, Harvey M. Vaile, Montfort C. Rerdell, Thomas J. Brady, and William H. Turner for Conspiracy*, vol. 1 (Washington, DC: Government Printing Office, 1882), 505–11, available online at http://hdl.handle.net/2027/hvd.32044086291325.

# Chapter 4

1. Richard R. John, *Spreading the News: The American Postal System from Franklin to Morse* (Cambridge, MA: Harvard University Press, 1995), 99–100; "The Romance of the Pony Express," *Joseph M. Adelman* (blog), April 14, 2015, https://josephadelman.com/2015/04/14/the-romance-of-the-pony-express/; W. Turrentine Jackson, "A New Look at Wells Fargo, Stage-Coaches and the Pony Express," *California Historical Society Quarterly* 45, no. 4 (December 1966): 291–324. For letter rates, see Steven C. Walske and Richard C. Frajola, *Mails of the Westward Expansion, 1803 to 1861* (Western Cover Society, 2015), 218; Sam Williamson, "Seven Ways to Compute the Relative Value of a U.S. Dollar Amount, 1774 to Present," Measuring Worth, 2019, https://www.measuringworth.com/uscompare/.

2. *1879 Annual Report of the Postmaster General* (Washington, DC: Government Printing Office, 1879), 19, 60–61.

3. For communications and mail during the colonial era, see Katherine Grandjean, *American Passage: The Communications Frontier in Early New England* (Cambridge, MA: Harvard University Press, 2015); Alejandra Dubcovsky, *Informed Power: Communication in the Early American South* (Cambridge, MA: Harvard University Press, 2016); Joseph M.

Adelman, *Revolutionary Networks: The Business and Politics of Printing the News, 1763–1789* (Baltimore: Johns Hopkins University Press, 2019). For a map and data of major postal routes in 1839, see Laura Eckstein, "Post Roads 1839," *Laura Eckstein Personal Blog* (blog), January 20, 2015, http://lauraneckstein.com/blog/1839postroads/; Laura Newman Eckstein, *Post Roads 1839*, 2015, https://github.com/lauraneckstein/postroads1839. The power to designate mail routes was part of Congress's role as what Kimberley Johnson describes as "the linchpin of Gilded Age and Progressive Era politics." Kimberley S. Johnson, *Governing the American State: Congress and the New Federalism, 1877–1929* (Princeton, NJ: Princeton University Press, 2006), 16.

4. See, for instance, petition of the citizens of Oregon, July 16, 1869 (referred to committee January 10, 1870), House Committee on the Post Office and Post Roads, NARA I RG 233, 41A, F19.6, folder 3: December 9, 1869 to January 28, 1870.

5. For a history of petitioning, see John, *Spreading the News*, 49–51; Richard R. John and Christopher J. Young, "Rites of Passage: Postal Petitioning as a Tool of Governance in the Age of Federalism," in *The House and Senate in the 1790s: Petitioning, Lobbying, and Institutional Development*, ed. Kenneth R. Bowling and Donald R. Kennon (Ohio University Press, 2002), 100–38.; Daniel Carpenter and Colin D. Moore, "When Canvassers Became Activists: Antislavery Petitioning and the Political Mobilization of American Women," *American Political Science Review* 108, no. 3 (August 2014): 479–98, https://doi.org/10.1017/S000305541400029X; Maggie McKinley, "Petitioning and the Making of the Administrative State," *Yale Law Journal* 127, no. 6 (April 2018): 1538–1637.

6. For an example of this legislative process, see discussion in HR 2628, March 3, 1883, 44th Congress, 2nd Session, *Congressional Record* 5, part 3:2222–23, 2224.

7. For the structure of the postal system during the Early Republic, see John, *Spreading the News*, 73–76.

8. John, *Spreading the News*, 160–61; US Postal Service Historian, "Rates for Domestic Letters, 1792–1863" (United States Postal Service, August 2008), https://about.usps.com/who-we-are/postal-history/domestic-letter-rates-1792-1863.pdf; 37th Congress, 3rd Session, "Ch. 71: An Act to Amend the Laws Relating to the Post-Office Department," Statutes at Large, March 3, 1863.

9. See David M. Henkin, *The Postal Age: The Emergence of Modern Communications in Nineteenth-Century America* (Chicago: University of Chicago Press, 2006), 15–41.

10. *1879 Annual Report of the Postmaster General*, 60–61. There were 2,846 miles of railway mail routes from Kansas westward in 1869 and 11,072 miles in 1879. For transit time, see United States Post Office Department, *1882 United States Official Postal Guide*, vol. 4, no. 1 (Washington, DC: Government Printing Office, 1882), 579–82.

11. There were 70,078 miles of star routes versus 11,072 miles of railway mail routes. *1879 Annual Report of the Postmaster General*, 60–61. Even by 1894, a quarter century after the transcontinental railroad was completed, the region's star routes still outdistanced its railway mail routes by more than 34,000 miles. *1894 Annual Report of the Postmaster General* (Washington, DC: Government Printing Office, 1894), 180–81. Note that all of these figures reflect the mileage of the routes themselves rather than the total miles traveled each year along those routes. By this second measurement, railway mail routes far outstripped star routes due to the fact that the mail traveled much, much faster along these routes and could therefore make many, many more trips each year.

12. Budget figures for 1871 were calculated from *1871 Annual Report of the Postmaster General*, 116–17. Per capita figures were calculated using state and territory population figures from the 1870 census: "List of U.S. States by Historical Population," *Wikipedia, the Free Encyclopedia*, February 13, 2015, http://en.wikipedia.org/w/index.php?title=List_of_U.S._states_by_historical_population. Figures for 1880 were calculated from *1880 Annual*

*Report of the Postmaster General* (Washington, DC: Government Printing Office, 1880), 558–59; "1880 United States Census," *Wikipedia*, July 7, 2017, https://en.wikipedia.org/w/index.php?title=1880_United_States_Census&oldid=789443640. The regional definitions reflect those designated by the US Census: US Census Bureau, Geography Division, "2010 Geographic Terms and Concepts—Census Divisions and Census Regions," 2010, https://www.census.gov/geo/reference/gtc/gtc_census_divreg.html.

13. *1880 Annual Report of the Postmaster General*, 558–59; "1880 United States Census." Letter-writing figures from *1880 Annual Report of the Postmaster General*, 87–89.

14. *1871 Annual Report of the Postmaster General*, 16–17; *1880 Annual Report of the Postmaster General*, 87–88. Figures reflect mail transportation costs west of the Kansas-Colorado border.

15. For the various costs associated with stocking and operating a long star route, see Mae Helene Bacon Boggs, *My Playhouse Was a Concord Coach: An Anthology of Newspaper Clippings and Documents Relating to Those Who Made California History During the Years 1822–1888* (Oakland, CA: Howell-North, 1942), 430–503. S. S. Huntley Company Records, folders 1–4, Montana Historical Society, Jared L. Sanderson, "The Memoirs of Jared L. Sanderson, 'Stagecoach King,' Part II," *Wagon Tracks (Santa Fe Trail Association Quarterly)* 20, no. 2 (February 2006): 12–21; Wayne R. Austerman, *Sharps Rifles and Spanish Mules: The San Antonio-El Paso Mail, 1851–1881* (College Station: Texas A&M University Press, 1985).

16. For grain prices, see Charles Mayhew to Henry Corbett, September 1, 1867, in Boggs, *My Playhouse Was a Concord Coach*, 501.

17. Arid conditions also left staging infrastructure vulnerable to fire. Silas Huntley to Charles Huntley, February 22, 1869, S. S. Huntley and Company Records, folder 1, Montana Historical Society; *Yreka Journal*, May 1, 1872, quoted in Boggs, *My Playhouse Was a Concord Coach*, 574.

18. Henry Corbett to John F. Sprague, September 24, 1866, quoted in Boggs, *My Playhouse Was a Concord Coach*, 459; Henry Corbett to W. H. Rhodehamel, November 7, 1866, quoted in Boggs, 467.

19. Henry Corbett to John Ferguson, September 25, 1866, quoted in Boggs, *My Playhouse Was a Concord Coach*, 460.

20. 44th Congress, 1st Session, "H. Rpt. No. 814: Management of the Post Office Department" (Washington, DC, August 9, 1876), 545.

21. 44th Congress, 1st Session, "Management of the Post Office," 416.

22. 44th Congress, 1st Session, "Management of the Post Office," iii, 109. See extracts from *Washington Daily Patriot* January 8, 1872, printed in 44th Congress, 1st Session, "Management of the Post Office," 400–409.

23. *The Official Register of the United States, 1873* (Washington, DC: Government Printing Office, 1873), 454–554.

24. Prentiss Cutler Dodge, *Encyclopedia Vermont Biography* (Burlington, VT: Ullery, 1912), 75–76.

25. For C. W. Lewis, see "Colonel Charles W. Lewis (Obituary)," *San Diego Union*, February 9, 1871, California Genealogy and History Archives, available online at http://www.rootsweb.ancestry.com/~cagha/obits/obits1/lewis-charles.txt; 42nd Congress, 1st Session, "Sen. Ex. Doc. No. 5: Letter of the Postmaster General Communicating, in Compliance with the Resolution of the Senate of the 20th Instant, Information in Relation to the Mail-Letting on Route No. 17401, from Santa Fe to El Paso" (Washington, DC, March 23, 1871), 5. The mail route proved to be a goldmine: within eight months, the department increased the frequency of service on the route, doubling the staging firm's compensation to $91,000 a year.

26. Charles Huntley wrote in one letter, "I shall without a doubt get [the contract], the service was let on a straw and I am the next bid to the straw. There is a big thing in either running or selling the contract; do not know which I will do yet." Charles Huntley to Silas Huntley, July 22, 1870,

S. S. Huntley and Company Records, folder 1, Montana Historical Society. See also Charles Huntley to Silas Huntley, July 11, 1870, 11, S. S. Huntley and Company Records, folder 1, Montana Historical Society. R.G. Dun & Co. Credit Report Volumes, Western Territories, vol. 3, p. 433, Baker Library Historical Collections, Harvard Business School.

27. 44th Congress, 1st Session, "Management of the Post Office Department," xciii–xcvi, 139, 176–78; 42nd Congress, 2nd Session, "Ex. Doc. No. 322: Offers of Land and Water Mail-Routes: Letter from the Postmaster General, Transmitting Abstracts of Offers Carrying the Mails Upon the Different Routes in the United States" (Washington, DC, May 17, 1872), 371–73; 43rd Congress, 1st Session, "H. Rpt. No. 738: Management of the Post-Office Department" (Washington, DC, June 22, 1874), 2. For more on Sawyer and his firm of Sawyer, Risher, and Hall, see Rex H. Stever, "Stagecoach Lines," in *Handbook of Texas Online*, June 15, 2010, http://www.tshaonline.org/handbook/online/articles/ers01; Austerman, *Sharps Rifles and Spanish Mules*; 44th Congress, 1st Session, "Management of the Post Office Department," 139.

28. Charles Huntley to Silas Huntley, July 22, 1870. See also R. G. Dun & Co. Credit Report Volumes, Western Territories, vol. 3, p. 433, Baker Library Historical Collections, Harvard Business School.

29. For Barlow's residence, see 44th Congress, 1st Session, "Management of the Post Office Department," 337, and R. G. Dun & Co. Credit Report Volumes, Washington DC, vol. 5, p. 182, Baker Library Historical Collections, Harvard Business School. For Sawyer's residence in Georgetown, see 44th Congress, 1st Session, "Management of the Post Office," 164. and R. G. Dun & Co. Credit Report Volumes, Washington, DC, vol. 4, p. 393, Baker Library Historical Collections, Harvard Business School. For Kittle quote, 44th Congress, 1st Session, "Management of the Post Office Department," 224.

30. Jared L. Sanderson, "The Memoirs of Jared L. Sanderson, 'Stagecoach King,' Part I," *Wagon Tracks (Santa Fe Trail Association Quarterly)* 10, no. 1 (November 2005): 17; 44th Congress, 1st Session, "Management of the Post Office Department," 326, 478–81.

31. In the words of one clerk, "A man that is present here at the Department can keep pressing a case. . . . He has an advantage of being better advised and better informed than a man who does not come here." 44th Congress, 1st Session, "Management of the Post Office Department," 193.

32. 44th Congress, 1st Session, "Management of the Post Office," 511–14.

33. 44th Congress, 1st Session, "Management of the Post Office," 384. John Y. Simon, ed., *The Papers of Ulysses S. Grant*, vol. 19, *July 1, 1868–October 31, 1869* (Carbondale: Southern Illinois University Press, 1994), 264–65.

34. See, for instance, the intensive in-person lobbying for a lucrative route running from Northern California to Oregon in 1870, one eventually won by Bradley Barlow: 44th Congress, 1st Session, "Management of the Post Office Department," 596–610.

35. *Yreka Journal*, June 7, 1867, quoted in Boggs, *My Playhouse Was a Concord Coach*, 491. Sawyer, for instance, wheedled a six-thousand-dollar penalty down to two thousand dollars. See 44th Congress, 1st Session, "Management of the Post Office Department," 188–90.

36. 44th Congress, 1st Session, "Management of the Post Office Department," 322, 480. For more on the Vermont Bank, see R. G. Dun & Co. Credit Report Volumes, Vermont, vol. 12, p. 40, 500. Baker Library Historical Collections, Harvard Business School.

37. 44th Congress, 1st Session, "Management of the Post Office," 366–67, 382. Other contractors included Grant Taggart and the staging firm Gilmore and Salisbury. See 44th Congress, 1st Session, "Management of the Post Office," 546–47.

38. 44th Congress, 1st Session, "Management of the Post Office Department," 366–69.

39. *Appendix to the Congressional Globe: Laws of the United States*, 41st Congress, 3rd Session, March 3, 1871, 390–91. Of course, straw bidders simply circumvented the 1871 legislation by either making bids that were less than five thousand dollars or submitting fraudulent

drafts with their bid. So the following year, Congress tightened these regulations to require checks or drafts for bids on any routes whose compensation for the previous term (not just the amount of the bid) exceeded five thousand dollars. See "Chap CXXV: An Act Relating to Proposals and Contracts for Transportation of the Mails, and for Other Purposes," *Appendix to the Congressional Globe: Laws of the United States*, 42nd Congress, 2nd Session, April 27, 1872, 702–3.

40. 44th Congress, 1st Session, "Management of the Post Office Department," 313. Congress further amended the legislation in 1872, including a suspicious amendment proposed by Senator George Edmunds, from Barlow's home state of Vermont. Whereas the earlier 1871 legislation required the 5 percent check or draft accompanying bids to come from "some reliable banking house or banking institution," that same check now had to come specifically from "some solvent national bank." Say, the Vermont National Bank. See "Chap CXXV: An Act Relating to Proposals and Contracts for Transportation of the Mails, and for Other Purposes," *Appendix to the Congressional Globe: Laws of the United States*, 42nd Congress, 2nd Session, April 27, 1872, 702–3. The amendment was introduced by George Edmunds (Republican, VT): *Congressional Globe*, 42nd Congress, 2nd Session, April 3, 1872, 2121; A. M. Gibson, "Report of the Attorney General on the Star Mail Service," in *Annual Report of the Postmaster General* (Washington, DC: Government Printing Office, 1881), 491–92.

41. Barlow profited in other ways from his position. As mail contractors congregated in Washington each winter to assemble and submit their bids to the department, Barlow offered them a financial service: he would issue checks to bidders and charge them interest. By 1876, he estimated that during each annual mail letting he issued anywhere from five hundred thousand to seven hundred thousand dollars in checks from the Vermont National Bank to various bidders. In doing so, Barlow managed to profit on mail contracts that he and his staging firm never even bid on. For the extent of Barlow's involvement as a financier, see 45thCongress, 3rd Session, "H. Mis. Doc. No. 16: Testimony Taken by the Committee on the Post Offices and Post Roads on the Post Office Department" (Washington, DC, 1878), 51–54, 164–67, 175–79. For Barlow's own recollection, see 44th Congress, 1st Session, "Management of the Post Office Department," 341.

42. Jockeying for increased service was commonplace amongst all mail contractors, even ones on smaller routes. One experienced California contractor claimed one thousand dollars from a smaller Southern California stage firm to compensate him for paying "Washington parties" for assistance in getting one of their routes increased. Thomas Flint to William Edward Lovett, June 27, 1868, William Edward Lovett Papers, box 1, folder 24, Bancroft Library, UC Berkeley.

43. Charles Huntley to Silas Huntley, July 22, 1870, S. S. Huntley and Company Records, folder 1, Montana Historical Society, Helena, Montana.

44. 44th Congress, 1st Session, "Management of the Post Office Department," 522–23.

45. 44th Congress, 1st Session, "Management of the Post Office," 303. For another case of fraudulent petitioning for increased service, see letter from F. C. Taylor dated August 9, 1875, quoted in "Notes from the Capitol," *New York Times*, September 4, 1875. Taylor all but admitted to its illegitimacy, closing his letter with "It will be best not to mention my name in it."

46. Petition of inhabitants of the Jeff County, New York, October 26, 1869, referred to committee on February 2, 1870, House Committee on the Post Office and Post Roads, NARA I RG 233, 41A, H9.2, folder 3.

47. 44th Congress, 1st Session, "Management of the Post Office Department," 250.

48. For one example, see 44th Congress, 1st Session, "Management of the Post Office," 534, 643.

49. When a California Congressmen helped secure faster mail delivery he was lauded in the local paper as "deserving of unanimous thanks of the people of Northern California and Oregon." *Yreka Journal*, July 24, 1872, quoted in Boggs, *My Playhouse Was a Concord Coach*, 577.

50. Routt was accused in 1871 of "openly interfering" in an Illinois senatorial election. See John Y. Simon, ed., *The Papers of Ulysses S. Grant*, vol. 21, *November 1, 1870–May 31, 1871* (Carbondale: Southern Illinois University Press, 1998), 119.
51. 44th Congress, 1st Session, "Management of the Post Office Department," 520–21, 561–63, 577.
52. 44th Congress, 1st Session, "Management of the Post Office," 527.
53. 44th Congress, 1st Session, "Management of the Post Office," 452–53, 584–85, 735. Between 1874 and 1876, four different men served as Postmaster General. See *Annual Report of the Postmaster General* from 1871 to 1875. President Grant's original appointment, John Creswell resigned in 1874 after five years in service. For his resignation letter and Grant's response, see *The Papers of John A. J. Creswell, 1819–1887*, vol. 17 (Library of Congress, 1931), A. C. 2410, Papers of John A. J. Creswell, Library of Congress, Washington, DC .
54. 44th Congress, 1st Session, "Management of the Post Office Department," 1–13, 28–36.
55. See "Abstract of Bids and Contracts for Carrying the Mail," House Committee on the Post Office and Post Roads, NARA I RG 233, 42A, F20.1, folder 1: August 4, 1871, West Virginia, North Carolina, Georgia, Florida, Alabama, Mississippi, Arkansas; 44th Congress, 1st Session, "Management of the Post Office," 83–97, 710–22.
56. 44th Congress, 1st Session, "Management of the Post Office," 18–19, 26–27, 218–19, 576–79, 582–83, 738–45.
57. This is especially damning because one of the clerks was the brother-in-law of John French, who at the time was the chief clerk and de-facto second assistant postmaster general as John Routt transitioned to the Colorado governorship. 44th Congress, 1st Session, "Management of the Post Office," 576.
58. The other mail contractor ended up being banned from bidding on mail contracts. See a letter from the Postmaster General to Jerome J. Hinds, July 14, 1875 in NARA I, RG 28, *Letters Sent, Postmaster General*, Volume 84, 121–23. 44th Congress, 1st Session, "Management of the Post Office," 738–45.
59. 42nd Congress, 2nd Session, "H. Rpt. No. 38: Contracts for the Transportation of the Mails" (Washington, DC, April 4, 1872); 43rd Congress, 1st Session, "H. Rpt. No. 738: Management of the Post-Office Department"; 43rd Congress, 1st Session, "H. Rpt. No. 775: Contracts for the Transportation of the Mails" (Washington, DC, June 20, 1874).
60. 44th Congress, 1st Session, "Management of the Post Office Department."
61. For Dorsey's earlier life, see Mari Grana, *On the Fringes of Power: The Life and Turbulent Career of Stephen Wallace Dorsey* (Helena, MT: TwoDot, 2015), 1–19. For bidding by the "Dorsey ring," see Sharon Lowry, "Portrait of an Age: The Political Career of Stephen W. Dorsey, 1868–1889" (PhD diss., University of North Texas, 1980), 253–65; Louise Horton, "The Star Route Conspiracies," *Texana* 7, no. 3 (1969): 220–33; J. Martin Klotsche, "The Star Route Cases," *Mississippi Valley Historical Review* 22, no. 3 (1935): 407–8, https://doi.org/10.2307/1892626; Earl Leland Jr., "The Post Office and Politics, 1876–1884: The Star Route Frauds" (PhD diss., University of Chicago, 1964), 29–36.
62. "Star Service Corruption," *New York Times*, April 25, 1881, 1, available online at https://timesmachine.nytimes.com/timesmachine/1881/04/25/98553855.html?pageNumber=1; Leland, "The Post Office and Politics," 45–51. For more information about the specific route, see 46th Congress, 2nd Session, "H. Mis. Doc. No. 31: Testimony Before the Committee on Appropriations in Relation to the Post Office Department" (Washington, DC, March 25, 1880), 192–93, available online at https://archive.org/stream/unitedstatescon255offigoog. "A Complete Specimen," *New York Times*, June 27, 1881, 4, available online at https://timesmachine.nytimes.com/timesmachine/1881/06/27/102752281.html?pageNumber=4; "A Star Route Civil Suit," *New York Times*, June 12, 1885, 4, available online at https://timesmachine.nytimes.com/timesmachine/1885/06/12/103022566.html?pageNumber=4.

63. Lowry, "Portrait of an Age," 266–67; Leland, "The Post Office and Politics," 76–84.

64. "Indiana's October Vote," *New York Times*, February 12, 1881, 2, available online at https://timesmachine.nytimes.com/timesmachine/1881/02/12/103398308.html?pageNumber=2; Leland, "The Post Office and Politics," 108–20; Grana, *On the Fringes of Power*, 27–31.

65. See, for example, "The Star Routers," *Dallas Daily Herald*, June 2, 1882, 1, available online at http://chroniclingamerica.loc.gov/lccn/sn83025733/1882-06-02/ed-1/seq-1/; "The Star Route Trial," *Memphis Daily Appeal*, August 4, 1882, 1, available online at http://chroniclingamerica.loc.gov/lccn/sn83045160/1882-08-04/ed-1/seq-1/.

66. Lowry, "Portrait of an Age," 292–324; Grana, *On the Fringes of Power*, 39–58; Klotsche, "The Star Route Cases," 415–18.

67. For treatment of these corruption scandals during this era, see Rebecca Edwards, *New Spirits: Americans in the Gilded Age, 1865–1905* (New York: Oxford University Press, 2006), 4, 30–31; Richard White, *The Republic for Which It Stands: The United States during Reconstruction and the Gilded Age, 1865–1896* (New York: Oxford University Press, 2017), 172–80, 255–66.

68. "Star Service Corruption," *New York Times*, April 25, 1881, available online at http://query.nytimes.com/mem/archive-free/pdf?res=9900EFDC133CEE3ABC4D51DFB266838A699FDE.

69. For the longer history of a statist developmental vision before the Civil War, see Brian Balogh, *A Government Out of Sight: The Mystery of National Authority in Nineteenth-Century America* (Cambridge: Cambridge University Press, 2009), 53–110; Ariel Ron, "Summoning the State: Northern Farmers and the Transformation of American Politics in the Mid-Nineteenth Century," *Journal of American History* 103, no. 2 (September 2016): 347–74, https://doi.org/10.1093/jahist/jaw316. For specifically the Republican Party, see Heather Cox Richardson, *West from Appomattox: The Reconstruction of America after the Civil War* (New Haven, CT: Yale University Press, 2007), 73, 155–58; Jay Sexton, "William H. Seward in the World," *Journal of the Civil War Era* 4, no. 3 (August 2014): 398–430, https://doi.org/10.1353/cwe.2014.0066; Steven Hahn, *A Nation Without Borders: The United States and Its World in an Age of Civil Wars, 1830–1910* (New York: Viking, 2016), 6, 284–85, 359, 391–400.

70. Karen Elizabeth Jenks, "Trading the Contract: The Roles of Entrepreneurs, Government, and Labor in the Formation of the Pacific Mail Steamship Company" (PhD diss., University of California, Irvine, 2012), 215; John Haskell Kemble, "A Hundred Years of the Pacific Mail," *Neptune* 10 (April 1950): 131.

71. *1872 Annual Report of the Postmaster General* (Washington, DC: Government Printing Office, 1872), 183.

72. "Pacific Mail and its Wonderful Lamp – the Arabian Nights of Wall Street," *New York Herald*, October 27, 1872, 8, available online at http://chroniclingamerica.loc.gov/lccn/sn83030313/1872-10-27/ed-1/seq-8/; "The Pacific Mail Subsidy, An Investigation Pending," *Chicago Tribune*, December 11, 1874, 1, available online at http://chroniclingamerica.loc.gov/lccn/sn84031492/1874-12-11/ed-1/seq-1/; Ryan Michael Stephens, "Tensions of Trade and Migration: The Origins of Transoceanic Steamship Companies and China-U.S. Exchange" (BA thesis, Pennsylvania State University, Schreyer Honors College, 2013), 25–29, https://honors.libraries.psu.edu/catalog/17816; 43rd Congress, 2nd Session, "H. R. Report No. 268: China Mail Service" (Washington, DC, February 27, 1875).

73. The tactics used by Republican congressmen to try and tack on commercial subsidies to the annual postal funding bill fits within what historian Gary Gerstle describes as a "surrogacy" strategy of using the relatively expansive powers of the post to enact unrelated policy. Gary Gerstle, *Liberty and Coercion: The Paradox of American Government from the Founding to the Present* (Princeton, NJ: Princeton University Press, 2015), 6, 101–4.

74. Kemble, "A Hundred Years of the Pacific Mail," 135; *1878 Annual Report of the Postmaster General* (Washington, DC: Government Printing Office, 1878), 371.

75. For an example of this legislative process, see discussion H.R. 2628, March 3, 1883, 44th Congress, 2nd Session, *Congressional Record* 5, part 3:2222–23, 2224.

76. Historian Nicolas Barreyre argues that sectionalism was one of the defining political divisions during this period. Nicolas Barreyre, *Gold and Freedom: The Political Economy of Reconstruction*, trans. Arthur Goldhammer (Charlottesville: University of Virginia Press, 2015), 2–10.

77. Senator George Edmunds speaking on March 24, 1876, 44th Congress, 1st Session, *Congressional Record* 4, part 2:1932; Senator Aaron Sargent speaking on March 24, 1876, 44th Congress, 1st Session, *Congressional Record* 4, part 2:1933.

78. Representative Christopher Upson speaking on April 1, 1880, 46th Congress, 2nd Session, *Congressional Record* 10, part 3:2042.

79. Representative Dudley Haskell speaking on February 25, 1880, 46th Congress, 2nd Session, *Congressional Record* 10, part 2:1133.

80. Quoted in Leland, "The Post Office and Politics," 55–56; Horton, "The Star Route Conspiracies," 221.

81. *Proceedings in the Trial of the Case of the United States vs. John W. Dorsey, John R. Miner, John M. Peck, Stephen W. Dorsey, Harvey M. Vaile, Montfort C. Rerdell, Thomas J. Brady, and William H. Turner for Conspiracy*, vol. 2 (Washington, DC: Government Printing Office, 1882), 2051, available online at http://hdl.handle.net/2027/hvd.32044086291325.

82. Representative John Stone speaking on April 1, 1880, 46th Congress, 2nd Session, *Congressional Record* 10, part 3:2045.

83. Between July of 1877 and June of 1878, the Post Office Department established 447 new post offices west of the Kansas/Missouri border. Just two years later, that same number was 1,139 new post offices established over 1879–1880. Figures tallied from *1878 Annual Report of the Postmaster General*, 44–45; *1880 Annual Report of the Postmaster General*, 56–57.

84. Klotsche, "The Star Route Cases," 409–10.

85. See, for instance, George Armstrong Custer, *My Life on the Plains; Or, Personal Experiences with Indians* (New York: Sheldon, 1876), 20–21; John Gregory Bourke, *On the Border with Crook* (Charles Scribner's Sons, 1891), 102. See also newspaper accounts in Austerman, *Sharps Rifles and Spanish Mules*, 226–308.

86. Col. William R. Shafter to Assistant Adj. Gen., June 5, 1871, NARA I, RG 393, Letters Sent, Fort Davis, Texas, quoted in Austerman, *Sharps Rifles and Spanish Mules*, 258.

87. In 1867, the postmaster general warned that conflict on the Plains threatened to suspend overland mail service through the region. See Postmaster General Alexander Randall to Ulysses S. Grant, May 18, 1867 in John Y. Simon, ed., *The Papers of Ulysses S. Grant*, vol. 17, *January 1–September 30, 1867* (Carbondale: Southern Illinois University Press, 1991). See also Silas Huntley to M. Hershfield, December 11, 1867, S. S. Huntley and Company Records, folder 1, Montana Historical Society; 44th Congress, 1st Session, "Management of the Post Office Department," 400.

88. 44th Congress, 1st Session, "Management of the Post Office Department," ii, xvii.

89. Mark W Summers, *The Era of Good Stealings* (New York: Oxford University Press, 1993), 304–5; Gregory P. Downs, *After Appomattox: Military Occupation and the Ends of War* (Cambridge, MA: Harvard University Press, 2015), 211–36.

90. *1881 Annual Report of the Postmaster General* (Washington, DC: Government Printing Office, 1881), 31.

91. Richard R. John has shown how a robust national postal system produced tensions in the antebellum period, including deep schisms over whether or not to carry the mail on the Sabbath along with the success of slaveholders in banning abolitionist material from the mail. John,

*Spreading the News*, 169–205, 257–80. Jo Guldi makes a similar point about the divisiveness of road building in Great Britain. Jo Guldi, *Roads to Power: Britain Invents the Infrastructure State* (Cambridge, MA: Harvard University Press, 2012), 18–22. In the western United States, Richard White makes the case that transcontinental railroads were built far ahead of demand. Richard White, *Railroaded: The Transcontinentals and the Making of Modern America* (New York: W. W. Norton, 2011).

## Chapter 5

1. The network's trademark instability continued unabated, as some 4,500 of the region's post offices also shut down over the same decade. Figures calculated from the *Annual Report of the Postmaster General* from 1880 to 1890.

2. Sacramento sent 1,054,248 letters and 3,423,472 total mail items, which ranked 58th among American cities, just between Jersey City, New Jersey, and Fort Wayne, Indiana. *1880 Annual Report of the Postmaster General* (Washington, DC: Government Printing Office, 1880), 87–89; "1880 United States Census," *Wikipedia*, July 7, 2017, https://en.wikipedia.org/w/index.php?title=1880_United_States_Census&oldid=789443640.

3. "The New City Post Office," *Sacramento Daily Union*, September 16, 1881, 3, available online at http://cdnc.ucr.edu/cgi-bin/cdnc?a=d&d=SDU18810916.2.18. For the Sacramento Post Office's employees, see *The Official Register of the United States, 1881*, vol. 2 (Washington, DC: Government Printing Office, 1881), 368, 612.

4. The Malakoff Diggins State Park has re-created McKillican's store and post office according to oral interviews conducted in the 1960s of old North Bloomfield residents. See State of California Department of Parks and Recreation, "Interpretive Prospectus and Interpretive Plan of the McKillican and Mobley Store, Malakoff Diggins State Historic Park," June 1969, box 14-M, Searls Library, Nevada City. For Crandall's salary, see *The Official Register of the United States, 1881*, vol. 2, 367.

5. Crandall listed his profession as "General Merchandise" in an 1880 census. Page no. 2, Supervisor's District no. 3, Enumeration District no. 64, in United States, Bureau of the Census and United States, National Archives and Records Service, *1880 California Federal Population Census Schedules—Nevada, Placer, and Plumas Counties*, vol. reel 0070, 10th Census, 1880, California [microform] (Washington, DC: National Archives and Records Service, General Services Administration, 1965), available online at http://archive.org/details/10thcensus0070unit.

6. There were 6,202 clerks in 1881 Official Register of the United States, excluding staff at Washington, DC headquarters. *The Official Register of the United States, 1881*, vol. 2, 610–78. Letter carriers were even less common, employed at only 0.3 percent of the country's more than 44,500 post offices. See *1881 Annual Report of the Postmaster General* (Washington, DC: Government Printing Office, 1881), 48. For the importance of urban post offices, see David M. Henkin, *The Postal Age: The Emergence of Modern Communications in Nineteenth-Century America* (Chicago: University of Chicago Press, 2006), 63–90.

7. Elisabeth Clemens makes a similar point in Elisabeth S. Clemens, "Lineages of the Rube Goldberg State: Building and Blurring Public Programs, 1900–1940," in *Rethinking Political Institutions: The Art of the State*, ed. Ian Shapiro, Stephen Skowronek, and Daniel Galvin (New York: New York University Press, 2006), 187–215.

8. For a canonical example of this approach, see Daniel Carpenter, *The Forging of Bureaucratic Autonomy: Reputations, Networks, and Policy Innovation in Executive Agencies, 1862–1928.* (Princeton, NJ: Princeton University Press, 2001).

9. James A. Garfield, *The Diary of James A. Garfield*, ed. Brown Williams, vol. 2 (East Lansing: Michigan State University, 1967), 213.

10. Mari Sandoz, *Old Jules* (Boston: Little, Brown, 1935), 181, 421.

11. For the relationship between politics and the US Post, see Richard R. John, *Spreading the News: The American Postal System from Franklin to Morse* (Cambridge, MA: Harvard University Press, 1995), 219–27; Dorothy G. Fowler, *The Cabinet Politician: The Postmasters General, 1829–1909* (New York: Columbia University Press, 1943).

12. John Joseph Wallis, "Table Ea894-903—Federal Government Employees, by Government Branch and Location Relative to the Capital: 1816–1992," in *Historical Statistics of the United States, Earliest Times to the Present*, ed. Susan B. Carter et al. (New York: Cambridge University Press, 2006).

13. Scott C. James, "Patronage Regimes and American Party Development from 'The Age of Jackson' to the Progressive Era," *British Journal of Political Science* 36, no. 1 (2006): 39, 49, https://doi.org/10.1017/S0007123406000032.

14. In 1871, 96 percent of the post offices were fourth-class offices that didn't require Senate confirmation. *1871 Annual Report of the Postmaster General* (Washington, DC: Government Printing Office, 1871), 85. In 1899, that figure was 94.4 percent of post offices. *1899 Annual Report of the Postmaster General* (Washington, DC: Government Printing Office, 1899), 822–23.

15. For more on the relationship between patronage and post offices, see Jon C. Rogowski, "Presidential Influence in an Era of Congressional Dominance," *American Political Science Review* 110, no. 2 (May 2016): 325–41, https://doi.org/10.1017/S0003055416000125. There is no way to have an exact count of the number of different postmasters who served in office. One back-of-the-envelope calculation, however, is to add up all of the postmasters that were removed, resigned, or died each year between 1865 and 1900, given that each of them needed to be replaced in office. This adds up to around 344,000 people. Some people may have been reinstated and then removed again, counting twice, but this number is almost certainly balanced out by the number of newly appointed postmasters for new post offices (more than 90,000 of which opened between 1867 and 1900).

16. Gary Gerstle, *Liberty and Coercion: The Paradox of American Government from the Founding to the Present* (Princeton, NJ: Princeton University Press, 2015), 162; Nicholas R. Parrillo, *Against the Profit Motive: The Salary Revolution in American Government, 1780–1940* (New Haven, CT: Yale University Press, 2013), 124; Stephen Skowronek, *Building a New American State: The Expansion of National Administrative Capacities, 1877–1920* (Cambridge: Cambridge University Press, 1982), 74. For contemporary coverage of assessments, see "A Joseph Surface President," *Los Angeles Herald*, July 13, 1878, 2, available online at https://cdnc.ucr.edu/cgi-bin/cdnc?a=d&d=LAH18780713.2.4&srpos=379.

17. For the cost of elections and the role of political parties in organizing them, see Gerstle, *Liberty and Coercion*, 159–68.

18. By the late 19th century, presidential postmasters had been moved entirely to a salary system, whereas before they could keep their letterbox rents. See, for instance, 52nd Congress, 2d Session, "H. Mis. Doc. No. 90: The Postal Laws and Regulations of the United States of America" (Washington, DC: Government Printing Office, 1893), 178–80. Isaac V. Fowler served as grand sachem of Tammany Hall and New York City's postmaster. He was accused of absconding with more than $150,000 in post office funds in 1863. David E. Meerse, "Buchanan, Corruption and the Election of 1860," *Civil War History* 12, no. 2 (1966): 122.

19. "A Memorial From Postmasters," written at Postmaster's Convention in Chicago, signed March 26, 1888. Senate Committee on the Post Office and Post Roads, NARA I RG 46, 49A, H20.1, box 97, folder: Various Subjects.

20. This was less than $2,600 in 2017 dollars, calculated using Sam Williamson, "Seven Ways to Compute the Relative Value of a U.S. Dollar Amount, 1774 to Present," Measuring Worth, 2017, www.measuringworth.com/uscompare/; *1887 Annual Report of the Postmaster General* (Washington, DC: Government Printing Office, 1887), 89–98. Even in 1901, around 50 percent of postmasters received less than a hundred dollars in annual commissions. *1901 Annual Report of the Postmaster General* (Washington, DC: Government Printing Office, 1901), 983.

21. Postmaster McKillican's quarterly commissions for 1889 were $110.44 on $150.88, $110.11 on $150.23, $105.29 on $142.15, and $120.31 on $170.62. Postal Account Book, 1887–1892, box 32, Malkoff Diggins State Park Historical Collection, California State Library, Sacramento, California. Once a postmaster's annual compensation reached $1,000 (the equivalent of $1,900 in receipts), their post office was reclassified from a "fourth-class" office to a "Presidential" office. Postmasters at these larger offices served four-year terms, were appointed by the president of the United States and confirmed by the Senate, and were broken into first-, second-, and third-class categories depending on the size of their post office. 52nd Congress, 2d Session, "1893 Postal Laws and Regulations," 177–80. This salary ranged from one thousand to eight thousand at New York City, the largest post office in the country. *1887 Annual Report of the Postmaster General*, 98.

22. Sandoz, *Old Jules*, 181.

23. For examples of "twelve dollar post office," see *Cape Girardeau Democrat*, January 21, 1893, 2, available online at http://chroniclingamerica.loc.gov/lccn/sn89066818/1893-01-21/ed-1/seq-2/; John Gregory Bourke, *On the Border with Crook* (New York: Charles Scribner's Sons, 1891), 70.

24. Walter M. Ferris, "Obstacles to Civil Service Reform," ed. Lorretus S. Metcalf, *The Forum* 9 (1889): 514.

25. It wasn't until the 20th century that most politicians began serving for longer tenures. By the 114th Congress in 2015–17, the average service time was almost nine years. Matthew Glassman and Amber Wilhelm, *Congressional Careers: Service Tenure and Patterns of Member Service, 1789–2015* (Washington, DC: Congressional Research Service, Library of Congress, January 3, 2015), 2–4, available online at http://digitalcommons.ilr.cornell.edu/key_workplace/1373.

26. The median time in office was 764 days. Varun Vijay calculated these figures while working as an undergraduate research assistant at the Stanford Center for Spatial and Textual Analysis during the spring of 2015. The larger dataset comes from 38,526 postmasters transcribed by Jim Wheat in Jim Wheat, "Postmasters and Post Offices of Texas, 1846–1930," December 28, 2006, http://www.rootsweb.ancestry.com/~txpost/postmasters.html, accessed January 10, 2013.

27. "Crossroads Post Office" was a recognizable phrase from the 19th century. See, for instance, Frank G. Carpenter, "The Fate of the Party . . . Lies in the Crossroads Post Office" in *The Gilded Age*, ed. Ari Arthur Hoogenboom and Olive Hoogenboom (Englewood Cliffs, NJ: Prentice-Hall, 1967), 166.

28. Residential mail delivery was only available in larger cities during this period. Even there, post offices were gathering places. Historian David Henkin argues that postage reductions made urban post offices some of "the most intensely promiscuous public spaces in nineteenth-century America." Richard R. John similarly remarks, "The local post office was far more than the place where you went to pick up your mail." Henkin, *The Postal Age*, 88; John, *Spreading the News*, 163.

29. Charles E. Henry to James Garfield, February 16, 1878 in James D. Norris and Arthur H. Shaffer, eds., *Politics and Patronage in the Gilded Age: The Correspondence of James A. Garfield and Charles E. Henry* (Madison: State Historical Society of Wisconsin, 1970), 204.

30. All data comes from *Colorado, New Mexico, Utah, Nevada, Wyoming and Arizona Gazetteer and Business Directory, 1884–1885* (R. L. Polk & Co. and A. C. Danser, 1884). "General Store" was listed 224 times for postmasters in this directory.

31. For connections between western general stores and post offices, see Linda English, *By All Accounts: General Stores and Community Life in Texas and Indian Territory* (Norman: University of Oklahoma Press, 2013), 8, 45, 72–73, 160.

32. Wayne F. Fuller, *American Mail: Enlarger of the Common Life* (Chicago: University of Chicago Press, 1972), 295–96.

33. Regulations stated: "No post-office shall be located in a bar-room or in any room directly connected with one." Arthur Harry Bissell and Thomas B. Kirby, *The Postal Laws and Regulations of the United States of America, Published in Accordance with the Act of Congress Approved March 3, 1879* (Washington, DC: Government Printing Office, 1879), 125. All data comes from *Colorado, New Mexico, Utah, Nevada, Wyoming and Arizona Gazetteer and Business Directory, 1884–1885* (R. L. Polk & Co. and A. C. Danser, 1884).

34. US Statutes at Large, 42nd Congress, 2nd Session, ch. 335, p. 286.

35. John, *Spreading the News*, 58–59, 123–24; Roman J. Hoyos, "The People's Privilege: The Franking Privilege, Constituent Correspondence, and Political Representation in Mid-Nineteenth Century America," *Law and History Review* 31, no. 1 (2013): 101–38, https://doi.org/10.1017/S0738248012000843; Matthew Glassman, *Franking Privilege: Historical Development and Options for Change* (Washington, DC: Congressional Research Service, Library of Congress, April 22, 2015), https://fas.org/sgp/crs/misc/RL34274.pdf.

36. Report for C. H. Pyle in R. G. Dun & Co. Credit Report Volumes, Washington DC, vol. 24: Santa Cruz, Shasta, Sierra, Siskiyou, p. 198, Baker Library Historical Collections, Harvard Business School. See also the report for R. S. Weston, of Forest City, on p. 281.

37. *Colorado, New Mexico, Utah, Nevada, Wyoming and Arizona Gazetteer and Business Directory.*

38. For 19th-century companies reaching out to postmasters for information, see Andrew Brown to Office of Wells, Fargo & Co's Express, April 20, 1893, and April 22, 1893, Andrew Brown Papers, Huntington Library, San Marino, California. For government agencies, see A. F. [Lucy] Hawley to Andrew Jackson Faulk, April 16, 1877, box 2, folder 15, in Andrew Jackson Faulk Papers, Yale Collection of Western Americana, Beinecke Rare Book and Manuscript Library, New Haven, Connecticut; Jamie L. Pietruska, *Looking Forward: Prediction and Uncertainty in Modern America* (Chicago: University of Chicago Press, 2017), 85–90; United States Pension Bureau, *Annual Report of the Commissioner of Pensions to the Secretary of the Interior* (Washington, DC: Government Printing Office, 1872), 7.

39. Several years after an Ohio man moved to northern California, for instance, his family grew worried after they hadn't heard from him in more than 18 months. Fearing the worst, one of them sent a letter from Ohio to the man's last known location asking for whereabouts and "whether he be dead or alive." Without knowing the name of a single person in the distant town, the family member simply addressed the letter to "Post Master, Orleans Bar, Klamath Co[unty] Cal[ifornia]." A month later, the family got a reply: the postmaster reported that the man had indeed left the previous year to chase gold in Washington Territory, and the post-master had forwarded their inquiry to the Walla Walla Post Office. After one more back-and-forth exchange, the Ohio family was eventually able to track down the wayward gold seeker. Jonathan Warner Jr. to Postmaster at Orleans Bar, January 5, 1863, folder 36; Bella Whipple Jenks to Jonathan Warner Jr., February 22, 1863, folder 37; Jonathan Warner Jr. to Postmaster at Orleans Bar, March 20, 1864, folder 38; Bella Whipple Jenks to George Washington Warner, May 12, 1864, folder 39; George Washington Warner to Jonathan Warner Jr., March 13, 1865, folder 40, box 1, Jonathan Warner Papers, Beinecke Rare Book and Manuscript Library, New Haven, Connecticut.

40. Examples from different cities include: "List of Letters," *Sacramento Daily Union*, November 11, 1881, p. 4, available online at https://cdnc.ucr.edu/cgi-bin/cdnc?a=d&d=SDU18811111.2.27.1&srpos=2; "Unclaimed Letters," *Waco Evening News*, March 25, 1893, p. 5, available online at http://chroniclingamerica.loc.gov/lccn/sn86088201/1893-03-25/ed-1/seq-5/; "List of Letters," *Daily Republican*, May 25, 1885, p. 1, available online at http://chroniclingamerica.loc.gov/lccn/sn84038114/1885-05-25/ed-1/seq-1/.

41. Henkin, *The Postal Age*, 72–81; John, *Spreading the News*, 152, 164–67; Winifred Gallagher, *How the Post Office Created America: A History* (New York: Penguin, 2016), 94–96.

42. Sec. 524, "Loungers in Post Offices" in Bissell and Kirby, *The Postal Laws and Regulations of the United States of America*, 125.

43. "Brief Reference," *Sacramento Daily Union*, October 21, 1875, p. 3, available online at https://cdnc.ucr.edu/cgi-bin/cdnc?a=d&d=SDU18751021.2.20&srpos=23.

44. "List of Letters," *Sacramento Daily Union*, November 11, 1881, p. 4, available online at https://cdnc.ucr.edu/cgi-bin/cdnc?a=d&d=SDU18811111.2.27.1&srpos=2. See also Los Angeles, "Advertised Letters Remaining in the Los Angeles Post-office, Feb. 26, 1882," *Los Angeles Daily Times*, February 26, 1882.

45. Beth Lew-Williams, *The Chinese Must Go: Violence, Exclusion, and the Making of the Alien in America* (Cambridge, MA: Harvard University Press, 2018), 17–89.

46. In Sierra Nevada logging camps, for instance, Chinese laborers made up some 90 percent of the workforce. Sue Fawn Chung, *Chinese in the Woods: Logging and Lumbering in the American West* (Urbana: University of Illinois Press, 2015), 1–16; Sue Fawn Chung, *In Pursuit of Gold: Chinese American Miners and Merchants in the American West* (Urbana: University of Illinois Press, 2011).

47. Mae M. Ngai, "Chinese Gold Miners and the 'Chinese Question' in Nineteenth-Century California and Victoria," *Journal of American History* 101, no. 4 (March 2015): 1094, https://doi.org/10.1093/jahist/jav112; Ping Chiu, *Chinese Labor in California, 1850-1880: An Economic Study* (Madison: State Historical Society of Wisconsin, 1967), 36–38. For the "Chinese quarter" in North Bloomfield: Charles Gaus Interview by Eric Leffingwell, 1967, California State Historic Parks Archives, p. 10, supplied to the author by Lola Aguilar; Sanborn Map Company, *North Bloomfield, California*, 1905, scale not given, 1905, Digital Sanborn Maps, 1867–1970, http://sanborn.umi.com.

48. "Scissors and Pen," *Grass Valley Daily*, December 12, 1882, p. 2, available online at https://www.mynevadacounty.com/DocumentCenter/View/6928/December-12-1882-The-Grass-Valley-Daily-Union-Newspaper-PDF_001.

49. "Chinese Sluice-Robber Killed," *Sacramento Daily News*, January 27, 1883, p. 1, available online at http://cdnc.ucr.edu/cgi-bin/cdnc?a=d&d=SDU18830127.2.5.1.

50. *Nevada City Transcript*, January 24, 1884, cited in Michel Janicot, *A History of Nevada County Post Offices, 1850–1994* (Nevada City, CA: Nevada County Historical Society, 1994), 28–29.

51. For episodes of anti-Chinese violence, see Jean Pfaelzer, *Driven Out: The Forgotten War Against Chinese Americans* (New York: Random House, 2007); Lew-Williams, *The Chinese Must Go*, 91-186.

52. See Record of Registered Letters Received and Delivered—1893, box 30, folder 5, and Money Order Applications, January–March 1895, box 6, folder 12, in Malakoff Diggins State Park Historical Collection, California Department of Parks and Recreation, Sacramento, California.

53. These are post office and postmaster names taken from a single year (1884) and a single state (Colorado). *Colorado, New Mexico, Utah, Nevada, Wyoming and Arizona Gazetteer and Business Directory*, 43–280.

54. James C. Scott, *Seeing Like a State: How Certain Schemes to Improve the Human Condition Have Failed* (New Haven, CT: Yale University Press, 1999).

55. Sec. 441, "Who May Be Postmaster" in US Post Office Department, *The Postal Laws and Regulations of the United States of America, Comp., Rev., and Pub. in Accordance with the Act of Congress Approved March 30, 1886* (Washington, DC: Government Printing Office, 1887). See also Marshall Henry Cushing, *Story of Our Post Office* (Boston: A. M. Thayer, 1893), 198.

56. For women's growing activity in public life during this period see Nell Irvin Painter, *Standing at Armageddon: A Grassroots History of the Progressive Era* (W. W. Norton, 1987), 62–64, 231–35; Rebecca Edwards, *Angels in the Machinery: Gender in American Party Politics from the Civil War to the Progressive Era* (New York: Oxford University Press, 1997), 12–58; Glenda Elizabeth Gilmore, *Gender and Jim Crow: Women and the Politics of White Supremacy in North Carolina, 1896–1920* (Chapel Hill: University of North Carolina Press, 1996), 31–60. Women also joined the Post Office Department's workforce in Washington, DC, in increasing numbers, especially in the Dead Letter Office and Topographer's Office. For more on female employees in the Dead Letter Office, see Cushing, *Story of Our Post Office*, 265–67. For more on women's entrance into the federal workforce, see Cindy Aron, *Ladies and Gentlemen of the Civil Service: Middle-Class Workers in Victorian America* (New York: Oxford University Press, 1987).

57. I used the Gender package in R (https://github.com/ropensci/gender) to infer the gender of presidential appointees from Scott James's dataset in James, "Patronage Regimes and American Party Development."

58. All of the percentages listed in this paragraph undercount the number of female postmasters. I used the Gender package in R (https://github.com/ropensci/gender) and assumed that any names the program could not associate with a gender were male. Oregon data came from a manual tabulation of female postmasters from Oregon using *The Official Register of the United States*, published every odd year.

59. Calculated from a list of 38,526 postmasters transcribed by Jim Wheat in Wheat, "Postmasters and Post Offices of Texas." I wrote a program to scrape data from Wheat's website and then used the Gender package in R (https://github.com/ropensci/gender) to infer the gender of postmasters. This analysis showed a similar growth in the overall percentage of female postmasters, from 1.67 percent in 1873 to 8.60 percent in 1893. An analysis of Scott James's dataset of presidential appointments in the Post Office Department between 1865 and 1900 shows a less pronounced increase, but an increase nonetheless in female postmasters at larger post offices.

60. Data from Chronicling America was generated on October 15, 2018, using the Bookworm interface developed by Benjamin Schmidt, Matt Nicklay, Neva Cherniavsky Durand, Martin Camacho, and Erez Lieberman Aiden at the Cultural Observatory: http://benschmidt.org/ChronAm/ -?%7B"words_collation"%3A"Case_Insensitive","search_limits"%3A%5B%7B"word"%3A%5B"postmistress"%5D,"publish_year"%3A%7B"%24gte"%3A1836,"%24lte"%3A1922%7D%7D%5D%7D. Data from HathiTrust was generated on October 15, 2018, using the Bookworm interface developed by Benjamin Schmidt, Matt Nicklay, Neva Cherniavsky Durand, Martin Camacho, and Erez Lieberman Aiden at the Cultural Observatory: https://bookworm.htrc.illinois.edu/develop/#?%7B%22search_limits%22:%5B%7B%22word%22:%5B%22postmistress%22%5D,%22date_year%22:%7B%22$gte%22:1840,%22$lte%22:1900%7D,%22language__id%22:%5B%221%22%5D,%22publication_country__id%22:%5B%221%22%5D%7D%5D,%22counttype%22:%22WordsPerMillion%22%7D. Data from Google Books was generated using the Google Books Ngram Viewer on October 15, 2018: https://books.google.com/ngrams/graph?content=postmistress&year_start=1840&year_end=1900&corpus=17&smoothing=3&share=&direct_url=t1%3B%2Cpostmistress%3B%2Cc0. Google Ngrams are not without problems, not least of which is the "black box" quality of what exactly is in its corpus. I use it cautiously as a supplement to other kinds of evidence. See Eitan Adam Pechenick, Christopher M. Danforth, and Peter Sheridan Dodds, "Characterizing

the Google Books Corpus: Strong Limits to Inferences of Socio-Cultural and Linguistic Evolution," *PLoS ONE* 10, no. 10 (October 2015): e0137041, https://doi.org/10.1371/journal.pone.0137041.

61. Sam Walter Foss, "The Postmistress of Pokumville," in *Dreams in Homespun* (Boston: Lee & Shepard, 1898), 180–82, available online at http://books.google.com/books?id=YiQ-AAAAYAAJ&pg=PA180. For "mails/males" jokes, see *Trinity Journal* (Yreka, CA), March 22, 1873, quoted in Mae Helene Bacon Boggs, *My Playhouse Was a Concord Coach: An Anthology of Newspaper Clippings and Documents Relating to Those Who Made California History During the Years 1822–1888* (Oakland, CA: Howell-North, 1942), 584; "Males and Mails," *United States Mail* 3, no. 33 (June 1887): 122.

62. "Fighting for a Post-Office," *Rocky Mountain News*, August 4, 1883, available online at http://infotrac.galegroup.com/itw/infomark/724/82/3675w16/purl=rc1_NCNP_0_GT3010049737&dyn=59!xrn_108_0_GT3010049737&hst_1?sw_aep=stan90222 For other complaints about postmistresses, see "A Woman Against the World," *United States Mail*, February 1887.

63. *Colorado, New Mexico, Utah, Nevada, Wyoming and Arizona Gazetteer and Business Directory*, 163, 498.

64. Cushing, *Story of Our Post Office*, 442.

65. The blurring of different kinds of work space and the opportunities this has provided for women can be seen especially clearly during times of war. See, for instance, Edwards, *Angels in the Machinery*, 12–38; Maurine Weiner Greenwald, "Working-Class Feminism and the Family Wage Ideal: The Seattle Debate on Married Women's Right to Work, 1914–1920," *Journal of American History* 76, no. 1 (1989): 118–49, https://doi.org/10.2307/1908346.

66. Patrick Henry Woodward, *The Secret Service of the Post-Office Department, as Exhibited in the Wonderful Exploits of Special Agents Or Inspectors in the Detection, Pursuit, and Capture of Depredators Upon the Mails* (Columbus, OH: Estill, 1886), 86, 438.

67. I explore this theme in more depth in Cameron Blevins, "Women and Federal Officeholding in the Late Nineteenth-Century U.S.," *Current Research in Digital History* 2 (2019), https://doi.org/10.31835/crdh.2019.08.

68. Opinion delivered by Augustus Garland on April 21, 1885. Augustus H. Garland, "Appointment of an Indian as Postmaster," in *Official Opinions of the Attorneys-General of the United States*, vol. 18 (Washington, DC: Government Printing Office, 1890), 181–85. Bluejacket earned $29.39 in 1883 and $61.51 in 1885. *The Official Register of the United States, 1883*, vol. 2 (Washington, DC: Government Printing Office, 1883), 430; *The Official Register of the United States, 1885*, vol. 2 (Washington, DC: Government Printing Office, 1885), 459. For more on the town of Bluejacket, see Craig County Genealogical Society, "Bluejacket," *The Encyclopedia of Oklahoma History and Culture*, www.okhistory.org/publications/enc/entry.php?entry=BL015, accessed July 20, 2017.

69. Nell Irvin Painter, *Exodusters: Black Migration to Kansas after Reconstruction*, repr. ed. (New York: W. W. Norton, 1992), 149–59; Quintard Taylor, *In Search of the Racial Frontier: African Americans in the American West, 1528–1990* (New York: W. W. Norton, 1998), 134–63; Norman L. Crockett, *The Black Towns* (Lawrence: Regents Press of Kansas, 1979), 174–77. Fletcher was a formerly enslaved person and Union Army veteran.

70. For Black political mobilization see Eric Foner, *Reconstruction: America's Unfinished Revolution, 1863–1877* (New York: Harper Perennial Modern Classics, 1988), ch. 6; Steven Hahn, *A Nation Under Our Feet: Black Political Struggles in the Rural South from Slavery to the Great Migration* (Cambridge, MA: Belknap Press of Harvard University Press, 2003), 163–264. For paramilitary violence, see Gregory P. Downs, *After Appomattox: Military Occupation and the Ends of War* (Cambridge, MA: Harvard University Press, 2015); Hahn, *A Nation Under Our Feet*, 265–314.

71. Eric Foner, *Freedom's Lawmakers: A Directory of Black Officeholders During Reconstruction*, rev. ed. (Baton Rouge: Louisiana State University Press, 1996), xiv; Willard B. Gatewood Jr., "Sunnyside: The Evolution of an Arkansas Plantation, 1840–1945," *Arkansas Historical Quarterly* 50, no. 1 (April 1991): 5–29, https://doi.org/10.2307/40022326. Few African American postmasters, if any, held office outside of the South's majority-Black communities and the handful of all-Black towns in the Great Plains. Deanna Boyd and Kendra Chen, "The History and Experience of African Americans in America's Postal Service," Smithsonian National Postal Museum, http://postalmuseum.si.edu/AfricanAmericanHistory/p2.html, accessed October 29, 2014.

72. Periodically communities would take collective action against postmasters. See, for example, *1885 Annual Report of the Postmaster General* (Washington, DC: Government Printing Office, 1885), 60.

73. John Roy Lynch, *The Facts of Reconstruction* (New York: Neale, 1913), 28–29.

74. US Post Office Department, *The Postal Laws and Regulations of the United States of America*. See also Wilking B. Cooley, *The Postmasters' Manual and Clerks' Assistant* (Washington, DC: C. R. Brodix, 1888), 12, available online at https://books.google.com/books?id=x8A_AAAAYAAJ; Cushing, *Story of Our Post Office*, 300–302. For more on the challenges of finding sureties in the South, see Cushing, *Story of Our Post Office*, 305.

75. Jennifer Lynch, "African-American Postal Workers in the 19th Century," United States Postal Service, January 2011, https://about.usps.com/who-we-are/postal-history/african-american-workers-19thc-2011.rtf; Historian of the United States Postal Service, "List of Known African-American Postmasters, 1800s," United States Postal Service, July 2010, https://about.usps.com/who-we-are/postal-history/african-american-postmasters-19thc-2010.pdf. See also Boyd and Chen, "The History and Experience of African Americans in America's Postal Service." There is no way to have an exact count of the number of different postmasters who served in office. One back-of-the-envelope calculation, however, is to add up all of the postmasters that were removed, resigned, or died each year between 1865 and 1900, given that each of them needed to be replaced in office. This adds up to around 344,000 people. Some people may be reinstated and then removed again, but this is almost certainly balanced out by the number of newly appointed postmasters for new post offices (more than 90,000 of which opened between 1867 and 1900).

76. *The Official Register of the United States, 1885*, vol. 2, 549; *Colorado, New Mexico, Utah, Nevada, Wyoming and Arizona Gazetteer and Business Directory*, 513–14.

77. Walter A. Friedman, *Birth of a Salesman* (Cambridge, MA: Harvard University Press, 2005), 56–87.

78. United States Post Office Department, *1882 United States Official Postal Guide*, vol. 4, no. 1 (Washington, DC: Government Printing Office, 1882), 56–87.

79. United States Post Office Department, *1882 United States Official Postal Guide*, vol. 4, no. 1, p. 2. For the role of postmasters as book agents, see Natalie Marine-Street, "Agents Wanted: Sales, Gender, and the Making of Consumer Markets in America, 1830–1930" (PhD diss., Stanford University, 2016), 154–56, 163–64, available online at https://searchworks.stanford.edu/view/11616850.

80. The phrase "universal service" was not widely used in the 19th century. Richard B. Kielbowicz, *Universal Postal Service: A Policy History, 1790–1970* (Postal Rate Commission, November 15, 2002), https://www.prc.gov/sites/default/files/papers/paper_0.pdf, 1.

81. For an overview of the tension between private and public mail delivery, see Richard R. John, "Private Mail Delivery in the United States during the Nineteenth Century: A Sketch," *Business and Economic History* 15 (1986): 135–47; Richard B. Kielbowicz, "Government Goes into Business: Parcel Post in the Nation's Political Economy, 1880–1915," *Studies in American Political Development* 8, no. 1 (1994): 150–72, https://doi.org/10.1017/S0898588X00000109.

82. Jesse L. Coburn, *Letters of Gold: California Postal History Through 1869* (Canton, OH: Philatelic Foundation, 1984). The Post Office Department even contracted with the company to transport the mail on its behalf, awarding a $1.75 million contract to run an overland mail route during the 1860s. *1868 Annual Report of the Postmaster General* (Washington, DC: Government Printing Office, 1868), 5–7.

83. For the lionization of Wells, Fargo & Co., see W. Turrentine Jackson, "A New Look at Wells Fargo, Stage-Coaches and the Pony Express," *California Historical Society Quarterly* 45, no. 4 (December 1, 1966): 291–324; W. Turrentine Jackson, "Wells Fargo: Symbol of the Wild West?," *Western Historical Quarterly* 3, no. 2 (April 1972): 179–96, https://doi.org/10.2307/967112; Philip L. Fradkin, *Stagecoach: Wells Fargo and the American West* (New York: Simon & Schuster, 2002), 24, 50, 145.

84. Quoted in John, "Private Mail Delivery in the United States," 139. Postal letters calculated from *1881 Annual Report of the Postmaster General,* 88–89.

85. There were 547 Wells, Fargo & Co. offices listed on July 1, 1880. Wells, Fargo & Co., "List of Offices, Agents, and Correspondents," July 1, 1880, in Pamphlets on California, Bancroft Library, F858.C18 v.3x. As of June 30, 1880, there were 2,023 post offices in Arizona, California, Idaho, Nevada, Oregon, Utah, and Washington. Calculated from *1880 Annual Report of the Postmaster General,* 57.

86. "The Parcels Post," *Harper's Weekly*, December 7, 1889, 970.

87. B. K. Sharretts, "The Legality of Wells Fargo's Letter-Carrying Business: Post Office Department, Wells, Fargo & Co's Letter-Express" (1880) in Richard John, *The American Postal Network*, vol. 2 (London: Pickering & Chatto), 284–87. . For other examples of postmasters acting as Wells, Fargo & Co. express agents, see B. B. Redding, S. K. Throckmorton, and J. D. Farwell, *Report of the Commissioner of Fisheries of the State of California, for the Years 1878 and 1879* (Sacramento: Legislature of the State of California, 1879), 5–6; *Colorado, New Mexico, Utah, Nevada, Wyoming and Arizona Gazetteer and Business Directory*, 505.

88. *An Illustrated History of Sonoma County, California: Containing a History of the County of Sonoma from the Earliest Period of Its Occupancy to the Present Time* (Chicago: Lewis, 1889), 725–26. For another example of the overlap between California postmasters and Wells, Fargo & Co., see Andrew Brown to Office of Wells, Fargo & Co.'s Express, April 22, 1893, Andrew Brown Papers, Huntington Library, San Marino, California.

89. Elizabeth Sanders, *Roots of Reform: Farmers, Workers, and the American State, 1877–1917* (Chicago: University of Chicago Press, 1999); Charles Postel, *The Populist Vision* (New York: Oxford University Press, 2009); Richard R. John, "Robber Barons Redux: Antimonopoly Reconsidered," *Enterprise and Society* 13, no. 1 (March 2012): 1–38, https://doi.org/10.1017/S1467222700010910.

90. Postel, *The Populist Vision*, 143–45; Richard R. John, *Network Nation: Inventing American Telecommunications* (Cambridge, MA: Belknap Press of Harvard University Press, 2010), 18–23, 121–22, 175–76, 395–405.

91. For the rural dimensions of the US Post, see Postel, *The Populist Vision*, 143–45. For the relationship between democratic politics and patronage, see Richard R. John, "Affairs of Office: The Executive Departments, the Election of 1828, and the Making of the Democratic Party," in *The Democratic Experiment: New Directions in American Political History*, ed. Meg Jacobs, William J. Novak, and Julian Zelizer (Princeton, NJ: Princeton University Press, 2003), 50–84.

92. Richard White, *The Republic for Which It Stands: The United States during Reconstruction and the Gilded Age, 1865–1896* (New York: Oxford University Press, 2017), 447–53.

93. *1887 Annual Report of the Postmaster General,* 16. For other examples of Vilas's attitudes regarding efficiency and organization, see Roy N. Lokken, "William F. Vilas as a Businessman," *Wisconsin Magazine of History* 45, no. 1 (October 1961): 32–39; *1887 Annual Report of the*

*Postmaster General*, 20–25, 36–37. For an overview of this attitude, see Alfred Chandler Jr., *The Visible Hand: The Managerial Revolution in American Business* (Cambridge, MA: Harvard University Press, 1977).

94. Fuller, *American Mail*, 256; Carpenter, *The Forging of Bureaucratic Autonomy*, 83–93, 102–12.

95. *1887 Annual Report of the Postmaster General*, 36–37; *1888 Annual Report of the Postmaster General* (Washington, DC: Government Printing Office, 1888), viii, 39.

96. For the circular, see "Mr. Vilas's Circular," *New York Times*, May 15, 1885, 4, available online at https://timesmachine.nytimes.com/timesmachine/1885/05/15/103015113. html?pageNumber=4; "Postmaster General's Circular," *Comet*, May 23, 1885, 2, available online at http://chroniclingamerica.loc.gov/lccn/sn89058128/1885-05-23/ed-1/ seq-2/. For figures on removals under Vilas, see Fred. Perry Powers, "The Reform of the Federal Service," *Political Science Quarterly* 3, no. 2 (1888): 269, https://doi.org/10.2307/ 2139033.

97. Fowler, *The Cabinet Politician*.

98. Ari Arthur Hoogenboom, *Outlawing the Spoils: A History of the Civil Service Reform Movement, 1865–1883* (Urbana: University of Illinois Press, 1961); Ari Hoogenboom, "The Pendleton Act and the Civil Service," *American Historical Review* 64, no. 2 (January 1959): 305, https://doi.org/10.2307/1845445; Skowronek, *Building a New American State*, 179.

99. *1888 Annual Report of the Postmaster General*, ix, 23–48. Inspector totals tabulated from *The Official Register of the United States, 1887*, vol. 2 (Washington, DC: Government Printing Office, 1887), 11–12. For more on inspectors, see Carpenter, *The Forging of Bureaucratic Autonomy*, 102–12. For the Comstock laws, see Helen Lefkowitz Horowitz, "Victoria Woodhull, Anthony Comstock, and Conflict over Sex in the United States in the 1870s," *Journal of American History* 87, no. 2 (September 2000): 403–34, https://doi.org/10.2307/ 2568758.

100. United States Postal Service Historian, "Pieces of Mail Handled, Number of Post Offices, Income, and Expenses Since 1789," United States Postal Service, January 2017, https:// about.usps.com/who-we-are/postal-history/pieces-of-mail-since-1789.pdf.

101. Cushing, *Story of Our Post Office*, 280–81. For one example of politicians' involvement with new post offices and their role as go-betweens, see L. Bradford Prince to C. W. Wildenstein, March 18, 1891, box 2, folder 1, L. Bradford Prince Papers, University of New Mexico Center for Southwest Research, Albuquerque, New Mexico. See also petition from citizens of Frio County, Texas, and accompany letter from L. S. White to S. B. Maxey, January 14, 1878, in Senate Committee on the Post Office and Post Roads, NARA I RG 46, 45A, H17.1, box 209, folder: Mail Routes, January 21–March 18, 1878.

102. Garfield, *The Diary of James A. Garfield*, 2:213.

103. Elisabeth Clemens makes this point in Clemens, "Lineages of the Rube Goldberg State." For the modern aversion to the "profit motive" for public servants, see Parrillo, *Against the Profit Motive*, 1–10. For "bureaucratic autonomy," see Carpenter, *The Forging of Bureaucratic Autonomy*, 66–73.

104. For Mobley's background, see Elaine Mobley, Oral History of the McKillican and Mobley General Store, interview by David A. Tucker, May 1, 1969, box 14-M, Searls Library, Nevada City. For Crandall, see Harry Laurenz Wells, *History of Nevada County, California; with Illustrations Descriptive of Its Scenery, Residences, Public Buildings, Fine Blocks, and Manufactories.* (Oakland, CA: Thompson & West, 1880), 215, available online at https:// archive.org/stream/historyofnevadac00well. For Mobley's sureties, see George W. Reed to Fred Brown, June 17th, 1892, in W. H. Taylor Collection, box 1, folder 3, Stanford University Special Collections. At the time, Robert McKillican was sheriff in Oakland: "McKillican's

Men," *San Francisco Call*, December 18, 1892, 7, available online at http://cdnc.ucr.edu/cgi-bin/cdnc?a=d&d=SFC18921218.2.52.

105. Elaine Mobley, Oral History of the McKillican and Mobley General Store, 61–62.

106. This was especially true in the case of postal money orders, in which the department explicitly tasked postmasters with positively identifying the recipient of a money order. See United States Post Office Department, *1880 United States Official Postal Guide*, vol. 2, no. 1 (Washington, DC Government Printing Office, 1880), 555.

107. United States Post Office Department, *1892 United States Official Postal Guide*, vol. 14, no. 1 (Washington, DC Government Printing Office, 1892), 759.

108. Record of Registered Letters Received and Delivered–1893, box 30, folder 5, Malakoff Diggins State Park Historical Collection, California Department of Parks and Recreation, Sacramento, California.

# Chapter 6

1. For weather and news see *Sacramento Daily Union*, February 11, 1895, 1, 3, available online at http://cdnc.ucr.edu/cgi-bin/cdnc?a=d&d=SDU18950211; "With Snow and Ice," *San Francisco Morning Call*, February 9, 1895, 2, available online at https://cdnc.ucr.edu/cgi-bin/cdnc?a=d&d=SFC18950209.

2. For a detailed recount of the store and its space, see Elaine Mobley, Oral History of the McKillican and Mobley General Store, interview by David A. Tucker, May 1, 1969, box 14-M, Searls Library, Nevada City; State of California Department of Parks and Recreation, "Interpretive Prospectus and Interpretive Plan of the McKillican and Mobley Store, Malakoff Diggins State Historic Park," June 1969, box 14-M, Searls Library, Nevada City. Money order data from Money Order Applications, January–March 1895, box 6, folder 12, Malakoff Diggins State Park Historical Collection, California Department of Parks and Recreation, Sacramento, California. For money order fees, see United States Post Office Department, *1896 United States Official Postal Guide* (Philadelphia: George F. Lasher, 1896), 901.

3. This includes both domestic and international money orders. *1895 Annual Report of the Postmaster General* (Washington, DC: Government Printing Office, 1895), 384–85, 601, 745. For details on the operations of the money order system, see Wilking B. Cooley, *The Postmasters' Manual and Clerks' Assistant* (Chicago: C. R. Brodix, 1888), 12–22, available online at https://books.google.com/books?id=x8A_AAAAYAAJ. Dollar values for 2019 were calculated using Sam Williamson, "Seven Ways to Compute the Relative Value of a U.S. Dollar Amount, 1774 to Present," Measuring Worth, 2019, https://www.measuringworth.com/uscompare/. By consumer price index (CPI), the 2019 equivalent of $169 million was $5.39 billion in 2019.

4. Marshall Henry Cushing, *Story of Our Post Office* (Boston: A. M. Thayer, 1893), 217.

5. For a general history of the system, see United States Post Office Department, *The United States Postal Money-Order System: A Survey of the System for the Purpose of Ascertaining Its Condition and Advancing Its Efficiency and Economical Administration* (Washington, DC: Government Printing Office, 1915); Tom Velk and Terence Hines, "The United States Post Office Domestic Postal Money Order System In The 19th Century: A Nascent Banking System," (Departmental Working Papers McGill University, Department of Economics, May 2009), https://ideas.repec.org/p/mcl/mclwop/2009-11.html; Terrence Hines and Thomas Velk, "The United States Post Office Domestic Money Order System in the 19th Century" (Blount Postal History Symposium, American Philatelic Center, Bellefonte, PA, 2011), http://www.postalmuseum.si.edu/symposium2011/papers/Hines_velk_2011_stamps.pdf; Terrence Hines and Thomas Velk, "Economic Activity Following the Civil War Indexed by

Postal Money Order Data" (Blount Postal History Symposium, American Philatelic Center, Bellefonte, PA, 2012), http://www.postalmuseum.si.edu/symposium2011/papers/Hines_velk_2011_stamps.pdf.

6. Seven years after the system was launched, Americans were transmitting $41.7 million in money orders domestically. *1871 Annual Report of the Postmaster General* (Washington, DC: Government Printing Office, 1871), 126–27.

7. "News of the Morning," *Sacramento Daily Union*, July 10, 1871, 2, available online at http://cdnc.ucr.edu/cgi-bin/cdnc?a=d&d=SDU18710710.2.8.

8. "Japanese Postal System," *Daily Alta California*, February 2, 1880, 1, available online at https://cdnc.ucr.edu/cgi-bin/cdnc?a=d&d=DAC18800202.2.8&srpos=596; Patricia L. Maclachlan, *The People's Post Office: The History and Politics of the Japanese Postal System, 1871–2010* (Cambridge, MA: Harvard University Asia Center, 2012), 36–40.

9. For the transatlantic dimensions of this network, see Daniel T. Rodgers, *Atlantic Crossings: Social Politics in a Progressive Age* (Cambridge, MA: Belknap Press of Harvard University Press, 1998). Foreign money orders were also part of a global turn within the Post Office Department that started in the 1860s. Richard R. John, "Projecting Power Overseas: U.S. Postal Policy and International Standard-Setting at the 1863 Paris Postal Conference," *Journal of Policy History* 27, no. 3 (July 2015): 416–38, doi:10.1017/S0898030615000172. By the end of the 19th century, Americans could mail a letter from San Francisco to some 50 different nations and colonies across six different continents, all for the price of a single five-cent stamp. *1899 Annual Report of the Postmaster General* (Washington, DC: Government Printing Office, 1899), 719; United States Post Office Department, *1899 United States Official Postal Guide* (New York: Metropolitan Job Print, January 1899), 1060.

10. The Hamilton postmaster's compensation in 1871 was $1,200, or the fifth-highest compensation in the state. *The Official Register of the United States, 1871* (Washington, DC: Government Printing Office, 1871), 682–83; "Nevada Items," *Daily Alta California*, October 5, 1872, 1, available online at https://cdnc.ucr.edu/cgi-bin/cdnc?a=d&d=DAC18721005.2.27; Walter Nettleton Frickstad and Edward W. Thrall, *A Century of Nevada Post Offices, 1852–1957* (Oakland, CA: Philatelic Research Society, 1958), 12.

11. All figures and calculations for Hamilton come from Register of Money Orders Issued at the Post Office of Hamilton, White Pine County, Nevada, MSS 2011/175 v.1, Bancroft Library, University of Berkeley, California. $19,718 was worth $529,996.19 by percentage increase in the consumer price index (CPI) between 1878 and 2019. Williamson, "Measuring Worth."

12. Figures reflect domestic, not international, money orders and were calculated for the fiscal year July 1880–June 1881 using *1881 Annual Report of the Postmaster General* (Washington, DC: Government Printing Office, 1881), 678–83; "1880 United States Census," *Wikipedia*, July 7, 2017, https://en.wikipedia.org/w/index.php?title=1880_United_States_Census&oldid=789443640.

13. John Joseph Giblin, *Record of the Fargo Family* (New York: American Bank Note Company, 1907), 22–23, available online at http://archive.org/details/recordoffargofam00lcgibl. The company started offering its own private money orders in 1882, almost two decades after the Post Office Department first launched the service.

14. As one financial textbook from the period reminded its readers, "Banks do not like to issue drafts for sums less than $5. Henry Thomas Loomis, *Spelling and Letter Writing: A Textbook for Use in Commercial Schools, Normal Schools, Colleges, Academies, and High Schools* ([Cleveland]: Spencer, Felton & Loomis, 1889), 158. The average order of a postal money order, meanwhile, was less than five dollars. *1880 Annual Report of the Postmaster General* (Washington, DC: Government Printing Office, 1880), 401.

15. Casting a wider net to include state banks, savings banks, trust companies, and private bankers increases the total number of financial institutions in the Far West to 259, still slightly

fewer than the number of money order post offices operating in the same region. Like national banks, these institutions were located in a much smaller range of places. United States Office of the Comptroller of the Currency, *Annual Report of the Comptroller of the Currency* (Washington, DC: Government Printing Office, 1880), cliv, cxviii; *1880 Annual Report of the Postmaster General*, 572. See also Richard H. Timberlake Jr., *The Origins of Central Banking in the United States* (Cambridge, MA: Harvard University Press, 1978), 87–88. Economic historians have since found that proximity to a national bank produced long-lasting increases in both agricultural production and manufacturing outputs. Matthew Jaremski, "National Banking's Role in U.S. Industrialization, 1850–1900," *Journal of Economic History* 74, no. 1 (March 2014): 109–40, https://doi.org/10.1017/S0022050714000047; Scott L. Fulford, "How Important Are Banks for Development? National Banks in the United States, 1870–1900," *Review of Economics and Statistics* 97, no. 5 (October 2015): 921–38, https://doi.org/10.1162/REST_a_00546.

16. For the creation of a national currency, see Stephen Mihm, *A Nation of Counterfeiters: Capitalists, Con Men, and the Making of the United States* (Cambridge, MA: Harvard University Press, 2009), 305–59. For the currency issue, see Richard White, *The Republic for Which It Stands: The United States during Reconstruction and the Gilded Age, 1865–1896* (New York: Oxford University Press, 2017), 281–84, 831–36; Nicolas Barreyre, *Gold and Freedom: The Political Economy of Reconstruction*, trans. Arthur Goldhammer (Charlottesville: University of Virginia Press, 2015).

17. Marshall Gramm and Phil Gramm, "The Free Silver Movement in America: A Reinterpretation," *Journal of Economic History* 64, no. 4 (2004): 1116.

18. For examples of paying in postage stamps, see advertisement for Red House Trade Union in *Sacramento Daily Union*, June 15, 1883, 1, available online at http://cdnc.ucr.edu/cgi-bin/cdnc?a=d&d=SDU18830615.2.5.2; Natalie Marine-Street, "Agents Wanted: Sales, Gender, and the Making of Consumer Markets in America, 1830–1930" (PhD diss., Stanford University, 2016), 187–88, available online at https://searchworks.stanford.edu/view/11616850. For the problems this posed for the Post Office Department, see *1876 Annual Report of the Postmaster General* (Washington, DC: Government Printing Office, 1876), xxiv; *1877 Annual Report of the Postmaster General* (Washington, DC: Government Printing Office, 1877), xxiv, 170.

19. For the introduction of postal notes, see 47th Congress, 2nd Session, "Ch. 123: An act to modify the postal money-order system, and for other purposes," Statutes at Large, March 3, 1883; Cushing, *Story of Our Post Office*, 214; *1884 Annual Report of the Postmaster General* (Washington, DC: Government Printing Office, 1884), 737.

20. Charles Postel, *The Populist Vision* (New York: Oxford University Press, 2009), 143.

21. United States Postal Service Historian, "Pieces of Mail Handled, Number of Post Offices, Income, and Expenses Since 1789," *United States Postal Service*, February 2020, https://about.usps.com/who-we-are/postal-history/pieces-of-mail-since-1789.htm. For a review of the annual finances of the Money Order Division from 1865–1892, see *1892 Annual Report of the Postmaster General* (Washington, DC: Government Printing Office, 1892), 240.

22. For Charles Macdonald's departure, see "Consul Macdonald's Services," *New York Times*, June 23, 1893, 4, available online at http://timesmachine.nytimes.com/timesmachine/1893/06/23/109701938.html.

23. *1893 Annual Report of the Postmaster General* (Washington, DC: Government Printing Office, 1893), 93, 688–89.

24. United States Post Office Department, *The United States Postal Money-Order System*, 10; "Legacy to Post Office Money Order Office," *New York Times*, September 25, 1902, 5, available online at https://timesmachine.nytimes.com/timesmachine/1902/09/25/101287474.html?pageNumber=5.

25. *1893 Annual Report of the Postmaster General*, 688-89; United States Postal Service Historian, "Pieces of Mail Handled, Number of Post Offices, Income, and Expenses Since 1789," *United States Postal Service*, February 2020, https://about.usps.com/who-we-are/postal-history/pieces-of-mail-since-1789.htm.

26. For the number of periodicals as a percentage of total mail matter, see *1890 Annual Report of the Postmaster General* (Washington, DC: Government Printing Office, 1890), 50-54; *1899 Annual Report of the Postmaster General*, 4–5; United States Postal Service Historian, "Pieces of Mail Handled, Number of Post Offices, Income, and Expenses Since 1789," *United States Postal Service*, February 2020, https://about.usps.com/who-we-are/postal-history/pieces-of-mail-since-1789.htm. For more on periodicals in the mail, see Richard B. Kielbowicz, "Postal Subsidies for the Press and the Business of Mass Culture, 1880–1920," *Business History Review* 64, no. 3 (October 1990): 458, https://doi.org/10.2307/3115736.

27. US Post Office Department, *The Postal Laws and Regulations of the United States of America, Comp., Rev., and Pub. in Accordance with the Act of Congress Approved March 30, 1886* (Washington, DC: Government Printing Office, 1887), 174–82; United States Post Office Department, *1892 United States Official Postal Guide*, vol. 14, no. 1 (Washington, DC: Government Printing Office, 1892), 822–23.

28. *1893 Annual Report of the Postmaster General*, xxxi, 688-91. For seed samples, see Kathy J. Cooke, "Who Wants White Carrots?: Congressional Seed Distribution, 1862 to 1923," *Journal of the Gilded Age and Progressive Era* 17, no. 3 (July 2018): 475–500, https://doi.org/10.1017/S1537781418000075.

29. "City Items," *Daily Alta California*, February 5, 1866, 1, available online at https://cdnc.ucr.edu/cgi-bin/cdnc?a=d&d=DAC18660205.2.2&srpos=1.

30. For a history of departmental requirements for money order offices, see Cushing, *Story of Our Post Office*, 217–19. See also *1892 Annual Report of the Postmaster General*, 240.

31. Figures for June 30, 1880. United States Post Office Department, *1880 United States Official Postal Guide*, vol. 2, no. 1 (Washington, DC: Government Printing Office, 1880). The Far West includes states and territories west of the Kansas/Colorado border.

32. Dina Hassan in the Stanford Center for Spatial and Textual Analysis conducted analysis of money order accessibility. Money order office data was transcribed from United States Post Office Department, *1880 United States Official Postal Guide*. Hassan classified the zones as follows: Zone 1 was the highest degree of accessibility—post offices that either were themselves money order offices or fell within 0–3 miles of a money order office. Zone 2 consisted of post offices that fell within 3–10 miles of a money order office. Westerners living in Zone 2 could presumably access the money order system within a single day by making between a round-trip journey on foot or horseback. Zone 3 consisted of post offices that fell within 10–20 miles of a money order office. These areas could technically access the money order system, but it would have required at least a full day or overnight round-trip journey. Finally, Zone 4 was made up of post offices that were effectively cut off from the money order system—those post offices that were more than 20 miles away from a money order office. An important caveat to note is that these distances reflect straight-line distances, not the actual routes that people would travel. This exaggerates the degree of accessibility within each zone, but it does serve as a rough proxy.

33. "Cisco," *Sacramento Daily Union*, February 5, 1867, 4, available online at https://cdnc.ucr.edu/cgi-bin/cdnc?a=d&d=SDU18670205.2.8&srpos=1. In 1871 Cisco's annual postmaster compensation was $12—the minimum amount disbursed by the Post Office Department. *The Official Register of the United States, 1871*, 508.

34. "Philipsburg Postal Matters," *New North-West*, November 9, 1877, 3, available online at http://chroniclingamerica.loc.gov/lccn/sn84038125/1877-11-09/ed-1/seq-3/. The Montana delegate was nothing if not persistent. Five years later, Macdonald found himself refusing yet

another request from Maginnis for money order facilities at yet another small post office in his territory. "Money Order Business," *Rocky Mountain Husbandman*, April 20, 1882, 6, available online at http://chroniclingamerica.loc.gov/lccn/sn83025309/1882-04-20/ed-1/seq-6/.

35. Representative Poindexter Dunn (AR), *Congressional Record*, 47th Congress, 1st Session, July 7, 1882, S. 6335.

36. Temple Bodley, "The Post Office Department as Common Carrier and Bank," *American Law Review*, 1884, 224.

37. *1882 Annual Report of the Postmaster General* (Washington, DC: Government Printing Office, 1882), xvi.

38. L. L. Fairchild, "The Money Order Business: A Public Convenience That Is a Heavy Tax on the Country Postmaster," *United States Mail*, March 1887; Cooley, *The Postmasters' Manual and Clerks' Assistant*, 12–22.

39. 52nd Congress, 2d Session, "H. Mis. Doc. No. 90: The Postal Laws and Regulations of the United States of America" (Washington, DC: Government Printing Office, 1893), 420. The 1893 Postal Laws and regulations are on page 420.

40. "A Memorial From Postmasters," written by Postmaster's Convention in Chicago, signed March 26, 1888; Senate Committee on the Post Office and Post Roads, NARA I RG 46, 49A, H20.1, box 97, folder: Various Subjects; James H. Curtis to Sarah Curtis and Delia Curtis, October 19, 1890, box 2, Curtis Family Correspondence, Huntington Library, San Marino, California.

41. Cushing, *Story of Our Post Office*, 218–19. *1893 Annual Report of the Postmaster General*, 69; *1892 Annual Report of the Postmaster General*, 240. For Wanamaker's role as a social reformer, see Nicole C. Kirk, *Wanamaker's Temple: The Business of Religion in an Iconic Department Store* (New York: NYU Press, 2018).

42. *1892 Annual Report of the Postmaster General*, 226–27; *1893 Annual Report of the Postmaster General*, 69.

43. For surrounding geography, see A von Haake, *Post Route Map of the States of California and Nevada, Showing Post Offices with the Intermediate Distances and Mail Routes in Operation on the 1st of June, 1896*, Pocket Map, 1:696,960 (Washington, DC: United States Post Office Department, June 1, 1896), available online at the David Rumsey Historical Map Collection, http://www.davidrumsey.com/luna/servlet/s/522v69. For more on the hydraulic mining court case and the famous "Sawyer decision," see Robert L. Kelley, "Forgotten Giant: The Hydraulic Gold Mining Industry in California," *Pacific Historical Review* 23, no. 4 (November 1954): 343–56, https://doi.org/10.2307/3634653. For information about North Bloomfield in the 1890s, see United States Census Office, *Report on the Population of the Eleventh Census: 1890; Part 1* (Washington DC: US Government Printing Office, 1895), 71; Harry Laurenz Wells, *History of Nevada County, California; with Illustrations Descriptive of Its Scenery, Residences, Public Buildings, Fine Blocks, and Manufactories* (Oakland, CA: Thompson & West, 1880), 58–59, available online at https://archive.org/stream/historyofnevadac00well; John Edmund Poingdestre, *Nevada County Mining and Business Directory, 1895* (Oakland, CA: Pacific Press Publishing Company, 1895), 20, 26.

44. For the establishment of money order facilities at North Bloomfield, see C. F. Macdonald to Postmaster at North Bloomfield, California, October 3, 1892, box 14, folder 25, Malakoff Diggins State Park Historical Collection, California Department of Parks and Recreation, Sacramento, California, "Postal Matters," *Sacramento Daily Union*, October 18, 1892, 7, available online at http://cdnc.ucr.edu/cgi-bin/cdnc?a=d&d=SDU18921018.2.46. In California alone the number of money order offices expanded by two-thirds over the course of a single year, from 322 to 540. Thank you to Terrence Hines for providing data related to the number of money order offices.

45. United States Post Office Department, *United States Official Postal Guide (1876)* (Washington, DC: Government Printing Office, 1876), 364; United States Post Office Department, *1882 United States Official Postal Guide*, vol. 4, no. 1 (Washington, DC: Government Printing Office, 1882), 524; United States Post Office Department, *1892 United States Official Postal Guide*, vol. 14, no. 1: 506; W. L. Nicholson, *Post Route Map of the States of California and Nevada* (Washington, DC: United States Post Office Department, 1885), National Archives and Records Association II (College Park).

46. Money order data was transcribed by Stanford research assistants Jenny Barin and Alex Ramsey from Money Order Applications—January–December 1895, box 6, folders 12–15, Malakoff Diggins State Park Historical Collection, California Department of Parks and Recreation, Sacramento, California. The months in this dataset include: February, March, April, June, August, September, October, and December of 1895. All future figures of money order information from North Bloomfield come from this source unless otherwise noticed.

47. For traditional large-scale economic histories of this era, see Richard Sylla, "Federal Policy, Banking Market Structure, and Capital Mobilization in the United States, 1863–1913," *Journal of Economic History* 29, no. 4 (December 1969): 657–86; John A. James, *Money and Capital Markets in Postbellum America* (Princeton, NJ: Princeton University Press, 1978); Naomi R. Lamoreaux, *The Great Merger Movement in American Business, 1895–1904* (New York: Cambridge University Press, 1985); John J. Binder and David T. Brown, "Bank Rates of Return and Entry Restrictions, 1869–1914," *Journal of Economic History* 51, no. 1 (March 1991): 47–66, https://doi.org/10.1017/S0022050700038353. For the importance of smaller scales of analysis in economic history, see Emma Rothschild, "Isolation and Economic Life in Eighteenth-Century France," *American Historical Review* 119, no. 4 (October 2014): 1080, https://doi.org/10.1093/ahr/119.4.1055. For thoughts on the relationship between historians and economic history, see William H. Sewell, "A Strange Career: The Historical Study of Economic Life," *History and Theory* 49, no. 4 (December 2010): 146–66, https://doi.org/10.1111/j.1468-2303.2010.00564.x.

48. Susan Strasser, *Satisfaction Guaranteed: The Making of the American Mass Market* (New York: Pantheon, 1989), 203–51; Lizabeth Cohen, "The Mass in Mass Consumption," *Reviews in American History* 18, no. 4 (December 1990): 548–55, https://doi.org/10.2307/2703053; Richard S. Tedlow, *New and Improved: The Story of Mass Marketing in America* (Boston, MA: Harvard Business School Press, 1996).

49. One industry manual described the Post Office Department's monthly postal guide as "the mail-order man's Bible." Samuel Sawyer, *Secrets of the Mail-Order Trade: A Practical Manual for Those Embarking in the Business of Advertising and Selling Goods by Mail* (New York: Sawyer, 1900), 20.

50. Grace Fairchild, *Frontier Woman: The Life of a Woman Homesteader on the Dakota Frontier*, ed. Walker Demarquis Wyman (River Falls: University of Wisconsin—River Falls Press, 1972), 19.

51. For an introduction to the literature on national consumer culture and the role of mail-order catalogs, see Cohen, "The Mass in Mass Consumption." For the standard account of mail-order houses and commercial integration, see Robert H. Wiebe, *The Search for Order, 1877–1920* (New York: Hill & Wang, 1967), 206; Alfred Chandler Jr., *The Visible Hand: The Managerial Revolution in American Business* (Cambridge: MA: Harvard University Press, 1977), 224–39; Strasser, *Satisfaction Guaranteed*, 211–21; William Cronon, *Nature's Metropolis: Chicago and the Great West* (New York: W. W. Norton, 1991), 333–40; Rebecca Edwards, *New Spirits: Americans in the Gilded Age: 1865–1905* (New York: Oxford University Press, 2006), 114.

52. Annette Kassis, *Weinstock's: Sacramento's Finest Department Store* (Charleston, SC: History Press, 2012).

53. Chandler, *The Visible Hand*, 224–39; Strasser, *Satisfaction Guaranteed*, 20–22; Howard R. Stanger, "The Larkin Clubs of Ten: Consumer Buying Clubs and Mail-Order Commerce, 1890–1940," *Enterprise and Society* 9, no. 1 (2008): 129. For a western exception, see Henry C. Klassen, "T. C. Power & Bro.: The Rise of a Small Western Department Store, 1870–1902," *Business History Review* 66, no. 4 (December 1992): 671–722, https://doi.org/10.2307/3116844.

54. "The Mechanic's Store," *Sacramento Daily Union*, May 29, 1878, 1, available online at http://cdnc.ucr.edu/cgi-bin/cdnc?a=d&d=SDU18780529.2.6.2.

55. Advertisement, *Eugene City Guard*, March 2, 1891, 3, available online at http://oregonnews.uoregon.edu/lccn/sn84022653/1891-05-02/ed-1/seq-3/. The number is almost certainly an exaggeration; the far larger Sears, Roebuck & Co. boasted a catalog circulation of 318,000 in 1897. John E. Jeuck and Boris Emmet, *Catalogues and Counters: A History of Sears, Roebuck & Co* (Chicago: University of Chicago Press, 1950), 92. See also Kassis, *Weinstock's*, 22. "Trying to Find It," *Pacific Rural Press*, March 20, 1886, 274, available online at http://cdnc.ucr.edu/cgi-bin/cdnc?a=d&d=PRP18860320.2.32.1.

56. Kassis, *Weinstock's*, 22–23; Olivia Rossetti Agresti, *David Lubin: A Study in Practical Idealism* (Little, Brown, 1922), 53. John Wannamaker, founder of Wannamaker's Department Store, also served as postmaster general from 1889 to 1893. For an analysis of another regional western department store, see Klassen, "T. C. Power & Bro." The 1900 census counted 29,282 people in Sacramento and 59,364 people in Hoboken, New Jersey. >>> "Sacramento, California," *Wikipedia, the Free Encyclopedia*, May 23, 2015, http://en.wikipedia.org/w/index.php?title=Sacramento,_California&oldid=663727740.

57. For examples of Weinstock, Lubin & Co. advertisements, see *Eugene City Guard*, March 2, 1891, 3, available online at http://oregonnews.uoregon.edu/lccn/sn84022653/1891-05-02/ed-1/seq-3/; "Trying to Find It." For second-class postage see United States Post Office Department, *1892 United States Official Postal Guide*, vol. 14, no. 1: 816–20; Kielbowicz, "Postal Subsidies for the Press"; Pamela Walker Laird, *Advertising Progress: American Business and the Rise of Consumer Marketing* (Baltimore: Johns Hopkins University Press, 1998), 57–100. My own research on one contemporary newspaper in Houston found that fully 29 percent of newspaper page space was dedicated to advertising. See Cameron Blevins, "Space, Nation, and the Triumph of Region: A View of the World from Houston," *Journal of American History* 101, no. 1 (June 2014): 139–40.

58. United States Post Office Department, *1892 United States Official Postal Guide*, vol. 14, no. 1: 816–20. Weinstock, Lubin & Co. offered to send their catalogs for free, whereas Sears, Roebuck & Co. charged between five and 15 cents for their catalog. See "Getting Their Catalogues," *Pacific Rural Press*, April 25, 1891, 403, available online at http://cdnc.ucr.edu/cgi-bin/cdnc?a=d&d=PRP18910425.2.22.1; Jeuck and Emmet, Catalogues and Counters, 92.

59. Weinstock, Lubin & Co., *Weinstock, Lubin & Co. Catalogue—Spring and Summer 1891, No. 31* (repr.; Sacramento, CA: Sacramento American Revolution Bicentennial Committee, 1975), 64, 76.

60. "Getting Their Catalogues.".

61. Weinstock, Lubin & Co., *Weinstock, Lubin & Co. Catalogue—Spring and Summer 1900* (Sacramento, CA: Weinstock, Lubin & Co., 1900), 4, 6, Bancroft Library, UC Berkeley.

62. Weinstock, Lubin & Co., *Weinstock, Lubin & Co. Catalogue - Spring and Summer 1891, No. 31*, 23.

63. Women were far more likely than men to use money orders for commercial purposes in North Bloomfield. Around three-quarters of their orders went to companies or other organizations rather than individual recipients, whereas men split their money orders evenly between the two.

64. Susan Porter Benson, *Counter Cultures: Saleswomen, Managers, and Customers in American Department Stores, 1890–1940* (Urbana: University of Illinois Press, 1986), 38–47, 289; Kathy Peiss, *Cheap Amusements: Working Women and Leisure in Turn-of-the-Century New York* (Philadelphia: Temple University Press, 1986), 139–62; Emily A. Remus, "Tippling Ladies and the Making of Consumer Culture: Gender and Public Space in Fin-de-Siècle Chicago," *Journal of American History* 101, no. 3 (December 2014): 751–77, https://doi.org/10.1093/jahist/jau650.

65. "A Business Maker," *Arizona Weekly Journal-Miner*, September 25, 1895, 3, available online at http://chroniclingamerica.loc.gov/lccn/sn85032938/1895-09-25/ed-1/seq-3/.

66. Weinstock, Lubin & Co., "Weinstock, Lubin & Co. Catalogue—Spring and Summer 1900," 6.

67. United States Post Office Department, *1892 United States Official Postal Guide*, vol. 14, no. 1: 817. Fourth-class mail made up a minuscule amount of the nation's mail. In both 1880 and 1890 it was estimated at less than 1 percent of all mailed items. See *1880 Annual Report of the Postmaster General*, 87–89; *1890 Annual Report of the Postmaster General* (Washington, DC: Government Printing Office, 1890), 52. *1880 Annual Report of the Postmaster General*, 87–89.

68. Richard B. Kielbowicz, "Government Goes into Business: Parcel Post in the Nation's Political Economy, 1880–1915," *Studies in American Political Development* 8, no. 1 (1994): 150–72, https://doi.org/10.1017/S0898588X00000109.

69. The Sacramento store had one additional advantage. Montgomery Ward refused to ship orders for less than five dollars, because "the cost of transportation would consume your saving," whereas Weinstock, Lubin & Co. actively encouraged these small-sized orders. In fact, the median size of a postal money order sent to the store from North Bloomfield was $4.20—a size that would have been too small for Montgomery Ward to fill. Weinstock, Lubin & Co., *Weinstock, Lubin & Co. Catalogue—Spring and Summer 1891, No. 31*, 64, 76, 80; Montgomery Ward, *Montgomery Ward & Co. Catalogue and Buyers' Guide—Spring and Summer 1895*, 2nd ed., vol. 57, 1895, 1.

70. Sven Beckert writes, "By 1900, no other recently captured region had been as thoroughly integrated into the national and global economy as the territory of the United States." Sven Beckert, "American Danger: United States Empire, Eurafrica, and the Territorialization of Industrial Capitalism, 1870–1950," *American Historical Review* 122, no. 4 (October 2017): 1149, https://doi.org/10.1093/ahr/122.4.1137. For the integration of language, see Rosina Lozano, *An American Language: The History of Spanish in the United States* (Berkeley: University of California Press, 2018), 27–28, 39. For industrial integration, see Noam Maggor, *Brahmin Capitalism: Frontiers of Wealth and Populism in America's First Gilded Age* (Cambridge, MA: Harvard University Press, 2017); Richard White, *Railroaded: The Transcontinentals and the Making of Modern America* (New York: W. W. Norton, 2011).

71. *1878 Annual Report of the Postmaster General* (Washington, DC: Government Printing Office, 1878), 17; *1895 Annual Report of the Postmaster General*, 132.

72. United States Post Office Department, *1878 United States Official Postal Guide*, vol. 16 (New York.: Houghton, Osgood, 1878), 29; United States Post Office Department, *1896 United States Official Postal Guide*, 901.

73. The nearest data available for mail transit times is from 1882 and 1894. The likely drop in transit time between 1878 and 1895 is almost certainly larger. United States Post Office Department, *1882 United States Official Postal Guide*, vol. 4, no. 1: 579; United States Post Office Department, *1894 United States Official Postal Guide* (Philadelphia: George F. Lasher, 1894), 779.

74. The Hamilton Post Office sent 571 money orders over February, March, April, June, August, September, October, and December, while the North Bloomfield Post Office sent 876 money orders over this same time frame.

75. Noam Maggor makes a similar point about the assumptions historians make regarding capitalist integration and political integration in Maggor, *Brahmin Capitalism*, 158, 177.
76. For more on the standardization of news, see Gerald J. Baldasty, *The Commercialization of News in the Nineteenth Century* (Madison: University of Wisconsin Press, 1992). I explore this theme in more depth in Blevins, "Space, Nation, and the Triumph of Region." Thomas Bender discusses how nationalism can enhance regionalism in Thomas Bender, *Community and Social Change in America* (New Brunswick, NJ: Rutgers University Press, 1978), 87–89.
77. *The Official Register of the United States, 1875* (Washington, DC: Government Printing Office, 1875), 965; *The Official Register of the United States, 1895*, vol. 2 (Washington, DC: Government Printing Office, 1895), 219; Frickstad and Thrall, *A Century of Nevada Post Offices*, 8, 9, 19, 22, 29, 30.

# Chapter 7

1. United States Postal Service Historian, "Pieces of Mail Handled, Number of Post Offices, Income, and Expenses Since 1789," United States Postal Service, February 2020, https://about.usps.com/who-we-are/postal-history/pieces-of-mail-since-1789.pdf, accessed April 23, 2020.
2. 37th Congress, 3rd Session, "Ch. 71: An Act to Amend the Laws Relating to the Post-Office Department," Statutes at Large, March 3, 1863.
3. The postmaster general's annual report lists 454 offices with City Free Delivery for the fiscal year ending 1889–1890. *1890 Annual Report of the Postmaster General* (Washington, DC: Government Printing Office, 1890), 255.
4. *1891 Annual Report of the Postmaster General* (Washington, DC: Government Printing Office, 1891), 82–88.
5. Wayne Edison Fuller, *RFD: The Changing Face of Rural America* (Bloomington, 1964); Winifred Gallagher, *How the Post Office Created America: A History* (New York: Penguin, 2016), 188–92, 204–7.
6. For RFD's impact on newspaper circulation, see Elisabeth Ruth Perlman and Steven Sprick Schuster, "Delivering the Vote: The Political Effect of Free Mail Delivery in Early Twentieth Century America," *Journal of Economic History* 76, no. 3 (September 2016): 791, https://doi.org/10.1017/S0022050716000784. For commercial and political effects of Rural Free Delivery, see Charles Postel, *The Populist Vision* (New York: Oxford University Press, 2009), 45–68; Fuller, *RFD*, 293–95. Rural residents could also purchase postal money orders from RFD mail carriers. See *1901 Annual Report of the Postmaster General* (Washington, DC: Government Printing Office, 1901), 128–30; "Postal Wagons for the Country," *San Francisco Call*, November 2, 1898, 9, available online at http://cdnc.ucr.edu/cgi-bin/cdnc?a=d&d=SFC18981102.2.114.
7. William R. Leach, *Land of Desire: Merchants, Power, and the Rise of a New American Culture* (New York: Pantheon, 1993), 182–84; Mary Beth Norton et al., *A People and a Nation: A History of the United States, Brief Edition* (Stamford, CT: Cengage Learning, 2014), 453; Christopher W. Wells, "The Changing Nature of Country Roads: Farmers, Reformers, and the Shifting Uses of Rural Space, 1880–1905," *Agricultural History* 80, no. 2 (April 2006): 143–66; Fuller, *RFD*.
8. Daniel P. Carpenter, "State Building through Reputation Building: Coalitions of Esteem and Program Innovation in the National Postal System, 1883–1913," *Studies in American Political Development* 14, no. 2 (2000): 121–55, https://doi.org/null; Daniel Carpenter, *The Forging of Bureaucratic Autonomy: Reputations, Networks, and Policy Innovation in Executive Agencies, 1862–1928.* (Princeton, NJ: Princeton University Press, 2001), 94–143; Samuel Kernell and Michael P. McDonald, "Congress and America's Political Development: The Transformation

of the Post Office from Patronage to Service," *American Journal of Political Science* 43, no. 3 (July 1999): 792–811, https://doi.org/10.2307/2991835.

9. Postel, *The Populist Vision*, 143–45; Wayne E. Fuller, "The Populists and the Post Office," *Agricultural History* 65, no. 1 (January 1991): 1–16. "The Omaha Platform: Launching the Populist Party," George Mason University, History Matters, http://historymatters.gmu.edu/d/5361/, accessed September 19, 2019.

10. *1890 Annual Report of the Postmaster General*, 40. For one example of Wanamaker's lobbying efforts, see his widely reprinted editorial in "Postal Delivery for County Districts," *Farmer's Review*, November 11, 1891, 714, available online at http://idnc.library.illinois.edu/cgi-bin/illinois?a=d&d=FFR18911111.2.8. For wider lobbying efforts conducted by both Wanamaker and agrarian reformers, see Carpenter, *The Forging of Bureaucratic Autonomy*, 123–31; Leach, *Land of Desire*, 182–85. For "country boy" see *1891 Annual Report of the Postmaster General*, 6.

11. Carpenter, *The Forging of Bureaucratic Autonomy*, 88–93, 96–98; *1889 Annual Report of the Postmaster General* (Washington, DC: Government Printing Office, 1889), 7; *1891 Annual Report of the Postmaster General*, 42–46.

12. William Dudley Foulke, *Fighting the Spoilsmen: Reminiscences of the Civil Service Reform Movement* (G. P. Putnam's Sons, 1919), 54–64.

13. *1893 Annual Report of the Postmaster General* (Washington, DC: Government Printing Office, 1893), ix; Carpenter, *The Forging of Bureaucratic Autonomy*, 131.

14. Fuller, *RFD*, 54–56.

15. For the growth of the Railway Mail Service as a bureaucratic beachhead within the US Post and its relationship to Rural Free Delivery, see Carpenter, *The Forging of Bureaucratic Autonomy*, 76–83, 98–102, 135.

16. *1880 Annual Report of the Postmaster General* (Washington, DC: Government Printing Office, 1880), 87–88; *1900 Annual Report of the Postmaster General* (Washington, DC: Government Printing Office, 1900), 264–65.

17. Fuller, *RFD*, 54–56.

18. *The Official Register of the United States, 1891*, vol. 2 (Washington, DC: Government Printing Office, 1891), 666.

19. Charles Roeser Jr. and R. A. Rock, *Post Route Map of the Territories of New Mexico and Arizona*, 1:833,000 (Washington, DC: United States Post Office Department, October 1, 1891), G4321. P8 1891.U55x, Norman B. Leventhal Map Center Collection, Boston Public Library, available online at https://collections.leventhalmap.org/search/commonwealth:cj82kj99g. For more on Bell Ranch, see David Remley, *Bell Ranch: Cattle Ranching in the Southwest, 1824–1947*, Revised edition (Las Cruces, NM: Yucca Tree, 2000).

20. George A. Howard, Office of the Auditor of the Post Office Department, to A. J. Tisdall, August 26, 1896; Second Assistant Postmaster General to Postmaster at Bell Ranch, San Miguel County, New Mexico, September 22, 1897; box 56, Red River Valley Co. Records, University of New Mexico Center for Southwest Research, Albuquerque, New Mexico.

21. A. von Haake, Topographer of the Post Office Department to Postmaster at Bell Ranch, San Miguel County, New Mexico, October 7, 1897, box 56, Red River Valley Co. Records, University of New Mexico Center for Southwest Research, Albuquerque, New Mexico.

22. C. W. Allen to A. J. Tisdall, May 20, 1897, box 56, Red River Valley Co. Records, University of New Mexico Center for Southwest Research, Albuquerque, New Mexico.

23. *1898 Annual Report of the Postmaster General* (Washington, DC: Government Printing Office, 1898), 155; *1900 Annual Report of the Postmaster General*, 116.

24. *1899 Annual Report of the Postmaster General* (Washington, DC: Government Printing Office, 1899), 203; *1903 Annual Report of the Postmaster General* (Washington, DC: Government Printing Office, 1903), 608.

25. Carpenter, *The Forging of Bureaucratic Autonomy*, 123–43.

26. For the longer history of post roads, see John Lauritz Larson, *Internal Improvement: National Public Works and the Promise of Popular Government in the Early United States* (Chapel Hill: University of North Carolina Press, 2001), 46–48; Richard R. John, *Spreading the News: The American Postal System from Franklin to Morse* (Cambridge, MA: Harvard University Press, 1995), 25–63.

27. Senator Davis speaking on February 9, 1883, 47th Congress, 2nd Session, *Congressional Record* 14, part 3:2334.

28. For "farce" see Senator Beck speaking on March 3, 1883, 47th Congress, 2nd Session, *Congressional Record* 14, part 4:3686. The legislation was passed with little fanfare or coverage. 48th Congress, 1st Session, "Ch. 9: An act making all public roads and highways post routes," Statutes at Large, March 1, 1884.

29. *1900 Annual Report of the Postmaster General*, 4.

30. For this and other letters from postmasters, see *1899 Annual Report of the Postmaster General*, 209–11.

31. Gallagher, *How the Post Office Created America*, 188–92; Fuller, *RFD*.

32. *1900 Annual Report of the Postmaster General*, 114. *1910 Annual Report of the Postmaster General* (Washington, DC: Government Printing Office, 1910), 342.

33. Daniel Carpenter, "From Patronage to Policy: The Centralization Campaign in Iowa Post Offices 1880–1910," *Annals of Iowa* 58, no. 3 (1999): 273–309; Fuller, *RFD*, 81–105; Judith Littlejohn, "The Political, Socioeconomic, and Cultural Impact of the Implementation of Rural Free Delivery in Late 1890s US" (master's thesis, The College at Brockport, State University of New York, 2013), 14, available online at http://digitalcommons.brockport.edu/hst_theses/10.

34. Gallagher, *How the Post Office Created America*, 206–7; Richard B. Kielbowicz, "Government Goes into Business: Parcel Post in the Nation's Political Economy, 1880–1915," *Studies in American Political Development* 8, no. 1 (1994): 150–72, https://doi.org/10.1017/S0898588X00000109; Gallagher, *How the Post Office Created America*, 204–7; Carpenter, "State Building through Reputation Building," 149–53; R. B. Kielbowicz, *Postal Enterprise: Post Office Innovations with Congressional Constraints, 1789–1970* (Washington, DC: Postal Rate Commission, 2000), 41–50.

35. Elisabeth S. Clemens, *The People's Lobby: Organizational Innovation and the Rise of Interest Group Politics in the United States, 1890–1925* (Chicago: University of Chicago Press, 1997), 41–99; Carpenter, *The Forging of Bureaucratic Autonomy*, 212–325; Brian Balogh, *The Associational State: American Governance in the Twentieth Century* (Philadelphia: University of Pennsylvania Press, 2015), 41–65, 89–138.

36. *1903 Annual Report of the Postmaster General*, 610; *1904 Annual Report of the Postmaster General* (Washington, DC: Government Printing Office, 1904), 583–84; *1902 Annual Report of the Postmaster General* (Washington, DC: Government Printing Office, 1902), 110–36. As of June 30, 1904, there were 24,566 RFD routes in operation across the United States.

37. Varun Vijay compiled spatial data about Rural Free Delivery routes established between 1896–1904 while working as an undergraduate research assistant at the Stanford Center for Spatial and Textual Analysis during the spring of 2015. The data was taken from US Postal Service Historian, "First Rural Routes by State" (United States Postal Service, April 2008), https://about.usps.com/who-we-are/postal-history/first-rural-routes.htm. The data only includes the originating post office (terminus) from which an RFD route operated, so multiple routes may have operated out of the same office.

38. In the words of political scientist Daniel Carpenter, "A triangular flow of information developed between the RFD inspector, the congressional representative, and department officials." Carpenter, *The Forging of Bureaucratic Autonomy*, 136. Brian Balogh makes a similar point

about the US Forest Service under Gifford Pinchot, whose technocratic, scientific management was also defined by a personal patronage network centered on the Yale Forestry School. Balogh, *The Associational State*, 41–65.

39. Kernell and McDonald, "Congress and America's Political Development."

40. Representative Maddox speaking on March 3, 1903, 58th Congress, 2nd Session, *Congressional Record* 38, part 1:262.

41. There were 456 routes in Georgia at the time. *1903 Annual Report of the Postmaster General*, 610. For more on the rollout of Rural Free Delivery in the South, see Wayne E. Fuller, "The South and the Rural Free Delivery of Mail," *Journal of Southern History* 25, no. 4 (November 1959): 499–521. For examples of the prevalence of political and partisan issues at the local level regarding new Rural Free Delivery routes, see papers, letters, and petitions in folder 693: Woodbury, CT Rural Free Delivery and folder 696: Rural Free Delivery, 1902–1904, box 54: Series II, Ebenezer J. Hill Papers (MS 279), Manuscripts and Archives, Yale University Library.

42. For the geography of Paloma and Palomas, see Rand McNally & Co., *Rand McNally & Co.'s Enlarged Business Atlas and Shippers' Guide, 1903* (Rand McNally & Co., 1903), 216–17, 227, 352–53, available online at http://www.davidrumsey.com/luna/servlet/s/cqm5i9; Harry L. Wilkey, *The Story of a Little Town: A History of Paloma, Illinois* ([n.p.]: W. A. Shanholtzer, 1934), 70–71, available online at http://archive.org/details/storyoflittletow00wilk. As late as 1916 there was one RFD route in the entire county of Yuma, Arizona (in which Palomas was located). *United States Official Postal Guide* (Washington, DC: Government Printing Office, 1916), 517–18. For the closure of the Palomas Post Office, see Alan H Patera and John S Gallagher, *Arizona Post Offices* (Lake Grove, OR: Depot, 1988), 226.

43. Wayne E. Fuller, "Good Roads and Rural Free Delivery of Mail," *Mississippi Valley Historical Review* 42, no. 1 (June 1955): 79–83, https://doi.org/10.2307/1898624; Wells, "The Changing Nature of Country Roads," 153–54, 157–58.

44. "Surrogacy strategy" is from Gary Gerstle, *Liberty and Coercion: The Paradox of American Government from the Founding to the Present* (Princeton, NJ: Princeton University Press, 2015), 6, 101–4. More infamous instances of this surrogacy strategy and the Post Office Department include the banning of abolitionist material from the mail and the anti-vice "Comstock Laws". John, *Spreading the News*, 257–80; Helen Lefkowitz Horowitz, "Victoria Woodhull, Anthony Comstock, and Conflict over Sex in the United States in the 1870s," *Journal of American History* 87, no. 2 (September 2000): 403–34, https://doi.org/10.2307/2568758.

45. Maurice O. Elridge, *Public-Road Mileage, Revenues, and Expenditures in the United States in 1904* (Washington, DC: Department of Agriculture, Office of Public Roads, 1907), 8–9.

46. Elridge, *Public-Road Mileage*, 8–9.

47. Carpenter, *The Forging of Bureaucratic Autonomy*, 66, 69, 73.

48. The total number of rural "fourth-class" post offices shrunk from 67,801 to 54,311 between 1898 and 1908. United States Post Office Department, *United States Official Postal Guide, 1898* (New York: Metropolitan Job, 1898), 1037, available online at https://babel.hathitrust.org/cgi/pt?id=pst.000003071618; United States Post Office Department, *United States Official Postal Guide, 1908* (Albany, NY: J. B. Lyon, 1908), 707, available online at https://babel.hathitrust.org/cgi/pt?id=uc1.b2919443.

49. Stephen Skowronek, *Building a New American State: The Expansion of National Administrative Capacities, 1877–1920* (Cambridge: Cambridge University Press, 1982), 178–79; "Executive Order 982: Amending Civil Service Rules to Limit Exceptions from Examination for Certain Postmasters," November 30, 1908, available online at https://en.wikisource.org/wiki/Executive_Order_982.

50. Thomas B. Catron to B. F. Pankey, April 16, 1912, box 1, Thomas B. Catron Papers, University of New Mexico Center for Southwest Research, Albuquerque, New Mexico.

51. B. F. Pankey to Thomas B. Catron, April 11, 1912, box 1, Thomas B. Catron Papers, University of New Mexico Center for Southwest Research, Albuquerque, New Mexico.

52. Thomas B. Catron to B. F. Pankey, April 16, 1912, box 1, Thomas B. Catron Papers, University of New Mexico Center for Southwest Research, Albuquerque, New Mexico.

53. Alfredo Lucero to Thomas B. Catron, May 10, 1912, box 1; Thomas B. Catron to George Curry, June 1, 1912, box 1; C. P. Grandfield, Office of First Assistant Postmaster General to Thomas B. Catron, June 6, 1912, box 1, Thomas B. Catron Papers, University of New Mexico Center for Southwest Research, Albuquerque, New Mexico.

54. José Salazar to Thomas B. Catron, June 28, 1912, box 1, Thomas B. Catron Papers, University of New Mexico Center for Southwest Research, Albuquerque, New Mexico.

55. C. P. Grandfield, Office of First Assistant Postmaster General, to Thomas B. Catron, June 25, 1912, box 1, Thomas B. Catron Papers, University of New Mexico Center for Southwest Research, Albuquerque, New Mexico.

56. Alfredo Lucero to Thomas B. Catron, July 6, 1912, box 1, Thomas B. Catron Papers, University of New Mexico Center for Southwest Research, Albuquerque, New Mexico.

57. *The Official Register of the United States, 1911*, vol. 2 (Washington, DC: Government Printing Office, 1911), 324, https://babel.hathitrust.org/cgi/pt?id=loc.ark:/13960/t4qj8681h.

58. James A. Garfield, *The Diary of James A. Garfield*, ed. Brown Williams, vol. 2 (East Lansing: Michigan State University, 1967), 213.

59. *1912 Annual Report of the Postmaster General* (Washington, DC: Government Printing Office, 1912), 87–88; Ari Hoogenboom, "The Pendleton Act and the Civil Service," *American Historical Review* 64, no. 2 (January 1959): 305, https://doi.org/10.2307/1845445; Skowronek, *Building a New American State*, 193–94. For contemporary coverage, see "Fourth Class Post Office," *Press Democrat*, May 30, 1913, available online at https://cdnc.ucr.edu/cgi-bin/cdnc?a=d&d=SRPD19130530.2.48; "Executive Order 1624: Amending Civil Service Rules to Limit Exceptions from Examination for Certain Postmasters," October 15, 1912, available online at https://en.wikisource.org/wiki/Executive_Order_1624; "Executive Order 1776: Amending Civil Service Rules Regarding Competitive Status for Fourth Class Postmasters," May 7, 1913, available online at https://en.wikisource.org/wiki/Executive_Order_1776.

## Conclusion

1. Daniel Calhoun Roper, *The United States Post Office: Its Past Record, Present Condition, and Potential Relation to the New World Era* (New York: Funk & Wagnalls, 1917), 312–14.

2. Roper, *The United States Post Office*, 312-14, 320.

3. Elisabeth Clemens forcefully make this point in Elisabeth S. Clemens, "Lineages of the Rube Goldberg State: Building and Blurring Public Programs, 1900–1940," in *Rethinking Political Institutions: The Art of the State*, ed. Ian Shapiro, Stephen Skowronek, and Daniel Galvin (New York: NYU Press, 2006), 188. See also Stephen W. Sawyer, "A Fiscal Revolution: Statecraft in France's Early Third Republic," *American Historical Review* 121, no. 4 (October 2016): 1144, https://doi.org/10.1093/ahr/121.4.1141.

4. Winifred Gallagher, *How the Post Office Created America: A History* (New York: Penguin, 2016), 221–36.

5. For the history of this period, see Gallagher, *How the Post Office Created America*, 239–54. For "rural allowance," see President's Commission on Postal Organization, *Towards Postal Excellence: The Report of the President's Commission on Postal Organization* (Washington,

DC: Government Printing Office, 1968), 137–38. For star route history, see United States Postal Service Historian, "Star Routes," May 2007, https://about.usps.com/who-we-are/postal-history/star-routes.pdf.

6. President's Commission on Postal Organization, *Towards Postal Excellence*, v, 24.

7. "Public Law 91-375, 91 Congress, Session 2, An Act: To Improve and Modernize the Postal Service, to Reorganize the Post Office Department, and for Other Purposes.," *U.S. Statutes at Large*, August 12, 1970, 719.

8. Gallagher, *How the Post Office Created America*, 256. For the wider shift from service to business, see Richard R. John, "History of Universal Service and the Postal Monopoly," Study on Universal Postal Service and the Postal Monopoly (School of Public Policy, George Mason University, November 2008).

9. "Public Law 91-375," 719.

10. United States Postal Service Historian, "First-Class Mail Volume since 1926," United States Postal Service, February 2020, https://about.usps.com/who-we-are/postal-history/first-class-mail-since-1926.htm.

11. "A Postal Primer: The Basics and Pivotal Issues Affecting the Future of the United States Postal Service," April 16, 2019, i–iii, 10–12, https://postalcouncil.org/wp-content/uploads/2019/04/C21-Postal-Primer-2019.pdf.

12. Outside the Box: Reforming and Renewing the Postal Service, Part II: Hearings before the U.S. Senate Committee on Homeland Security & Governmental Affairs, 113th Cong. (September 26, 2013) (testimony of Dean Baker), available online at https://www.hsgac.senate.gov/imo/media/doc/Testimony-Baker-2013-09-26.pdf.

13. "United States Postal Service FY2019 Annual Report to Congress" (United States Postal Service, 2020), https://about.usps.com/what/financials/annual-reports/fy2019.pdf.

14. Lisa Rein, "Postal Service Names 3,700 Post Offices That Could Be Closed," *Washington Post*, July 26, 2011, available online at https://www.washingtonpost.com/politics/postal-service-names-3700-post-offices-that-could-be-closed/2011/07/26/gIQARk3tbI_story.html; "Statement on Delay of Closing or Consolidation of Post Offices and Mail Processing Facilities," United States Postal Service, December 13, 2011, https://about.usps.com/news/national-releases/2011/pr11_1213closings.htm.

15. "Tester Blasts Postmaster General for 'Lack of Transparency,'" U.S. Senator for Montana Jon Tester, October 12, 2011, https://www.tester.senate.govp=press_release&id=1542.

16. "Management and Oversight of Highway Contract Routes" (Office of Inspector General: United States Postal Service, September 30, 2016), 1–2, https://www.oversight.gov/sites/default/files/oig-reports/NL-AR-16-006.pdf.

17. "New Strategy to Preserve the Nation's Smallest Post Offices," United States Postal Service, May 9, 2012, https://about.usps.com/news/national-releases/2012/pr12_054.htm; "A Postal Primer\."

18. Jennifer Collins, "First Village Post Office Debuts in Malone," *Marketplace* (blog), August 10, 2011, https://www.marketplace.org/2011/08/10/first-village-post-office-debuts-malone/; Patrick Oppmann, "The New Face of the U.S. Post Office," CNN News, September 12, 2011, https://www.cnn.com/2011/US/09/12/mini.mart.post.office/index.html.

19. Brian Balogh, *The Associational State: American Governance in the Twentieth Century* (Philadelphia: University of Pennsylvania Press, 2015), 128–99.

20. Gareth Davies and Martha Derthick, "Race and Social Welfare Policy: The Social Security Act of 1935," *Political Science Quarterly* 112, no. 2 (1997): 232–35, https://doi.org/10.2307/2657939; Gary Gerstle, *Liberty and Coercion: The Paradox of American Government from the Founding to the Present* (Princeton, NJ: Princeton University Press, 2015), 243–45; C. Lowell Harriss, *History and Policies of the Home Owners' Loan Corporation* (New York: National

Bureau of Economic Research, 1951), 140, available online at https://www.nber.org/books/harr51-1.

21. Aaron L. Friedberg, *In the Shadow of the Garrison State: America's Anti-Statism and Its Cold War Grand Strategy* (Princeton, NJ: Princeton University Press, 2000), 222–35, 296–345; Gerstle, *Liberty and Coercion*, 253–55, 262–65.

22. Elizabeth Hinton, *From the War on Poverty to the War on Crime: The Making of Mass Incarceration in America* (Cambridge, MA: Harvard University Press, 2016), 14–17.

23. Matthew Glassman, Laura A. Hanson, and Carla N. Argueta, *Federal Land Ownership: Overview and Data* (Washington, DC: Congressional Research Service, Library of Congress, March 3, 2017), https://fas.org/sgp/crs/misc/R42346.pdf; "Public Land Statistics 2018" (U.S. Department of the Interior, Bureau of Land Management, August 2019), https://www.blm.gov/sites/blm.gov/files/PublicLandStatistics2018.pdf.

24. James R. Skillen, *The Nation's Largest Landlord: The Bureau of Land Management in the American West* (Lawrence: University Press of Kansas, 2009), ix. The BLM continues to face geographical challenges to regulation and enforcement: V. William Scarpato, "Don't Tread on Me: Increasing Compliance with Off-Road Vehicle Regulations at Least Cost," *Environs: Environmental Law and Policy Journal* 36, no. 2 (May 2013): 135–69; Brian C. Steed, "Collaboration with State and Local Partners," (information bulletin, Washington, DC: United States Department of the Interior: Bureau of Land Management, March 2, 2018), https://www.blm.gov/policy/ib-2018-037.

25. "First Inaugural Address of Ronald Reagan," January 20, 1981, available online at the Avalon Project, https://avalon.law.yale.edu/20th_century/reagan1.asp.

26. In 2017, there were 4.1 million people categorized as contractors and another 1.2 million as "grant employees," compared to the roughly 3.8 million direct government employees or active-duty military personnel. Paul Light, *The Government-Industrial Complex: The True Size of the Federal Government, 1984–2018* (Oxford: Oxford University Press, 2019), 36–42. For literature on government contracting, see Jody Freeman and Martha Minow, eds., *Government by Contract: Outsourcing and American Democracy* (Cambridge, MA: Harvard University Press, 2009); Jocelyn M. Johnston and Barbara S. Romzek, "The Promises, Performance, and Pitfalls of Government Contracting," in *The Oxford Handbook of American Bureaucracy*, ed. Robert F. Durant (Oxford University Press, 2010), 396–420, https://doi.org/10.1093/oxfordhb/9780199238958.001.0001; Suzanne Mettler, *The Submerged State: How Invisible Government Policies Undermine American Democracy* (Chicago: University of Chicago Press, 2011).

27. Manan Ahmed et al., "Textures," *Torn Apart / Separados* 1 (June 25, 2018), http://xpmethod.plaintext.in/torn-apart/volume/1/textures.html; "Department of Homeland Security, U.S. Immigration and Customs Enforcement Budget Overview: Fiscal Year 2018" (Washington, DC: Department of Homeland Security, 2018), https://www.dhs.gov/sites/default/files/publications/ICE%20FY18%20Budget.pdf.

28. Department of Homeland Security Office of the Inspector General, "ICE Does Not Fully Use Contracting Tools to Hold Detention Facility Contractors Accountable for Failing to Meet Performance Standards" (Washington, DC: Department of Homeland Security, January 29, 2019), 7, https://www.oig.dhs.gov/sites/default/files/assets/2019-02/OIG-19-18-Jan19.pdf.

29. Office of Management and Budget, "Analytical Perspectives, Budget of the United States Government, Fiscal Year 2019," Analytical Perspectives (Washington, DC: U.S. Government Publishing Office, 2018), 65, https://www.whitehouse.gov/wp-content/uploads/2018/02/spec-fy2019.pdf.

30. Cathy O'Neil, *Weapons of Math Destruction: How Big Data Increases Inequality and Threatens Democracy* (New York: Crown, 2016); Lee Raine and Janna Anderson, "Code-Dependent: Pros and Cons of the Algorithm Age" (Pew Research Center, February 8,

2017), https://www.pewinternet.org/2017/02/08/code-dependent-pros-and-cons-of-the-algorithm-age/. For Facebook altering user attitudes, see Adam D. I. Kramer, Jamie E. Guillory, and Jeffrey T. Hancock, "Experimental Evidence of Massive-Scale Emotional Contagion through Social Networks," *Proceedings of the National Academy of Sciences* 111, no. 24 (June 17, 2014): 8788–90, https://doi.org/10.1073/pnas.1320040111; Elise Hu, "Facebook Manipulates Our Moods for Science and Commerce: A Roundup," *All Tech Considered* (NPR blog), June 30, 2014, https://www.npr.org/sections/alltechconsidered/2014/06/30/326929138/facebook-manipulates-our-moods-for-science-and-commerce-a-roundup.

31. "1889 Annual Report of the Postmaster General" (Washington, DC: Government Printing Office, 1889), 7; O'Neil, *Weapons of Math Destruction*; Safiya Umoja Noble, *Algorithms of Oppression: How Search Engines Reinforce Racism* (New York: NYU Press, 2018); Julia Angwin et al., "Machine Bias: There's Software Used Across the Country to Predict Future Criminals. And It's Biased against Blacks.," *ProPublica*, May 23, 2016, https://www.propublica.org/article/machine-bias-risk-assessments-in-criminal-sentencing; Pauline Kim, "Data-Driven Discrimination at Work" (SSRN Scholarly Paper, Rochester, NY: Social Science Research Network, April 19, 2017), https://papers.ssrn.com/abstract=2801251; Miranda Bogen, "All the Ways Hiring Algorithms Can Introduce Bias," *Harvard Business Review*, May 6, 2019, https://hbr.org/2019/05/all-the-ways-hiring-algorithms-can-introduce-bias; Rachel Courtland, "Bias Detectives: The Researchers Striving to Make Algorithms Fair," *Nature* 558 (June 20, 2018): 357–60, https://doi.org/10.1038/d41586-018-05469-3; Dillon Reisman et al., "Algorithmic Impact Assessments: A Practical Framework for Public Agency Accountability" (AI Now Institute, April 2018), https://ainowinstitute.org/aiareport2018.pdf.

# Index

*For the benefit of digital users, indexed terms that span two pages (e.g., 52–53) may, on occasion, appear on only one of those pages.*

Page numbers followed by *f* refer to figures.